Financial Planner's Guide to Estate Planning

Third Edition

Paul J. Lochray, J. D.

College For Financial Planning
Denver, Colorado

Prentice Hall, Englewood Cliffs, New Jersey 07632

Library of Congress Cataloging-in-Publications Data

LOCHRAY, PAUL J.
    Financial planner's guide to estate planning / Paul J. Lochray.—
    3rd ed.
        p.   cm.
    Includes bibliographical references and index.
    ISBN 0-13-318502-8
    1. Estate planning—United States. 2. Inheritance and transfer tax—Law and legislation—United
States. I. Title.
    KF750.L6 1992   91-3537
    343.7305'3—dc20   CIP
    [347.30353]   Rev.

Editorial/production supervision and interior design: *Jean Lapidus*
Cover design: *Butler/Udell Design*
Pre-press buyer: *Mary Elizabeth McCartney*
Manufacturing buyer: *Susan Brunke*
Copy editor: *Maria Caruso*
Acquistion editor: *Bernard Goodwin*
Editorial assistant: *Diane Spina*

 © 1992 by Prentice-Hall, Inc.
A Simon & Schuster Company
Englewood Cliffs, New Jersey 07632

The publisher offers discounts on this book when ordered
in bulk quantities. For more information, write:

Special Sales/Professional Marketing
Prentice Hall
Professional & Technical Reference Division
Englewood Cliffs, NJ 07632

ISBN 0-13-318502-8

Printed in the United States of America

10 9 8 7 6 5 4

ISBN 0-13-318502-8

PRENTICE-HALL INTERNATIONAL (UK) LIMITED, *LONDON*
PRENTICE-HALL OF AUSTRALIA PTY. LIMITED, *SYDNEY*
PRENTICE-HALL CANADA INC., *TORONTO*
PRINTICE-HALL HISPANOAMERICANA, S.A., *MEXICO*
PRENTICE-HALL OF INDIA PRIVATE LIMITED, *NEW DELHI*
PRENTICE-HALL OF JAPAN, INC., *TOKYO*
SIMON & SCHUSTER ASIA PTE. LTD., *SINGAPORE*
EDITORA PRENTICE-HALL DO BRASIL, LTDA., *RIO DE JANEIRO*

*This book is dedicated to my mother,
Rita Joyce Marlow Lochray,
who taught me the meaning of perseverance.*

CONTENTS

PREFACE

The past five years have seen enormous changes in the laws affecting the viability of estate planning. The Tax Reform Act of 1986, the Omnibus Budget Reconciliation Act of 1987, the Technical and Miscellaneous Revenue Act for 1988, the Revenue Reconciliation Act of 1989, and the Revenue Reconciliation Act of 1990 all brought numerous technical changes in the area of estate planning for clients as well as for financial planners. As a result of these numerous tax changes, financial planners need to be aware of new opportunities that were unavailable to most clients prior to the enactment of these specific laws. In addition, tax law changes have made some techniques that were previously attractive less so because of adverse income, estate, or gift tax consequences stemming from the new legislation.

These changes are the reasons for this third edition. The *Financial Planner's Guide to Estate Planning, third edition,* provides the financial planner with updated information on a variety of estate planning techniques. This text provides the financial planner with both quantitative and qualitative information for estate planning purposes, including such topics as counseling techniques that elicit additional information from the client, wills and characteristics of wills, will substitutes and their uses in estate planning, characteristics and tax implications of using trusts as part of the estate plan, postmortem planning techniques, charitable transfer techniques, forms of property ownership, and special estate planning considerations for the disabled.

Paul J. Lochray

ACKNOWLEDGMENTS

Special thanks and acknowledgment are extended to the following people without whose assistance this book would not be possible.

To Sally Robben, who provided me with word processing and assisted in the physical production of the book.

To Keith Fevurly, J. D., CFP, and Kathryn Ioannides, J. D., CLU, ChFC, who provided me with technical assistance and content resources for the chapter, "Community Property: Estate Planning Concepts." This chapter had its genesis in the publication, "Community Property in the Estate Planning Process," originally published by the College For Financial Planning® in August, 1985. Copies of the publication are available from the College For Financial Planning.®

To Brett H. Nelson, who unknowingly provided me with advice and support at times when it was needed most.

1

CLIENT COUNSELING, ESTATE ANALYSIS, AND THE ESTATE PLANNING PROCESS

INTRODUCTION

The art of estate planning involves the implementation and coordination of various skills by the financial planner. It requires the ability to gather data and analyze it, and it requires the planner to become a "counselor" in the sense of knowing when the client is being honest and when the client is holding back information that is essential to the proper formation of an estate plan. Estate planning requires organizational and data gathering skills that give the financial planner an idea of the client's current financial condition before any additional techniques are implemented. It also requires the financial planner to coordinate his or her efforts with attorneys, trust officers, accountants, life underwriters, and others as a part of an estate planning team. Finally, estate planning requires the financial planner to be a realist in the sense that every estate plan ultimately requires the client to recognize that death is inevitable. The role of the financial planner may be to ease the client into an awareness of eventual death and to help the client in repositioning assets in such a way that the client's estate planning objectives are ultimately fulfilled. This is no easy task if the client still has difficulty in accepting the finality of death.

In order to enhance the role of the financial planner as a part of the estate planning team, the financial planner must have a thorough understanding of the role played in the estate planning process. The financial planner must know what information must be obtained during the initial data gathering interview, and must also be trained to know when vital information is missing that may have a bearing on the legality or effectiveness of the estate plan. In addition, the financial planner must be able to assist the client in establishing and identifying estate planning goals, and must be prepared to analyze the client's goals in order to determine whether they are realistic in light of the client's total asset ownership, lifetime financial needs and other limiting factors.

The financial planner must also have an estate planning "team" at his or her disposal to assist in the implementation of the estate plan. Attorneys, trust officers, accountants, investment advisors, and life insurance agents may all be a part of this team. With their assistance, the financial planner can more readily implement the plan and assure the client that the plan achieves the client's objectives.

Finally, the financial planner must be aware of the client's changing needs or changing factual patterns. A significant change in the client's life style (e.g., a divorce, birth of a subsequent child, or death of a family member) may make all or a part of the estate plan obsolete. In addition, changes in tax laws and inheritance and probate laws may cause the client's estate plan to become outdated. As a result, the financial planner needs to remain current in various aspects of law that could affect the vitality of the client's estate plan.

This chapter will focus on several aspects of the estate planning process. First, an overall estate planning process or methodology will be presented to assist the financial planner in developing, implementing, and monitoring an estate plan for a client. Each step of the process will be reviewed, with significant emphasis placed on data gathering and what the data gathered reveals about the client. Then, analysis of the data will be coordinated with the estate planning objectives of the client, which have been previously identified and prioritized. After data have been identified and quantified, the client's limitations or constraints will be examined to help in the selection of one or more estate planning techniques that achieve the client's objectives. After one or more techniques have been selected, they will be "tested" to determine whether or not they meet the client's objectives. Finally, monitoring of the plan will occur to ensure that the estate plan has not become outmoded or inappropriate for the client.

In addition to these quantifiable steps, this chapter will also examine client counseling skills and techniques that improve communication skills between the financial planner and the client, and help the planner deal with the client who is reluctant to start planning the estate. In addition, counseling skills and recommendations will be discussed to assist the financial planner who needs to assist a client with the development of an estate plan. Especially important are questions designed to elicit further information when the client may be reluctant to discuss certain items related to estate planning.

THE ESTATE PLANNING PROCESS

The estate planning process is a methodology used to develop estate plans for all clients, regardless of their income level, asset ownership, or economic sophistication.

The overall estate plan should be one that analyzes the client's current financial condition. It should be one that can also project the client's future economic needs. The estate planning techniques selected should be appropriate to accomplish the client's objectives. Finally, the estate plan should be flexible enough for amendments or revisions which are dictated by the client's changing factual pattern.

When discussing the formation of an estate plan with the client, the financial planner needs to keep the following issues in mind:

1. Be aware of the rate of *inflation,* and the impact it can have on any estate plan.
2. Structure a plan that provides the estate with *liquidity*. It is not enough that the estate has sufficient assets to pay any potential estate tax liability. What is important to realize is that the estate may have to sell off specific properties (bequests) that were supposed to go to certain individuals in an attempt to pay off the debts and expenses of the estate. Liquidity becomes an important concern for the financial planner.
3. The financial planner needs to keep in mind that no estate plan is ever truly "final" or "complete." A number of changes can occur which can make the client's present estate plan outdated, inappropriate, or cause it to pay unneeded estate or gift taxes. *Periodic review* of the estate plan is essential to ensure that what the client *wants* and what the client *has* are, in fact, the same.

The steps presented on the following pages are intended to serve as guidelines for the estate planning methodology. By using this process, the financial planner should be able to structure an estate plan for any client, provided the planner is supplied with complete and accurate information. The ultimate test for whether the estate planning techniques selected are appropriate is by examining the client's estate planning objectives. If the selected technique accomplishes the estate planning objective, then it can be considered appropriate in light of all other information.

STEPS IN THE ESTATE PLANNING PROCESS

The estate planning process may be thought of as a series of steps that are used to develop and monitor a comprehensive estate plan for the client. The following steps are involved in the estate planning process.

1. Gather significant data form the client.
2. Establish and prioritize estate planning objectives.
3. Identify the factors that limit or affect the selection of estate planning techniques.
4. Identify estate planning weaknesses before selecting a technique.
5. Select an appropriate estate planning technique.
6. Implement the estate planning technique.
7. Monitor the plan for revisions and modifications.

Step 1: Gather Significant Data

The financial planner initiates the estate planning process by gathering significant data from the client, data that affect the selection and implementation of a comprehensive estate plan. The significant data gathered by the financial planner usually include whether or not the client has a will, how the client wishes to have his property divided upon death, the identity and relationship of those individuals considered to be the heirs or takers of the client's property, the manner in which title to property is held, and a list of all assets and interests held by the client that would be included in the client's gross estate and the includable value of each item. Also important is the amount of the client's debts and liabilities and how these amounts may reduce the size of the distributable estate to heirs or intended beneficiaries. There may be other significant information that also has a bearing on the creation of the estate plan, such as the health and life expectancy of the client and the client's family members, and whether there are any special health problems that may affect the creation of an estate plan. An accurate and thorough data gathering form should be used to obtain most of the significant estate planning information needed to properly plan for the client's estate.

Step 2: Establish and Prioritize Estate Planning Objectives

Once essential information has been gathered, the financial planner assists the client in identifying and prioritizing estate planning objectives. The greatest obstacle to identifying and prioritizing estate planning objectives occurs when a client has two or more objectives that the client would like to see fulfilled but has limited economic resources that prevent one or more objectives from being achieved. The financial planner's role is to make the client aware that limited resources make fulfillment of all objectives unlikely or unrealistic. The financial planner can assist the client by suggesting other alternatives. For example, the financial planner may suggest that the objectives be reordered in terms of their priority, or that one or more objectives be deferred until a later time. The client may then select other options which allow most of the objectives to remain intact. However, if none of the client's objectives are realistic in light of his or her resources, then the client may have to identify new objectives. Through analysis of the client data, the financial planner may be able to suggest a course of action that permits one or two objectives to be accomplished immediately and the remaining objectives to be accomplished in five years if the client's financial resources permit. Alternatively, the financial planner may suggest to the client that the remaining objectives be discarded because they are highly unrealistic in light of the client's limited resources.

Step 3: Identify Factors That Limit or Affect the Selection of Techniques

Once objectives have been identified and prioritized, the financial planner identifies those factors that may limit or affect the selection of estate planning techniques. The factors that have the potential for affecting the selection of an estate planning technique that accomplishes the client's estate planning objectives are the following:

1. Value of the gross estate
2. Amount of estate or gift tax liability
3. Health and life expectancy of the client
4. Financial needs of the client during life
5. Types of properties included in the client's estate
6. Title to properties included in the client's estate
7. Competency of the client's beneficiaries
8. The client's marginal income tax bracket
9. State law of the client's domicile

Some of these factors may have a greater capacity for influencing the selection of an appropriate estate planning technique than others. But taken as a whole, all nine factors restrain or affect what the client ultimately selects as an estate planning technique.

For example, a client may be 55 years old and in good health. His primary estate planning objective is to distribute his estate, valued at $1 million, to his wife and two children in three equal shares. He wants his wife and children to live at the standard of living to which they are accustomed. The factors that determine the selection of an appropriate estate planning technique for the client are the following:

1. Value of the gross estate: gross estate valued at $1 million
2. Amount of estate or gift tax liability: estate tax liability is $345,800 before subtracting applicable deductions and credits
3. Health and life expectancy of the client: good health; client has life expectancy of 19 more years
4. Financial needs of the client: client needs $2500 per month in today's dollars for living expenses and savings for retirement
5. Types of properties included in the estate: client's estate consists largely of a farming operation which has appreciated greatly since its acquisition 35 years ago; the farm is income-producing though it would be difficult to find a buyer for the entire farming interest if the client dies in the near future
6. Title to properties included in the estate: most assets, including the farm, held solely by the client which permits both lifetime control and testamentary disposition of the property
7. Competency of the client's beneficiaries: client's spouse is legally, mentally, and financially competent; client's children are legally and mentally competent but lack investment experience and are not considered financially competent
8. Client's marginal income tax bracket: client is in a 31 percent marginal tax bracket
9. State law of the client's domicile: client is domiciled in a common law property state.

A detailed discussion of these factors and how they affect the selection of an appropriate estate planning technique follows.

Value of the gross estate.   The value of the client's gross estate is a significant factor in the selection of an appropriate estate planning technique. If the client's gross estate exceeds the amount of the exemption equivalent, the client may be·subject to estate tax liability if deductions and available credits are not used. For example, if a client had a gross estate valued at $1 million and was not married and did not make charitable testamentary contributions, the client's estate tax liability would be $153,000 ($345,800 minus $192,800 in unified credit) if the client died in 1987 or in a later year. On the other hand, if the client was married and specified a marital deduction amount of $400,000, the client would have no estate tax liability because of the use of both the marital deduction and the unified credit for the client's estate. If the client's gross estate is a major concern because of the tax liability that could arise, the client may wish to select particular techniques that could reduce this tax liability, such as a charitable technique or one or more trusts that utilize the marital deduction and the unified credit—a combination of a marital and nonmarital trust.

Amount of estate or gift tax liability. The amount of estate or gift tax liability could be a significant factor in terms of what the client selects as an appropriate estate planning technique. If the client's tax liability is potentially large, it could have an impact on the client's plans for distribution of the remainder of the estate to family members, spouse, and other beneficiaries. Obviously, any savings in estate or gift tax liability means that there will be a greater amount of the net estate remaining that can be distributed to family members. Thus, if the client faces a projected estate tax liability, the client may wish to implement particular techniques to achieve a greater amount of net estate that can be distributed to the client's spouse and family members (e.g., special use valuation on real estate held in a closely held farming or ranching operation or alternate valuation on assets that can be expected to have a lower value six months after the date of the decedent's death than they do on the date of the decedent's death).

Health and life expectancy of the client. The client's health and life expectancy can affect the selection of an estate planning technique that achieves the client's objectives. For example, if the client is in poor health or has a short life expectancy, the use of a single life private annuity would be more appropriate than some other types of estate planning techniques, such as life insurance. If the client is in excellent health and has a long life expectancy, various techniques may be appropriate to achieve the client's objectives; a life insurance trust could be an appropriate technique as well as a cross-purchase agreement used to provide funds for the purchase of a closely held business interest. Obviously, in these situations the financial planner is attempting to reduce estate tax liability and to avoid probate. If the recommended technique does not remove the asset from the gross estate or does not avoid probate, then it may be inappropriate in light of the client's objectives.

Financial needs of the client. The financial needs of the client may determine, to some extent, whether a particular estate planning technique is appropriate. For example, if a client has living expenses of $30,000 annually and has additional projected savings needs of $12,000 annually for retirement purposes, then any estate planning technique that would transfer any portion of the client's assets that exceeds this amount for purposes of an estate plan would seriously disrupt the client's current financial needs. The need for retirement income, coupled with the need to match current living expenses, could prevent certain estate planning techniques from being selected. If a client has financial needs of $42,000 annually, this need ordinarily would prevent the creation of an irrevocable living trust into which a significant portion of the client's estate would be contributed, as long as such a trust would prevent current financial needs from being met. An appropriate estate planning technique would be one that would allow the client to achieve particular estate planning objectives, while permitting him to live within his means.

Types of properties included in the estate.   The types of properties included in a client's estate can often determine whether a particular estate planning technique is appropriate. For example, if a client owns a closely held incorporated business that has appreciated greatly in value and he wishes to peg the value of the business for federal estate tax purposes while also locating a successor for the business at his death, then a buy-sell agreement may be the most appropriate estate planning technique.

Property considerations that may influence the selection of an appropriate estate planning technique include the following:

1. Whether or not the property is difficult to value
2. Whether or not the property can be easily divided (e.g., can the property be partitioned so that a portion could be sold to pay debts and taxes?)
3. Whether or not the property is liquid and has a market in the event it must be sold
4. Whether or not the property is appreciating in value
5. Whether or not the property is depreciating in value
6. Whether or not the death of the client-owner will impair or reduce the value of the property

All of these considerations can play an important part in the selection of an estate planning technique that is most appropriate for the types of property included in the client's gross estate.

Title to properties included in the estate.   The manner in which title to properties is held may also influence the selection of an appropriate estate planning technique. If property is held by the client as sole owner, this form of ownership provides the client with the greatest flexibility as well as postmortem control. If the bulk of the client's estate is held in joint tenancy with right of survivorship, this prevents the client from exercising any postmortem control over the property if the client predeceases the other joint tenant. Thus, if a client wishes to transfer property to his son, yet the property is currently held in joint tenancy with right of survivorship with the client's spouse, this form of ownership prevents the client from making a testamentary transfer of the property to his son if the client dies, survived by his spouse. Since the client exercises no postmortem control should he predecease his spouse, the client may not wish to keep the property titled in this form if he wishes to transfer the property to his son. Thus, some other form of property ownership may be necessary to achieve the specific estate planning objectives of the client.

Competency of the client's beneficiaries. The competency of the client's beneficiaries can be an important factor in the selection of an appropriate estate planning technique. A beneficiary can be said to be *legally competent* if he is not a minor; thus, all adults are legally competent. A beneficiary can be said to be *mentally competent* if he has not been adjudicated to be mentally incompetent by a court, has not been confined to a mental institution, or has not undertaken any other conduct that would raise questions about his competence. The most significant type of competence from a financial planning point of view is a beneficiary's *financial competence.* Financial competence includes the ability of the beneficiary to invest in and manage assets, provide for other family members, and supervise and administer assets. If the beneficiary possesses financial competency, it could be considered appropriate for him to serve as administrator or executor of the estate, or he could be named as a co-trustee or trustee of a trust, or he could be named as a guardian or conservator on behalf of minors and other incompetent family members.

Thus, a beneficiary considered financially competent could serve as a trustee for a particular type of trust that serves the best interests of a class of beneficiaries, for example, minor children. On the other hand, if the same beneficiary is considered financially incompetent, an outright transfer of property to that individual would be inappropriate.

Client's marginal income tax bracket. A client may wish to reduce his or her income tax liability through the use of one or more estate planning techniques. For example, if a client is in a high-marginal income tax bracket and wishes to reduce it, then several types of estate planning techniques may be appropriate to reduce the tax liability (e.g., an outright gift of income-producing property to the donee, or, in the case of a closely held business interest, a family partnership). Any technique that would not reduce the client's marginal tax bracket or reduce the income tax liability on the income produced by it would be inappropriate for the client's estate planning objectives.

State law of the client's domicile.   State law can be a significant factor in the selection of an estate planning technique. A state that has a system of community property laws may have very different estate tax and estate planning consequences for a client than a state that has a system that follows the common law property concepts. In a community property state, the decedent spouse might have to include a provision in his will that leaves his portion of the community residence to his spouse, whereas, in a common law property state there would be no need for a will provision bequeathing the property to the spouse if the property were held in joint tenancy with right of survivorship.

Other differences in state law can have a significant impact on a client's estate plan. Among the differences in state law that can influence the creation of an estate plan are the following:

1. Whether or not the state has a mortmain statute, which prohibits excessive charitable bequests when the decedent is survived by spouse and children,
2. Whether or not the state permits holographic (handwritten) wills,
3. Whether or not the state permits the surviving spouse to elect to take the entire amount of the decedent's estate, or whether the elective share is limited to a certain dollar amount,
4. Whether or not the state has state inheritance taxes,
5. Whether the state has a homestead allowance or a homestead exemption, and, if so, what the dollar amount of the allowance or exemption is.

Because there are 50 sets of state laws that can affect an estate plan, the financial planner should consult with an attorney to determine the impact of state law on a client's estate plan.

Step 4: Identify Present Estate Planning Weaknesses

Once all factors that have the potential for limiting the selection of an estate planning technique have been identified, the financial planner needs to evaluate the client's present situation in order to identify weaknesses which may exist before other estate planning techniques may be implemented.

A weakness can be defined as any situation in the client's present estate plan that is in conflict with an estate planning objective. For example, a client may wish to leave his business property to his children (objective) but is unable to do this because the title to the property is currently held in joint tenancy with right of survivorship with the client's business partner. Thus, the client's present situation conflicts with his estate planning objective. This is a weakness in the present plan. It needs to be modified if the client expects to transfer the property to his children, as he wishes.

Conversely, if the estate planning objective conflicts with any of the factors discussed so far, the objective may need to be modified or revised.

Step 5: Select an Appropriate Technique

Using the client's estate planning objectives and the limiting factors previously discussed as guidelines, the financial planner selects estate planning techniques that are appropriate for the client's situation. Techniques that do not meet the client's objectives are eliminated, as are techniques that are inconsistent with the client's financial needs, marginal tax bracket, types of property, title to property, and the other factors previously discussed.

For example, a client may have two estate planning objectives: (1) to reduce his own estate tax liability, and (2) to ensure that the property passes to children from a prior marriage while qualifying the property for the marital deduction.

Using the client's objectives and limiting factors as guidelines, the most appropriate estate planning technique for the client is the qualified terminable interest property trust (Q-TIP) because it is the only technique that accomplishes both objectives. If elected by the client's executor, the Q-TIP trust reduces estate tax liability by qualifying for the marital deduction in the client's estate; yet, it also allows the client to transfer the property to his children from a previous marriage after the death of his present spouse. Since the Q-TIP trust is the only technique that accomplishes *all* of these objectives, it is the most appropriate. Any technique that accomplishes fewer than all of the objectives is not the most appropriate estate planning technique.

Step 6: Implement the Estate Planning Technique

Once the most appropriate estate planning technique is selected, the technique is implemented. Usually, implementation involves the use and coordination of an estate planning team of attorneys, financial planners, accountants, insurance agents, and others. An estate plan needs to be properly implemented so that the client's objectives are achieved, tax liability is reduced, and the property is ultimately transferred to the intended beneficiaries. If the estate plan is not properly implemented, there can be adverse income, estate, and gift tax consequences for the owner of the property, as well as disruption of the owner's plans. In addition, if the financial planner attempts to implement the plan without the assistance of an attorney or an accountant, the financial planner may be liable for any acts considered to be the unauthorized practice of law or the unauthorized practice of accountancy.

Step 7: Monitor the Plan for Revisions

No estate plan can ever be said to be total or final. Changes in the client's family situation, testamentary intentions, or changes in the tax laws may make an estate plan that was once appropriate an outmoded plan. Thus, every estate plan needs to be monitored to ensure that the client's plan and objectives are consistent.

The monitoring process involves a periodic review (e.g., every 6 months or every year) of a client's plan with the client to ensure that the financial planner is aware of changes in the client's family situation, asset ownership, or other factors. When changes do occur, the entire estate plan is reviewed and modified where necessary so that the plan is once again appropriate for the client's objectives and circumstances.

ENCOURAGING THE CLIENT TO PLAN AN ESTATE

Many financial planners may discuss risk management, investments, and tax planning with their clients with relative ease. Yet, when it comes to discussing estate planning, the client may indicate no desire to have the subject broached, or may show extreme discomfort when it is discussed. This can become disheartening to the financial planner who sees a client who is in desperate need of an estate plan of some type.

The financial planner should keep in mind that there may be several reasons why the client has not prepared an estate plan, or has not thought about the prospect of distributing the estate after death. Following are some common reasons why people fail to plan their estates:

1. The topic of death is an unpleasant one. Many people have not psychologically come to terms with the inevitability of their death. As a result, if they do not plan for it, they do not have to think about it. Many people assume that the distribution of their property after their deaths will become someone else's problem and they would rather not have anything to do with it while they are alive.

2. Many people are aware of the immense family problems that will result from their planning; will contests, family arguments over particular assets, and delays and disputes over estate distribution, executor's commissions and probate-related fees can all have a detrimental effect on the planning of an estate. Many people, knowing the temperament of other family members, are deterred from planning

an estate because of the unpleasantness that they fear will ens\ They avoid planning their estates, assuming that, when they die, they will not have to worry about the rest of the family.

3. Many people have complicated business matters and their involvement with their business affairs is so time consuming that they do not give much thought to what will happen when they die. If an individual owns a growing business that is appreciating rapidly in value, he may be so involved in running the business and making day-to-day decisions that the activity leaves him with little time to consider what will happen when he dies. Some people who have considered what will happen when they die may not have answers to the questions they have about their business: How do I keep the appreciation out of my estate? Who will take the property after I die? How can I make a tranquil disposition of the business to other family members when I retire? What if no one in the family shows any interest in running the business? Rather than attempting to answer these questions through careful planning, many business owners do not allow themselves to address these issues and ignore estate planning as a result.

4. Many people are physically mobile and, because of their frequent relocations, do not think about planning their estates. For the young professional mobile client, estate planning is a concept he will consider in the future, at some point in time when the client finally settles in one place, starts a family, and makes permanent ties in the community. Many people have not yet reached that point; a person who lives in three or four states in a 10-year period does not have a concept of permanence. For this type of client, estate planning is a remote concept because of the finality of making a will, naming an executor, naming guardians and conservators, or planning estate tax savings.

Despite these reasons, the financial planner should encourage the client to plan an estate, especially if the client's assets indicate the possibility of an estate tax problem. If the client is reluctant to discuss estate planning, the financial planner should delicately and diplomatically provide the client with several compelling reasons why the client should have an estate plan. The following are some reasons why an individual should have an estate plan:

1. If the client has minor children, the welfare of the children can be structured and supervised through formal estate planning. Trusts, guardianships, and conservatorships can all ensure that the minor children are properly provided for; in addition, proper estate planning

can ensure that the client's assets are preserved for the children and their needs.

2. Proper estate planning can minimize estate taxes, thereby leaving a greater amount of property available to family members, heirs, friends, and others.

3. If the client owns a business, proper estate planning can provide for an orderly distribution of the business to another key individual, employee, or competent family member. Without estate planning for the business asset, the business could be distributed according to the laws of intestacy, and could end up going to an individual who shows little interest in running the business. Even worse, the business could be dissolved.

4. Proper estate planning is necessary to guarantee that the person's estate is liquid. If the estate has insufficient liquidity, major assets such as real estate or assets that have sentimental value for one or more family members might have to be sold to satisfy creditors and pay estate taxes and administrative expenses.

5. Proper estate planning can actually resolve many intrafamily problems that could occur on the death of the individual. Estate planning, if properly structured for a client, can dispose of particular assets to certain named beneficiaries, bequeath general legacies or sums of money to other beneficiaries, allocate property to trusts in such a way that minimizes estate tax liability, and provide a stream of income to the surviving spouse and minor children for living expenses during probate of the estate. If the estate is planned properly, will contests and other intrafamily disputes can be avoided, in most cases.

6. Proper estate planning can provide continuity of income in the event of the client's disability or in other emergency situations. Should the client and the client's spouse both die, or should one of them die while the other becomes disabled, a properly arranged estate plan can provide a life income stream to the surviving spouse, provide for the payment of medical expenses or other debts, and provide for the benefit and welfare of any minor children or other family members.

Given these reasons and others, the client should be encouraged to initiate the planning of his or her estate.

A more difficult situation occurs when the client provides the financial planner with an incomplete picture of the client's estate plan. For whatever reasons, the client may only provide the financial planner with some of the information needed that is necessary for the proper planning of an estate. It is the responsibility of the financial planner to obtain as accurate a picture as possible of the client's complete estate plan.

For this reason, the financial planner may need to implement certain questions that are designed to elicit additional information to the planner about the client's state of affairs. The client may not understand why these questions are being asked and lacking that understanding, may be reluctant to provide the financial planner with the appropriate information. For this reason, the financial planner needs to understand the implications of these questions and the reason underlying the asking of the question. Better understanding of the client's estate plans and objectives is the end result of asking questions of this nature.

The following types of questions are designed to elicit the information necessary for completion and implementation of the client's estate plan. These questions may be added to the financial planner's client interview form, or they may be asked in a separate interview of the client. The financial planner should pay special attention to the reasons for which the question is being asked, since the nature of the question may reveal possible estate problems for the client, or may reveal a possible income, estate or gift tax problem for the client if the present estate plan is not changed. The questions that follow should be thought of as representative in nature, not all-inclusive.

Question: At present, do you (the client) have a will?

Reason for asking question: If the answer is no, the client's property will pass to heirs under the laws of intestate succession. It is possible that one or more individuals for whom the client had strong bonds of admiration or affection may receive nothing from the client unless the client has a will executed to make specific provisions for the individual in question. Otherwise, the laws of intestate distribution will pass all property to the client's surviving spouse, children, grandchildren, parents, brothers and sisters, or other family members who meet the definition of being an heir.

Question: If the client has a will, when was the will executed (written)?

Reason for asking question: It is possible that if the will was executed prior to September 12, 1981, it will have to be amended in order to achieve the client's objective of leaving a greater portion of the estate to the client's spouse as property qualifying for the marital deduction. Since the unlimited marital deduction became available for estates of decedents dying after December 31, 1981, who had wills executed on or after September 12, 1981, it would be necessary to have an attorney write a new will or attach a codicil to the present will if the client's estate planning objective is to give the surviving spouse a greater portion of the estate as marital deduction property. Under the law that existed prior to September 12, 1981, the maximum amount that could qualify for the marital deduction was $250,000 or 50 percent of the adjusted gross estate, whichever amount was greater. Thus, if the client wishes to leave any amount greater than this to the surviving spouse where the will was written before this date, the will must be revised to ensure that the marital deduction amount available to the client also coincides with the unlimited marital deduction amount. The law does not automatically revise the written provisions of a will to make it coincide with the present tax law, since it is assumed that a will is a voluntary instrument—in other words, if the maker of the will wishes to have the will reflect his or her true intentions, the maker usually has the opportunity to amend or revise the instrument. Thus, any tax laws and estate laws enacted after the date of the will execution will not apply to the provisions of the will, unless otherwise noted by the specific provisions of the law. For this reason, the will of the client has to be changed in order to comply with the client's specific estate planning objectives.

Question: If the client is married, did the client ever live in a community property state at any time during the course of the marriage?

Reason for asking question: If the couple resided in a community property state at any time during the marriage (Arizona, California, Idaho, Louisiana, Nevada, New Mexico, Texas, Washington, and beginning in 1986, Wisconsin, which has a statutory form of marital property known as marital partnership property) and acquired property in that state, the property retains its status as community property even though the couple may subsequently move to a common law property state. This can be of significance for a client and the client's spouse for estate planning purposes. Unless the couple elects to treat the property as some form of property other than community property, which can be accomplished through a separate property agreement, the property will be divided according to community property principles. If a separate property agreement is not entered into between the parties, the parties could be making a dangerous assumption about the classification of the property for estate planning purposes.

Question: Does the client have property in more than one state?

Reason for asking question: If the client has property in more than one state, and has no lifetime plans for disposition or transfer of the property, the client's estate will be subject to a secondary probate for any real estate located in a state other than the state of client's domicile (personal property is usually probated in the state of the decedent's domicile and does not cause the problem of an ancillary probate procedure that is caused by real estate). Thus, to avoid additional time delays and the expenses related to the administration of the secondary or ancillary estate, the client may wish to avoid this procedure. If this is the case, the client needs to be aware of specific estate planning techniques that can be used to avoid an ancillary probate procedure for example, creation and funding of a revocable living trust that has as its corpus the property located outside the state of the client's domicile.

Question: Does the client live in a state that has adopted material provisions of the Uniform Probate Code?

Reason for asking question: Although the answer to this question could be determined easily by consulting with an attorney, the financial planner needs to be aware of the estate tax implications of property transfers in a state that has adopted the Uniform Probate Code (UPC). Especially significant is the definition of the "augmented estate" for the surviving spouse. The augmented estate is a formula used in UPC states to determine the amount of property that can be used to satisfy the elective share of the surviving spouse's property. The augmented estate can include such lifetime property transfers made by a decedent such as property placed into a revocable living trust, property gratuitously placed into a joint form of ownership with someone other than the surviving spouse (e.g., placing property into joint tenancy with right of survivorship with a nonfamily member who provided none of the consideration for the property), and certain amounts of cash and other liquid assets that were gifted away in the two year time period preceding the client's death. The net effect of including these assets in the property constituting the augmented estate is to give the surviving spouse a greater net percentage of the decedent's estate than she would otherwise receive if her elective share of his estate only consisted of the actual assets owned outright by the decedent at the time of his death. Basically, the concept of the augmented estate protects the surviving spouse from a decedent who attempted to make large lifetime transfers of property to nonrelated individuals and thereby deprived the surviving spouse of that share of the decedent's estate that she would have otherwise received. To determine whether the client's state of domicile is one which has adopted the Uniform Probate Code, the financial planner should consult with the attorney who forms part of the estate planning team.

Question: Does the client own property that passes to a named beneficiary outside the will?

Reason for asking question: If the client has property that passes to a named beneficiary outside the will, such as life insurance, IRA accounts, or other property transfers known as "will substitutes," this property will avoid the probate process and will result in a reduction of probate costs and expenses. Since many clients wish to avoid the time delay usually associated with the distribution of assets through the probate process and since many administrative fees, including attorney's fees, are usually based on a percentage of the probate estate, these fees could be reduced by transferring property in such a way that avoids probate altogether. Thus, a client may wish to consider the use of one or more techniques that may avoid probate.

Question: Has the client previously been married and are there living children from that marriage?

Reason for asking question: If the client wishes to transfer property to children from a prior marriage but plans on doing so indirectly through bequests made by his second wife under the terms of her will to these children, the client needs to seriously consider the interpersonal relationships among all the parties before considering the permanency of this arrangement. Even if the children from the first marriage and the second spouse are on good terms now, this relationship could deteriorate in the future and the children could be totally disinherited. This could occur because, once the client bequeathed all of his property to his second wife, she would then be free to dispose of the property as she saw fit. This could mean that she could leave all of the property to the children born of the second marriage; or, if none were born from that marriage, she could leave all of the property to her children from her first marriage. What is important to recognize is the possibility that the client's children from his first marriage could be effectively disinherited. To avoid this possibility, the client should consider seriously the use of an estate planning technique that would prevent the children from the first marriage from being disinherited, for example, use of a Q-TIP trust.

Question: Does the client wish to leave bequests to a charity or charities? Are there current provisions in the client's will that leave sizeable bequests to one or more charities?

Reason for asking question: Charitable transfers serve to reduce the client's federal estate and gift tax liability because they take advantage of the estate tax charitable deduction as well as the gift tax charitable deduction. If a client has a will that leaves a sizeable portion of the client's estate to one or more charities, it is possible that a portion of the bequest could be claimed by the client's heirs or other interested parties. This is possible if the state in which the client dies has a mortmain statute, the purpose of which is to avoid excessive charitable bequests when the client is survived by a spouse, children, or other dependents. If the state has a mortmain statute that prohibits a transfer of more than 20 percent of the decedent's net estate to a qualified charity when the client is survived by a spouse, children, or other dependents, then it is possible that any of these parties could file a claim with the court seeking to set aside that portion of the charitable bequest which exceeds 20 percent of the net estate (e.g., a charitable bequest which left 30% of the net estate to a qualified charity could be set aside to the extent of the amount that exceeds the maximum charitable bequest under the mortmain statute—in this case, 10% could be claimed by the spouse, children, or other interested parties).

Question: Does the client or the client's spouse have significant investment or business experience?

Reason for asking question: If either the client or the client's spouse has significant investment experience or business managerial experience, this factor may determine the appropriateness of a particular estate planning technique, for example, if either the client or the client's spouse has the managerial experience required to invest and manage assets, the use of a trust in which the spouse or grantor is named as trustee could be an appropriate estate planning technique. If either the spouse or the client lacks such experience, it might be more appropriate to name a trust company or other corporate trustee as the party responsible for managing assets and making investment decisions. If the client and the client's spouse both have the ability to manage, but lack the desire to do so, then naming a professional trust company to manage the assets with a family member named as co-trustee might be more appropriate.

Question: Does the client wish to make an anatomical gift of his organs after his death?

Reason for asking question: Many clients wrongfully assume that they will be able to make a gift of their organs or their bodies to science when they die and include such a provision in the will to that effect. Unfortunately, most wills are not read until long after the death of the decedent or certainly at a time when it is too late to be able to make the proper donations of the bodily organs to science or for research purposes. In order to properly comply with the wishes of the client, the financial planner should direct the client to an attorney to make the proper plans for such gifts while the donor is still alive. The financial planner should stress the importance of not placing such instructions in the terms of the will. Rather, donations of bodily organs to science or for other specified purposes should be done under the terms of a separate letter of instructions to be delivered to the executor, spouse, or personal representative at some time prior to death or immediately after death to ensure that the wishes of the donor can be fulfilled.

Figure 1.1 is a sample client questionnaire that may prove helpful, in eliciting essential planning information.

Figure 1.1a Form A, Personal Data*

CLIENT

NAME: _____ LAST _____ FIRST _____ INITIAL

AGE _____ BIRTHDATE _____ BIRTHPLACE (City and State) _____ SOCIAL SECURITY NUMBER _____

SOCIAL SECURITY STATUS: COVERED _____ NOT COVERED _____ COMMENT _____

RESIDENCE ADDRESS: STREET _____ CITY _____ STATE _____ ZIP _____ OWN/RENT _____ TELEPHONE NO. _____

RESIDENCE SINCE: _____ PRIOR RESIDENCE ADDRESS (if less than five years) _____

OFFICE ADDRESS: STREET _____ CITY _____ STATE _____ ZIP _____ OWN/RENT _____ YEARS _____ TELEPHONE NO. _____

EMPLOYER _____ OCCUPATION _____ AREA OF EXPERTISE _____ NUMBER OF YEARS _____

DAY OFF _____ BEST HOURS TO PHONE _____ SECRETARY'S NAME _____

SEND MAIL TO: HOME: _____ OFFICE: _____ OTHER: _____

MARITAL STATUS (CHECK ONE):

MARRIED _____ SINGLE _____ DIVORCED _____ SEPARATED _____ WIDOWED _____

DATE OF MARRIAGE _____

ANY FORMER MARRIAGE(S): Yes _____ No _____ COMMENT: _____

EDUCATION:

GRADUATE SCHOOL: _____ DEGREE _____ YEAR _____

COLLEGE: _____ DEGREE _____ YEAR _____

PROFESSIONAL DESIGNATION: _____ YEAR _____

OTHER: _____ YEAR _____

Figure 1.1b Form A, Personal Data

SPOUSE _____

NAME: _____
            LAST   FIRST   INITIAL

AGE _____ BIRTHDATE _____ BIRTHPLACE (City and State) _____ SOCIAL SECURITY NUMBER _____

SOCIAL SECURITY STATUS: COVERED _____ NOT COVERED _____ COMMENT _____

RESIDENCE ADDRESS: _____ STREET _____ CITY _____ STATE _____ ZIP _____ OWN/RENT _____ TELEPHONE NO. _____

RESIDENCE SINCE: _____ PRIOR RESIDENCE ADDRESS (if less than five years) _____

OFFICE ADDRESS: _____ STREET _____ CITY _____ STATE _____ ZIP _____ OWN/RENT _____ YEARS _____ TELEPHONE NO. _____

EMPLOYER _____ OCCUPATION _____ AREA OF EXPERTISE _____ NUMBER OF YEARS _____

DAY OFF _____ BEST HOURS TO PHONE _____ SECRETARY'S NAME _____

SEND MAIL TO:
HOME: _____ OFFICE: _____ OTHER: _____
MARITAL STATUS (CHECK ONE):
MARRIED _____ DATE OF MARRIAGE _____ SINGLE _____ DIVORCED _____ SEPARATED _____ WIDOWED _____
ANY FORMER MARRIAGE(S): Yes _____ No _____ COMMENT: _____

EDUCATION:
GRADUATE SCHOOL: _____ DEGREE _____ YEAR _____
COLLEGE: _____ DEGREE _____ YEAR _____
PROFESSIONAL DESIGNATION: _____ YEAR _____
OTHER: _____ YEAR _____

21

Figure 1.1b Form A, Personal Data (Continued)

DEPENDENT CHILDREN (List Eldest First)

NAME	AGE	BIRTHDATE	SOC. SEC. #	THIS MARRIAGE	ADOPTED	MARITAL STATUS

NON-DEPENDENT CHILDREN	AGE	BIRTHDATE	SOC. SEC. #	THIS MARRIAGE	ADOPTED	MARITAL STATUS

OTHER RELATIVES:	LIVING YES/NO	AGE	DEPENDENT YES/NO	NAME	HEALTH	CAUSE OF DEATH (If Deceased)
C-Mother						
C-Father						
C-Brother/Sister						
Other						
S-Mother						
S-Father						
S-Brother/Sister						
Other						

C = Client   S = Spouse

Figure 1.1b Form A, Personal Data (Continued)

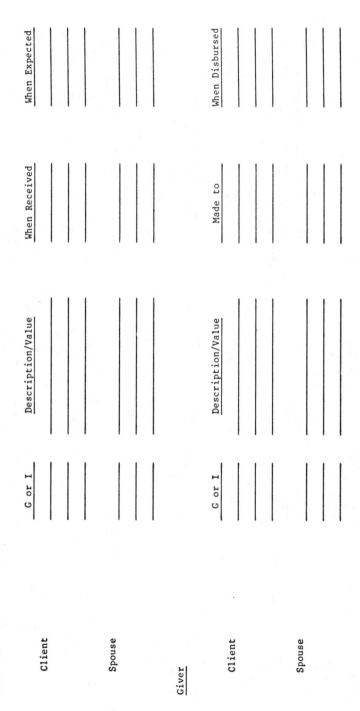

GIFTS (G) AND INHERITANCES (I)

Receiver

G or I	Description/Value	When Received	When Expected

Client

Spouse

Giver

G or I	Description/Value	Made to	When Disbursed

Client

Spouse

Figure 1.1b Form A, Personal Data (Continued)

LIST OF ADVISERS & FREQUENCY OF CONTACT (e.g., once a year etc.)

ATTORNEY:
NAME _____
ADDRESS _____
TELEPHONE NO. _____
CONTACT FREQUENCY _____

ACCOUNTANT:
NAME _____
ADDRESS _____
TELEPHONE NO. _____
CONTACT FREQUENCY _____

BANKER:
NAME _____
ADDRESS _____
TELEPHONE NO. _____
CONTACT FREQUENCY _____

REAL ESTATE BROKER:
NAME _____
ADDRESS _____
TELEPHONE NO. _____
CONTACT FREQUENCY _____

LIFE INSURANCE AGENT:
NAME _____
ADDRESS _____
TELEPHONE NO. _____
CONTACT FREQUENCY _____

TRUST OFFICER:
NAME _____
ADDRESS _____
TELEPHONE NO. _____
CONTACT FREQUENCY _____

STOCK BROKER:
NAME _____
ADDRESS _____
TELEPHONE NO. _____
CONTACT FREQUENCY _____

OTHER:
(Specify)
NAME _____
ADDRESS _____
TELEPHONE NO. _____
CONTACT FREQUENCY _____

COMMENTS: _____

LOCATION OF IMPORTANT PAPERS: R = Residence;   S = Safe Deposit;   O = Other (Specify)

Original Will _____
Copy of Will _____
Original Trust _____
Copy of Trust _____
Naturalization Papers _____

Real Property Deeds _____
Insurance Policies _____
Military Papers _____
Security Certificates _____
Adoption Papers _____

Business Agreements _____
Pension Certificates _____
Marriage License _____
Birth Certificates _____
Divorce Papers _____

Figure 1.1c Form AA, General Questions

1. Have you ever had a financial evaluation? Yes _____ No _____ If yes, how did you feel about it? _____

2. In your opinion, are you living within your means? Yes _____ No _____

3. Do you currently have any financial concerns? Yes _____ No _____
   Explain _____

4. What is your career goal? (e.g., What position do you think you will hold in five years?) _____

5. What is a conservative estimate of your base salary for the next five years? _____

6. Does your spouse know all the details of your financial affairs? Yes _____ No _____

7. What value do you place on your spouse's investment ideas? _____

8. Do you tell your spouse of your financial decisions before or after they are implemented? _____

9. In your opinion, if your spouse were left on his/her own, would his/her judgment and emotional stability serve the best interests of the family? _____

Figure 1.1c Form AA, General Questions (Continued)

10. To what degree are the members of your family capable of managing financial affairs? _____

11. Is there anyone, other than your spouse, providing you with financial advice at this time? Yes _____ No _____
Give details. _____

12. What are your immediate financial goals? _____

13. Have any of your current assets been earmarked for future use? Give details. _____
_____
_____

14. Do you have any immediate plans to remodel your current residence? Yes _____ No _____
Give details. _____
_____

15. Do you anticipate the purchase of a second residence, new automobile, new appliances, boat, etc., in the next three years? Yes _____ No _____ Give details. _____
_____

16. Over the next five years, do you anticipate the sale of your current residence? Yes _____ No _____
If so, what are the reasons for the sale? _____

Figure 1.1c Form AA, General Questions (Continued)

17. What are your long range (beyond five years) financial goals?

   Client _____

   Spouse _____

18. Are you presently in the military service? Yes _____ No _____

   Period of service _____

   Branch _____

   Highest Rank _____

19. Is your spouse presently in the military service? Yes _____ No _____

   Period of service _____

   Branch _____

   Highest Rank _____

20. Are you a veteran of military service? Yes _____ No _____

   Period of service _____

   Branch _____

   Highest Rank _____

21. Is your spouse a veteran of military service? Yes _____ No _____

   Period of service _____

   Branch _____

   Highest Rank _____

Figure 1.1d Form B, Insurance Policies

CODES

Ownership/Beneficiary

C – Client
S – Spouse
Ch – Children
O – Other (Explain)

Mode of Payment

A – Annual
S – Semi-Annual
Q – Quarterly
M – Monthly
AP – Automatic Payment

Type of Policy

WL – Whole Life
DT – Decreasing Term
T – Term
GI – Group Individual
GF – Group Family
I – Individual
R – Renewable

LIFE POLICIES

CLIENT:

INSURER AND POLICY NUMBER	OWNER	AGE AT ISSUE	FACE AMOUNT	PREMIUM/ MODE OF PAYMENT	TYPE OF POLICY CODE	CURRENT CASH VALUE	BENEFI- CIARY CODE
				/			
				/			
				/			
				/			
				/			

Totals

Comments (Loans, Dividend Status, Riders, etc.)

Figure 1.1d Form B, Insurance Policies (Continued)

LIFE POLICIES

SPOUSE:

INSURER AND POLICY NUMBER	OWNER	AGE AT ISSUE	FACE AMOUNT	PREMIUM/ MODE OF PAYMENT	TYPE OF POLICY CODE	CURRENT CASH VALUE	BENEFI- CIARY CODE
				/			
				/			
				/			
				/			
				/			

Totals

Comments (Loans, Dividend Status, Riders, etc.)

CHILDREN:

				/			
				/			
				/			
				/			
				/			

Totals

Comments (Loans, Dividend Status, Riders, etc.)

Figure 1.1e Form C, Cash, Checking, Savings Accounts, etc.

How much are you and your spouse systematically saving each month? $ _____
How? (Payroll Deduction, etc.)

ASSET	INTEREST RATE	OWNERSHIP*	BANK NAME AND LOCATION	ACCOUNT NUMBER	AVERAGE MONTHLY BALANCE	PRESENT BALANCE
Cash on Hand:						
Checking						
Checking						
Savings						
Savings						
Savings						
Credit Union						
Money Market Fund						
Other						
				TOTAL IN PERSONAL ACCOUNTS		$

*Ownership   Joint Tenants = JT   Community Property = CP
Tenancy in Common = TC   Client's Name = C
Spouse's Name = S

Figure 1.1f Form D, Securities: Stocks, Bonds, Mutual Funds, Government Issues, etc.

STOCKS

TITLE/ OWNERSHIP*	STOCK(S) CORPORATE NAME	NO. OF SHARES	** P/C	CURRENT DIVIDEND	DIV. RE.***	PURCHASE DATE	PRICE/SH. COST	TOTAL COST	CURRENT PRICE/SH.	TOTAL MKT. VALUE

FOR OFFICE USE ONLY (over CURRENT PRICE/SH. and TOTAL MKT. VALUE columns)

TOTAL _____   TOTAL _____

BONDS

TITLE/ OWNERSHIP*	ISSUER'S NAME	# OF UNITS	UNIT FACE VALUE	COUPON INT. RATE	MATURITY DATE	PURCHASE DATE	UNIT COST	TOTAL COST	CURRENT PRICE/UNIT	TOTAL MKT. VALUE

FOR OFFICE USE ONLY (over CURRENT PRICE/UNIT and TOTAL MKT. VALUE columns)

TOTAL _____   TOTAL _____

*TITLE/OWNERSHIP: Joint Tenants = JT   Spouse's Name = S   Community Property = CP

Tenancy in Common = TC   Client's Name = C

**PREFERRED/COMMON
***DIVIDEND REINVESTED

31

Figure 1.1f Form D, Securities (Continued)

MUTUAL FUNDS

							FOR OFFICE USE ONLY	
TITLE/ OWNERSHIP*	ISSUER'S NAME	NO. OF UNITS	MON./QTR. SYSTEMATIC PURCHASE PLAN	CAPITAL GAINS REINVESTED	DIV. RE.**	PURCHASE DATE	UNIT COST	TOTAL COST

	CURRENT PRICE/UNIT	TOTAL MKT. VALUE

TOTAL _____ TOTAL _____

GOVERNMENT ISSUES

									FOR OFFICE USE ONLY	
TITLE/ OWNERSHIP*	ISSUER'S NAME	NO. OF UNITS	DENOMIN- ATION	INT. RATE	ISSUE DATE	MATURITY DATE	PURCHASE DATE	UNIT COST	TOTAL COST	CURRENT PRICE

TOTAL MKT. VALUE

TOTAL _____ TOTAL _____

Are any of these securities pledged as collateral? Yes _____   No _____
If yes, explain _____

*TITLE/OWNERSHIP: Joint Tenants = JT   Spouse's Name = S   Community Property = CP
                  Tenancy in Common = TC   Client's Name = C

**DIVIDENDS REINVESTED

32

Figure 1.1g Form I, Client and Spouse Assets Summary

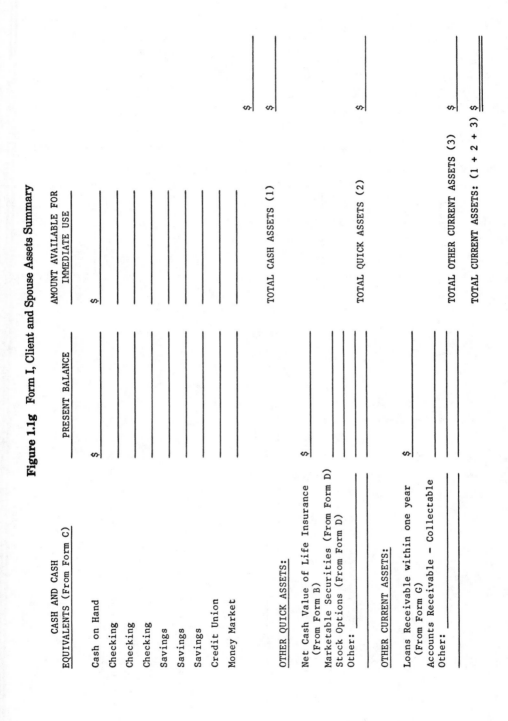

CASH AND CASH
EQUIVALENTS (From Form C)

PRESENT BALANCE

AMOUNT AVAILABLE FOR
IMMEDIATE USE

Cash on Hand $ $

Checking

Checking

Checking

Savings

Savings

Savings

Credit Union

Money Market

TOTAL CASH ASSETS (1) $

OTHER QUICK ASSETS:

Net Cash Value of Life Insurance
(From Form B) $

Marketable Securities (From Form D)

Stock Options (From Form D)

Other:

TOTAL QUICK ASSETS (2) $

OTHER CURRENT ASSETS:

Loans Receivable within one year
(From Form G) $

Accounts Receivable – Collectable

Other:

TOTAL OTHER CURRENT ASSETS (3) $

TOTAL CURRENT ASSETS: (1 + 2 + 3) $

Figure 1.1g Form I, Client and Spouse Assets Summary (Continued)

INVESTMENT ASSETS:
(Include Trust Deeds, etc.)

General Partnership Interests (From Form E) _____
Limited Partnership Interests (From Form E) _____
Closely held Corporate Stock (From Form E) _____
Loans Receivable Over One Year (From Form G) _____
Keogh Plan Assets (From Form E) _____
IRA (From Form E) _____
Corporate Pension and/or Profit Sharing Accounts
   (From Form E) _____
Other: _____ _____

TOTAL INVESTMENT ASSETS $_____

REAL PROPERTY - FORM F

Residence(s)/Vacation Homes _____
Income Producing Property _____
Unimproved Real Property _____

TOTAL REAL PROPERTY ASSETS $_____

BUSINESS INTERESTS - FORM H

Close Corporation Stock _____
Other Business Interests _____

TOTAL BUSINESS INTERESTS $_____

Figure 1.1g Form I, Client and Spouse Assets Summary (Continued)

OTHER PERSONAL PROPERTY - FORM F

	PURCHASE PRICE	DATE OF PURCHASE	FAIR MARKET VALUE	APPRAISAL YES/NO
Automobiles			$	
Motorcycles/Motorhomes, etc.				
Boat				
Airplane				
Household Furnishings				
Jewelry, Furs, Antiques, etc.				
Hobby Assets (Coins, Stamps, etc.)				
Other				
Proprietary Rights/Interests				

Comments: _____

_____

_____

Figure 1.1h Form J, Client and Spouse Liabilities

	ORIGINAL LOAN AMOUNT	DATE MADE MO/YR	SECURED BY	INTEREST RATE	TERM OF LOAN	MONTHLY PAYMTS.*	BALANCE OF LOAN TERM	BALANCE DUE
MORTGAGE/TRUST DEED LOANS:								
AUTO LOANS:								
BANK LOANS:								
PRIVATE LOANS:								

*Indicate whether payment includes more than principal and interest (i.e., taxes, insurance).

Figure 1.1h Form J, Client and Spouse Liabilities (Continued)

	ORIGINAL LOAN AMOUNT	DATE MADE MO/YR	SECURED BY	INTEREST RATE	TERM OF LOAN	MONTHLY PAYMTS.*	BALANCE OF LOAN TERM	BALANCE DUE
OTHER LOANS:								
CHARGE ACCOUNTS:								
UNSETTLED DAMAGES & CLAIMS:								
							TOTAL	

*Indicate whether payment includes more than principal and interest.

Figure 1.1i Form K, Client and Spouse Assets and Liability Summary*

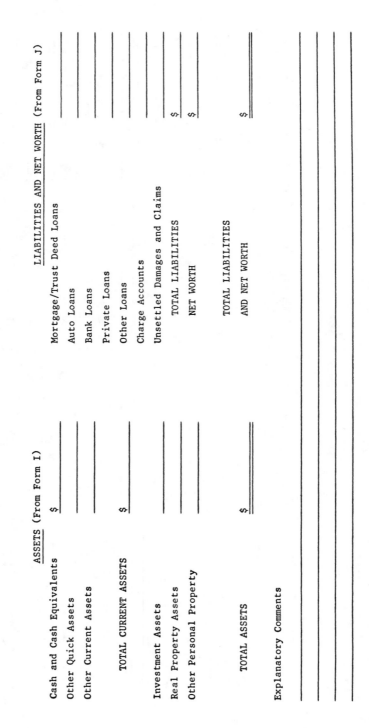

ASSETS (From Form I)

Cash and Cash Equivalents $ _____

Other Quick Assets _____

Other Current Assets _____

TOTAL CURRENT ASSETS $ _____

Investment Assets _____

Real Property Assets _____

Other Personal Property _____

TOTAL ASSETS $ _____

Explanatory Comments

LIABILITIES AND NET WORTH (From Form J)

Mortgage/Trust Deed Loans _____

Auto Loans _____

Bank Loans _____

Private Loans _____

Other Loans _____

Charge Accounts _____

Unsettled Damages and Claims _____

TOTAL LIABILITIES $ _____

NET WORTH $ _____

TOTAL LIABILITIES

AND NET WORTH $ _____

*Excludes Business Interests

Figure 1.1j Form N, Retirement Plans

CLIENT _____

| TYPE | PERSONAL ANNUAL CONTRIBUTION | COMPANY ANNUAL CONTRIBUTION | AMOUNT VESTED/WHEN | RETIREMENT DISBURSEMENTS | | DEATH BENEFITS | | |
				LUMP SUM	MONTHLY ANNUITY BEGIN/END	LUMP SUM	MONTHLY ANNUITY BEGIN/END	BENEFICIARY
Individual Retirement Account			___/___		___/___		___/___	
Keogh Plan			___/___		___/___		___/___	
Qualified Profit Sharing Plan			___/___		___/___		___/___	
Qualified Pension Plan			___/___		___/___		___/___	
Qualified Thrift Plan			___/___		___/___		___/___	
Nonqualified Deferred Compensation			___/___		___/___		___/___	
Government Pension			___/___		___/___		___/___	
Social Security			___/___		___/___		___/___	

Do any of the above plans have provisions for premium payments in the event of disability? _____ Explain. _____

_____
_____
_____
_____

Figure 1.1j Form N, Retirement Plans (Continued)

SPOUSE

TYPE	PERSONAL ANNUAL CONTRIBUTION	COMPANY ANNUAL CONTRIBUTION	AMOUNT VESTED/WHEN	RETIREMENT DISBURSEMENTS		DEATH BENEFITS		
				LUMP SUM	MONTHLY ANNUITY BEGIN/END	LUMP SUM	MONTHLY ANNUITY BEGIN/END	BENEFICIARY
Individual Retirement Account	___	___	_/_	___	_/_	___	_/_	___
Keogh Plan	___	___	_/_	___	_/_	___	_/_	___
Qualified Profit Sharing Plan	___	___	_/_	___	_/_	___	_/_	___
Qualified Pension Plan	___	___	_/_	___	_/_	___	_/_	___
Qualified Thrift Plan	___	___	_/_	___	_/_	___	_/_	___
Nonqualified Deferred Compensation	___	___	_/_	___	_/_	___	_/_	___
Government Pension	___	___	_/_	___	_/_	___	_/_	___
Social Security	___	___	_/_	___	_/_	___	_/_	___

Do any of the above plans have provisions for premium payments in the event of disability? _____ Explain. _____

Figure 1.1k Form DD, Retirement Questions

CLIENT

1. At what age do you wish to retire? _____

2. What do you estimate your net worth will be at retirement? _____

3. If your net worth at retirement was exactly the same as it is today, how would you feel? _____

4. What is the minimum you would need for retirement income (based upon present day costs)? _____

5. What income would you consider ample during your retirement years? _____

6. Do you feel that your present retirement program adequately provides for your retirement? _____ Explain.

_____
_____
_____
_____

Figure 1.1k Form DD, Retirement Questions (Continued)

SPOUSE

1. At what age do you wish to retire? _____

2. What do you estimate your net worth will be at retirement? _____

3. If your net worth at retirement was exactly the same as it is today, how would you feel? _____

4. What is the minimum you would need for retirement income (based upon present day costs)? _____

5. What income would you consider ample during your retirement years? _____

6. Do you feel that your present retirement program adequately provides for your retirement? _____ Explain.

_____

_____

_____

Figure 1.11 Form EE, Estate Planning, Management, and Distribution Questions

1. Wills: CLIENT: Yes _____ No _____   SPOUSE: Yes _____ No _____

   A. Date of Execution?   C _____ S _____
   B. Date Late Reviewed?   C _____ S _____
   C. Do the wills contain testamentary trusts?   C _____ S _____

2. Trusts:

Established by	Type	Date of Execution	Trustee	Beneficiary
_____	_____	_____	_____	_____
_____	_____	_____	_____	_____
_____	_____	_____	_____	_____

3. In terms of your own priorities, indicate the importance of having adequate funds to accomplish the following:
   (Rate the top priority #1, the next priority #2, etc.)

   Enjoy retirement   C _____ S _____
   Provide college education for children   C _____ S _____
   Be financially secure during a period of disability   C _____ S _____
   Provide for family in the event of sudden death   C _____ S _____

4. Briefly state the relative importance of the following considerations in your estate planning. (Use not important, important, very important.)

   Retaining full control of your assets during your lifetime   C _____ S _____
   Minimizing taxes at death   C _____ S _____
   Preserving a percentage of your assets to be passed on to
      your heirs after death   C _____ S _____

5. Do you and/or your spouse consider any of your present assets to be the sole property of one or the other of you?

   Yes _____   No _____   Explain. _____

43

Figure 1.11 Form EE, Estate Planning, Management, and Distribution Questions (Continued)

6. What is the minimum monthly income your family would need replaced in the event of your death:

	CLIENT	SPOUSE
Prior to providing education funds?	$_____	$_____
While providing education funds?	$_____	$_____
After providing education funds?	$_____	$_____

7. Does your spouse have training for a specific occupation? _____ Explain. _____

8. Would you expect your spouse to support the family in the event of your death? _____

9. Is it important that your spouse not be dependent on your children in the event of your death? _____

10. If something happened to you and/or your spouse, would you want your family to live in the same neighborhood, go to the same schools, and engage in the same social activities? _____

11. Would your family be able to live in the present home? _____

    How would the mortgage and other expenses be paid? _____

12. How do you feel about your spouse remarrying in the event of your death? _____

13. Have you and your spouse discussed trusts and trust management? _____

44

Figure 1.11 Form EE, Estate Planning, Management, and Distribution Questions (Continued)

14. What are your hopes for your children and what are their capabilities? _____

    Client _____

    Spouse _____

15. Should your heirs be permitted to consume the principal of your estate or only the income? _____

    Client _____

    Spouse _____

16. How and when should your estate capital be distributed? _____

    Client _____

    Spouse _____

17. In your estate planning, should any special problems be considered or special allowances made (handicaps, personalities, abilities)? _____

    Client _____

    Spouse _____

18. What educational and/or business opportunities do you wish to provide for your heirs? _____

    Client _____

    Spouse _____

19. Who would you select as guardian of your minor children in the event of the death of you and your spouse? _____

_____

Figure 1.11 Form EE, Estate Planning, Management, and Distribution Questions (Continued)

20. If you could leave a legacy to your favorite church or other charitable organization, how would it make you feel?

    Client _____

    Spouse _____

21. Detail briefly the manner in which you would desire your estate to be distributed in the event of:

    Client's death _____
    _____

    Spouse's death _____
    _____

    Common disaster _____
    _____

22. Who would you select as the executor of your estate? Client _____

    Spouse _____

23. What do you expect your estate settlement costs will be:

    Client's death first _____ $_____
    Spouse's subsequent death __ $_____
    Spouse's death first _____ $_____
    Client's subsequent death __ $_____

2

WILLS, INTESTACY, AND THE PROBATE PROCESS

INTRODUCTION

Having a valid will is one of the most fundamental steps in establishing an estate plan. A transfer of property through a will is used when the owner of property wishes to dispose of an interest in a manner that differs from the laws of intestacy. Because intestate distribution of a decedent's assets could result in one or more beneficiaries being disinherited, when this is not the client's intent, a financial planner needs to be aware of how an estate could be distributed in the absence of a will. Accordingly, if a property owner chooses to distribute the assets in some fashion other than how they would be distributed in the absence of a will, then a will is a necessary technique for the property owner. A complete schedule of a typical intestacy scheme of distribution is provided later in this chapter in order to give the financial planner an idea of how an estate might be distributed in the absence of a will.

A valid complete will can properly take care of many of a client's concerns, but the financial planner should be aware that there are specific objectives that cannot be accomplished through the use of a will. These objectives will be reviewed later in this chapter. In addition, specific estate planning pitfalls that are often the result of improper will drafting will be emphasized so that the financial planner can prevent these pitfalls from occurring in the client's estate plan.

Finally, it should be noted that, because a will is a legally binding instrument, it must be drafted and implemented by a licensed, competent attorney. Ordinarily, the financial planner is not in a position to draft wills, unless he also happens to be an attorney. Nevertheless, the financial planner needs to be aware of the legal requirements for valid execution of the will, as well as the pitfalls that can occur in a will if a completed will review checklist is not used in the data gathering process. For this reason, a sample will review checklist is included in this chapter in order to give the financial planner a sample list of the "problem areas" that can occur which may require the will to be amended.

DEFINITION OF A WILL

A will is a validly executed document that disposes of an individual's property and other owned interests when he dies. The will leaves the property to specifically named individuals, known as *beneficiaries*. The property transferred pursuant to the terms of the will is known as a *bequest*. Ordinarily, wills distribute property according to a specific pattern of distribution which usually differs from the *laws of intestacy*, that is, the laws of the state that determine how a decedent's property is distributed in the absence of a will.

In most states, there is a requirement that the will be in writing. Oral wills (known as noncupative wills) are generally not permitted. In addition to being in writing, there are also other requirements for a valid will. These requirements, known as execution requirements, control whether the will is valid. Failure to comply with all of the execution requirements, as well as any other requirements as determined by state law, causes the will to be treated as an invalid instrument, and the property distributions contained in the will are null and of no effect. In such a situation, the property will be distributed according to the laws of intestate succession if the will is not redrafted prior to the death of the property owner (known as the *maker*).

Though written during the lifetime of the maker, the will is *testamentary* by nature; it takes effect only upon the death of the maker. Therefore, it is a *revocable* instrument, one that can be amended, altered, or revoked a number of times prior to the maker's death. If it is revoked prior to the maker's death, and another valid will is not executed to take the place of the prior will, the decedent's property will be transferred according to the rules of intestate succession.

Since a will is revocable, it is possible to revise a will a number of times prior to the decedent's death. Many wills are revised by the use of a *codicil,* an instrument that must be executed according to the same execution formalities of a will. However, a codicil may be thought of as a more convenient method of revising a will, since it can be used to make changes in a will and yet remain relatively simple—most codicils are only one or two pages in length, and are not as costly as having the entire will revised. For these reasons, codicils are frequently used to make minor changes in a will at a reduced cost.

A will can and should be revised if any of the following situations occurs:

1. Changes in the client's family situation (marriage, divorce, birth or death of individuals, adoptions, etc.)
2. Changes in the client's business situation (the sale or acquisition of an asset, an increase or decrease in the value of a business asset or a closely held business)
3. Changes in the tax laws that could result in significant estate tax savings if implemented; or, conversely, detrimental estate tax liability that could result if the provisions of the will are not amended

In addition, there could be other reasons for having a will amended, and these reasons will be explored when examining what a will can and cannot accomplish.

The financial planner should be aware that the law of each state governs the validity of will provisions, execution formalities, and other requirements. The requirements for one state may not be identical to those of another state; therefore, the assumption should not be made that what works in one state necessarily works in another. For this reason, the financial planner should consult an attorney as a part of the overall estate planning team when attempting to implement the client's estate plan. Though valid execution requirements differ from state to state, as a general rule, the following can be considered typical execution requirements for the maker of a will:

1. The maker must be of sound mind when executing the will.
2. The maker must either be of age (no minors) or if married, a minor who is considered to have reached the age of majority because of the marriage.
3. The will must be in writing (this can either be typewritten, as is required by many states, or can be in the maker's own handwriting, referred to as a *holographic* will, which is also allowed by certain states).
4. The will must be signed by the maker, or, if the maker suffers a severe handicap and cannot sign, then it may be signed by someone other than the maker at the express command of the maker.

5. The will must be declared to be the last will and testament of the maker. This recitation is usually cited at the top of the instrument and is also declared again, usually within the first paragraph of the document.

6. The will must be witnessed by two (or three) competent individuals who serve as witnesses. The witnesses must: (a) sign the will at the request of the maker, (b) sign in the presence of the maker, and (c) sign as a witness in the presence of each of the other witnesses. Some states may have a minimum age requirement for a person serving as a witness. For example, some states require that an individual must be at least 16 years old in order to serve as a competent witness. States that have recognized holographic wills as valid may not have a witness requirement.

7. In addition, some states may require an attestation clause to validate a will. The attestation clause normally states that the will was validly executed according to the state's statutory execution requirements, and has been validly witnessed. In states where the attestation clause is not required, it is still recommended to include such a clause since a will is presumed valid when such a clause is used.

Other variations in local law may have a direct impact on the validity of the will. In some states, the divorce of a maker and the maker's spouse has no effect on the validity of the will. As a result, the property will be bequeathed to the ex-spouse unless the will is expressly revoked, or unless the will is amended to revise the provisions that bequeathed property to the ex-spouse. In other states, the divorce of the maker and the spouse will automatically invalidate only those portions of the will that left property to the ex-spouse, and all other portions of the will remain valid. Still, in other states, the effect of a divorce is to render the entire will invalid. The laws of each particular state must be consulted to determine the legal effect of a divorce or dissolution on the validity of a will.

Revocation of a will may also vary, according to state statute. There are a number of means by which a will can be revoked, but all states do not recognize all the means by which a will can be revoked. Therefore, it is advisable to consult with a local attorney to see what methods of will revocation are generally permitted.

The most frequent means of revoking a will are the following:

1. Revocation by cancellation: This involves a formal revocation of a prior will, and is usually a signed, witnessed statement. Frequently, the cancellation of a preexisting will occurs in a written instrument, which contains an express statement that all previous wills executed are cancelled and revoked at the time the statement of cancellation is validly executed.

2. Revocation by destruction: This involves the tearing, burning, or obliteration of a will by its maker. The destruction must be accompanied by an intention by the maker to have the will revoked. If intention to revoke the will cannot be proved, then the will is still deemed to be a valid instrument. Thus, in cases of individuals who have had their wills destroyed without an intention to revoke the will (e.g., floods, natural disasters, house fires, etc.), the will is assumed to be a valid, binding instrument, even if it has been destroyed. In cases like this, the court will attempt to follow the provisions of the will if the contents of the will can be proven from another source (e.g., an unsigned copy of the will kept by the attorney).

3. Revocation by execution of a subsequent will: This is perhaps the most frequently used method of cancelling a prior will. In most circumstances, this involves a formal declaration or statement in the subsequent will that all prior wills and codicils are revoked as of the date the subsequent will is validly executed. It is important for an individual to revoke prior wills on the subsequent execution of another will, since a person may only have one validly executed will which disposes of the maker's property at death. In those situations where a maker has two apparently valid executed wills, and neither is dated so that it cannot be determined which will supersedes the other, neither will be given effect and the estate of the deceased will be distributed according to the laws of intestacy.

It should be recognized that some states do not recognize all of the above as valid methods of will revocation. For example, some states may not recognize the revocation of a will by means of burning, tearing, or obliteration (due largely in part to the difficulty of proving the maker's intent to revoke, which must accompany the physical act of destruction). Nevertheless, if a part of a will is destroyed by any one of the three mentioned methods of destruction, the effect may be that the court will not give effect to the obliterated portions of the will; the net result could easily be that a part of the decedent's estate passes according to the laws of intestacy.

For a client who wants to ensure that all of his or her property passes according to the terms of a will, a *conditional revocation* may be a solution. For example, a client wants to ensure that all of the property interests are distributed according to the terms of a will. This client makes changes in the estate plan which call for a different scheme of distribution of estate assets. The client revokes the first will on subsequent execution of the second will. The second will contains a statement that expressly revokes the first will. Yet, to ensure that the property will pass according to the terms of a will (should, for any reason, the second will prove to be invalid), the maker can have a conditional revocation statement inserted into the second will. This statement indicates that if, for any reason, the second will is deemed to be an invalid instrument, then the revocation clause contained in that will which purported to revoke the first will is null and void, and the first will is still a validly binding instrument. In this way, the maker ensures that his property will not be distributed according to the terms of intestacy. Other solutions, which vary from state to state, may be available to assist the maker of the will in dealing with specific revocation problems.

WHAT A WILL CAN ACCOMPLISH

Generally, the maker of a will can dispose of his or her property in any manner of distribution. This is the most obvious advantage in having a will. In the will, the maker decides who will receive the property. In the absence of a will, the state decides who will receive the property and the property is distributed according to the intestate succession statutes of the state in which the decedent resided. With a few noted exceptions which will be discussed later, the maker of the will can determine who the ultimate beneficiaries of the estate will be.

In addition, a will can accomplish all of the following, if the will provisions are worded properly:

1. A will can leave a specific bequest to the surviving spouse and minor children for living expenses during the period of probate administration.
2. A will can allocate property to specific trusts that will ensure a stream of income to family members or others for a designated period of time.
3. A will can allocate the payment of estate taxes, state inheritance or death taxes, administrative costs, and debts and attorney's fees out of a specific portion or portions of the estate.
4. A will can structure the transfer of the decedent's estate so that it escapes all federal estate tax liability, by coordinating the use of the unified credit, the marital deduction, and the charitable deduction.
5. A will can bequeath a portion of the estate to a qualified charity for educational, medical, scientific, charitable, or other express purposes.
6. A will can name specific individuals to serve in a fiduciary capacity to take care of the decedent's personal interests, naming: guardians to take care of minor children, conservators or custodians to take care of the financial concerns of minors or incapacitated adults, trustees to supervise and control business interests or personal interests for the surviving family members, and executors or other qualified individuals to serve the legal interests of the decedent's estate.

7. A will can create a presumption of survivorship in the event it cannot be determined who died first, the decedent or the decedent's spouse: this presumption can have an effect on how the estate is distributed and who the ultimate beneficiaries of the decedent's property will be.

8. A will can create and specify the investment authority of the executor for the decedent's assets, thus permitting the executor greater investment authority than that permitted under most state statutes.

There may be other specific objectives that can be accomplished by the use of a will. This list is not intended to be all-inclusive. The flexibility that each of these objectives gives to the decedent's estate (as opposed to an estate being probated through intestacy) shows why it may be advantageous to have a will.

WHAT A WILL CANNOT ACCOMPLISH

Just as there are client objectives that can be accomplished through the use of a will, there are also specific objectives which cannot be accomplished with a will. One of the most commonly cited client objectives which cannot be achieved by use of a will is the disinheritance of a spouse. A decedent may attempt to disinherit his or her spouse under the terms of the will, but most states do not recognize this attempt. Most states specifically provide the surviving spouse protection under a "right of election" statute or an "elective share" statute, the specifics of which vary according to the formula used in each state. Typically, these statutes enable the surviving spouse to make an election within a specified time following the death of the first spouse and to take a specified percentage of the value of the decedent's estate, even if the decedent chose to leave no property to the surviving spouse under the terms of the will. Most state legislatures protect the surviving spouse against the improvident or unscrupulous conduct of a decedent, and most elective share statutes are premised on such a recognition, stemming from the common law concepts of dower and curtesy.

Unless the surviving spouse specifically enters into some type of antenuptial agreement and expressly waives the right to take a share of the estate against the will, the estate owner may not prevent the surviving spouse from receiving a portion of the decedent's property. For decedents who die without a will, the surviving spouse is still afforded protection by means of the intestacy survivorship statutes. These statutes enable the surviving spouse to take a specified percentage of the decedent's net estate. The amount of the estate that can be claimed by the surviving spouse depends on such factors as: (1) whether the decedent was survived by any children, (2) whether the decedent was survived by one or both parents, and (3) the dollar amount of the decedent's net estate.

In only a few limited situations could one spouse disinherit the other. Conceivably, in a community property state where the marriage was of short duration and there was no acquisition of property with community held assets and there was no appreciation of either spouse's separate property due to the efforts or skills of the other spouse, it is possible that one spouse could leave his or her property to someone other than the surviving spouse. This assumes, of course, that there was no property held in joint tenancy with right of survivorship and that the state does not have a statute which entitles the surviving spouse to take a specified percentage of the deceased spouse's estate. Other estate planning objectives that cannot be achieved through the use of a will include the following:

1. **Transfers that occur by operation of law:** A will cannot effectively transfer property to another individual when the transfer of such property is controlled by operation of law. Most notably, this affects property held either in joint tenancy with right of survivorship or tenancy by the entirety. By its very nature, the survivorship feature of joint tenancy permits transfer of the property only to the surviving joint tenant. Tenancy by the entirety property also has this survivorship feature. Upon the death of one of the tenants, any provision in his or her will which leaves the property to someone other than the surviving joint tenant (or surviving spouse, in the case of tenancy by the entirety) is a void provision. This usually nullifies only that portion of the will which attempted to convey the jointly held property rather than nullifying the entire will.

2. **A trust established to last indefinitely for noncharitable beneficiaries:** A will that contains a trust provision in violation of the rule against perpetuities is inoperable. Basically, the rule against perpetuities provides that a trust created for a named noncharitable beneficiary or class of beneficiaries can exist only for a given length of time. The duration of the trust cannot be for an indefinite time period. The trust cannot exceed the lives of any of the beneficiaries who were alive at the time the trust was created plus 21 years and 9 months. If a trust exceeds this time period for a beneficiary that is not a charity, the trust is deemed to be invalid. (The 21 years and 9 months is for the benefit of any trust beneficiary who is born after the trust is established. The 9 months is for the benefit of any trust beneficiary who was *in vitro* at the time the trust was established). While it is not the financial planner's responsibility to structure the terms of a trust, the planner should be aware of the consequences that could occur if a trust were structured to take effect for a class of beneficiaries, all of

whom are not yet in existence. Proper counseling with an attorney can avoid this problem.

3. Excessive bequests to charities: In some states it is not possible for a decedent to bequeath his or her entire estate to qualified charities due to "the mortmain statute." The statute prohibits excessive charitable bequests when the decedent is survived by a spouse, children, or other heirs. Typically, the mortmain statute provides that if a charitable bequest exceeds a certain percentage of the net estate (25% is a common percentage) then a spouse, child, grandchild, parent, or other recognized heir has a right to make an election and set aside that portion of the net estate going to charity which exceeds the statutory percentage limit; for example, if a decedent's will leaves 35 percent of the net estate to a given charity, a designated heir could elect to set aside that portion of the charitable bequest in excess of the statutory limit, in this case, 10 percent of the net estate. By being able to set aside the amount of the excessive charitable bequest, the effect of a statute of this type is similar in nature to the surviving spouse's right to take against the will. Since some states have abolished this statute in recent years, consultation with an attorney is important to determine whether the mortmain statute is applicable to the client's situation.

4. Wishes and desires that are not the decedent's to make: A will cannot be used to express a command or personal choice of the decedent that is not the decedent's to make. A typical decision of this type occurs in situations in which the decedent names a particular attorney to serve as the attorney for the estate at the time of its probate. Technically, no court has to comply with this command or directive, since the selection of an attorney to represent the estate is the choice of the executor or personal representative (in situations where the decedent dies without a will).

5. Disinheritance of a child: In many states, a decedent cannot disinherit a child unless there is an express intention to do so. Many states have *pretermitted heir statutes* which provide protection to a child born after the time when the will was drafted. These statutes are based on the premise that the decedent did not intend to disinherit his or her child and, due to inadvertence, had not revised the will to include the after-born child. Only when there is an express indication that the maker of the will intended to disinherit such a child will such a provision in a will be given effect. Typically, a provision of this sort leaves a minimal amount to the child, for example, $1,000 is common, or such a provision includes a statement that the act of disinheriting a particular child is intentional.

Only in Louisiana can a child not be intentionally disinherited.

This is because Louisiana has a forced heirship statute which requires that a specified percentage of the decedent's estate be transferred to the decedent's children. This forced heirship statute is similar in concept to the surviving spouse's right to take a portion of the decedent's estate.

6. Provisions which violate the law: Any will provision which bequeaths property to a specific beneficiary on the condition that the beneficiary commit an act prohibited by law is null and void. Will provisions that leave property to a specific beneficiary *only if* that beneficiary does not marry are void and against public policy since such conditions are an alienation of the right of an individual to marry. Similarly, provisions which grant property to a charity on conditions that the property be used for a public charitable trust can be null and void if the terms of the public trust discriminate against a particular class of beneficiaries on religious, racial, ethnic, or gender-based grounds. Because of legal variances in the consequences of these will provisions, the financial planner should notify the client to seek the advice of an attorney when structuring a will.

PROVISIONS TO INCLUDE IN A WILL

Once it is understood that there are certain objectives that can and cannot be accomplished through the use of a will, a will can be constructed containing those provisions that accomplish particular client objectives. Among the provisions which can be placed in a will are the following:

1. Bequests of property to specified beneficiaries, including both general devises and specific bequests (e.g., "my 1988 Buick Skyhawk to my nephew, Jeremy")
2. Provisions that allocate payment of estate taxes to particular portions of the estate or beneficiaries (e.g., "The payment of all of my estate tax liability is to come from the residuary estate after which any remaining property is to be distributed to my niece, Anne.")
3. Provisions that utilize both the unified credit and the marital deduction (e.g., "That portion of my estate which equals the exemption equivalent in the year of my death shall go to my children in equal shares; the rest of my estate shall go to my surviving spouse, Mary.")
4. Provisions that name specific guardians for minor children (e.g., "In the event that both my wife and I are killed, then I hereby name my brother, Randy, to serve as guardian of our minor children.")
5. Provisions that provide a presumption of survivorship (e.g., "In the event that it cannot be determined who died first, and we both die in

the same disaster or accident, then it shall be presumed that I predeceased my wife.")

6. Provisions that name an executor ("I hereby appoint my sister, Amy, to serve as executrix of my estate and in the event my sister Amy predeceases me, then I hereby name my brother, Christopher, as my executor.")

7. Provisions for distribution of a portion of the estate to a qualified charity (e.g., "I hereby bequeath $40,000 to the American Diabetes Association for purposes of research and education.")

8. Allocation of the remainder or residue of the estate to prevent partial intestacy (e.g., "I hereby bequeath all the rest, residue, and remainder of my estate to my wife, Edith.")

9. Provisions for income distribution to the surviving spouse and other family members (e.g., "In the event of my death, I hereby allocate my income-producing stock portfolio to the XYZ trust, the terms of which direct that $1000 per month shall be distributed to my surviving spouse, and in the event my spouse shall predecease me, then I direct that $1000 per month shall be distributed to my children until they shall reach the age of majority.")

In addition, other specific provisions may be inserted in the will which achieve the client's specific estate planning objectives. Therefore, this list should not be considered an all-inclusive list of will provisions.

PITFALLS OF INSUFFICIENT ESTATE PLANNING

A number of estate planning pitfalls can occur if there is not sufficient estate planning for a client who already has a will or who is considering amending the will. These pitfalls are highlighted so that the financial planner may aid the client in identifying these problems; then, the attorney is called in to solve these problems through proper drafting.

Ancillary Probate

A will normally can only dispose of the decedent's *personal* property interests and those *real* property interests that are located in the state of the decedent's residence. It cannot dispose of real estate located in a state other than that of the decedent's residence, unless the property is subjected to a separate probate proceeding. If a will attempts to dispose of real estate located in another state, the provisions of the will may direct to whom the real property will be transferred, but a separate probate procedure called an *ancillary probate procedure* will be necessary. Thus, the maker of a will cannot avoid a double probate procedure—one in the state of the decedent's residence and another in the state where the real property was located. If a property owner wants to avoid an ancillary probate procedure for the real property located in another state, the property will have to be gifted to another person or placed in a trust at some point in the decedent's lifetime. A provision in the will which attempts to dispose of the property in an attempt to avoid an ancillary probate procedure is null and of no effect. A will cannot avoid an ancillary probate procedure and the owner of property located in a state other than the state of residence should plan accordingly to dispose of the property to avoid the time delays and costs of an ancillary probate procedure.

Partial Intestacy

A will should be drafted so that it properly disposes of the *entirety* of a decedent's estate. Many makers of wills do not realize that they may unintentionally be creating a situation in which a portion of the estate may pass through intestacy. If the maker of a will does not include a residuary clause in the will that bequeaths all residuary property to a named individual, it is possible that a portion of the estate could pass through partial intestacy. This is especially important if the maker of a will acquires property after the will is executed. In the absence of a residuary clause, the property will pass to those individuals who would take the property if there were no will. Thus, to avoid a partial intestacy problem, the maker of a will should include a provision that bequeaths the rest, residue, and remainder of the estate to a specified individual.

Court-Imposed Guardians and Conservators

Many individuals with wills make the mistake of failing to name a contingent guardian or conservator. The maker may name a guardian or conservator to take care of minor children or the legal and financial interests of children or others, but should the individual named in the will predecease the maker, there is no individual to serve as guardian or conservator of the maker's estate. Therefore, in most states, a special court hearing must be held to name a guardian, conservator, or other fiduciary. The same problem holds true if the maker of the will fails to name a contingent executor or executrix for the estate. Contingent beneficiaries and executors should always be named in the event any one of them predeceases the maker of the will.

The disadvantage of having a court name the guardian or executor lies in the fact that the guardian or conservator named may be someone whom the maker may not have wanted to serve in that capacity. The individual named by the court may be a closely related heir or other family member but may also be someone whom the maker had grave reservations about serving in that capacity. An estate owner can avoid these pitfalls through proper planning.

Adverse Tax Consequences

Wills can be structured to properly take care of estate tax liability through the optimal use of both the unified credit and the marital deduction. Many makers of wills, especially since the enactment of ERTA in 1981, believe that their estates will have no estate tax problems if everything is left to the surviving spouse. Technically, this is true since the unlimited marital deduction is available for the estates of spouses dying on or after January 1, 1982 who are survived by a spouse to whom the property is left.

By structuring an estate in this fashion, the estate of the first decedent spouse will pay no federal estate tax because everything will qualify for the marital deduction. However, upon the death of the surviving spouse, there will be no marital deduction available to offset the estate tax. As a result, the estate tax liability on the estate of the second spouse may be greater than if the first estate had utilized *both* the unified credit and the marital deduction. Rather than wasting the unified credit available to the first estate, the estate should be structured so that it takes advantage of both the unified credit *and* the marital deduction, thus achieving an overall reduction in estate tax liability.

Assuming that a decedent dies in 1987 or later with a gross estate valued at $1 million, the following chart shows the overall estate tax savings achieved through the use of the marital deduction *and* the unified credit available for that year, as opposed to leaving everything to the surviving spouse through use of the marital deduction.

	Using Unified Credit	Not Using Unified Credit
Amount of estate	$1,000,000	$1,000,000
Exemption equivalent used	600,000	-0-
Marital deduction used	400,000	1,000,000
Amount of tax paid by decedent	-0-	-0-
Amount of taxable estate transferred to surviving spouse	400,000	1,000,000
Amount of tax payable on estate of surviving spouse	121,800	345,800
Amount of surviving spouse's unified credit (for 1987 and later years)	192,800	192,800
Surviving spouse's tax payable	-0-	153,000
Overall tax savings	$153,000	

Abatement and Ademption Problems

If there are insufficient assets in an estate so that the bequests of the maker cannot be distributed in accordance with the maker's intentions, then a procedure known as *abatement* applies. This frequently occurs when the decedent's debts or taxes exceed the amounts originally anticipated at the time the will was drafted, or, can often occur if the surviving spouse or an after-born child elects to take a portion of the estate against the will, thus reducing the amount of property available to other beneficiaries.

Abatement is a procedure by which the testamentary wishes of the maker are reduced for each devisee so that each ultimately receives a portion of the estate but receives a reduced amount of the estate in order to distribute the assets to all of the beneficiaries as intended by the maker. The maker of the will can create his or her own abatement procedure within the terms of the will. If an abatement procedure is not established within the terms of the will, then the abatement procedure will follow a statutory pattern similar to the following:

1. If there is property left in the estate that has not been disposed of, undisposed property is first used to satisfy debts and expenses of the estate.
2. If all of the property has been disposed of, then assets from the residuary estate are used to satisfy debts, obligations, or the surviving spouse's or after-born child's share.
3. If there is no residuary estate remaining, then general devises are used (e.g., a bequest of cash).
4. If there are no general devises remaining, then specific devises are used (e.g., a bequest of specific property, such as "a 1988 Mercedes to my nephew, John") to satisfy debts, expenses, and other claims.
5. If there are no specific bequests remaining, then the property passing to the surviving spouse is used to satisfy debts and expenses (except for *exempt* property which may not be attached by creditors for satisfaction of claims.)

In addition to abatement problems, there may be a problem with *ademption*. If a decedent leaves a specific bequest of property to a certain individual (e.g., "my 1988 Mercedes to my nephew, John") but gives the car to his nephew in his lifetime rather than waiting to bequeath it under the terms of the will, then the property is said to have *adeemed* to its ultimate intended beneficiary. As a result, because the intended beneficiary actually received the property prematurely, then the beneficiary (in this case, nephew John) will not receive another Mercedes at the time the maker of the will dies. This is known as *ademption by satisfaction*.

On the other hand, if the car was destroyed before it could be bequeathed to the nephew, there is no car to be bequeathed to the nephew under the terms of the will. This is known as *ademption by extinction* and if the maker of the will does not provide for an alternate bequest to the nephew (e.g., "In the event the car cannot be delivered to the nephew, then $30,000 shall be distributed in lieu of the car.") then the nephew will receive nothing. For this reason, alternative distribution plans should be considered if the maker wishes to leave the equivalent of the specific bequest to the intended beneficiary. Some states may allow the nephew to receive insurance proceeds for the value of the car in the event the insured car is destroyed.

Precatory Language

One consideration that must be fully examined when constructing an estate plan for a client with a will is the problem of *precatory language*. Ideally, the language of the will should be making express commands and directions to various individuals, such as the executor. If there is any language in the will that does not express a directive or a command, but is instead indicative of a *wish* or *hope* or *desire,* such language may not be given recognition by a court because it cannot be determined whether the maker really meant to have the wish carried out. As a precautionary measure, clients should be advised to state their intentions in terms of commands and directives rather than hopes and desires.

Will Contests

The maker of a will should realize that he or she cannot, in most circumstances, avoid a will contest. Will contests are usually initiated by a disenchanted beneficiary or a disinherited beneficiary who seeks a greater portion of the decedent's estate. Such contests are usually based on one of several grounds:

1. That the maker of the will was not of sound mind at the time the will was drafted.
2. That the maker was unduly influenced by another individual at the time the will was drafted and this undue influence has a direct impact on the distribution of the estate.
3. That the maker was fraudulently deceived, and as a result of the fraud disinherited a person who ordinarily would have taken a greater share of the estate.
4. That the maker suffered from an insane delusion at the time the will was drafted. An insane delusion differs from a state of "unsound

mind" in the following sense: to be of unsound mind, the maker must not know who the maker is, or doesn't know the extent of his or her property ownership, or doesn't know who the natural objects of his or her affection are, or doesn't know that he or she is making a will and giving away his or her property. An "insane delusion," on the other hand, may be a situation in which the maker knows who his or her heirs or family members are (e.g., a man knows that his daughter is, in fact, his daughter but disinherits her because he suffers from an insane delusion that she is trying to kill him).

In only one limited situation is it perhaps possible to avoid a will contest. That is a situation in which a beneficiary is left a certain portion of property ($50,000) on the grounds that if the beneficiary attempts to contest the will in the hopes of gaining a greater portion of the estate, then the beneficiary will be totally disinherited. Such clauses have generally been upheld in situations where the beneficiary is someone other than the surviving spouse.

Funeral Arrangements and Plans

Generally, it is advisable not to include funeral provisions in the will. Most wills are not read or formally admitted to probate until some time after the decedent's death. If the decedent specifies particular funeral arrangements in the will, that is, burial versus cremation, or requests burial in a specific location, for example, "next to my parents in the cemetery in Oakland County," then it may not be possible to achieve the last wishes or hopes of the maker. Funeral arrangements and directives should be put in a separate written instrument and left with a trusted family friend or close relative. They should not be placed in a safe deposit box since there may be difficulties in obtaining permission to open the box prior to the funeral.

TYPES OF WILLS

Wills may be categorized according to the various characteristics they possess. The following are the most common types of wills:

1. A *simple will* is a will in which the maker leaves everything to only a few devisees. Frequently it is used by one spouse to leave all property to the surviving spouse. With a few noted exceptions where specific bequests are made to other individuals, all remaining property is usually left to the surviving spouse. Used frequently when the decedent does not own an estate larger than the exemption equivalent.

2. A *holographic will* is a will written in the handwriting of the maker, as opposed to being typewritten or printed. Permitted in some states but not all.

3. A *codicil* is an attachment or formal amendment to a will; required by law to follow the same execution requirements that are required of a will.

4. A *noncupative* (oral) *will* is a "verbal" will which bequeaths the decedent's property, generally not permitted in most states because the execution requirements have not been satisfied. May be permitted in some states if the maker is on his or her deathbed, or in an emergency situation where the maker is not expected to live. Most oral wills can only dispose of personal property (not real estate or land) and are often limited to a maximum dollar amount, such as $1000.

5. A *joint will* is one document that serves as the last will and testament for two individuals. Spouses are generally advised not to have a joint will because the first decedent spouse's property interests are often construed as being terminable interests, and thus are prohibited from qualifying for the marital deduction. Also, with a joint will it is often questionable whether the survivor has the ability to change the terms of the will once the first spouse dies.

6. A *mutual will* is a will executed by one individual pursuant to an agreement with another individual. Both individuals agree to dispose of their property in a particular way. This type of will may be inadvisable because of the difficulty of enforcing the agreement after the first decedent dies. Sometimes referred to as a "contractual will."

7. A *reciprocal will* is a will executed by one person who agrees to leave his or her property to another person; in turn, the other person agrees to leave his or her property to the other maker. This will is often entered into between spouses, each of whom "reciprocates" and leaves his or her property to the other spouse in the event of death. Sometimes referred to as the "I love you" will.

8. A *"living" will*—This is not actually a will as a testamentary disposition of property. It is an arrangement to ensure that artificial or prolonged means are not used to keep an individual alive should the person suffer from a permanent debilitating condition. Frequently recognized by many state legislatures to prevent prolonged comas or other severe medical conditions. The provisions for a "living will" are usually put in writing and are signed and witnessed by at least one individual, similar to a will. The wishes of the individual not to have his or her life prolonged may not necessarily be followed by a court. But the language and signature of the document do give the court and other family members some indication of the *intentions* of the individ-

ual should the person be incapacitated and unable to speak for himself or herself in the event of a serious accident. More and more state legislatures are recognizing the validity of the "living will" especially since the court decisions that have been handed down since the Karen Ann Quinlan case in the mid-1970s.

DETERMINING WHETHER A WILL NEEDS TO BE AMENDED

Though the actual revision or amendment of a will is a responsibility for a licensed attorney, the financial planner must also be knowledgeable about those situations which may call for the amendment of a will. The financial planner can help the client avoid most of the estate planning pitfalls previously discussed by proper use of some reference-based criteria which assist the client in determining whether the will needs to be amended.

Many financial planners use some form of a will review checklist to assist them in making a determination as to whether the will needs to be amended. Most will review checklists are designed to pinpoint the "critical areas" in a client's life that could justify the changing of a will, such as acquisition or disposition of property interests and business interests, changes in the family situation, the birth, death or adoption of one or more individuals, changes in health and life expectancy of one or more individuals, changes in the tax laws, and so on.

The will checklist which appears in this chapter is not intended as an all-inclusive list. Rather, it is designed to provide the financial planner with some guidelines as to what areas are of primary concern to both the client and the financial planner. A complete review of these areas of concern may indicate one or more factual situations which justify an amendment to the will. Once these areas have been identified and the proper estate planning solution has been discussed thoroughly with the client, the attorney then implements the appropriate changes in the will which will achieve the client's objectives.

The following is a sample will review checklist that can be used by the financial planner.

Checklist to Determine Whether Will Needs to be Amended*

Use the following checklist in conjunction with the information provided by the client. Place a check on the line in front of each statement that indicates a material change in the client's situation and may indicate the need for an amendment to the will.

_____ Review of will by an attorney has not occurred in the past 12 months.

_____ Execution requirements have not been satisfied.

_____ Will was drafted prior to ERTA (1981) and contains a limited marital deduction clause.

_____ Change of one or more beneficiaries named in the will is desired.

_____ Change in the amounts bequested to one or more beneficiaries is desired.

_____ Change in the type of property bequested to one or more beneficiaries is desired.

_____ Addition of/deletion of beneficiaries is desired.

_____ Change in the amount of the marital deduction or in the amount of life income to the surviving spouse is desired.

_____ Change in residuary clause is desired.

_____ Cancellation of debts by a will provision is desired.

_____ Change in marital status of testator or a member of testator's family has occurred since the last review.

_____ Change in the health of testator or a member of the testator's family has occurred since the last review.

_____ Birth or adoption of children/grandchildren has occurred since the last review.

_____ There has been a change in the value of the testator's estate since the last review.

_____ There are one or more assets that have appreciated greatly since the last review.

_____ The estate faces a potential liquidity problem.

_____ There has been an acquisition/change in ownership of life insurance, qualified pension plans, or other retirement benefits since the last review.

_____ There has been a significant change in a business situation since the last review.

_____ There have been business liquidity or continuity problems since the last review.

_____ Change of a guardian, executor, or trustee designation is desired.

_____ Addition of a successor guardian, executor, or trustee is desired.

_____ There has been a change in the status of a fiduciary since the last review (divorce, deterioration of health, disability, relocation).

_____ There has been a change in the form of property ownership or a change on one or more deeds of ownership since the last review.

_____ There has been a change in the state of residency since the last review.

_____ Additional property has been acquired in a state other than the state of residency since the last review.

_____ There have been significant tax law changes since the last review.

_____ The will needs to be reviewed for additional reasons.

INTESTACY

If an individual dies without a will, the property belonging to the decedent is distributed to his heirs according to a predetermined pattern. This pattern is defined by state law for each of the 50 states, and these state laws are referred to as the *intestate succession statutes*. The purpose of such statutes is to provide some protection to those individuals who are considered the natural objects of the decedent's love and affection (e.g., surviving spouse, children, grandchildren, parents, brothers and sisters, and other collateral relatives). Theoretically, these individuals take priority over other individuals who do not have a blood relationship to the decedent, such as friends and creditors. Accordingly, persons related to the decedent by a blood relationship take most, if not all, of the decedent's estate at the time the estate is distributed. Creditors may be afforded some protection by the provisions of creditors' rights laws in each of the 50 states, but friends of the decedent who are related by neither marriage nor blood will receive nothing. For this reason, if a property owner wishes to transfer property to a friend or to a charity, that individual should either have a will or plan on making a lifetime gift of the property to the unrelated beneficiary.

In order for a financial planner to appreciate the pattern of distribution for estate assets of a decedent dying without a will, he should have some familiarity with the intestate distribution statutes for the state in which he resides. Only by examining the pattern for intestate distribution can the financial planner realize the difference for asset distributions that can be achieved through the use of a will.

Typically, the intestate succession statutes provide for a specified percentage of the estate to pass to the surviving spouse. The amount of the estate and the type of property that passes to the surviving spouse often depend on the dollar amount of the decedent's estate as well as whether the decedent was survived only by the spouse or whether the decedent was survived by a spouse and children.

A typical intestacy statute might provide the following to the surviving spouse if both the spouse and children survive the decedent:

1. One-third the value of all real property possessed by the deceased during the marriage to which the surviving spouse has not relinquished any rights (e.g., no antenuptial agreement was signed) *plus*
2. All exempt personal property (determined by the exempt property statutes of each particular state) *plus*
3. One-third of all other nonexempt personal property after payment of debts and expenses
4. If the total of all of the above does not equal a stated dollar amount, for example, $100,000, then so much additional property which, when added to the above, equals $100,000 (after payment of debts and expenses).

If the surviving spouse did not have any living children at the time of the decedent's death, then the intestate succession statute might provide the following to the surviving spouse:

1. One-third the value of all the decedent's real property interests held during the marriage to which the surviving spouse relinquished no rights *plus*
2. All exempt personal property *plus*
3. One-third of all nonexempt personal property after payment of debts and charges
4. If the total of all of the above does not equal a stated dollar amount, for example, $100,000, then so much additional property which, when added to the above, equals $100,000, plus one-half of the net estate for any amounts in excess of $100,000.

After the surviving spouse's portion of the estate has been satisfied, the balance of the decedent's estate is distributed in the following pattern; or, if there is no surviving spouse, then the entire estate of the deceased is distributed in a pattern which may resemble the following:

1. In equal shares to the decedent's surviving children; if any child has predeceased the decedent, then that child's share passes to his or her children (the grandchildren of the decedent).
2. If no children survive and there are no grandchildren born to the decedent, then to the decedent's surviving parents; if only one parent survives, then all to the surviving parent.

3. If neither children, grandchildren nor parents survive, then one-half goes to those individuals who would have taken the property if the decedent's mother had survived; the other one-half goes to those individuals who would have taken the property if the decedent's father had survived.

4. If no persons can be found to take the property on either the mother's side or on the father's side, then the rest and remainder shall pass to either side which has takers for the property.

5. If no persons can be found on either side who would have taken the property from either the mother or the father, then the balance shall go to the decedent's surviving spouse; if there is no surviving spouse, then the property shall pass to any heirs that can be found, to be divided in equal shares.

6. If no persons can be found to inherit the property, then the property *escheats* to the state.

From this representative intestate succession statute, it is clear that distribution of assets to any one other than a lineal heir (blood related) or a blood ancestor (parent, grandparent, or any one of their descendants) is not permissible. Further, no bequests or allocations of property can be distributed to qualified charities or other qualified organizations in an attempt to reduce the decedent's estate tax liability. As a result, a will is highly recommended for any individual who chooses to bequeath his or her property in any manner inconsistent with the state intestacy statutes. Figure 2.1 is a graphic illustration of the distribution of a decedent's estate if he were to die without a will.

THE PROBATE PROCESS

Much has been written about the advantages of avoiding the probate process, and for a time, avoiding probate was thought of as a highly successful strategy in minimizing payment of state inheritance or estate taxes and administrative expenses. Now, with the enactment of ERTA, it is possible to have a large gross estate and still avoid payment of federal estate taxes, mainly because of a graduated increase in the amount of the exemption equivalent for the estates of decedents dying on or after January 1, 1982 and in years thereafter. A deceased's estate is able to avoid payment of any federal estate tax on a gross estate up to $600,000 in value in 1987 and following years. The unlimited marital deduction also makes it possible for the estate of the first decedent spouse to avoid payment of any federal estate tax, regardless of the dollar amount of the estate. As a result, concern with payment of federal estate tax is not as great as it used to be,

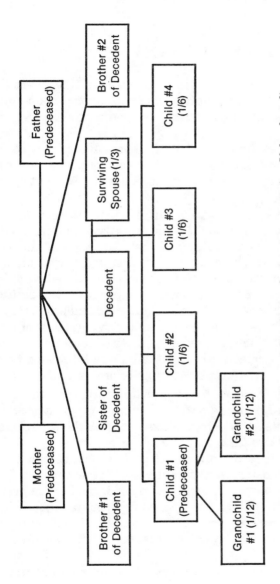

Figure 2.1 Typical scheme of distribution for intestate succession. If decedent dies, surviving spouse takes 1/3, remaining 2/3 to each child, or 1/6 each. Child #1 predeceased decedent, so Child #1's share is divided equally, or 1/12 to each grandchild. If no children outlived decedent, remaining 2/3 would have gone to parents (1/3 each). If parents predeceased decedent, remaining 2/3 would go to their lineal descendants—brothers and sisters of decedent would get 22.2% each. If no brothers and sisters of decedent survived, surviving spouse would receive rest. If there were no brothers or sisters, nieces or nephews, parents, surviving spouse, children or grandchildren or other lineal descendants (including cousins), property would escheat to state.

and many estate owners no longer find advantages in avoiding probate. As the number of estates transferred through probate increases, the financial planner should become familiar with the characteristics of the probate process.

Characteristics of the Probate Process

Though each state has its own specific procedures that affect the probate process, the states also have characteristics in common. Generally, the probate process is characterized by the following procedures:

1. In the case of a decedent dying with a will, the will is filed with the probate court. Generally, this occurs in the county where the decedent resided at the time of death. If the decedent dies without a will, no document is filed.

2. In the case of a decedent dying with a will, a petition to have the will admitted to probate is filed with the court. This petition initiates the probate administration of the estate, and both the will and the petition must be filed with the court within a stated period of time following the death of the decedent. In the case of a decedent dying without a will, probate administration is initiated by filing a petition for the appointment of a personal representative or other fiduciary to administer the probate estate. Although the surviving spouse often is named as the petitioner for both testate estates (estates with a will) and intestate estates (estates without a will), any interested party may file the petition and initiate the probate process.

3. Once a will has been filed with the probate court, it is generally admitted to probate. Interested parties then have a stated period of time in which to challenge or set aside the probate of the will. Generally, most states require that, once the will is admitted to probate, notice must be given to all interested parties. Notice can occur through written notification (letter) or publication (newspaper). (The reader should note, however, that in June, 1988, the U.S. Supreme Court ruled that mere publication in a newspaper was insufficient where the estate had actual knowledge of the creditor's existence and had failed to provide written notice or actual notice of the deadline for filing creditor's claims. Thus, to avoid litigation by unnotified creditors, attorneys and other representatives of the estate should provide written notice or actual notice to all creditors of a decedent's estate.) If an interested party is not given notice, the actions of the personal representative can be challenged. It is possible in some states for an interested party to waive the written notice requirement. Generally, once an interested party has been given notice and fails to contest the

probate process within the specified period of time, for example, 6 months from the date of the last publication that the will has been admitted to probate, the interested party is barred from raising any further challenges to the probate of the will. Generally, for estates of decedents dying without a will, the process is similar. The individual named as personal representative of the estate is required to give notice to all interested parties, informing them that the personal representative has been appointed by the court and that they are interested parties. This notice is usually published in a local newspaper.

4. In both estate and intestate estates, all creditors of the estate have an opportunity to file their claims with the probate court. Generally, if a creditor fails to file a claim within a stated period of time following the admission of the will to probate (e.g., 6 months), or following the appointment of the personal representative (e.g., 6 months), the creditor's claim is barred.

5. Once all claims are filed and the personal representative has been given letters testamentary (a letter of authority given to a person by the court to act on behalf of the estate as fiduciary), further administration of the estate can proceed.

6. For estates of decedents dying with a will, an additional procedural step is necessary. The will that has been admitted to probate must be proven to be a valid document. This requires either a hearing at which proof of valid execution of the will must be established or a signed statement from witnesses, declaring that the will was validly executed. Generally, this means the will must comply with the execution requirements for that state, or it must meet the execution requirements for the state in which it was executed, if a state other than the state of the decedent's residence. Frequently, this requires proof that the decedent intended the document to serve as his or her last will and testament, that the decedent signed or acknowledged the document as his or her last will and testament, that the decedent signed it in the presence of two or more disinterested witnesses, and that the witnesses signed and acknowledged it in the presence of the maker of the will. This statement can be waived if the will contains a self-proving affidavit. The self-proving affidavit contains the sworn statements of the witnesses that the will met all valid execution requirements for the state in which it was executed. As a result, a strong presumption arises that the will was validly executed.

7. Once the will has been proved to be a valid document and letters testamentary have been issued to the personal representative, administration of the probate estate occurs. For the personal representative of either the testate or intestate estate, administration usually

involves an inventory of all probate assets, payment of creditors' claims and distribution of the probate estate according to the terms of the decedent's will, or according to the laws of intestacy, if the decedent dies without a will. Payment of federal estate and state inheritance and estate taxes also occurs at this time. One or more accountings are filed with the court to notify the court of those probate assets that have already been distributed as well as those claims of creditors that have already been filed and paid. The accounting also informs the court of any additional expenses incurred by the estate as a part of the probate process, such as appraisal fees for probate assets, court filing fees, attorney's fees, and other administrative expenses. If specific deeds are necessary to transfer title to real estate or other properties, those deeds are issued by the probate court prior to completion of probate. Beneficiaries or heirs who receive property from the estate are usually required to sign a written receipt that verifies that they have actually received the property.

8. Once all claims and debts have been paid, all taxes have been paid, and all property has been distributed, the estate may be closed. This usually occurs after a final accounting or report is filed with the court. A petition to discharge the personal representative is usually filed with the court. If the personal representative was required to file a bond or oath with the court, it is usually released at this point. The court approves the discharge of the personal representative if it is satisfied with all accountings and other reports. Once the estate is probated and the personal representative has been discharged from his or her duties, the probate is normally completed. However, there are circumstances in which the estate may be reopened, for example, there are newly discovered assets, an accounting is discovered to be incomplete, or one of the interested parties has perpetrated a fraud on the court.

In many states, it is possible to bypass the formalities of all of the above probate procedures by having the estate probated through a small estate administration, which normally occurs if the value of the decedent's gross estate is minimal (e.g., the gross estate is valued at less than $25,000). If the value of the gross estate is small, and the decedent dies without a will, or dies with a will that names as his or her sole beneficiaries a spouse, parent, or children, it is possible to have the estate probated in a relatively simple procedure.

Despite the usefulness of the probate process, there may be reasons why an estate owner may want to avoid probate. Among those reasons are the following:

1. The estate owner may wish to avoid the publicity associated with the probate of the estate. When a will is probated, the will and all documents filed with the probate court become public records unless specific instructions or court orders are obtained. Therefore, many estate owners choose not to have their intentions made public knowledge and avoid the publicity by transferring their property interests in such a way that avoids probate.

2. The estate owner can avoid lengthy time delays by transferring property to beneficiaries in a way that avoids probate. It is not unusual for the probate process to extend over a period of several years because of complications involving property disputes, tax returns, accountings, or property receipts. Many estate owners choose to avoid this delay by eliminating probate.

3. Costs involved in the probate of an estate are likely to be higher than if probate is avoided because most administrative and attorney's fees are based on a percentage of the value of the probate estate. Therefore, the greater the amount of property that is transferred outside the probate estate, the smaller the amount of administrative and legal expenses incurred by the estate. Additional costs also may be involved if the probate procedure includes appointments of guardians, conservators, or appraisers. Many of these costs can be eliminated if the probate process is avoided; for example, it is less expensive to transfer a sum of money to an individual who is named beneficiary of a whole life insurance policy as opposed to a transfer made to a beneficiary of a testamentary trust.

Conversely, there are several reasons why an estate should be probated, including the following:

1. In situations involving disputes between beneficiaries or between a surviving spouse and the personal representative, or between any other interested parties, the dispute can be judiciously settled by going through the probate court. The dispute can be resolved by an impartial decision-making body. Once a decision has been rendered, it is normally final unless one of the parties to the dispute chooses to appeal it.

2. In many situations, probate of an estate involving real estate serves as a document of title for the real property. In cases involving title disputes, the probate process can be important because it produces evidence of legal title or at least writings that enable a party to defend title to the real estate. This can be valuable to a client who wishes to prove his or her status as legal titleholder. In many jurisdictions, once

the title has been resolved, the owner receives an executor's deed which serves as proof of legal title.

3. Probate provides publicity in situations where the client wishes to have some degree of publicity surrounding the disposition of his or her assets, specifically for charitable purposes.

In addition, there may be other reasons for having the estate probated and the above-mentioned list is not all-inclusive. The financial planner should become familiar with the reasons for either having the estate probated or having it avoid probate to help the estate owner implement a plan that is consistent with his or her objectives and limitations. If the estate owner truly wishes to avoid probate, then serious consideration should be given to the use of will substitutes. These are discussed at length in Chapter 9.

3

FUNDAMENTALS OF TRUSTS AND THEIR USES IN ESTATE PLANNING

DEFINITION OF A TRUST

An essential technique to be considered in the structure of an estate plan is the trust. Because of the flexibility and convenience that can result from proper implementation of a trust, trusts have become extremely popular as estate planning techniques. Tax savings can also occur if a trust is implemented properly, and the tax savings can occur in lifetime (both income and gift tax savings) as well as at death (estate tax savings).

Basically, a trust arrangement is one in which one party (the trustee) holds legal title to property for the benefit of one or more beneficiaries. The beneficiaries are the equitable owners of the trust in the sense that they are entitled to the enjoyment of the trust property or, if income-producing, the income produced by the trust property. The party serving as trustee has a fiduciary obligation to the beneficiaries. As legal title holder of the trust property (commonly called the *corpus,* the *principal* or the *res*), the trustee has certain administrative responsibilities and management authority over the trust assets. As a fiduciary, the trustee must hold the property, invest it, distribute its income, pay the trust's income tax liability, accumulate income, if necessary, and render any services required by law to ensure that the beneficiaries receive the enjoyment and use of the property in an equitable manner.

A trust can be as complex or as informal as the individual establishing it (commonly referred to as the *grantor, settlor,* or *donor*) wishes it to be. If only personal property (e.g., stocks, bonds, cash, other income-producing property that is not real estate) is placed into the corpus of a trust, there is no requirement that the terms of the trust be put into writing. If the corpus includes real estate, there is a requirement that the trust terms be put into writing so that they do not violate the Statute of Frauds. Some types of trusts, by their very nature, are required to be in writing (e.g., a testamentary trust which is contained in the terms of a will) while others (e.g., a revocable living trust) might possibly bypass the written requirements. In general, however, it is usually preferable to place the terms of the trust in writing because the written language removes any ambiguity or misunderstanding as to the identity of the beneficiaries, the identity of the trustee, the terms under which income is to be distributed, conditions under which the income is to be accumulated, and other questions regarding the breadth and depth of the trustee's responsibilities and authority. Most trusts are, in fact, reduced to writing, either through the use of a will (for testamentary trusts) or through the use of a written trust agreement (for various types of living trusts).

In order to have a valid trust, the following elements are necessary in most states:

1. There must be specific property, the corpus or res, which is placed into the trust. The property must be specifically identified as the property constituting the corpus of the trust.

2. There must be at least one or more readily ascertainable beneficiaries, who will receive equitable ownership of the income through their use and enjoyment of it; in the case of property that is nonincome producing, the beneficiary must receive at least the use and enjoyment of the corpus. Though the beneficiaries must be ascertainable, there is no requirement that they be named individually in the trust agreement. A common example of trust beneficiaries whose identities are ascertainable but who are not named in the trust itself would be a *class* of beneficiaries, for example, "the grantor's grandchildren."

3. There must be a trustee who will hold legal title to the property and who will administer the property for the benefit of the beneficiaries. Though usually identified in the terms of the trust agreement, many states do not require the identity of the trustee to be established. In the event the trustee is not identified in the terms of the trust agreement, or if the designated trustee has predeceased the grantor, most states will permit a trustee to be appointed by the court. Most courts take the position that, if it was the intent of the grantor to create a trust, the trust will not fail for having failed to designate a trustee.

4. There must be an intention to create a trust which is clear from the grantor's language or actions. Though the use of the words, "trust," "trustee," or "trust arrangement," may not be required, the language must indicate the clear intention of the grantor to separate legal and equitable titles in the property while having one party serve as fiduciary for the other(s). It is not enough that a grantor in his will leaves the property to another with the *hope* or *desire* that the recipient create a trust. Usually, no trust arrangement is evidenced by this language.

5. If the trust is of a type that is required to be in writing (e.g., a trust involving real estate or a trust that is testamentary in nature), then the written requirements must be complied with.

6. Finally, most trusts are required to have terms or conditions under which the trust will terminate or fail. If the trust does not have conditions or terms under which it will terminate, so that the trust could conceivably be of infinite duration, then the trust will violate the rule against perpetuities and will fail unless the trust beneficiary is a charity.

WHAT TRUSTS CAN ACCOMPLISH

Trust arrangements can be used for a variety of purposes. If a client wishes to reduce potential estate tax liability, this objective can be achieved through utilization of various combinations of trusts (e.g., coordination of a marital and nonmarital trust). Both trusts reduce estate tax liability by taking advantage of the grantor's marital deduction amount (the marital trust) and unified credit (the nonmarital trust).

If a client wants to provide that the income from a trust be distributed to specified beneficiaries (e.g., children) with the remainder being distributed to a charity, a trust can accomplish this purpose (e.g., a charitable remainder annuity trust or a charitable remainder unitrust).

If the client wishes to have professional management of the assets and knows that the surviving spouse and other family members have little professional investment or business experience, the use of a trust can assure the client that someone with professional asset management experience can serve in that capacity.

If the client wants to provide income to a specified beneficiary, but knows that the beneficiary cannot control money or is improvident and cannot manage money wisely, then the client can structure the trust in such a way that the beneficiary cannot transfer his or her interest in the income until it is actually received. In this way, the beneficiary's creditors cannot reach the trust or the income produced by the trust until the income is actually distributed to the trust beneficiary (e.g., a spendthrift trust).

If the client wishes to provide income to one or more beneficiaries but is not in a position at present to determine whether the beneficiaries actually *need* the income or what the income tax liability will be for such beneficiaries, then the client can use a trust in which the trustee has the discretion to distribute income or corpus to the beneficiaries. Since the income needs of the beneficiary are subject to change, the trustee may be in a better position to determine the actual needs of the beneficiaries instead of the grantor, who may be deceased. The trustee can then distribute income as it is needed by trust beneficiaries and in such a manner that is least detrimental for the beneficiary's income tax liability.

If a client wishes to assist another family member who has suffered disability through an accident or who has been disabled since birth or childhood (e.g., a developmental disability), a trust arrangement can be used that enables the disabled beneficiary to receive assistance in such a way that does not disqualify the disabled person from receiving public assistance benefits, Medicare, or other forms of supplemental assistance. A trust, if properly structured, can achieve these objectives. For more information as to specifics of a trust for the developmentally disabled, see Chapter 10.

In short, a client can use a trust for any legitimate purpose that is not considered to be in violation of public policy. Therefore, trusts that have been established *solely* for the purpose of carrying on an illegal business, or solely for the purpose of defrauding creditors are examples of illegal trusts. Similarly, a public charitable trust that violates some provision of the law, for example, the Civil Rights Act, is an illegal trust if the effect of the trust is to discriminate against a class of beneficiaries on the basis of race, religion, national origin, or gender. Likewise, a trust that would require the trustee to perform criminal or tortious acts, or a trust that would require the beneficiaries to commit tortious or criminal acts as a condition for receiving income or corpus would be an illegal trust. If a trust is considered illegal it will not be enforced.

TYPES OF TRUSTS

It is difficult to quantify the various types of trusts that can be used as part of an estate plan. Just as the tax laws change, so do the types of trusts that are available to meet a specific client objective. The number of trusts available for usage as part of an estate plan varies, and will continue to vary, according to the grantor's needs, the size of the grantor's gross estate, the amount of estate tax the grantor would pay, and the specific identifiable objectives of the client. What follows is a brief description of the major types of trusts available for use as part of an estate plan, and the situations in which the use of the particular trust might be appropriate.

All trusts can generally be characterized as taking effect during the grantor's lifetime (*a living trust*) or as taking effect upon the death of the grantor (*a testamentary trust*). Testamentary trusts are always part of a decedent's last will and testament and are always in writing. Living trusts may or may not be in writing but, as previously discussed, it is preferable to execute them in writing so that the terms of the trust are clearly understood by the grantor, the trustee, and the beneficiary.

Trusts may also be characterized as *revocable* (capable of being terminated by the grantor at some point in time after the trust is created) or *irrevocable* (a trust which cannot be revoked by the grantor in the grantor's lifetime, even in the event of an emergency or some other situation requiring the trust to be terminated). Revocable trusts have the advantage of being flexible, and the terms of the trust can be amended, altered, or revoked in their entirety by the grantor if the grantor finds that the terms of the trust are not fulfilling the grantor's estate planning objectives. Revocable trusts also provide the grantor with the flexibility needed in the event the corpus needs to be consumed by the grantor or the grantor's family. A revocable trust provides the grantor with greater ease in amending the trust should the grantor become dissatisfied with the way in which the trust is operating. The primary disadvantage of a revocable trust is that the assets placed into the corpus of such a trust are included in the gross estate of the grantor and do not escape estate tax liability or income tax liability.

An irrevocable trust has as its primary advantage the reduction of the grantor's estate tax liability. As long as the grantor establishes an irrevocable trust, and retains no incidents of ownership over the property and retains no powers over the corpus of the trust that could be construed as ownership, then the assets placed into such a trust will escape inclusion in the gross estate of the grantor. (The only exceptions to this rule are when certain types of property are transferred to the irrevocable trust and the grantor dies within 3 years of the date of the transfer such as life insurance policies owned by the grantor; transfers of property over which the grantor reserved a right to alter, amend or revoke; transfers of property in which the grantor reserved a lifetime right to use or enjoy the property; and transfers of property wherein the transfer took effect upon the death of the grantor.) An irrevocable trust established over particular assets is considered a completed gift and the property is ordinarily removed from the grantor's gross estate. Thus, there may be gift tax liability on the value of the assets transferred to the corpus of such a trust. Another disadvantage of this type of trust is that such an arrangement lacks flexibility. Once it is established and funded, the irrevocable trust cannot be altered or terminated by the grantor, even in the event of a medical emergency. Special court orders would have to be obtained in order to revoke the trust, since the grantor has terminated any ability to change, alter, or revoke the terms of the trust. Should the client's financial situation change drastically so that the corpus or income are needed by the client, the irrevocable trust can be a serious detriment for the client whose estate plan requires greater flexibility.

Certain types of trusts, which are irrevocable by nature, may provide the grantor with certain benefits such as a grantor retained annuity trust (GRAT) or a grantor retained unitrust (GRUT) either of which may provide the trust grantor with income from the trust assets.

It should be noted that an irrevocable living trust can only be established during the life of the grantor. Since all testamentary trusts are, by nature, irrevocable (since the grantor is dead when the trust takes effect), the term "irrevocable" is usually applied only to trusts that are established during the lifetime of the grantor.

A trust can distribute its income to one or more beneficiaries according to a fixed schedule of distribution or at the discretion of the trustee. Under such terms, the beneficiary is usually entitled to a fixed sum for each period of trust distribution (e.g., $1000 per month, to be distributed four times per year, once every three months). A trust can also distribute its income according to the needs of the trust beneficiary, as determined by the trustee. A trust that vests the distribution of income or corpus to beneficiaries according to the authority of the trustee is known as a *discretionary trust,* since it is up to the trustee's discretion as to whether any income or corpus is distributed. A trust that permits the trustee to distribute income or corpus among various beneficiaries, according to the needs of the beneficiaries, is sometimes referred to as a trust with sprinkling provisions or a *sprinkling* or *spray trust.* Under the terms of such a trust, the trustee has the discretion to determine whether a particular beneficiary needs any income, and if such a need is determined, the amount that the beneficiary will receive. Accordingly, a sprinkling trust could provide Beneficiary A with $5000 in Year One, $0 in Year Two, $10,000 in Year Three, and $8000 in Year Four. During the same time period, Beneficiary B could receive $10,000 per year for years One through Four, and Beneficiary C could receive no income in years One, Two, and Three, while receiving $25,000 in income in Year Four. The primary advantage of a sprinkling trust is the flexibility it provides to the trustee in making income distributions to beneficiaries who may not have a need for income in one year but could have such a need in a subsequent year.

A trust that is established solely for the purpose of providing income to a beneficiary in discharge of the grantor's obligation of support to the beneficiary is referred to as a *support trust.* Such a trust seldom provides the grantor with any significant tax advantages, as will be discussed later in this chapter. Such trusts are used primarily as a means of providing a fixed stream of income to the beneficiary for which the grantor has an obligation of support. A commonly used example of a support trust is one established pursuant to the terms of a dissolution of marriage. In such an arrangement, the grantor parent would establish a support trust for the benefit of the grantor's minor children. The trust would distribute a fixed stream of income to the custodial parent on behalf of the minor children in lieu of the grantor's legal obligation of support. The trust would terminate when the youngest of the minor children reached the age of majority. Usually, the children would receive the remainder interest.

Sometimes a grantor wishes to establish a trust that can benefit several generations within the same family. The trust is established primarily to take advantage of estate and gift tax savings for the grantor, when the grantor is extremely wealthy. A *generation-skipping trust* can be used to achieve this purpose. The generation-skipping trust can provide income to the grantor's spouse for the spouse's lifetime; upon the death of the spouse, or simultaneous with the income distribution to the spouse, the children of the grantor can receive income for their lives; upon the deaths of all of the children, the outright title to the property in the corpus passes to the grandchildren of the grantor. In order to be an effective means of saving estate and gift taxes for the grantor, the trust must possess the following characteristics:

1. The trust must be irrevocable in nature.
2. The trust income may be distributed to the grantor's spouse and children, but the absolute title to the property must "skip" at least one generation (that generation being the children of the grantor, also referred to as "the deemed transferors").
3. The outright title to the trust property must pass to someone who is separated from the grantor's generation by at least two generations (it must be the grandchildren).
4. Prior to 1976, this type of trust arrangement was structured primarily to avoid estate or gift tax liability in the child's estate had the property been transferred directly from the grantor to the grantor's children. Thus, a direct transfer to the next succeeding generation was avoided, and estate and gift taxes were also minimized. However, since 1976, when Congress imposed a generation-skipping tax on transfers of this sort, the attractiveness of such an arrangement for the extremely wealthy has diminished greatly. However, for a grantor with moderate wealth, the generation-skipping trust is still an effective means of transferring property to the children and grandchildren of the grantor. This is because the generation-skipping tax laws permit an exemption of $1 million per transferor for the value of any assets placed in a generation-skipping trust. Thus, a grantor could fund a trust with $1 million and all of it would avoid the generation-skipping transfer tax.
5. The generation-skipping transfer tax is only imposed on those trans-

fers deemed to be either taxable terminations or taxable distributions. Thus, the tax is imposed in a situation where the income beneficiary's interest in the trust terminates, and the property is transferred from one generation to a member of another generation.

6. The generation-skipping transfer tax was not imposed on direct skips of property from the grantor to the grantor's grandchildren prior to the Tax Reform Act of 1986 (TRA '86). Under TRA '86, the generation-skipping transfer tax was imposed on direct skips of property interests that passed from the grantor to the grantor's *grandchildren.* However, there was a special $2 million exemption for the grantor for *each* transfer deemed to be a direct skip. (Note that this special $2 million exemption applied only to the grantor's grandchildren, not to all trust beneficiaries of a generation-skipping transfer.) This exemption expired after December 31, 1989. After that date, the grantor was still entitled to the $1 million exemption per transferor for all transfers.

A trust can be used for the benefit of minor children. There are a variety of trusts that can be used to benefit minors. The most informal of these is truly not a trust, but is actually a custodial account established for the benefit of a minor beneficiary pursuant to the Uniform Gifts to Minors Act (UGMA), or the Uniform Transfers to Minors Act (UTMA). In this type of fiduciary relationship, the property is placed in an account which bears the name of the minor as the legal title holder. The property is then held by an adult who has "custody" of the property until the minor reaches the age of majority. These custodial accounts, or UGMA or UTMA accounts, as they are sometimes called, are convenient and relatively inexpensive to administer. They do not have significant administration costs or accounting expenses as do more formal trust arrangements.

Special trusts that are structured for the benefit of minors include both 2503(b) and 2503(c) trusts. These are trusts which meet the requirements of these Code sections in order to qualify annual additions to these trusts for the gift tax annual exclusion. A *2503(b) trust,* named after the specific Internal Revenue Code section, provides a minor with a stream of income during the time in which the beneficiary is a minor. The trust must pay out a specified sum of income to the minor at least once annually, and there is a mandatory income distribution requirement annually. Because of this mandatory income distribution requirement, a part of the income distribution may use the gift tax annual exclusion. The corpus of a 2503(b) trust need not be distributed to the beneficiary when the beneficiary reaches the age of majority. In fact, there is no requirement that the beneficiary of the trust ever receive the corpus. This type of trust provides the grantor with greater flexibility over the distribution of the corpus. If the grantor wishes to distribute the corpus to the beneficiary, but does not want to do so until the beneficiary is 30 years old, then a 2503(b) trust may be appropriate.

A *2503(c) trust* is also a trust used for minors but it differs from the 2053(b) trust in several significant respects. Unlike the 2503(b) trust, in which the corpus need not be distributed to the beneficiary when the beneficiary reaches the age of majority, the corpus of a 2503(c) trust *must* be available for distribution to the beneficiary when the beneficiary reaches the age of 21. However, the child may choose not to make withdrawals from the trust corpus, and if the child chooses to leave the corpus intact, the trust will continue until such time as the terms of the trust agreement dictate. The second major difference is that the 2503(c) trust does not require a current mandatory distribution of income, like the 2503(b) trust. Rather, income can be accumulated and added to the corpus of the trust. However, both the current income and all accumulated income which has been added to the corpus must be available for distribution when the beneficiary reaches the age of 21. Thus, for a grantor who wishes to delay absolutely the distribution of the trust corpus until such time that the beneficiary has demonstrated an ability to manage it, the 2503(b) trust may be more appropriate than the 2503(c) trust. However, for the grantor who is reluctant to provide the income beneficiary with an absolute right to immediate distribution of the income while the beneficiary is a minor, the 2503(c) trust may be more appropriate than the 2503(b).

Certain trusts for minors can be structured to take advantage of the gift tax annual exclusion. These trusts, which normally accumulate trust income for the benefit of minor beneficiaries until such time as the minors reach the age of majority, qualify for the gift tax annual exclusion because the gifts of income or corpus are considered gifts of a present interest. Both the 2503(b) and 2503(c) trusts are examples of trusts that qualify for the annual exclusion. However, if the trust is properly structured so that the minor beneficiary can demand the lesser of the amount transferred annually to the trust, or the maximum amount allowed under a five and five power (the greater of $5000 or 5% of the value of the corpus), then the minor beneficiary has what is known as a Crummey right of withdrawal over the trust. The effect of adding a Crummey provision to a trust is to make annual additions to the trust a gift of a present interest, thereby qualifying them for the gift tax annual exclusion. Such a trust, called a *Crummey trust,* can provide the grantor with valuable gift tax savings for the value of the assets added to the trust.

Just as trusts can be used to benefit minor beneficiaries, they can also be used to benefit a qualified charity. These so-called *charitable trusts* have varying characteristics, which will be touched on only briefly here. A *charitable lead trust* is one which pays a fixed income stream to a qualified charity for a period of years (usually no more than 20 years). At the expiration of the stated time period, the remainder interest passes to one or more noncharitable beneficiaries. The charitable lead trust can provide the grantor with either income or estate tax savings, depending on when the use of such a technique is employed. An immediate income tax deduction can be obtained by the grantor for a charitable lead trust established during the grantor's lifetime when the grantor is considered the owner of the trust income. The deduction is measured by the present value of the income stream passing to the charity for the stated time period. Any gift tax that would occur on such a transaction would be absorbed by the gift tax charitable deduction. If the charitable lead trust is structured to take effect upon the death of the grantor, the grantor's estate will receive a charitable deduction for the present value of the income stream passing to the charity.

A *charitable remainder annuity trust* (CRAT) is one in which the qualified charity receives the remainder interest in the corpus after distribution of a fixed stream of income, known as a sum certain, to one or more noncharitable beneficiaries. The CRAT can receive only one initial contribution of corpus. No subsequent additions can be made to the corpus of a CRAT. In addition, the amount of the annuity or income stream paid to the noncharitable beneficiary does not change in subsequent trust years (e.g., at least 5% of the corpus as valued in the initial year that the trust was established).

A *charitable remainder unitrust* (CRUT) is also used to provide an income stream, a fixed percentage, to a noncharitable beneficiary while transferring the remainder interest to a qualified charity. Unlike the CRAT, however, the CRUT can receive subsequent additions to its corpus. Thus, the corpus of a CRUT can continue to receive assets in later years. The CRUT also differs from a CRAT since the stream paid out by the CRUT trust must be at least 5 percent of the annual reappraised value of the corpus. Thus, where the CRAT pays a sum certain of income that never varies in amount, the CRUT can distribute greater or lesser amounts of income, depending on the reappraised value of the corpus and accumulated income. If the value of the corpus and income continues to appreciate, the amount of the payment to the noncharitable beneficiary can increase with each succeeding year. This makes the CRUT an effective means of fighting inflation. If, however, the value of the assets continues to depreciate over a period of years, the CRUT can actually pay less income to the noncharitable beneficiary than was originally intended. If a grantor wishes to ensure an annual increase in the value of the income payment to the noncharitable beneficiary, the grantor should fund the corpus of such a trust with assets that pay a guaranteed rate of return such as U.S. Treasury notes that pay interest tied to a specific rate of return.

Sometimes a grantor will establish a trust with the intention that all or a part of the income is to be distributed to the grantor. Such a trust is not used primarily to minimize income, estate, or gift taxes. If a trust is structured to provide all of its income to the grantor as the trust beneficiary, such a trust is referred to as a *grantor annuity trust*. The income from such a trust is fully taxable to the grantor, and the assets that make up the corpus are fully includible in the gross estate of the grantor, even if the trust is irrevocable. Since the receipt of income from such a trust is considered the retention of a life estate in the transferred property, the full value of the property in the trust is included in the gross estate of the grantor. The primary purpose of such a trust is to provide the grantor with a fixed stream of income rather than to minimize any tax liability.

When the grantor wishes to receive a specified percentage of the income from a trust (e.g., "$20,000 per year or 10% of the corpus, whichever is less, with the excess to be distributed to my sister"), such a trust is referred to as a *short-term annuity trust*. A short-term annuity trust ensures that the grantor receives a certain sum of income for each period of income distribution, but has the added advantage of specifying that any excess amounts shall be distributed to another named beneficiary. If structured properly, the trust can avoid gift tax liability on the excess amount of income that is distributed to other beneficiaries.

Some trusts that were formerly used to benefit family members, which are now seldom used, are mentioned only briefly to alert the reader that these trusts, if implemented prior to March 1, 1986, are still valid. A *short-term (Clifford) trust,* if structured and funded prior to March 1, 1986 or if funded pursuant to a binding property settlement entered into by the parties to a marital dissolution prior to March 1, 1986, could be used to transfer income to family members in lower marginal income tax brackets. The short-term (Clifford) trust was structured to last at least 10 years and one day. During that time the trust was irrevocable. The income produced by the trust assets was distributed to family members who were usually in a lower marginal tax bracket than the grantor. There was overall income tax savings achieved by transferring the income to another family member. There was also tax savings achieved by having the income taxed at a lower marginal tax bracket instead of at the grantor's. Upon termination of the trust, the corpus reverted back to the grantor; thus, there was no significant estate tax savings achieved by the use of a *Clifford* trust. It should be noted that the terms of a Clifford trust had to last for at least 10 years plus one day if the grantor was to avoid being taxed on the income produced by such a trust (where such trusts have been funded prior to March 1, 1986). The only exception to this situation occurred when the trust beneficiary died before the term of the trust was completed. Under these circumstances, the grantor would not be taxed on the income produced by the trust for the term of the trust.

Another type of trust that was effectively used to benefit other family members prior to March 1, 1986 was the *spousal remainder trust*. If implemented prior to March 1, 1986, the spousal remainder trust was structured somewhat similarly to the Clifford trust, except that the trust need not have lasted 10 years and one day; it could last for a lesser duration. The income produced by the trust was distributed to family members in a lower marginal tax bracket than that of the grantor. Usually, the trust beneficiaries were individuals in lower marginal tax brackets, such as college-age children of the grantor who used the trust income for their college-related expenses. Upon the child's graduation from college, the trust terminated and the remainder interest in the trust passed to the spouse of the grantor for the spouse's exclusive use and enjoyment. None of the corpus or income from the trust could be used to benefit the grantor, either directly or indirectly. The remainder interest passing to the spouse of the grantor was transferred without gift tax liability because of the unlimited gift tax marital deduction available between spouses. Prior to March 1, 1986,the spousal remainder trust became popular as a result of the unfavorable tax treatment accorded to interest-free and low-interest loans.

Another frequently used type of trust is the *life insurance trust*. The life insurance trust can be funded or unfunded, revocable or irrevocable, and is used primarily as a receptacle for life insurance proceeds and other assets belonging to the decedent. The trust is structured to receive either a life insurance policy or the death benefits payable upon the death of the insured. The trustee is named the beneficiary on the policy designation form so that the trust becomes funded when the insured dies. In an irrevocable life insurance trust, the trustee is designated as both the owner of the policy and beneficiary of the policy. As an alternative, the grantor can establish and fund the trust with other assets during the grantor's lifetime in addition to the life insurance policy(ies). The death benefit proceeds are then added to the corpus of the trust when the insured dies, and the terms of the trust control the distribution of income and corpus. Life insurance trusts are often popular estate planning techniques because they avoid probate.

Another type of trust that is popular because it can avoid probate is the *pourover trust*. A pourover trust is established during the grantor's lifetime. Its primary function is to receive assets from a variety of sources such as life insurance benefits, qualified retirement plan proceeds, retirement plan benefits, IRA accounts, Keogh plan accounts, and assets pouring into it under the terms of a will. With the exception of property passing into such a trust from a will, all of the above-mentioned sources of funding such a trust would avoid probate. The pourover trust can receive assets from a variety of sources where the assets themselves are usually liquid in nature. The trust can then distribute the assets and the income produced by them in accordance with the terms and provisions of the trust. A pourover trust can either be revocable or irrevocable, depending on the grantor's preferences. The pourover trust provides professional management and supervision of the assets and can ensure that one or more improvident beneficiaries will not consume the entire corpus or all of the income.

A variety of trusts that take advantage of a decedent's unified credit amount as well as the marital deduction can also be used as a part of a client's estate plan. A *marital trust,* also known as a *power of appointment trust,* can provide the decedent's spouse with absolute control over some or all of the decedent's property. The entire amount placed into a marital trust will avoid estate tax liability in the estate of the first decedent spouse since it qualifies for the marital deduction.

A *nonmarital* or *bypass trust* is appropriate in situations where the grantor wishes to leave a life income interest to his spouse as well as other family members, such as children or grandchildren. Upon the death of the grantor's spouse absolute ownership of the property passes to other individuals such as the children of the grantor or the grandchildren of the grantor. The nonmarital trust is usually funded in an amount equal to the exemption equivalent. While the value of the corpus in such a trust remains in the taxable estate of the grantor it usually avoids estate tax liability because the tax on such an amount is equal to the amount of unified credit available to the grantor. The use of a bypass trust is also appropriate when the grantor wishes to leave ownership of the property to someone other than the surviving spouse.

A *qualified terminable interest property trust* or Q-TIP trust is appropriate when the grantor wishes to provide a stream of income to a spouse for the life of the spouse, but wishes to pass the remainder interest in such property to someone other than the surviving spouse, usually children from a previous marriage. The income stream passing to the surviving spouse ensures the grantor that the surviving spouse will receive income for life, yet the value of the property placed in the trust may escape estate tax liability in the grantor's estate because it can be made to qualify for the marital deduction. However, for this to occur, the property or a portion of it must be elected by the executor as qualifying for the marital deduction. Because the property in the trust is a qualified terminable interest property, the grantor of the Q-TIP trust is allowed postmortem control over the trust property by determining who the ultimate beneficiaries of the trust property will be after the death of the surviving spouse.

The grantor may also wish to consider the use of an *estate trust* in special circumstances where the grantor wishes to qualify the property in the trust for the marital deduction but where the donee spouse already has a sizeable estate and does not need or want the income or corpus from the trust. In such circumstances, the grantor can employ an estate trust which will provide income to the grantor's spouse only when the trustee deems it proper. The corpus and the majority of the income will not be distributed to the donee spouse in the spouse's lifetime. Yet, the property will qualify for the marital deduction since the surviving spouse has a general power of appointment over the corpus of the trust and can determine who will receive the property when the surviving spouse dies.

Finally, the grantor may wish to consider a *disclaimer trust,* which is used in situations where the surviving spouse wishes to file a *qualified disclaimer* over a portion of the property passing to the survivor from the grantor's estate. A disclaimer trust is frequently used when the surviving spouse wishes to have the decedent's estate take full advantage of the unified credit available to it or when the survivor has no need for property bequeathed to the survivor under the terms of the decedent's will. This most often occurs in situations in which the decedent's estate has overqualified the estate for the marital deduction and has failed to take full advantage of the unified credit. By taking advantage of a disclaimer trust, the surviving spouse disclaims a portion of the assets that would have been received from the grantor's estate. Instead, these assets pass into a disclaimer trust, the income from which can be used to benefit the surviving spouse (not unlike a nonmarital trust). The property that is disclaimed remains in the taxable estate of the decedent and takes full advantage of the unified credit, so there is usually little if any estate tax liability for the grantor's estate. In effect, the property contained in the disclaimer trust usually passes to someone other than the surviving spouse in order to take advantage of *both* the unified credit (the disclaimed portion) and the marital deduction (that portion of the property which is not disclaimed but which instead is enjoyed by the spouse or is that property over which the spouse enjoys postmortem control). The exercise of the disclaimer trust by the surviving spouse is an important postmortem election since it ensures both estates of overall estate tax savings by using the combined estate tax savings provided by use of both the marital deduction and the unified credit. For example, a disclaimer of some property by the surviving spouse would cause the disclaimed property to be included in the grantor's gross estate, thus using the grantor's unified credit, while the property not disclaimed would qualify for the marital deduction in the grantor's estate. The property disclaimed would not be included in the survivor's estate, thus reducing the survivor's estate tax liability as well. The ultimate ownership of the property disclaimed is transferred to a nonspousal beneficiary who may not receive the property until the surviving spouse has fully enjoyed a life income interest in the property (similar to a nonmarital or bypass trust). (**Note:** for the disclaimer to be qualified, for federal estate tax purposes, the property disclaimed cannot pass to other beneficiaries by the direction, control, or command of the surviving disclaimant.)

Two specific types of trusts may occur by operation of law. A *resulting trust* is a trust occurring in favor of the grantor when a trust originally designed for another beneficiary fails because all beneficiaries have died or when the trust has been declared void. The grantor becomes the beneficiary in such a trust arrangement. A *constructive trust* is one which arises by operation of law in favor of a person who is unjustly deprived of property by another individual who is unjustly enriched as a result of fraud, undue influence, or breach of a confidential relationship. An example of a constructive trust would be a situation in which an individual was fraudulently induced into signing over property rights in a conveyance of real estate. Had the owner of the property truly known of the facts relevant to the transfer of the property, the owner would not have conveyed the property. In such a situation, a court will impose a constructive trust on the property in such a way that the benefits and enjoyment of the property will be returned to its original owner.

One final trust that is worthy of consideration is the *standby trust*. The standby trust is important because it is a trust specifically structured to take effect if the grantor becomes temporarily or permanently disabled. Since the statistical probability of becoming disabled is eight times greater than dying in any given year, this type of trust can prove extremely important in settling or structuring an estate plan.

A standby trust is usually structured to take effect when the owner is no longer capable of managing the assets. Frequently, this occurs in situations where the grantor has become disabled or where the grantor has left the country for a period of time (e.g., 3 years leave of absence to develop a business enterprise in a foreign country). The standby trust is usually revocable in nature.

If the grantor suffers a permanent disability, the trust can be made to become irrevocable. The trustee of such a trust can use the trust assets to provide for the disabled grantor's living expenses, financial needs, and medical care. Though the grantor of such a trust will be taxed on the income from such a trust, and though the corpus of such a trust would be included as an asset in the grantor's estate, the standby trust is important because of the professional management experience it provides should the grantor become physically or mentally disabled and unable to take care of his or her business interests.

POWERS OF A TRUSTEE

Ordinarily the terms of the trust agreement or the will determine the duties and powers of a trustee. Though the powers of a trustee may vary from state to state, the general powers that a trustee may hold include the following:

1. Power to collect trust property, settle claims, and sue or be sued
2. Power to sell, acquire or manage trust property in such a manner that is in the best interests of the trust
3. Power to vote corporate shares
4. Power to borrow money and use the trust corpus as collateral, if approved by the court

5. Power to enter into contracts and leases that do not exceed the duration of the trust
6. Power to make payments to a beneficiary of the trust
7. Power to make required divisions and distributions of trust property
8. Power to receive additional assets into the corpus of the trust

Generally, if there are two or more trustees, all trustees must act unanimously. If the trustees cannot agree upon a unanimous course of action for the trust, a special hearing will have to be held in order to determine the effectiveness of the trust and the conditions under which one or more trustees may step down or resign.

DUTIES OF A TRUSTEE

While the powers of a trustee are variable—the grantor can determine the extent of the trustee's powers in the trust agreement or in the will—the trustee must thoroughly understand the duties which accompany the title of legal owner of the trust assets. The duties of a trustee may vary from state to state, but in general, a trustee's duties include the following at a minimum:

1. The trustee has a duty to carry out the trust in accordance with the terms of the trust agreement or will.
2. The trustee has a duty not to delegate the trustee's duties to another individual—any duty which calls on the trustee to exercise skill and judgment may not be delegated (e.g., investment responsibilities). However, this duty does not prohibit the trustee from hiring professional experts, for example, professional investment advisors to evaluate the suitability and nature of trust investments.
3. The trustee has a duty to exercise a reasonable degree of skill and care in the management of the trust assets. The trustee should administer the trust with the degree of skill and care that would be required if the trustee were dealing with his or her own assets.
4. The trustee owes a duty of loyalty to the beneficiaries to administer the trust solely in their best interests. This duty of loyalty prohibits the trustee from self-dealing with the trust.
5. The trustee has a duty to possess, protect, and preserve the trust property. The trustee must use ordinary diligence and care in the prosecution of claims and in the collection of income and other receivables. The trustee has a general duty to defend the trust and the interests of the beneficiaries against those who challenge the validity

of the trust. While the trustee is not an insurer of the corpus, the trustee must use reasonable care and diligence in preserving and protecting the property (e.g., obtaining insurance on the property if an ordinary, reasonable, prudent individual would do the same).

6. The trustee has a duty to separate and earmark trust property. A trustee is required to keep trust property separate from the trustee's own property. If a trustee commingles his or her own property with the trust property, the trustee is liable for any losses resulting from the commingling.

7. The trustee has a duty to make the trust property productive. The standards normally used to make the trust property productive are controlled by a "prudent person" investment rule. Included under the prudent person investment rule are actions in which the trustee may acquire, invest, reinvest, exchange, sell, and manage trust property in the same manner in which people of ordinary, reasonable, and prudent standards would manage it.

8. The trustee has the duty to treat all beneficiaries impartially. If a trustee has the duty to distribute income according to the trustee's discretion, the trustee's decision will be sustained if made in good faith. The trustee must avoid behavior which favors one beneficiary over another. If one beneficiary is favored over another, and the trustee cannot show good faith, the trustee may be liable for any harms that can be proven by the beneficiary whose interests were injured.

INCOME TAX IMPLICATIONS OF TRUSTS

There are significant income tax implications for trusts. The implications for these trusts vary, depending upon the type of trust. Trusts that are required to distribute all of their income in the present year (*simple trusts*) are taxed differently from trusts that are not required to distribute all of their income in one year (*complex trusts*). Though the specifics of these trusts may be beyond the scope and purpose of this book, the financial planner should be aware of the variations in the tax treatment of these trusts.

For tax purposes, both the trust and the trust beneficiary are separate entities. Thus, it is possible that the trust may have to file an income tax return and pay income tax in the same year that the trust beneficiary does. Both the trust and the trust beneficiary would pay income tax on the amount of taxable income distributed to each; however, unlike a corporate situation, in which double taxation occurs on the corporate earnings (where tax is paid by the corporation and is taxed again to the shareholders when received by them) the trust income is not subject to double taxation. The trust receives a deduction for any income that is actually distributed to the trust beneficiaries, so that the income is taxed only once.

The Internal Revenue Code allows a trust a deduction for the amount of income that is required to be distributed currently to beneficiaries. This trust qualifies as a simple trust provided there is no distribution of corpus. If any portion of the corpus of such a trust is distributed, it ceases to be treated as a simple trust and is taxed as a complex trust. Thus, for any trust which terminates and distributes its corpus, the trust will be treated as a complex trust in the year of the distribution of the corpus.

The trust beneficiary is taxed on income that is required to be distributed to the beneficiary, regardless of whether the income is actually received. If the income accumulates in the trust and is retained by the trust, the trust pays the income tax on it. When the trust passes the income to the beneficiaries, the trust receives a distribution deduction and the beneficiaries must pay the tax on the distribution. In effect, the beneficiary is taxed on his or her proportional share of the distributable net income (DNI).

A trust can sometimes be subjected to the payment of income tax on property other than undistributed income. Section 644 of the Code provides that if a sale or exchange of appreciated property occurs within 2 years after the property is initially transferred to the trust and before the time of the grantor's death, the trust will pay income tax on the "built-in gain." Rather than paying the tax at the trust's tax rates, however, the trust will pay the tax at the grantor's marginal tax bracket, which is usually somewhat higher than that of the trust. This tax pitfall can be properly avoided if the terms of the trust agreement prohibit the trustee from selling or exchanging the property within 2 years from the date it is acquired by the trust. Including a provision of this type in the terms of the trust agreement can result in overall tax savings of the trust since the built-in gain that is subject to the tax at the grantor's tax rates is either: (1) the gain recognized by the trust on the sale or exchange of the property or (2) the excess of the fair market value of the property at the time of its initial transfer into the trust minus its adjusted basis immediately after the transfer, whichever amount is less. Avoidance of this tax is important since it is a tax imposed on the trust in addition to any other tax payable by the trust.

For complex trusts, a trust is entitled to a distribution deduction which equals the combined amounts of income that are required to be distributed currently and any other amounts, whether they be income or corpus, that are actually paid, credited, or distributed during the taxable year. The complex trust differs from the simple trust in respect to the treatment of capital gains. Whereas capital gains are *not* treated as a part of the distributable net income of a simple trust, they are treated as a part of the distributable net income of a complex trust if they are paid, distributed, or set aside for a beneficiary. As with a simple trust, a complex trust cannot take a distribution deduction that exceeds the value of the trust's DNI.

An important concept that is frequently employed in the taxation of trusts is the concept of the *throwback rule*. Basically, this rule is designed to tax the beneficiary of a trust that accumulates income. The throwback rule taxes that portion of the accumulated income as if the income had been distributed. The throwback rule applies only in certain situations, however, and applies only where the actual distributions from the trust exceed the amount of the distributable net income.

Generally, a trust beneficiary is only taxed on distributions that equal the amount of DNI, not on amounts that exceed the DNI. However, in order to prevent tax avoidance through the accumulation of income in a trust at tax rates that are lower than what the beneficiary would pay if the income were distributed, the throwback rules are applied in those situations where certain distributions are in excess of DNI. The amount of any distribution which exceeds the DNI in any given year is referred to as an *accumulation distribution,* and such a distribution is treated as having been distributed in prior years to the extent that the trust accumulated income in those years.

Not all distributions that exceed the amount of the DNI are considered accumulated distributions, however, and the following types of distributions are not subject to the throwback rules:

1. Gifts or bequests of a specific sum of money or property (e.g., "$10,000 cash to my niece, Sara")
2. Any amount set aside, paid or used for a qualifying charitable purpose (e.g., "$15,000 to the American Humane Society, to prevent cruelty to animals")
3. Income that is *required* to be distributed currently even though the income exceeds the amount of DNI
4. Distributions of income that accumulate before the beneficiary's birth or before the beneficiary reaches the age of 21
5. Distributions that do not exceed the trust's *accounting* income.

For years in which the income is accumulated, the trust pays the income tax on such accumulations at the trust's regular marginal tax bracket. When the trust pays out its accumulated income to the beneficiary in current years, the beneficiary is taxed on the income as though it had been distributed to the beneficiary on the last day of the year in which the income accumulated in the trust. The net effect of the throwback rule is to ensure that the trust beneficiary pays his or her share of the income tax on such income at the same rates that would have been paid if the income had actually been distributed rather than accumulated. It avoids the undue accumulation of income in a trust in an attempt to avoid the payment of income tax on it.

GRANTOR TRUST RULES

Specific sections of the Internal Revenue Code govern the income taxation of trusts. Specifically, these sections provide that a grantor of the trust (rather than the trust itself or the trust beneficiary) will be taxed on the income produced by the trust in a number of situations. Basically, the grantor will pay the income tax on any income produced by the trust if the following conditions occur:

1. The grantor receives the income directly.
2. The grantor may have the income payable to him, under the terms of the trust.
3. The grantor indicates that the income from the trust is to be paid to the grantor's spouse.
4. The grantor indicates that the income is to accumulate for the benefit of the grantor, or the grantor's spouse.
5. The grantor indicates that the income is to be used to pay life insurance premiums for a policy owned by the grantor or the grantor's spouse.
6. The grantor indicates that the income is to be used to satisfy a legal obligation of support for a family member of the grantor (e.g., minor children) or for the grantor's spouse.
7. The grantor has the ability to revoke the trust or alter its terms so that the trust terminates or reverts back to the grantor at any time.
8. The grantor retains the power to control the beneficial enjoyment of the trust property, including the power to determine who shall receive the property and the terms under which the property can be enjoyed (e.g., "$20,000 per year to my son, Charles, age 24, as long as he achieves good grades in his medical studies but if he should not achieve good grades in his medical studies then the income shall terminate upon the discretion of the grantor").
9. The grantor possesses specific administrative powers over the trust; he is allowed to borrow against the trust and use the trust corpus as collateral.

If any of these conditions are present, the grantor will be deemed to be the recipient of the income produced by the trust and will be liable for income tax on any income produced by the trust. If the grantor wishes to avoid being taxed on trust income, the grantor should avoid any of the nine situations described.

TRUSTS AND ESTATE TAX LIABILITY

Generally, when a grantor establishes a revocable living trust, the grantor should understand that the assets in such a trust are still included in the grantor's gross estate. Because the grantor can terminate the trust at will, or revoke it at any time the grantor is dissatisfied with the operation of this trust, the grantor possesses incidents of ownership over the trust and its corpus and undistributed income. The ability to revoke the trust will cause the inclusion of the corpus and all undistributed income in the gross estate of the grantor. Thus, such a trust should be thought of primarily for its flexibility and not as a saver of estate tax.

With certain noted exceptions, the creation of an irrevocable living trust will successfully remove the property placed in the trust from the gross estate of the grantor. An irrevocable living trust constitutes a total completed gift of the property placed in such a trust, and the grantor has made a complete severance of all rights and interests in the property. Where this has occurred, the property placed in the trust and all future appreciation of it are removed from the gross estate of the grantor.

There are a few situations in which the creation of an irrevocable living trust will not result in removing the property from the gross estate of the grantor. The following examples demonstrate this type of situation:

1. The grantor transfers the property to the trust but retains a life income or the right to use or enjoy the property for the rest of the grantor's life (retention of a life estate).
2. The grantor establishes the trust but fails to specify beneficiaries to receive the trust income or property in the event the primary beneficiary dies, so that the property in the trust reverts back to the grantor or has a possibility of reverting back to the grantor (a "reversionary interest") that is greater than 5 percent of the value of the property at the inception of the trust.
3. The grantor establishes a trust over which he or she has the ability to direct where the property will go and to whom. Basically, any situation in which the grantor can exercise a general power of appointment will cause the property to be included in his gross estate.
4. The grantor establishes an irrevocable living trust and funds it with life insurance policies but dies before 3 years have passed from the date the policies were transferred. The policies, valued at their face

amount, will be included in the gross estate of the grantor as one of the classes of property that is included in the gross estate of the grantor if transferred within 3 years of death.

5. The grantor establishes a trust into which life insurance policies are transferred. The grantor retains the right to change the beneficiary designation, determine the settlement options and pay out schedule, or can determine the conditions under which the beneficiary shall receive the proceeds. When the grantor retains incidents of ownership in the policy, the face value of the proceeds will be included in the gross estate of the grantor.

6. The grantor retains specific interests in the trust property, such as having the trust property pledged as collateral for a loan where the grantor is the obligated party, or any other situation in which the grantor could be construed, directly or indirectly, as retaining a specific interest in the trust property. Retention of these interests will cause the property in the trust to be included in the gross estate of the grantor.

GIFT TAX IMPLICATIONS OF TRUSTS

In general, a revocable trust is not considered a completed gift because the grantor has not parted with dominion and control over the property. Thus, a revocable trust will not be subject to gift tax liability. However, because the grantor has not parted with ownership of the property it will be included in the grantor's gross estate, even if the trust is a life insurance trust.

An irrevocable living trust will normally result in some form of gift tax liability. The gift is the fair market value of the property at the time it is transferred into the trust, not its value at the date of the grantor's death. Thus, if the grantor has property that is highly appreciable in nature, it might be a good idea to transfer the property into the irrevocable living trust in order to avoid having the future appreciation included in the gross estate of the grantor. If the trust pays income, it may qualify for the annual exclusion amount on the stream of income being distributed to the beneficiary. As long as the income *must* be distributed to the beneficiary, or as long as the beneficiary has a demand right of the greater of $5000 or 5 percent of the corpus, or can demand the lesser of an annual addition to trust corpus, or the maximum amount allowable under a five and five power (5% of the value of the corpus, or $5000, whichever is greater) the income produced by such trusts qualifies for the gift tax annual exclusion amount and can reduce the grantor's gift tax liability. In trusts where the beneficiary does not have a demand right over a portion of the corpus, or where the income from such a trust must accumulate, the gift tax annual exclusion is not available to offset any gift tax liability the grantor may have to pay.

In situations where the value of the property transferred to the corpus is sizeable (e.g., greater than the amount of the exemption equivalent), there can be significant gift tax liability for the grantor. In most trusts, the corpus is distributed to remaindermen at some point in the future. Such a gift of the corpus is a gift of a future interest and does not qualify for the annual exclusion amount. If the grantor uses all of his or her unified credit to absorb the gift tax liability on the value of the property at the time it is transferred to the trust, the grantor could face gift tax liability at the time the trust is created. Careful structuring and funding of the trust should be planned so that the grantor does not face any unintended gift tax liability.

SPECIAL SITUATIONS: GRANTOR RETAINED ANNUITY TRUSTS AND GRANTOR RETAINED UNITRUSTS

In late 1990, Congress passed the Revenue Reconciliation Act of 1990. One of the most significant aspects of this piece of legislation was the repeal of Code Section 2036(c), which dealt with valuation of intrafamily estate freezes for federal estate tax purposes. Concurrent with the retroactive repeal of Code Section 2036(c), Congress enacted a new Chapter 14. Chapter 14 attempts to value intrafamily freeze techniques for gift tax purposes, and establishes particular rules for the valuation of retained interests in recapitalized corporations, family partnerships involving freezes, certain trusts and life estates, and lapses of certain rights.

Among the trusts that were affected by the provisions of Chapter 14 were grantor retained income trusts, also known as GRITs. Under the gift valuation rules of Chapter 14, the retained income interest held by the grantor in a GRIT is valued *for gift tax purposes* at zero. Essentially, this means that the value of the gift being made to the remaindermen of the GRIT is not its actuarial value, based on the present value of the remainder interest to be received by the remaindermen. Instead, the value of the gift is the *fair market value* of any assets placed in trust (since the retained interest is deemed to have a value of zero, the entire fair market value of any assets in trust is the value of the gift for federal gift tax purposes). The net result of new Chapter 14 is that the use of a GRIT will no longer expose its grantor to any retained interests for federal estate tax purposes; however, the use of a GRIT could expose the grantor to substantial gift tax liability, since the gift is measured as the fair market value of any assets transferred to the trust rather than just the value of the remainder interest eventually received by the remaindermen of the trust. This gift tax liability could pose problems for the grantor if the grantor has previously used all of his or her unified credit on prior lifetime gifts.

However, Chapter 14 does contain a number of exceptions for trusts where the retained income interest held by the grantor will *not* be valued at zero. Instead, if the grantor retained income trust is structured so that the income payments received by the grantor meet the definition of a "qualified interest," then the retained interest will be valued according to the appropriate valuation tables found for valuing annuity trust and unitrust amounts. Generally, these valuation tables are located in Publication 1457 at Table S for a single life and at Table R(2) for joint lives for an *annuity* amount, and in Publication 1458 at Table U(1) for a single life and at Table U(2) for joint lives for a *unitrust* amount.

A "qualified interest" is defined under Chapter 14 as the right of the grantor to receive an income distribution from a trust established by the grantor where: (1) the grantor has a right to receive fixed amounts payable at least once annually (an annuity amount); or (2) the grantor has a right to receive amounts payable at least once annually, where the value of such payments is a fixed percentage of the annually reappraised value of the trust property (a unitrust amount); or (3) where the grantor has a noncontingent remainder interest if all other interests in the trust are structured as either an annuity amount or a unitrust amount.

If the grantor retained income trust is structured as an annuity (a GRAT), then the value of the retained income interest will be measured by the appropriate valuation tables from either Table S or Table R(2). If the grantor retained income trust is structured as a unitrust (a GRUT), then the value of the retained income interest will be measured by the appropriate valuation tables from either Table U(1) or Table U(2). (See Appendix A for Tables S and U(1) for proper use of these tables to determine the value of GRATs and GRUTs for gift tax purposes.)

Unless a grantor retained income trust is structured as either a GRAT or a GRUT, the retained income interest held by the grantor will be valued at zero. As a result, should the grantor establish a grantor retained income trust that is structured neither in an annuity amount nor a unitrust amount, the grantor will be treated as if he or she had made a gift of the fair market value of all property transferred to the trust. If this amount exceeds $600,000, the grantor could be subject to gift tax liability on the value of any portion of the assets in trust that exceeds the exemption equivalent amount. Furthermore, these assets will be contained in the grantor's post-1976 adjusted taxable gift amounts and could prevent the amount of the grantor's estate tax liability from decreasing.

Thus, if a grantor wishes to use a grantor retained income trust, he or she should be sure that the trust is structured so that the income payments received by the grantor meet the definition of a "qualified interest."

WHEN THE USE OF A PARTICULAR TRUST IS APPROPRIATE

With the great numbers of trusts that are available to a client, it is sometimes difficult to determine which trust is the most appropriate. After carefully analyzing a client's objectives, there may be one or more trusts that are appropriate in light of the client's estate planning goals and the client's limiting factors (such as dollar size of the gross estate, financial, legal, and mental competency of beneficiaries, amount of income needed for current living needs and for retirement purposes).

After analyzing all relevant client data, the following guidelines should be used to decide which form of trust may be most appropriate.

1. If the grantor wishes to avoid estate tax liability on property while also removing all future appreciation on the value of the asset, then an irrevocable living trust is appropriate since it removes the property from the grantor's estate (provided, of course, that the grantor retains no incidents of ownership or control over the property, pursuant to the grantor trust rules and outlives the transfer of a life insurance policy to the trust by more than three years).

2. If the grantor wishes to retain some degree of flexibility and control over the property, or chooses to alter, amend or vary the terms of the trust after it has been established, then a revocable living trust may be the most appropriate.

3. If the grantor wishes to avoid income tax liability on the value of the income produced by the trust, then the grantor may use any trust that is not in violation of the grantor trust rules (e.g., an irrevocable living trust that does not distribute its income to the grantor).

4. If the grantor wishes to avoid estate tax liability on the value of the income or the corpus placed in the trust, then some form of trust will be required that takes the value of the corpus and the income out of the grantor's gross estate (e.g., an irrevocable living trust of some sort, such as an irrevocable living pourover trust or an irrevocable living life insurance trust).

5. If the grantor wishes to avoid gift tax liability on the value of income or corpus, then some form of trust will be required that results in little or no gift tax liability. A revocable living trust avoids gift tax liability because there is no completed gift, but the value of the corpus will be included in the grantor's gross estate.

6. If the grantor wishes to retain some degree of postmortem control, yet

also wishes to provide a stream of income to the surviving spouse, then either a nonmarital trust or Q-TIP trust will be appropriate, especially since both trusts allow the decedent to determine who the ultimate beneficiaries of the property will be. In addition, both trusts enable the decedent to provide a stream of income to the surviving spouse. The distinction between the use of the nonmarital trust as opposed to the use of the Q-TIP trust is that the nonmarital trust is designed to achieve maximum use of the unified credit amount, whereas the Q-TIP trust is designed to achieve maximum use of the marital deduction. If both the unified credit and the marital deduction are used, or if the decedent intends to use both as part of an overall estate plan, then both trusts may be appropriate.

7. If the decedent grantor wishes to provide his or her spouse with little or no income produced from a trust, but wishes that the surviving spouse have postmortem control over the corpus of the trust and all undistributed income, then the estate trust may be the most appropriate choice of a trust since the surviving spouse seldom obtains any lifetime income yet has postmortem control over the corpus and income.

8. If a decedent grantor wishes to provide his or her spouse with a degree of postmortem control over the property while also providing the surviving spouse with a stream of income, the marital trust may be the most appropriate form of trust arrangement.

9. If the grantor has a relatively modest-sized estate (valued at less than $1 million) and wishes to provide a stream of income to his or her spouse and children, yet leave the remainder of the estate to grandchildren, then the generation-skipping trust may be the most appropriate trust arrangement in terms of accomplishing these objectives.

10. If the grantor wishes to give his or her surviving spouse the option of receiving assets that would otherwise pass to the surviving spouse (and otherwise qualify for the marital deduction) so that the surviving spouse may elect not to receive them and prevent the surviving spouse's estate from receiving assets that could subject the survivor's estate to estate tax liability, then a disclaimer trust may be the most appropriate trust technique, since it still allows the surviving spouse to receive a stream of income from the disclaimed property, yet it avoids inclusion in the surviving spouse's gross estate (similar to a nonmarital trust).

Other trusts may also be used, depending on the specific estate planning objectives of the client.

TERMINATION OF TRUSTS

Trusts are usually structured to last for a stated period of time or until a certain set of conditions expires, at which time they terminate and the corpus and all undistributed income either revert to the grantor or pass as a remainder interest to someone other than the grantor. Since there can be significant tax implications if a trust is terminated in a fashion other than intentionally (e.g., a constructive trust is imposed in cases of fraud), the conditions under which a trust can terminate ought to be examined.

1. Termination of Trust Purpose: Most trusts terminate in an orderly fashion, according to the terms of the trust agreement. Thus, the trust will terminate when the stated condition in the trust agreement happens to occur. For example, a nonmarital trust may last as long as the surviving spouse is alive. *Upon the surviving spouse's death,* the trust terminates and the remainder interest in the property passes to the children of the decedent and spouse (the income recipient of the nonmarital trust). When the specified condition occurs upon which the trust will terminate, the corpus and all undistributed income must be distributed to one or more designated remaindermen; or, conversely, all undistributed income and corpus must be distributed to the grantor as a reversionary interest. If the property reverts back to the grantor and the grantor is deceased at the time the trust terminates, then the grantor's will normally provides who shall take those interests owned by the grantor. If the grantor's will is silent on these reversionary interests, then the laws of intestacy will determine who receives the grantor's reversionary interests in one or more trusts.

2. Trusts that Violate the Rule Against Perpetuities: A trust that is established for a *non*charitable beneficiary must be capable of being measured. The trust cannot be perpetual but can only last for a period of time that is measured by the lives of any persons alive at the time the trust is created (plus any life *in vitro*) plus 21 additional years. Thus, a trust can only last for a time period that does not exceed the life of any person in existence at the time the trust is created, plus a period of 21 years and 9 months (to account for any lives *in vitro*). If the trust is structured to last longer than this time period, then the trust is in violation of the rule against perpetuities and is regarded as void from its inception.

3. Termination by Agreement of the Beneficiaries: If all of the beneficiaries are legally and mentally competent, all beneficiaries can agree to terminate the trust and distribute the corpus and undistributed income, *provided* the material purpose of the trust has first been

achieved. In most states, the grantor's intentions take precedence over the wishes of the beneficiaries, however, if the grantor has a specific purpose for creating the trust and that purpose has yet to be achieved or has not been substantially achieved, then the decision by the beneficiaries to terminate the trust will not be binding. Where the material purpose has already occurred ("to provide financial assistance to my children and grandchildren so that they may attend college"), then the beneficiaries of the trust by agreement may terminate the trust and receive the corpus and undistributed income.

4. Illegal Purpose of the Trust: Should the trust or any of its purposes be designed for an illegal activity, so that the trustee or any of the beneficiaries must commit an act that is illegal (a crime) or that would be considered an example of tortious conduct, the trust is illegal and will terminate on the occurrence of the act deemed illegal or tortious. A trust that is designed for the sole purpose of evading the grantor's creditors is an act of fraud (a tort) and the creditors may reach the assets in trust or the court may declare the trust to be invalid; subsequently, the trust terminates when the grantor attempts to use it in an attempt to defraud a creditor.

5. Merger of Legal and Equitable Title in the Same Beneficiary: In some states, when the trustee and beneficiary of the trust are the same individual, there may be a merger of legal and equitable title in the individual. When this occurs, the trust may terminate by operation of law because of the merger. In order for a trust to be properly recognized, there should be a vesting of the legal title in the trustee; the equitable title should be in possession of the trust beneficiary. When these titles merge in the same person, there may no longer be a reason to have a trust. Therefore, in some states, when merger occurs, the trust terminates. As long as there are multiple trustees and multiple beneficiaries, the trust will still be operative. Also, if there is one trustee but several beneficiaries, or there are several trustees and one beneficiary, the trust will still be an operative instrument. It is when the sole trustee is also the sole beneficiary that the merger doctrine applies and at that point the trust may cease to exist.

6. Termination Due to Impossibility of Purpose: If the purpose for which a trust was created cannot be performed due to impossibility of the purpose, then the trust will terminate if a similarly related purpose cannot be found. For example, if a private trust (noncharitable trust) were created for the sole purpose of providing a stream of income to a disabled beneficiary to provide that beneficiary with living expenses and assistance, but the beneficiary died shortly after the trust was created, the trust would terminate unless the terms of the trust specifically provided either: (1) that the trust would continue in the

event of the death of the beneficiary, or (2) that the trust would continue for the express purpose of providing living expenses and assistance to other disabled persons living within the same metropolitan area (defined by the trust as all disabled persons living within a 100-mile radius from the original trust beneficiary). If neither of these provisions was contained in the terms of the trust agreement, then the trust could fail because of impossibility of purpose.

There may be other reasons why a trust could terminate (e.g., establishing a public charitable trust that violates the terms of the Civil Rights Act by discriminating against a class of trust beneficiaries on the basis of race, national origin, religion, creed, or gender). The variations and possibilities that could occur require the consultation of an attorney who is licensed to practice in a particular state. The examples in Exhibits A, B, and C are used only as guidelines and should serve to assist the financial planner by making him aware of the problem areas that could occur by the use of a particular trust. The examples are intended to be representative in nature, not all-inclusive.

Exhibit A A COMPARISON OF THE TAX CHARACTERISTICS OF TRUSTS
Below is a list of the tax characteristics of various types of trusts. These characteristics should be considered carefully by the financial planner when assisting the client in selecting an appropriate trust arrangement.

Type of Trust	Included in Grantor's Gross Estate	Grantor Subject to Income Tax?	Grantor Subject to Gift Tax?
Irrevocable Living Trust	Ordinarily, no— not if grantor gives up all dominion and control	No	Yes
Revocable Living Trust	Yes	Yes	No
Generation-skipping Trust	No—if created in grantor's lifetime	No—if grantor receives no income	Possibly—on initial transfer of corpus to trust
Spendthrift Trust	1) Yes—if grantor retains incidents of ownership	Yes	No
	2) No—if grantor gives up all dominion and control	No	Yes

(continued)

Exhibit A *(continued)*

Type of Trust	Included in Grantor's Gross Estate	Grantor Subject to Income Tax?	Grantor Subject to Gift Tax?
Support Trust	1) No—if irrevocable in nature	Yes	Yes—if irrevocable
	2) Yes—if grantor can revoke	Yes	No
2503(b) Trust	No—as long as grantor has no reversionary interest in corpus	No	Yes
2503(c) Trust	No	No	Yes
Crummey Trust	No—if trust is irrevocable and grantor retains no control	No	Yes
Grantor or Short-Term Grantor Annuity Trust	Yes	Yes	No
Short-Term Clifford Trust (before 3/1/86)	Yes—but only the present value of the reversionary interest	No	Yes—on the value of the income stream
Disclaimer Trust	Yes—if disclaimer exercised by surviving spouse	No	No
Marital Trust (in will)	Yes—but qualifies for marital deduction	No	No
Nonmarital Trust (in will)	Yes—but usually funded in an amount equal to the exemption equivalent	No	No
Q-TIP Trust (in will)	Yes—but qualifies for marital deduction if elected	No	No
Estate Trust (in will)	Yes—but qualifies for marital deduction	No	No

Exhibit B   *HOW DISTRIBUTABLE NET INCOME IS CALCULATED FOR A SIMPLE TRUST*

During a taxable year, the income of a trust is required to be distributed to the grantor's spouse during the spouse's life. Capital gains are allocated to the corpus and all expenses are charged against the corpus.

During the taxable year, the trust has the following income:

Dividends from stock		$40,000
Rents		20,000
Taxable interest		20,000
Tax-exempt interest		20,000
Long-term capital gains		20,000
Trustee's commissions and other expenses allocated to corpus		10,000
The DNI for this trust is calculated as follows:		
Dividends from stock		$40,000
Rents		$20,000
Taxable interest		$20,000
Tax-exempt interest	$20,000	
Less: Expenses allocated to tax-exempt interest	2,000	18,000
(20,000/100,000 × $10,000)		
TOTAL		$98,000
Less: Expenses ($10,000 total minus $2,000 allocated to tax-exempt interest)		$ 8,000
Distributable Net Income		$90,000

The DNI is that income which must be reported as *taxable income* in the year received by the trust beneficiary. Any amount that is distributed to the beneficiary that exceeds the amount of $90,000 is subject to the throwback rule, as long as the trust beneficiary is not a minor.

It should be noted that when income for a simple trust is calculated, long-term capital gains are not included in income.

To arrive at DNI of $90,000, the following modifications were made to the trust's taxable income: No deductions were allowed for distributions to beneficiaries, no deductions were allowed for the personal exemption of the trust, capital gains were allocated to the corpus of the trust and were not distributed to the beneficiaries, and the tax-exempt interest and dividend exclusion of $100 were included as income.

In computing the DNI of $80,000, the taxable income of the trust was calculated with the following modifications: no deductions were allowed for distributions to beneficiaries and for the personal exemption to the trust; capital gains were allocated to the corpus of the trust and were not distributed to the beneficiaries, and the tax-exempt interest and dividend exclusion of $50 were included as income.

Exhibit C *HOW DISTRIBUTABLE NET INCOME IS CALCULATED FOR A
COMPLEX TRUST*

Under the terms of a trust, one-half the trust income is to be paid currently to the grantor's wife for her life. The remaining trust income may be distributed to the grantor's son, or it may accumulate. When the wife dies, the trust terminates and the corpus and undistributed income are payable to the son.

During the taxable year, the trust has the following income:		
Dividends from stock		$30,000
Rents		$30,000
Taxable interest		$15,000
Tax-exempt interest		$15,000
Capital gains (long-term)		$10,000
Trustee's commissions allocated to corpus		$ 2,000
Trustee's commissions allocated to income		$ 2,000
Expenses attributed to rental income		$ 6,000
The DNI for this trust is calculated as follows:		
Dividends from stock		$30,000
Rents		$30,000
Taxable interest		$15,000
Tax-exempt interest	$15,000	
Less: Trustee's commissions allocated to tax-exempt interest		
(15,000/90,000 × $4,000) = $667 (rounded)		$14,333
	TOTAL	$89,333
Deductions:		
Rental expenses		$ 6,000
Trustee's commissions (4,000 minus $667		$ 3,333
allocated to tax-exempt interest)		$ 9,333
Distributable Net Income		$80,000

4

FORMS OF PROPERTY OWNERSHIP AND THEIR USES IN ESTATE PLANNING

INTRODUCTION

Many individuals mistakenly believe that the key to having a completed estate plan lies in having a will. While a will does control the testamentary disposition of an individual's probatable assets, the manner in which a person's property is titled is also a significant factor in developing an estate plan. A client should not assume that a will can properly take care of all of the individual's estate planning objectives, especially if the person owns real estate or other property that can be transferred without probate. In the data gathering process, the financial planner should determine the nature of all property owned by the client, the way in which titles are held, and the identity of all owners.

The manner in which property is titled can be a significant estate planning factor for the following reasons:

1. The way in which the property is titled can determine the amount of the property owner's estate tax liability upon death.
2. The way in which the property is titled can determine the amount of administrative expenses and attorney's fees that the estate of the property owner pays.

3. The way in which the property is titled can determine the amount of the decedent's property that is subject to probate administration.
4. The way in which the property is titled can determine who will ultimately receive the property upon the owner's death.
5. The way in which the property is titled can determine the extent of both income tax and gift tax liability for the owner of the property.
6. The way in which the property is titled can determine the extent to which the property owner's estate is transferred through a will.

This chapter will focus on the various forms of property ownership, emphasizing the characteristics of sole ownership, joint tenancy with right of survivorship, tenancy by the entirety, and tenancy in common. Because of the complexities involved in community property, an entire chapter will be devoted to a discussion of community property in Chapter 5.

In addition to the characteristics of each of these forms of property ownership, this chapter also features the income, estate, and gift tax implications of each of the various forms of property ownership. Advantages and disadvantages of each of these forms of property ownership are also discussed, as is the issue of when it is most appropriate to use each form of property ownership when developing an estate plan.

SOLE OWNERSHIP

The primary characteristic of property held in sole ownership is that one individual has absolute ownership and control of the property. This means that if the owner wishes to sell it or make a lifetime gift of the property to someone else, the owner has an absolute, unqualified right to do so. If the owner wishes to retain the property and make a testamentary transfer of it, either by transferring it through a will or into a testamentary trust, the owner also has that option. Clearly, both lifetime control and postmortem control of property are characteristics of property held in sole ownership.

If the solely owned property produces income, all income attributable to the solely owned property must be reported by the owner, even if the owner makes gifts of the income to others. Presumably, the owner is in constructive receipt of the income and has the power and control over the property to determine who will receive its benefits. Therefore, all of the income produced from the property is taxable to the owner.

Should the owner of solely owned property choose to make a gift of the income to a nonowner, the owner could face potential gift tax liability on the amount of the transfer. If the amount in question exceeds the annual exclusion amount, the owner will have to use his or her unified credit amount to absorb the gift tax liability on the amount of the taxable gift.

Likewise, if the owner of solely owned property chooses to make a gift of a part of the property, thus creating either a joint tenancy with right of survivorship, or a tenancy in common, the owner could face potential gift tax liability on the amount of the gift that exceeds the annual exclusion amount. Since transfers of this type seldom occur over a period of years and are usually one-time transactions, the amount of gift tax liability could be significantly greater because the annual exclusion amount will only be utilized once. As a result, a greater amount of the donor's unified credit will be used to absorb any gift tax liability.

For estate tax purposes, the entire amount of the solely owned property will be included in the sole owner's gross estate. Unless some special valuation technique is used, such as alternate valuation or special use valuation, the includible value of the solely owned property will be its fair market value as of the date of the owner's death. Unlike jointly held property or tenancy in common property, which may only be partially included in the estate of the deceased owner, there is no opportunity to include only a fractional portion of the property in the estate of the sole owner. Depending on the size of the estate of the sole owner, this could be a disadvantage for estate tax purposes.

The owner of solely held property needs to plan properly for the transfer of such property when he dies. The sole owner may leave the property to whomever he wishes, and may make a specific bequest of the property to one or more individuals in his will. One special *caveat* should be issued, however. If the sole owner happens to be married and bequeaths the property to someone other than the surviving spouse, the surviving spouse may file an election to take a statutory percentage of the decedent's estate, instead of taking the property bequeathed to the spouse under the terms of the decedent's will. If the surviving spouse does choose to elect to take against the will, the surviving spouse may take, as his or her percentage of the decedent's estate, the solely owned property or some portion of it. Therefore, if the sole owner wants to guarantee the transfer of the property to a specific individual other than the surviving spouse, proper planning would suggest that the sole owner convert the property into joint tenancy with right of survivorship with the specific individual at some point in the sole owner's lifetime. Otherwise, an individual who is left the solely owned property under the terms of the will could unexpectedly have the property taken by the surviving spouse, since many elective share statutes disrupt the testamentary plans of the owner of the solely held property.

If the sole owner does not have a will and dies, the solely owned property will pass to the decedent's heirs and beneficiaries, according to the rules of intestate succession. Each state has its own separate statutes for intestate succession. These statutes frequently determine the order in which the property passes to the heirs and the amount of the decedent's property that goes to each. Should the decedent die without a will and without living heirs or designated beneficiaries, the property will *escheat* to the state. If the sole owner wishes to avoid this consequence, or wishes to make a testamentary disposition of this property to a charity or some other beneficiary, the sole owner should have a will.

Because administrative expenses and attorney's fees are frequently calculated as a specific percentage of the decedent's probate estate, the fact that the decedent was sole owner of a sizeable amount of property could cause these expenses to be greater than they would be if the property were held in some form of joint tenancy or tenancy in common. If the owner of solely owned property wants to ensure that these expenses are reduced, one possible solution would be to place the property in some form of ownership other than sole ownership. Likewise, solely owned property is fully includible in the probate process and, as a result, there could be considerable expenses and time delays before the solely owned property is transferred to its ultimate beneficiary.

Though it would appear that sole ownership has significant disadvantages, it should be remembered that sole ownership provides advantages that no other form of ownership provides. It is the most flexible form of property ownership and can be transferred with the least amount of inconvenience and time delay. Sole ownership provides the owner with the absolute dominion and control over the property; the owner can sell, gift, convey, or pledge the property without the consent of other individuals. If the property is income-producing, only the owner is entitled to receipt of the income. The sole owner can enjoy the property fully, knowing that only the sole owner's creditors can attach the property for payment of the obligation, unlike some forms of jointly held property, where a creditor can attach the property for a debt incurred by only one of the joint owners.

When is it appropriate to use solely owned property as a form of property ownership? Generally, there are no absolute rules for determining the answer to this question. But it can be said that if holding the property as sole owner achieves the maximum number of the client's estate planning objectives, then it can be said to be the most appropriate.

Generally, sole ownership is appropriate if the owner wants absolute control over the property, or needs all of the income from the property if it is income-producing. If the owner's estate is small enough so that it is less than the amount of the exemption equivalent, and there will be no adverse estate tax consequences, then sole ownership could be appropriate. If the owner wishes to retain ownership, but wants others to enjoy and use the property without the responsibilities of ownership, then sole ownership could be appropriate. This is frequently the case with an individual who owns real estate as sole owner, and who wishes to provide his or her elderly parents with a place to live without subjecting the parents to the burdens of property upkeep, improvements, payment of property taxes, or other matters directly connected to ownership. Rather than having the parents named as joint owners or as tenants in common (and thus avoiding the adverse estate tax consequences that could occur if the parents predecease their child), the property could be held by the child as sole owner. This form of ownership would keep the asset out of the parents' estates and would allow the child to control the ultimate disposition of the property after the parents' deaths. As long as the parents pay a reasonable amount of rent to the child for leasing the property, the parents should face no adverse income, estate, or gift taxes in this transaction.

JOINT TENANCY WITH RIGHT OF SURVIVORSHIP (WROS)

This form of property ownership is frequently held between spouses and many clients mistakenly believe that it can only be held between spouses. However, property can be held between joint tenants with rights of survivorship between parent and child, brother and sister, and business partner and business partner. In addition, joint tenancy with right of survivorship can also be held by husband and wife. It is important to note that the income, estate, and gift tax implications of jointly held property can vary, depending on who the other joint tenant(s) is (are). These implications will be discussed in greater detail later in this chapter.

The primary characteristics of property held in joint tenancy with right of survivorship are the following:

1. Unlike sole ownership, property held in joint tenancy with right of survivorship is shared by several owners. While it is frequently held by two owners, it is not uncommon to have the property held by three or more owners. This causes lifetime control to be divided among two or more joint tenants. Control, ownership, and enjoyment of the property are shared equally by all of the joint tenants.

2. Income from income-producing property that is held in joint tenancy with right of survivorship is split equally among all the joint tenants. Thus, if the property produces income of $18,000 annually, and is held by two joint tenants, each joint tenant would report income of $9,000. While this would be of no consequence to a husband and wife who file a joint income tax return, it could be an effective means of splitting income between joint tenants who are not married.

3. The distinguishing feature of joint tenancy is its survivorship feature. Upon the death of the first joint tenant, the property immediately passes to the surviving joint tenants in equal shares. Thus, if there is only one surviving joint tenant, the surviving joint tenant owns full and absolute title to the entire property. Holding property

in this form of ownership excludes the possibility of any post-mortem control by the first joint tenant who dies. This can be especially problematic for a joint tenant who wants to leave the jointly held property to children from a prior marriage; yet, in its current form of ownership, there is no guarantee that the children from the prior marriage would receive the property, especially since the surviving spouse, who is unrelated to the children, could use, consume or expend the property or gift the property to a third party. If the joint tenants are not in agreement as to whom to dispose the property after their deaths, or if one of the joint tenants is not on especially good terms with would-be beneficiaries, then this form of ownership is inappropriate since the first decedent spouse has no postmortem control over the jointly held property.

4. The automatic survivorship feature of joint tenancy with right of survivorship means that such property is not controlled by the terms of a will. Rather, such property passes automatically to the surviving joint tenant(s) and passes outside the terms of a will. For that reason, it does no good to place a provision in a will that controls the disposition of jointly held property after the owner's death. Unless this survivorship feature is properly understood, an owner of joint tenancy property could improperly develop his or her estate plan.

5. The survivorship feature of joint tenancy property causes such property to be excluded from the probate estate of the decedent. Thus, if an individual wants to transfer the property immediately upon his or her death to another individual outside of probate, the owner of such property should place it in joint tenancy with right of survivorship at some time during life.

As mentioned earlier, the tax implications of holding property in this form of ownership can vary, depending on the relationship between the joint tenants. As stated earlier, joint tenancy property can result in a splitting of income produced by such property. If the joint tenants are not married, or if the joint tenants are married and file separate income tax returns, the income produced from this form of property ownership can be split among all joint tenants, thus reducing income tax liability for each joint tenant as opposed to having the entire amount of income reported by the sole owner.

If the property is initially acquired by nonmarried or separately filing married joint tenants with right of survivorship, each joint tenant takes as his or her basis in the property the amount of actual contribution. Thus, if property is acquired and titled in joint tenancy with right of survivorship, and each joint tenant provides an equal amount of the cost basis, the gain produced by the property upon subsequent sale would be divided equally. If the original contribution of each joint tenant were split in a two-thirds/one-third ratio, then the gain reported on a subsequent sale of the property would be divided in a two-thirds/one-third proportion.

However, if the joint tenants each originally contributed one-half of the cost basis in the property but agreed to divide the subsequent sale proceeds in a manner inconsistent with their proportion of their original bases in the property, the amount of reportable gain would remain the same. Thus, if two joint tenants purchased a parcel of income-producing property and each provided $5000 of the original basis, each would report a taxable gain of $35,000 if the property were subsequently sold for $80,000. The amount of gain reported by each would still remain the same even if the parties agreed to split the gain in any manner other than a 50-50 split of the gain.

Placing property into joint tenancy with right of survivorship can also result in gift tax liability. If proper planning does not occur, the original donor can face unexpected gift tax liability if the gift is one of stocks, bonds, or real estate. Generally, if the owner of solely owned property converts the title to joint tenancy with right of survivorship with another tenant who provides no consideration or value for the property converted, the donor has made a gift of one-half the value of the property to the noncontributing joint tenant. There may be gift tax liability if the value of the property contributed exceeds the annual exclusion amount. In addition, in those situations where the transfer occurs between spouses, there is no gift tax liability because of the unlimited gift tax marital deduction available for interspousal gifts made after 1981.

If nonspousal joint tenants enter into a joint tenancy arrangement, and subsequently sell the property at a gain, there may also be potential gift tax liability. For example, if two unmarried joint tenants acquire property as joint tenants with right of survivorship, and each contributes one-half of the original basis, each is entitled to one-half the reported gain upon a subsequent sale of the property. However, if one of the joint tenants receives more than one-half of the gain on a subsequent sale, the tenant who received less than one-half the gain is deemed to have made a gift of the difference to the other. Thus, if two joint tenants each provided one-half the original basis of $5000 for a parcel of real estate held in joint tenancy, and subsequently sold the property at a price of $80,000 but divided the proceeds so that one joint tenant received $60,000 and the other received $20,000, then the joint tenant who received $20,000 is deemed to have made a gift of $20,000 to the joint tenant who received the $60,000. Since the proceeds should have been divided equally, with each joint tenant receiving $40,000, the $20,000 difference between what should have been received and what was actually received would be a gift to the tenant receiving the excess amount. After applying the annual exclusion amount, this results in a $10,000 taxable gift being made. Consequently, the joint tenant who received the lesser amount of the proceeds would be liable for the gift tax liability on a taxable gift of $10,000, and the unified credit would have to be used to absorb the gift tax liability. However, if the tenants happen to be married, and split the sale proceeds according to this sample, there would be no gift tax liability because of the unlimited gift tax marital deduction. For joint tenants who are not spouses, careful planning is necessary to avoid unintended gift tax liability.

The estate tax implications of holding property in joint tenancy with right of survivorship are somewhat more complicated. According to Internal Revenue Code Section 2040(a), except for joint tenants who are husband and wife, the full value of jointly held property is included in the gross estate of the first joint tenant to die unless the survivor can prove contribution to the acquisition of the property or unless the survivor can establish ownership of some portion of the property before the joint tenancy was created. Thus, unless accurate records are kept and the survivor can prove contribution to the cost of the property, the entire amount will be included in the estate of the first decedent joint tenant.

To avoid this adverse tax consequence, all joint tenants should keep meticulous records which prove the amount of their original contribution, any subsequent contributions or subtractions, or the cost of any additional improvements and the amount contributed by each joint tenant. Since no one knows who will die first, it is prudent to keep records in order to protect the interests of all joint tenants. Joint tenants such as parent and child, partner and partner, or nonspousal joint tenants need to be reminded that the joint tenancy status of the property does not automatically result in the inclusion of only one-half the amount of the joint tenancy property in the decedent's gross estate. Unless the survivor can prove contribution, the entire amount will be included in the decedent's gross estate.

Since 1981, spouses who hold joint tenancy property have had an estate tax advantage. For property acquired by spouses as joint tenants with right of survivorship, Section 2040(b)(1) of the Internal Revenue Code provides that only one-half the value of qualified joint tenancy property will be included in the gross estate of the first decedent spouse. Presumably, this property will also qualify for the marital deduction because it passes to the surviving spouse. As a result, the estate of the first decedent spouse will face no estate tax liability on such property, even though one-half the value of the jointly held property is included in the decedent's gross estate. The entire value of the property will be included in the surviving spouse's gross estate without the advantage of the marital deduction to offset estate tax liability. Unless the surviving spouse disposes of the property or consumes it in its entirety during life, the full value of it, plus any appreciation on it, will be included in the gross estate of the surviving spouse.

For nonmarried joint tenants who can prove contribution to the acquisition of joint tenancy property, a "fractional interest rule" applies. Basically, this rule provides that, where nonspousal joint tenants can prove contribution, the amount of property included in the gross estate of the decedent joint tenant will be the value of the property which correlates to the decedent's original contribution to the property. For example, if the decedent acquired the property with an original contribution of 25 percent of the value of the property, and the property later appreciated in value, 25 percent of the appreciated value of the property at the date of the decedent's death would be included as an asset in the decedent's gross estate. Thus, for property acquired by the decedent joint tenant at a cost of $5000 (with a total value of $20,000) which later appreciated in value to $100,000 at the time of the decedent's death, 5000/20,000 or 25 percent of the value of the property, or $25,000 (.25 × $100,000) would be included as an asset in the gross estate of the decedent. Of course, this is assuming that the surviving joint tenant can prove contribution of 75 percent of the value of the joint tenancy property, or at least 3/4 of the original basis.

When is it most appropriate to use property held in joint tenancy with right of survivorship? Although there are no hard and fast rules regarding the appropriateness of title, the following circumstances indicate that holding property in joint tenancy with right of survivorship may be appropriate

1. when the owner wants to ensure that the property passes to a specific individual upon the owner's death. If property is held in joint tenancy with right of survivorship, title passes to the surviving joint tenant immediately upon the death of the first joint tenant. If the surviving spouse is not the surviving joint tenant, usually not even the surviving spouse can set aside the transfer of the property to the surviving joint tenant, unlike a surviving spouse who can elect the property by taking against the will or by taking an elective share of the decedent's estate if the decedent owns the property as sole owner. (An important exception exists in states that have adopted the Uniform Probate Code under the "augmented estate" concept.)

2. when the owner wants to avoid probate. Joint tenancy property bypasses the probate process, which means that title vests immediately in the survivor. There are no time delays, administrative costs, or legal fees associated with the transfer of the property to the surviving joint tenant.

3. when the owner wants to reduce administrative costs and attorney's fees. Use of joint tenancy can be effective since these fees are often calculated as a percentage of the probate estate. If the property is held between spouses, only one-half the value will be included in the decedent's gross estate. If the property is held between nonspouses,

only that portion that is attributable to the contributions of the decedent will be included in the gross estate.

4. when the owner wants to qualify property for the marital deduction and holds the property as sole owner. The property should be converted to joint tenancy property with the spouse in order to minimize the estate tax liability of the decedent and maximize the use of the marital deduction for the surviving spouse.

5. when the owner wants to minimize income tax liability. This can be achieved by splitting the income with other joint tenants, with a resultant tax savings for each joint tenant, as opposed to having all of the income reported by a sole owner.

6. when the owner wants to minimize gift tax liability. A transfer of the property to joint tenancy with right of survivorship can be an effective means of achieving this objective, especially with a transfer of the property to a spouse.

A final concern regarding joint tenancy property is the manner of terminating the ownership form. How is a joint tenancy normally terminated, and what are the tax consequences of such a termination?

Generally, a joint tenancy can be terminated unilaterally by one of the joint tenants. This causes a severance of the characteristics of joint tenancy property; namely, an undivided interest in the *entire* property as well as an interest in *one-half* the property (assuming there are only two joint tenants). Joint tenants normally acquire the same interest in the same property at the same time, and normally take possession simultaneously. (These interests are usually referred to as the four unities of time, title, interest, and possession). Since these interests were acquired by the joint tenants at the same time, a transfer of one joint tenant's interests in the property to another individual severs the four unities and causes a tenancy in common to be formed. The severance of joint tenancy property does not require the consent of all joint tenants; it can be done by one joint tenant without the consent of other joint tenants. However, as a practical matter, it is always prudent to obtain the signature of the nonconsenting joint tenant on a deed transfer form, especially if the joint tenants are spouses. Otherwise, the nonconsenting joint tenant spouse could assert survivorship rights in the property that was sold to a third party. The only way these rights can be defeated or extinguished is by obtaining the consent of the other spouse.

It is important to note that, in particular circumstances, there can be potential estate and gift tax problems upon termination of the joint tenancy. If the joint tenancy is terminated, and the proper record keeping has not been preserved, adverse estate tax consequences can occur for the estate of the tenant who receives the property upon termination of the joint tenancy. Similarly, if a joint tenancy is created and later terminated within 3 years of the death of one of the joint tenants, with a resultant gift tax liability stemming from the fact that one of the joint tenants provided no consideration, the value of these gift taxes paid must be added back to the gross estate of the contributing joint tenant pursuant to the "gross-up rule."

When *converting* joint tenancy property to property held as tenants in common, there are no adverse estate or gift tax consequences as long as the proportional interests in the joint tenancy property remain the same in the tenancy in common property. Thus, if each joint tenant owned a one-half interest in the property and contributed one-half of the original cost of the property, there will be no adverse estate or gift tax consequences as long as they convert their shares into equal one-half interests in the property held as tenants in common. For jointly held property held between spouses, there will be no adverse estate or gift tax consequences because of both the unlimited marital deduction for the value of property included in the estate, and the unlimited gift tax marital deduction available for post-1981 lifetime gifts made from one spouse to another.

TENANCY BY THE ENTIRETY

Though there are only a handful of states that still retain this form of property ownership, tenancy by the entirety can still be a form of property ownership available as a means of planning the distribution of an estate. Tenancy by the entirety is a form of joint tenancy property between husband and wife and, as such, possesses many of the characteristics of property titled in joint tenancy. The survivorship feature that is characteristic of joint tenancy property is also found in tenancy by the entirety. Upon the death of the first tenant, the property automatically passes to the survivor outside the terms of the decedent's will and outside the probate process. For estate tax purposes, the property is divided between the spouses equally, with only one-half the value of the property included in the gross estate of the first tenant to die, and the full value of the property included in the gross estate of the surviving tenant.

Property held in tenancy by the entirety does differ from joint tenancy property in two significant aspects.

1. Only husband and wife may hold the property as tenants by the entirety. This form of property ownership cannot be held between siblings, parent and child, or business partners.
2. Unlike property held in joint tenancy, which can be severed through the unilateral action of one of the joint tenants, property held in

tenancy by the entirety can only be severed with the consent of both spouses. One spouse, acting alone, cannot sever the ownership form and transfer his or her share to a third party. Such an attempt could be challenged as a fraudulent conveyance in violation of the other spouse's survivorship rights.

With these characteristics in mind, one might ask the question of why anyone would want to hold title to property in this form of ownership? The primary reason in doing so would be to safeguard one spouse and protect that spouse from a severance of the property that could arise if the other spouse chose to sever the joint tenancy and convert the property into a tenancy in common arrangement. Presumably, this protection could make the value of the property higher than it would be if either joint tenant had the ability to unilaterally sever the joint tenancy and transfer the property to a third party. At the same time, this inability to sever the property without the consent of the other spouse could be considered a disadvantage, especially if one of the spouses was cash poor and needed to sell his or her one-half interest to generate revenue or cash for various reasons. Both spouses should be fully aware of the advantages and drawbacks to using this form of property ownership in those states where it is still retained.

One final observation should be made in respect to both joint tenancy property and property held in tenancy by the entirety. For income tax purposes, the estate of the surviving spousal joint tenant or the estate of the surviving spouse who holds the property by the entirety is entitled to receive a step up in basis on only the decedent spouse's share of the property. Thus, if a husband and wife acquired property at an original cost of $20,000 and held it as joint tenants with right of survivorship or as tenants in common, the surviving spouse would only be able to claim a step up in basis on the one-half of the property held by the decedent spouse. Thus, if the property had appreciated in value to $100,000 at the time of the decedent spouse's death, only the decedent's half would receive a step up in basis (from $10,000 to $50,000). If the surviving spouse were to sell the property for its fair market value of $100,000 shortly thereafter, he or she would have to report a gain on an amount of $40,000. This $40,000 sum represents the increase in gain on the survivor's one-half share of the property (the difference between the survivor's original basis of $10,000 and its subsequent fair market value of $50,000). Only the decedent's half would receive a step up in basis; therefore, no gain would be reported on the one-half interest representing the decedent's share of the property. Whether this gain would have to be reported as taxable income would depend on the nature of the property (e.g., a personal residence, in some circumstances, could escape income tax liability pursuant to the $125,000 capital gains exclusion on the sale of a personal residence for persons over age 55).

The advantages and disadvantages of holding property in some form of joint tenancy or tenancy by the entirety would have to be carefully weighed and considered before implementing a comprehensive estate plan for an individual client and his or her family.

TENANCY IN COMMON

Tenancy in common is a way in which property can be owned by several owners simultaneously. Property held in tenancy in common differs from joint tenancy property in several significant aspects. First, there may be several tenants in common who hold title as such. These tenants in common each own an undivided interest in the property. (The undivided interest may be a one-half, one-third, or one-fourth interest, depending on the number of tenants in the specific relationship. It is also possible for one tenant in common to hold a two-thirds interest while another tenant in common holds a one-third interest in the property.) What this means is that each tenant in common, rather than owning a fractional share of some specific portion of the property (e.g., the northern one-half acre of the township), owns an undivided one-half interest in any portion of the tenancy in common property. Unless the tenants in common agree to a specific allocation of their property rights in a partition of the property, each tenant in common continues to own a fractional undivided interest in any portion of the property at any given time.

Tenants in common are entitled to a division of income from income-producing property according to their respective interests in the property. If each tenant in common owns an undivided one-third interest in the property, each will be entitled to one-third of the income from that property. If the tenants in common agree to divide the income in any manner other than according to their respective interests in the property, the portion received by each tenant in common that is in excess of their proportional share of ownership will be considered a gift, and the tenant in common who receives less than his or her proportional share of the property may be subject to gift tax liability on the excess gifted to another.

Tenants in common are free to transfer their respective shares of the property to other individuals. The property retains its status as tenancy in common property and the consent of the other tenants in common is generally unnecessary when transferring title. In fact, it is not unusual for all of the tenants in common to be unrelated by blood to the other tenants in common. If a conveyance of the entire property is desired, then the signature of all tenants in common would be required, but there is no requirement that all of the property be conveyed at once. However, if the tenants in common are unrelated and are in positions where their interests in the property are potentially adverse to those of the other tenants in common so that a desired sale of the entire property to a third party is difficult, the property may receive a discount in valuation because of this inability to agree on a sale or conveyance. Such a discount is referred to as a co-ownership discount.

For estate tax purposes, there are no survivorship rights in property held in tenancy in common. For the holder of such an interest, this means that upon the death of the holder, his or her respective share of the entire property is included as an asset in the holder's gross estate. Additionally, it means that the property will pass to whomever the deceased holder names in a will. If the deceased died without a will, the deceased's share of the property will pass to heirs, according to the local intestate succession statutes. There are no survivorship rights in the tenancy in common property for the surviving cotenants. Therefore, they will receive nothing upon the death of the first cotenant unless they happen to be named in the will, or are related by blood or are heirs of the deceased tenant in common.

For the estate of the deceased tenant in common, only that portion of the property owned by the deceased will be included in the gross estate. Thus, if the value of an entire property was $90,000 and the deceased tenant in common owned a one-third interest, then $30,000 of the property will be included in the estate of the tenant in common. Holding property in this form may be advantageous if the owner's objective is to minimize the size of the gross estate and any resultant tax liability.

However, it should be kept in mind that, unless the surviving tenant in common also happens to be decedent's spouse and the decedent's share of the property is specifically allocated to the surviving tenant in common, the property ordinarily will not qualify for the marital deduction. If the property is bequeathed to the surviving tenants in common, one of whom is the surviving spouse, then the property will not qualify for the marital deduction because the spouse is not the sole recipient of the property.

As previously stated, upon the death of one tenant in common, the decedent's property passes to the tenant in common's heirs or lineal descendants unlike joint tenancy property, which passes by operation of law to the surviving joint tenant(s). This variation causes the tenant in common's property interest to be included in his or her probate estate. Thus, unlike joint tenancy property, it does not bypass probate, and the tenant in common's share is fully includible for purposes of calculating administrative expenses and attorney's fees.

When reviewing the advantages and disadvantages of placing property in tenancy in common, the following advantages encourage the use of this form of property ownership.

1. Tenancy in common can split income among several tenants in common; if the tenants are members of the same family, this can be an effective means of splitting income among family members.

2. Tenancy in common provides a readily available and convenient means of transfer. The consent of other tenants in common is not necessary to effect a transfer of a particular tenant in common's interest.

3. Tenancy in common can result in a reduced reportable amount of property in the gross estate of the decedent, as opposed to joint tenancy property or sole ownership property (e.g., one-fourth of the property as a tenant in common instead of one-half as a joint tenant or all of it as sole owner).

4. Tenancy in common can serve as a means of transferring the property to an intended beneficiary under the will. The property does not pass automatically to the surviving tenants in common.

5. Unlike joint tenancy property, which can result in unexpected distribution problems in the event of the simultaneous death of both joint tenants, the tenancy in common does not pose these problems. With joint tenancy property, the simultaneous death of both joint tenant spouses will cause the property to be divided equally between the lineal descendants of each spouse. In effect, if both spouses die simultaneously so that it cannot be determined who died first, the joint tenancy property will be divided equally and half the property will be included in the gross estate of each. In effect, the property will have the same testamentary disposition as if it were tenancy in common property. The unintended results that could stem from this arrangement could be disadvantageous to the estates of the joint tenants, especially if neither joint tenant had contemplated this possibility. Unintended beneficiaries could receive some of this property. This would not occur with property held in tenancy in common, which would pass to whomever the deceased named in his or her will.

The determination of whether tenancy in common is appropriate in a given situation can only be determined by carefully examining the client's objectives. If a client wishes to reduce potential estate tax liability and income tax liability while ensuring that the property is transferred to a designated beneficiary, then this form of titling property could be appropriate. A close analysis of all of the client's objectives as well as his or her limitations as gathered from the client data would have to be examined before making this selection. To assist the financial planner in advising the client on which form of property ownership is most appropriate, the advantages and disadvantages of the major forms of property ownership are presented in Table 4.1. The tax characteristics as well as disposition aspects of each of these forms should be considered in order that the most appropriate form of property ownership for the client may be selected.

Table 4.1 A COMPARISON OF THE ADVANTAGES AND DISADVANTAGES OF SOLE OWNERSHIP, JOINT TENANCY, AND TENANCY IN COMMON PROPERTY

	Sole Ownership	Joint Tenancy WROS	Tenancy In Common
Avoids probate?	No	Yes	No
Can be disposed of by will?	Yes	No	Yes
Does decedent have postmortem control?	Yes	No	Yes
Receive a step up in basis at decedent's death?	Receives step up in basis on entire amount when it passes to beneficiary or heir	Yes—on the portion attributable to the decedent only	Same as sole ownership on the tenant's proportional interest
Consent of others needed prior to conveyance?	No	Yes—if there is a spousal joint tenant it is advisable; otherwise, no	No
Amount included in gross estate of decedent?	All	One-half if spouses; otherwise, the portion or percentage which is proved as actual contribution; if survivor cannot prove contribution, then all	Tenant's undivided fractional interest

Survivorship rights upon death of decedent owner?	No	Yes	No
If gifted, subject to payment of gift tax?	Yes	No—if gifted to spouse; otherwise, yes	Yes
Effective means of splitting income?	No	Yes	Yes
Reduced administrative expenses and costs?	No	Yes	No
Difficult to dispose of or convey?	Generally, no	Generally, no	Can be a problem if tenants in common cannot agree to buy or sell their interest to others—can result in a co-ownership discount
Can interest qualify for marital deduction?	Only if bequeathed to spouse in decedent's will or if transferred to spouse pursuant to intestacy statute	Yes—if surviving joint tenant is spouse	Yes—if tenant in common bequeaths it to spouse in will or if transferred to spouse pursuant to intestacy statute
Subject to creditors' claims?	Yes	No—possibly free in some states, but state law must be checked	Yes
Lifetime control?	Yes—total	Yes—partial	Yes—partial

5

COMMUNITY PROPERTY:
Estate Planning Concepts

INTRODUCTION

One significant form of property ownership that was not covered in Chapter 4 was the concept of community property. Because of the complexities in the income, estate, and gift tax implications for this form of property ownership, a separate chapter is necessary. In addition, the complexities of this form of property ownership require a thorough and analytic examination, since the migration of a married couple from a community property state to a common law property state, or vice versa, can trigger significant tax implications that affect the viability of the couple's estate plans. For these reasons, a separate chapter is devoted to the topic of community property.

Among the issues discussed in this chapter are the following:

1. A discussion of the characteristics of community property as opposed to common law property forms
2. Identification of property as either community, solely held, or some other form of jointly held property
3. Classification of assets as either community assets or noncommunity assets for estate planning purposes

4. Estate planning strategies that can be implemented to effectively plan for an estate containing community property
5. Income, gift, and estate tax implications of community property
6. The effect of moving from a community property state to a common law property state, and vice versa, and how such a move affects the couple's estate plans
7. Special community property situations in the state of Wisconsin.

In addition, other issues involving community property as a part of the estate planning process are discussed in this chapter. Because each community property state has developed its own laws affecting marital rights in such property, the financial planner should refer the case to an attorney who can consult the laws of each of the community property states before taking legal action or seeking to alter or amend an estate plan. *It is important that the reader not assume that the community property laws of each state are identical.* The effect of moving from one community property state to another community property state can alter a couple's estate plan or cause changes in the income tax treatment of such property. For these reasons, a client in a community property state should always consult an attorney licensed in that state.

COMMUNITY PROPERTY DEFINED

Community property is a form of ownership held by husband and wife in the nine community property states: Arizona, California, Idaho, Louisiana, Nevada, New Mexico, Texas, Washington, and in 1986, Wisconsin. With property held in community property, both husband and wife own a separate, undivided, equal interest in the property. Each spouse has a separate interest acquired in the property during marriage. Thus, the presumption usually arises that any property acquired by the spouses during the term of the marriage is to be divided equally between them should one of the spouses die or should the couple obtain a divorce after acquiring the property.

Even if only one of the spouses initially acquires property or earns income that is used to benefit the couple, community property states emphasize the efforts of both spouses that directly or indirectly lead to the acquisition of property or income. As a result, even if only one of the spouses is an income earner, it is presumed that the efforts of the nonworking spouse contributed to the benefit of the marital property; as a result, all property acquired by the spouses during the marriage is presumed to be community property.

Community property differs significantly from most common law forms of property ownership—joint tenancy with right of survivorship, tenancy in common, and tenancy by the entirety—in its income, estate, and gift tax implications. Most of the significant differences occur between community property and joint tenancy with right of survivorship property. These differences will be discussed more fully in this chapter.

CLASSIFICATION OF ASSETS AS COMMUNITY OR SEPARATE

The general rule for classification of assets as community property or separate property depends on when the property was acquired and how the property was titled at the time it was acquired. If the property was acquired *prior* to the marriage by either spouse as separate property, it retains its status as separate property even after the marriage unless the parties by agreement decide to classify it otherwise. If property is acquired by the spouses at any time *subsequent* to the marriage, it is presumed to be community property unless the couple specifically titles the property in some other form of ownership. The parties are allowed to classify the property as community or separate, according to their own agreement. However, in the absence of an agreement or in the absence of acquiring the property with separately owned assets, the property is classified as community property.

If property is acquired by either spouse by gift or inheritance, the gifted or inherited property retains its status as separate property and retains its separate character throughout the marriage. Thus, if one of the spouses (husband) receives a $30,000 inheritance from his father's estate, the property remains the separately owned property of the husband; in most circumstances, the wife will be unable to claim that any portion of the inheritance is legally hers, nor will any portion of it be included in her gross estate. Similarly, property acquired with the separate assets of either spouse retains its character as the separately owned property of the spouse providing the consideration.

While each state has local variations on the classification of assets (e.g., in Texas, the proceeds of a lawsuit for personal injuries of a spouse are a separately owned asset of that spouse), there are general presumptions regarding the classification of community property that apply in all nine of the community property states. These presumptions are

1. All property acquired during the marriage is presumed to be community property.
2. The community property presumption can be overcome by clear and convincing evidence presented by the party seeking to claim the property as separate; for example, the presumption of community

property can be overcome by evidence that only one spouse provided all of the consideration for the property with separately owned assets, or that the parties had previously entered an agreement declaring the property to be the separate property of the spouse seeking to overcome the presumption.

3. If separate and community property are mixed so that it is no longer possible to determine which is separately owned and which is community property, the property will be treated as community property.

4. If property has been established as separately owned property, it will retain this characterization until clear and convincing evidence is presented that establishes that the property is no longer separately owned.

Normally, the evidentiary proof needed to classify property as community or separate is provided by furnishing records, purchase receipts, deeds of title, and records of deposit or withdrawal. These records establish the fact that the purchaser provided all consideration for the property, or that the property was purchased with the separately owned assets of one of the spouses, or that the property was initially titled in sole ownership or joint tenancy with right of survivorship, or that the property was acquired with the funds acquired by one of the spouses through gift or inheritance. If this evidentiary burden is met, the property will be classified as separate rather than community, even though acquired during the marriage. Since neither spouse can be certain of whether he or she will survive the other, and thereby acquire the property through the laws of intestate succession, each spouse should carefully document all property acquisitions and should maintain a meticulous record keeping system.

MANAGEMENT OF COMMUNITY PROPERTY

Traditionally, the husband, though only owning half the community property assets, has been determined to be the manager of community property assets. As manager of the property, the husband made investment decisions and other decisions deemed to be in the best interests of the community. As such, the husband had a fiduciary duty of loyalty to the wife and was legally responsible to her in the event his investment decisions were counterproductive or if they resulted in an actual loss due to his mismanagement.

Today, most community property states have removed the requirement that the husband be the manager of the community property assets. Most community property states have enacted statutes permitting either spouse to manage the community property assets. In fact, each spouse is usually deemed to be the manager of his or her portion of the assets held in community, unless the parties agree to manage the property in some other manner.

The management of community property by the spouses has resulted in certain property transactions that may not be entered into without the permission or consent of the other community property tenant. For example, if one community property tenant attempted to sell or convey a community property held asset (such as real estate) to a third party, the sale could not be completed without the consent and signature of the other spouse on a real estate deed. A third party buyer in such a situation would ordinarily demand the consent and signature of both community property tenants in order to establish that one of the spouses was not responsible for mismanagement of the property and did not perpetrate a fraud on the property rights of the nonconsenting spouse.

While both spouses are now presumed to have equal management rights in community property, there are exceptions to this rule. For example, if a closely held business interest is operated or managed by one of the spouses, even though acquired during the course of the marriage, the spouse who operates the business will have management and control of the business interest as a community property asset. In some community property states, such as California, this stated principle is true. In other community property states, such as Louisiana, if one of the spouses is sole manager of the community property business asset, that spouse has the exclusive right to convey, transfer, or mortgage any personal property assets (not including real estate) if the name of the other community property tenant is not on the deed, registration, or other form indicating ownership.

Because of variations in local law regarding the management rights of community held assets, the financial planner should always consult with a licensed attorney to determine the effect of assigning management of community held assets to one of the spouses. Generally, it can be said that one spouse's ability to manage and control assets is more likely to occur with personal property assets than with real estate.

RIGHTS OF SPOUSES IN THE EVENT OF A LIFETIME DISPOSITION

Most community property states permit one of the spouses to make a gift of community property assets to a third party as long as the amount of the gift is reasonable and the gift itself does not perpetrate a fraud on the nondonor spouse. For example, a wife could make a gift of $300 to a niece or nephew as a graduation present without the consent or formal approval of the husband, even though the source of the present is a community held checking account. As long as the amount of the gift is reasonable, there are no adverse legal implications for the donor spouse. Some states have even gone so far as to define the term "reasonable gift" in terms of a stated dollar amount, such as $500 in any calendar year.[1]

However, if the amount of the gift is deemed unreasonably large, the gift could well be construed as one that is made fraudulently, in violation of the other community tenant's property rights. In such cases, the spouse making the gift will be required to reimburse the community for the value of the gift that constituted an injury to the nondonor spouse's community interest. For example, if the donor spouse made a gift of $10,000 that constituted an unreasonable gift that harmed the nondonor's community property interests, the donor spouse would be required to reimburse the nondonor spouse in an amount equal to $5,000.

Some states avoid this type of problem by prohibiting a gift of community property without the consent of the other spouse. For example, in California, Washington, and Idaho, one spouse is prohibited from making a gift of community property to a third party without consent of the other spouse.[2] If such a gift is actually made, it is treated as an illegal attempt to make a gift and the entire transaction is deemed void. In such situations, the donee of the gift would be required to return the property to the married couple. If the state has a statue that permits the gift to be made, but requires reimbursement to the injured nonconsenting spouse, then the donor spouse would be required to reimburse the other spouse for one-half the value of the gifted amount.

Of course, if a spouse owns separately owned property that is not considered community in nature, then that spouse is entitled to gift the property, regardless of amount, to any third party. In such cases, the owner of the property is not required to reimburse the other spouse for a gift of separately owned property to a third party.

RIGHTS OF SPOUSES IN THE EVENT OF ONE SPOUSE'S DEATH

Generally, each spouse owns an undivided one-half interest in the community property assets. When one of the spouses dies, that spouse's gross estate contains one-half the value of all assets held by the community. Each spouse controls the ultimate disposition of the assets contained in the estate, and, in this aspect, community property differs significantly from property held in joint tenancy with right of survivorship. With joint tenancy property held between spouses, the one-half interest owned by the decedent passes by operation of law to the surviving spouse. The decedent spouse retains no postmortem control of the property. In community property, the one-half interest owned in the property is controlled by the decedent spouse, who can either bequeath it to the surviving spouse under the terms of the decedent's will, or can bequeath it to any third party that is a beneficiary of the decedent.

In addition, if the decedent should die without a will, the property would be left to the decedent's heirs according to the state's intestate succession statutes. Conceivably, the surviving spouse could obtain a portion of the decedent's community property interest, but the decedent's children and other heirs would also receive a portion of it. (It should be noted that some community property states may have special statutes that leave the decedent's community property interests to the surviving spouse when the decedent dies without a will.) Thus, if it is a decedent's wish that the surviving spouse receive the *entire* community property, the decedent should include a provision in the will that leaves the property to the surviving spouse. Because such property is bequeathed to the surviving spouse, it qualifies for the marital deduction and avoids estate tax liability in the estate of the first decedent spouse.

It is important to note that with community property, each spouse controls the one-half interest owned. It does not pass by operation of law to the surviving spouse in the absence of a special statute to that effect. Therefore, if a spouse wants to pass the property to the surviving spouse, it will be necessary to bequeath it to the spouse under the terms of the decedent's will.

If a decedent spouse attempts to bequeath the entire community property interest to a third party rather than the one-half interest actually owned by the decedent, the surviving spouse's remedy is to file a statutory election by which the surviving spouse can defeat the decedent's attempt to dispose of the entire community property interest. This statute allows the surviving spouse to protect his or her *own* ownership interest in the community property rather than attempting to prohibit the decedent's estate from transferring the portion of the property that was actually owned by the decedent. As a result of filing this election, the surviving spouse protects his or her own ownership interest in the community property which prevents the decedent's estate from bequeathing or transferring the entire interest in the community property. As a result, this statute enables the decedent to effectively convey only one-half of the community property.

ESTATE TAX IMPLICATIONS
OF COMMUNITY PROPERTY

For purposes of inclusion in a decedent's gross estate, property is treated as separately owned or community property according to the state in which the property was acquired, or where the spouses resided at the time of death, or according to the terms of a property agreement entered into by the parties during the course of the marriage.

All types of community property are included in the gross estate of a decedent spouse, provided they are community in nature at the time originally acquired. For example, a decedent's gross estate would include one-half the value of a residence, stocks, bonds, personal property, and one-half of the cash surrender value of a life insurance policy on the life of a third party or one-half the value of the death benefit proceeds of a life insurance policy that was obtained on the life of one of the spouses when community property was used to pay the premiums on the policy.

In addition to the above items, in some states the concept of quasi-community property applies, and this may have an affect on the estate tax liability of the individual owning property that falls under this classification. By definition, quasi-community property is property acquired by the spouses in a common law property state. If the couple originally acquiring this property subsequently moves to Arizona, California, Washington, or Idaho, the property acquired in a common law property state will be treated as community property. Upon termination of the marriage by the death of one of the spouses, one-half the property will be included in the gross estate of each spouse in California, Washington, and Idaho; in Arizona, the property is divided into two one-half shares upon the dissolution of the marriage, but it is not divided as such in the event one of the spouses dies.

For state inheritance tax purposes, quasi-community property is divided equally between the estates of the spouses and one-half of the value of the quasi-community property is subject to probate administration in the estate of each spouse. This differs from the federal estate tax treatment of quasi-community property, which is fully includible in the estate of the decedent providing all of the consideration or value for the property. Therefore, if one spouse originally acquired the entire value of the property while the couple resided in a common law property state, and subsequently moved to California, Washington, or Idaho where they resided until the time of the death of the acquiring spouse, the entire value of the property will be included in the gross estate of the spouse who originally acquired it for federal estate tax purposes, even though for state inheritance tax and estate planning purposes one-half the value of the quasi-community property will be included in the gross estate of each spouse.

The distinction between the federal estate tax treatment and state estate tax treatment of quasi-community property is a significant one and should be kept in mind by the financial planner so that there are no adverse tax consequences which may prevent fulfillment of the client's estate planning objectives.

DIVISION OF COMMUNITY PROPERTY IN THE ESTATE

In general, the value of any community property asset is included in the decedent spouse's estate to the extent of the decedent's one-half interest. For a decedent who dies owning a community held checking account with a balance of $12,000, $6000 of the account balance would ordinarily constitute the decedent's one-half interest in the community property. Without an agreement to characterize the account as the separate property of either spouse, $6000 would be included in the estate of each spouse. At death, each community property tenant is free to transfer, bequeath, or convey his or her one-half interest to whomever the decedent wishes. This feature of community property distinguishes it from property held in joint tenancy with right of survivorship, which must pass to the surviving tenant spouse.

For a life insurance policy held by the spouses as community property, the value of the policy is divided equally between the spouses. For the life insurance policy held by the spouses on the life of an insured third party, one-half of the interpolated terminal reserve value (the policy's fair market value plus any unearned premiums) is included in the deceased spouse's gross estate. The other one-half of the value is included in the gross estate of the surviving spouse. For a policy held on the life of the insured decedent spouse, one-half the value of the death benefit or face amount of the policy is included in the decedent's gross estate. The remaining one-half is included in the gross estate of the surviving spouse.

Community assets contained in the gross estate of a decedent spouse are disposed of according to the terms of the decedent's will. The community property does not pass automatically to the surviving spouse. If a decedent dies without a will, the property is transferred to the decedent's heirs according to the intestate succession statutes of the decedent's state of domicile. A minority of the community property states do permit the surviving spouse to have survivorship rights in the decedent's community property interests,[3] though this is the exception rather than the rule. In effect, these states permit· a couple, if they wish, to create a right of survivorship in each other for the community property interests held by the other spouse. Such rights of survivorship allow the community property interests to be transferred without the necessity of probate administration. In all other community property states, a probate administration will be necessary to transfer the community property interests held by the decedent to another individual, including the spouse.

DEDUCTIONS FOR FUNERAL
AND ADMINISTRATIVE EXPENSES

Deductions for expenses of administration, funeral expenses and debts, and uninsured losses are allowed to the extent such expenses and losses can be allocated to the decedent's portion of the community property. If the administrative expenses, funeral expenses, and other expenses of estate administration are solely attributable to the decedent's one-half of the community property, the full amount of those expenses are deductible. If, however, the entire community property is administered, then deductions are limited to one-half of all expenses that are not specifically allocated to the decedent's share of the community property. Usually, appraisal fees for valuing the assets contained in the decedent's gross estate are fully deductible, as are funeral expenses as long as the decedent's estate is fully liable for payment of those expenses. If however the spouse of the decedent is obligated to make the payments, or if the entire community is liable for the expenses, then only one-half the amount of the funeral expenses may be deducted on the decedent's federal estate tax return. Deductions for uninsured losses are deductible to the extent of the decedent's interest in the lost property. Thus, if the decedent owned an antique automobile as a community property asset and the automobile was destroyed in a fire after the death of the decedent, the estate's deduction for a loss on the community held asset is limited to one-half the amount of the loss, provided the automobile was not insured.

THE MARITAL DEDUCTION

For estates of decedents dying after December 31, 1981, there is an unlimited marital deduction for the value of any community property passing to the surviving spouse. If a decedent dies in 1982 or later and leaves the decedent's one-half interest in the community property to the surviving spouse, the one-half interest passing to the surviving spouse qualifies for the marital deduction.

     Prior to 1982, the marital deduction was available for community property only in very limited circumstances. For example, prior to 1977, a decedent's estate that consisted solely of community property assets was not entitled to qualify any of it for the marital deduction. Because community property was not included under the definition of an "adjusted gross estate," none of its value could qualify for the marital deduction.

     Between 1977 and 1982 it was possible for an estate containing community property to qualify some of it for the marital deduction. For the 1977–1982 time period the amount qualifying for the marital deduction was based on a formula that took into consideration the amount of community property and the dollar amount of funeral, administrative, and other related expense deductions that could be allocated to community property. As long as the allowable deductions could be allocated to a specified portion of the community property, that portion of the community property qualified for the marital deduction. Spouses who have not amended their wills since 1982, or who had their wills drafted in the 1977–1982 time period should consult an attorney to ensure that the estate is taking advantage of the optimal marital deduction for the community property interests.

For an estate containing community property, the unified credit is available to offset any potential estate tax liability. In addition, the other types of tax credits available to an estate containing noncommunity property interests are also available to the estate containing community property (e.g., credits for payment of state death taxes, taxes on prior transfers, and foreign death taxes).

ESTATES CONTAINING SEPARATE AND COMMUNITY ASSETS

There may be special problems in classifying an asset as separate or community. If an asset is acquired by spouses with funds that come from the community as well as the separately owned funds of each spouse, there may be a problem in determining how much of the property is community, how much is separate, and how the property will be treated for estate planning purposes.

For most estate planning purposes, if an estate asset is purchased with a lump sum payment that consists of both community property funds and separately owned funds, the value of the property will be apportioned according to the overall percentage of community assets and separate assets that were used to purchase it. For example, if stocks worth $40,000 are purchased with a lump sum payment of $40,000, and $10,000 is contributed from community property funds and the remaining $30,000 is contributed by the wife, then one-fourth of the stock ($10,000 out of a total of $40,000) is a community property asset and the remaining three-fourths ($30,000 out of a total of $40,000) is a separately owned asset of the wife. If the husband dies after the stock is acquired and paid for, then one-half the value of the community property interest in the stock, or $5000, is included in the husband's gross estate. If the wife dies after the stock is acquired, then her gross estate will not only include the value of her separately owned interest of $30,000 but will also include one-half the value of the community property interest of $5000 in the stock. Thus, her estate will contain a total of $35,000 worth of the total value of the stock.

Separately owned property acquired by either spouse *prior* to the marriage can also pose special problems. If the property appreciates significantly in value during the course of the marriage and the appreciation can be attributed to the efforts of the nonacquiring spouse, then a portion of the appreciation may be regarded as community property and may be included in the gross estate of the nonacquiring spouse for state inheritance and estate tax purposes. As a result, any portion of the appreciation that is directly attributable to the efforts of the nonacquiring spouse is not included in the gross estate of the spouse who originally acquired the property. This may result in a significant difference in estate tax liability on a state inheritance tax or estate tax return. It differs from the tax treatment of the property as reported on the federal estate tax return. On Form 706, any property originally acquired as the separate property of that spouse retains its character as separate property. Therefore, the entire value of the property, including all appreciation, is included as an asset in the gross estate of the spouse who originally acquired it. Since complications can arise because of this variance in federal and state estate tax treatment of the appreciation on this type of property, an attorney should always be consulted for proper planning.

ESTATE PLANNING STRATEGIES USING COMMUNITY PROPERTY

Because of the complications inherent in community property, proper planning is necessary to take advantage of the estate planning benefits available with this type of property. For a resident of a community property state, or for an individual who acquires community property while residing in a community property state, a financial planner should be aware of the following information when creating an estate plan.

1. If the spouses are uncertain of the status of property as community or separate due to the passing of time, they should enter into an agreement specifying their respective interests in the property. Since most states regard such agreements as valid, the spouses may elect to treat an asset as community or separate, depending on which choice provides their estate plans with the greatest flexibility and overall tax savings.

2. If a couple chooses to implement a revocable living trust as part of their estate plan and funds the trust with community property assets, the terms of the trust agreement should specify that the property is to retain its character as community property in the event of revocation. To further protect the status of the property as community property, both husband and wife should have the power to revoke the trust and this revocation power should be expressly stated in the terms of the trust agreement.

3. Since some states, most notably Idaho, Louisiana, and Texas, characterize the income produced by separately owned property as community property, the income produced by such property should be regu-

larly withdrawn or separated from the separate property to avoid commingling the separate and community property interests. This separation provides an accurate method of accounting for community and separate property assets, especially interest-bearing accounts, savings accounts, and certificates of deposit. In addition, it may save expenses and time on probating the estate of a decedent spouse.

4. Community property has a distinct income tax advantage because of the step up in basis afforded to both halves of the community property when either spouse dies. To take advantage of this step up in basis, the couple may wish to convert separately owned property or property held either in joint tenancy or tenancy in common to community property. This step up in basis can usually be achieved through a lifetime conversion of the property to community property. This conversion can greatly reduce income tax liability on an appreciated asset. A subsequent sale of the property at a price equal to its fair market value on the date of death of one of the spouses would result in no income tax liability because of the step up in basis that the entire property receives upon the death of either spouse. If the property had been held in joint tenancy with right of survivorship, only the one-half of the property held by the decedent would receive a step up in basis. In that case, if the surviving spouse had subsequently sold the property at a price equal to its fair market value on the date of death, he would have to report a taxable gain on the difference in value between the fair market value of his initial one-half interest and his basis in the property at the time the joint tenancy was created (usually, his cost basis if purchased or the donor's basis if gifted to the surviving spouse).

5. With the availability of the unlimited marital deduction for community property since 1982, it may seem attractive to qualify all property for the marital deduction so that the estate of the first decedent spouse has little or no estate tax liability. However, if this occurs, the decedent may be unintentionally overqualifying his or her estate for the marital deduction and burdening the survivor's estate with all of this property in addition to whatever property the surviving spouse owned individually. Since the surviving spouse will have only the unified credit available to offset estate tax liability, unless he or she remarries, the survivor's estate may be subjected to an unnecessarily large amount of taxation. This dilemma can be avoided by having the estates of both spouses pay a portion of the estate tax liability. By fully utilizing two unified credits rather than wasting the unified credit available to the first estate, the taxable estate is divided between both spouses with a resultant lower amount of tax liability. This strategy achieves greater estate tax savings as opposed to hav-

ing the first estate paying no estate tax and having the second estate paying a greater amount of estate tax.

6. For a spouse owning community property who wishes to take advantage of some of the marital deduction available for this type of property, the spouse should be certain that he or she has a will that is dated *after* December 31, 1981. A serious pitfall can occur if the maker of a will presumes that the unlimited marital deduction automatically applies to community property contained in the decedent's gross estate.

For the unlimited marital deduction to successfully apply to community property interests, the will must be dated *after* September 12, 1981; otherwise, the amount of marital deduction available for community property interests is limited to the amount available at the time the will was drafted. This may be less than the amount intended by the decedent spouse and could subject the estate to unintended and unnecessary estate tax liability. It is especially important that a community property tenant have his or her will rewritten if the will was written prior to 1977, since no part of the community property could qualify for the marital deduction prior to that time. In order to avoid subjecting the decedent's estate to unwarranted estate tax liability because of an outdated will, the will should be redrafted to take advantage of the marital deduction amount that is considered optimal in achieving the specific estate planning objectives of the spouse.

GIFT TAX IMPLICATIONS
OF COMMUNITY PROPERTY

The gift tax implications of a gift of community property depend on a number of variables, including the amount of the total gift, the identity of the donee, and whether the donor has used any unified credit on prior lifetime gifts. In addition, the classification of the gift as a gift of a present interest or future interest can also have varying gift tax implications.

For federal gift tax purposes, a gift of community property made to a nonspousal third party is treated as two gifts—a gift made by each spouse to the donee and a gift of one-half the value of the property to the donee. Each spouse is subject to gift tax liability on one-half the value of the gift. If the gift is one of a present interest, the transfer made by each spouse is entitled to the use of the annual exclusion amount. Thus, for a gift of community property valued at $40,000 to a third party donee, each spouse has made a *taxable* gift of $10,000 to the donee. The total gift of $40,000 has been made by both spouses; so each spouse has made a total gift of $20,000 and is entitled to use the annual exclusion amount of $10,000, and is thereby liable for a taxable gift of $10,000. The donors would each use their separate unified credits to offset any gift tax liability on the $10,000 taxable gift.

When a gift of community property is made from one spouse to the other spouse, there is no gift tax liability. The gift has the effect of transferring a one-half interest in the property from one spouse to the other, thereby making the donee spouse the sole owner of the property. Since the gift of property qualifies for both the annual exclusion and the gift tax marital deduction, there is no gift tax liability for a donor who chooses to gift his or her one-half interest in the community property to the other spouse. For a gift of this type, it is not necessary to file a federal gift tax return.[4]

An agreement by spouses to treat future income as the separate property of each spouse rather than as community property may be a gift. For example, if a husband and wife enter into an agreement that treats all income as the separately earned income of the respective spouse, this could constitute a gift. Assume in 1992 that the husband earns $60,000 and the wife earns $80,000. The community property interest of each in the community income is $70,000 (one-half the combined income totals of $140,000). Since the husband can now only claim $60,000 as his separately owned property pursuant to the agreement, he constructively makes a gift of $10,000 to his wife (the difference between the community property interest of $70,000 and the $60,000 actually received as separate property). However, because of the gift tax annual exclusion and the gift tax marital deduction, the husband would incur no gift tax liability even if the amount of the gift exceeded $10,000.

Special attention must be given to the particular laws of each state when determining whether a spouse had made a gift of property to the other spouse. California has recently enacted legislation that creates a legal presumption treating all property acquired during the marriage as community property.[5] The presumption of community property ownership can be rebutted only by clear evidence to the contrary, including a statement to that effect in the deed or other evidence of title. For gift tax purposes, the law provides that where there is a division of community property, the spouse shall be reimbursed for his or her contributions to the acquisition of the community property to the extent that the spouse can trace his or her respective contributions to a separate property source.[6] This provision negates any presumption that one spouse made a gift to the other of the value of any contribution traced to the separate property. California now requires that reimbursement be made to a contributing spouse for any amount traced to the separate property of either spouse rather than presuming that the contributing spouse intended to make a gift of such property to the other spouse. Community property tenants in other states should consult an attorney in their state to see whether the laws of their state create a presumption of a gift or whether such laws require reimbursement to the contributor spouse.

INCOME TAX IMPLICATIONS OF COMMUNITY PROPERTY

Perhaps the most significant income tax implication of community property is the step up in basis it affords *both* holders of the community property; both the decedent's one-half of the community property and the surviving spouse's one-half of the community property receive a step up in basis upon the death of the first decedent spouse. As previously discussed, this can result in an overall income tax savings for the surviving spouse who subsequently sells either the *entire* community property interest or the one-half interest owned by the survivor. Since both halves of the property receive a stepped-up basis, if the decedent decides to bequeath his or her one-half interest to the surviving spouse, the survivor does not have to report *any* taxation on the asset because the entire value of the property receives a step up in basis equal to the fair market value of the property on the date of the decedent's death. This significant income tax advantage can be obtained only with community property; it cannot be obtained with any other type of property ownership.

With the enactment of the Tax Reform Act of 1984, there are also advantageous income tax implications for holders of community property should the couple divorce or dissolve the marriage. Specifically, the Code provides that there will be no income tax consequences stemming from any transfer of property as a result of a divorce. Therefore, any transfer due to the severance of the community property is a nontaxable event.[7]

Prior to 1987, a significant income tax advantage stemming from the step up in basis of community property assets was that property received from the decedent spouse's estate was deemed to have been held for the time required to make it a long-term capital gain holding. Thus, even though the surviving spouse may have held the property for one month at the time the estate was probated, the property received from the decedent was treated for tax purposes as if it had been held for more than one year. Thus, the surviving spouse who received property from the decedent received favorable income tax rates (long-term capital gain treatment) on property that received a stepped-up basis. With enactment of the Tax Reform Act of 1986, the tax rate distinction between capital gain treatment of property and ordinary income treatment of property was eliminated, however, the taxation of capital gains was frozen at 28 percent while the taxation of ordinary income rose to 31 percent after the Revenue Reconciliation Act of 1990.

COMMUNITY PROPERTY AND THE MIGRATING CLIENT

The classification of property as community or separate (all other property forms) can sometimes become a difficult task. This process can become even more complicated if the client acquires the property in a community property state and then migrates to a common law property state. What effect does the act of migration have on the status of the property as community or separate?

Generally, the character of property acquired as community property in one of the nine community property states does not change if the couple subsequently moves to a common law property state. Thus, if a husband and wife obtain a residence as a community property asset and subsequently sell the home and move to a common law property state, the sale proceeds from the residence will retain their character as community property, even though the couple no longer lives in the community property state.

The opposite is also true; if an asset is acquired as a separate property in a common law state and the couple subsequently moves to a community property state, the status of the property does not change. Thus, if a couple establishes a residence in a common law property state and purchases the home and places the title in joint tenancy with right of survivorship, the sale proceeds obtained upon a sale of the residence are deemed to be the separate assets of either spouse and their character as separate assets does not change even though the couple may subsequently move to a community property state.

This illustration demonstrates the rule, *not* the exception. The general rule regarding the status of community property is that separately owned assets retain their character as separate assets and community property retains its character as community property, even though its form may change. The major exception to this rule is the concept of *quasi-community property,* previously discussed, which applies only in Arizona (upon dissolution of the marriage), California, Washington, and Idaho. Thus, if a couple acquires separate property in a common law state and later moves to one of these four states, the property will be treated as community property even though originally acquired as separate property.

One important protection that may be lost to the surviving spouse is the right to claim an elective portion of the decedent's community property assets as belonging to the surviving spouse. This occurs when the couple originally acquires the property in a common law state and subsequently moves to a community property state that does not afford protection to the surviving spouse in the form of quasi-community property.

Assume, for example, that a husband and wife reside in Oregon, a common law property state, and the husband acquires substantial assets which are placed in his name. In addition, he is the sole wage earner and his wife remains at home to take care of the children. At a later date, the couple moves to Nevada, a community property state that does not afford protection to the surviving spouse in the form of quasi-community property. Since the property was acquired as the separate property of the husband, it retains this character when the couple moves to Nevada. The husband executes a will and leaves the property to someone other than the surviving wife. Conceivably, the wife can be disinherited in this situation because she owns none of the property and is afforded no protection as the surviving spouse in the separately owned assets of the husband. If the spouse owned any community property, she would be afforded protection to the extent of the community property she owned. However, in the absence of a specific statute authorizing the survivor to take an elective share of the decedent's separately owned assets, the surviving spouse could be totally disinherited. For this reason, a couple needs to properly plan their estates when moving from a common law state to a community property state.

COMMUNITY PROPERTY IN WISCONSIN

In 1984, the Wisconsin legislature enacted a bill establishing a system of marital partnership property for all interests held by husband and wife. Though modifications to the original bill are still occurring as of this writing, the act is significant because it establishes a community property system of property law in this state. Thus, Wisconsin becomes the ninth state to adopt a system of community property laws. These laws took effect on January 1, 1986.

The new statutes[8] presume all property acquired by spouses during the course of the marriage to be marital property unless the property falls within one of several express exceptions. Properties that retain their status as separately owned properties even though acquired during marriage include property acquired by gift or inheritance, property received in exchange for the proceeds of separately owned property, and appreciation of separately owned property that is not directly attributable to the efforts and labor of the other spouse. Additionally, any property received as a result of a property settlement or whose status is converted by agreement of the parties retains its status as separately owned property.

The estate tax implications of owning property are similar to those in other community property states (e.g., each spouse has a 50% interest in the value of each item of marital property). Upon the death of either spouse, the marital property is divided equally and one-half the value of such property is included in the gross estate of each spouse. When a spouse dies, his will determines who will ultimately receive the one-half share of the property; there are no survivorship rights in the property which automatically transfer it to the surviving spouse. The decedent may either bequeath it to the surviving spouse, or a portion of it may pass to the surviving spouse by operation of law under the state's intestate succession statutes. If the deceased spouse bequeaths his or her interest in the property to a third party, the successor becomes a tenant in common with the surviving spouse to the property.

Income earned by the couple is presumed to be the community property of both spouses if it is earned by the couple during the marriage and is earned after December 31, 1985, or after the date on which the couple establishes a marital domicile in the state of Wisconsin. Normally, the income would be split between the spouses with each reporting one-half of it, though if the couple files a joint income tax return, there is virtually no significance in splitting the income equally. If the spouses choose to treat separate income or income produced from separately owned property as marital property, the parties are free to enter into an agreement to this effect for any property acquired prior to the marriage or for any property acquired through gift or inheritance.

Wisconsin permits property acquired before January 1, 1986 or before the date the couple established a marital domicile in Wisconsin to be treated as quasi-community property. Thus, property acquired in another state as separate property that would have been marital property if it had been acquired in Wisconsin is treated as if it were marital property.

The sole management and control by one spouse of property belonging to the community does not determine the character of the property as separate or marital. Thus, one spouse acting alone may manage and control the property, but this management does not alter or convert the property into the separate property of the manager. Both spouses retain legal rights in the property.

If property that was originally acquired as the separate property of either spouse is improved through a substantial contribution of labor, skill, or intellectual or managerial creativity of the other spouse, the property can be converted from separate property to marital property. The conversion occurs if the contributing spouse has not received reasonable compensation for the services rendered and if the efforts of the nonowner spouse have caused the value of the property to appreciate significantly.

A gift of property from one spouse to another spouse is free of gift tax liability because of the annual exclusion and the gift tax marital deduction. A gift of property made by one spouse to a third party is not subject to reimbursement proceedings by the nondonor spouse unless the amount of the gift exceeds $500 in any calendar year, or unless the gift is considered unreasonable when the economic positions of the parties are considered.

Presumably, this would permit one spouse to make small gifts of marital property to a third party without the other spouse seeking reimbursement. Where the amount of the gift exceeds $500 or any amount considered reasonable, the donor spouse would be subject to reimbursing the nondonor spouse.

If any debts or obligations are incurred by a couple and the marital property is obligated, it is presumed that the debts and obligations are incurred in the interest of both spouses. Thus, if an obligation is incurred by one spouse during the marriage that is not for the benefit of the marriage but can be attributed to an obligation incurred prior to the marriage or on separate property, the economic benefit of the marriage has been harmed. In such situations, the unobligated spouse may seek reimbursement from the obligated spouse to the extent the obligation incurred infringes on the nonobligated spouse's enjoyment and interest of the marital property.

There are a variety of remedies available for one spouse against the other for impairment of the nonobligated spouse's right to use and enjoy the marital property. The remedies include such alternatives as a court ordered accounting of the marital property, the addition of a spouse's name on separate property in order to compensate the nonobligated spouse for the marital property that was encumbered, as well as court orders declaring marital property to be the separately owned property of the nonobligated spouse or orders removing the obligated spouse as the manager of the marital property. In short, all remedies are provided that afford the nonobligated spouse the right to reclaim the fair market value of the marital property that was encumbered by the debts and obligations of the other spouse.

CONCLUSION

Because of the complex income, estate, and gift tax consequences that can stem from community property ownership, the financial planner needs to be aware of these consequences as well as the consequences stemming from a client's move from a community property state to a common law state, and vice versa. The advice of a competent attorney should always be obtained when attempting to structure a client's estate plan.

FOOTNOTES

1. For example, the state of Wisconsin permits one spouse, acting alone, to make a gift of property up to an amount of $500 per year to a third party without requiring the donor spouse to compensate the nondonor spouse. Wisconsin Statutes Section 766.53(1).

2. California Civil Code Section 5125(b) (West Pub. 1981 Supp.); Washington Revised Code Section 26.16.030(2) (1979); *Koenig v. Bishop,* 409 P.2d 102 (Idaho 1965).

3. Nevada Revised Statutes Section 111.064 (1981).

4. Internal Revenue Code Section 6019 provides that no gift tax return need be filed if the gift qualifies for a deduction allowable under Section 2523 (the gift tax marital deduction).

5. California Civil Code Sections 4800.1 and 4800.2 (1984 West Supp.).

6. California Civil Code Section 4800.2 (1984 West Supp.).

7. Internal Revenue Code Section 1041 (1984).

8. Originally enacted as 1983 Wisconsin Act 186, a portion of the bill amends the old Chapter 766 and specifies the rights of marital parties to property acquired during the course of the marriage while domiciled in Wisconsin or married in another jurisdiction and later moving to Wisconsin. For a comprehensive discussion of the provisions of this act, see Wisconsin Statutes Chapter 766, Sections 1 through 70.

6

POWERS OF APPOINTMENT, THE MARITAL DEDUCTION, AND MARITAL AND NONMARITAL TRUSTS IN ESTATE PLANNING

INTRODUCTION

A large part of estate planning for the married client involves the use and coordination of general and special powers of appointment, as well as the use and coordination of marital and nonmarital transfer forms. Foremost among the forms of marital and nonmarital transfers are the marital and nonmarital trusts, but outright bequests or transfers that are marital or nonmarital in nature also are an important part of estate planning. Since the nature of a power of appointment as general or special determines whether the property subject to that power qualifies for the marital deduction, it is important to learn the characteristics of various types of powers of appointment.

This chapter will describe the characteristics of general powers of appointment as well as special powers of appointment. The tax implications of a general power of appointment as well as a special power of appointment will be reviewed so that the financial planner may properly understand the income, estate, and gift tax implications of these powers. The tax implications for the exercise, lapse, or release of general powers and special powers will be reviewed so that the financial planner may better understand their estate tax treatment and the consequences of exercising or releasing these powers, as well as the consequences of allowing these powers to lapse.

This chapter will also describe the characteristics of property that qualify it for the marital deduction. A distinction will be drawn between property that qualifies for the marital deduction and property that fails to qualify for the marital deduction. Special attention will be given to terminable interests—those interests or properties that cease to provide income or use and enjoyment to the donor's spouse on the occurrence of a specified event. Some of these terminable interests qualify for the marital deduction while others do not. Those terminable interests that are eligible for the marital deduction, known as qualified terminable interests, will be reviewed. The reasons for treating these terminable interests as marital deduction property will be reviewed, as well as the reasons why such interests are not given marital deduction treatment.

Finally, this chapter will focus on the use of various marital and nonmarital transfer forms. The characteristics of marital, nonmarital, Q-TIP, and estate trusts will be reviewed, as will the estate tax implications of the use of each of these trusts. The use of the most appropriate trust arrangement, including the use of various trust combinations, will be highlighted so that the financial planner can decide which trust combination achieves the greatest number of estate planning objectives.

POWERS OF APPOINTMENT

By definition, a power of appointment is an interest held by a person (the holder) which gives the holder the ability to determine who shall enjoy, use, and possess the property subject to the power. The power of appointment can be held by the holder in the holder's lifetime or can be held by the holder's estate or can be exercised by the holder as a postmortem power.

A power is classified as "general" or "special" depending on the conditions and circumstances under which the power may be exercised. If the holder can exercise the power without any conditions or restrictions placed on the ability to exercise the power, the power is known as a *general power of appointment*. If the holder can exercise the power only under certain conditions, or only for a special group of beneficiaries, or only for a limited period of time, the power is known as a *special (or limited) power of appointment*. The distinction between property that is subject to a general power of appointment and property that is subject to a special, or limited, power of appointment is a very important one, since property subject to a general power of appointment is included in the gross estate of the holder; whereas, property that is subject to a special power of appointment is not included in the gross estate of the holder. Generally, the distinction between a general power of appointment and special power of appointment may be thought of in terms of *restrictions*; if there are any "strings attached" to the exercise of the power, then it is considered a special power of appointment. If there are "no strings attached," the power will be considered a general power of appointment.

General versus Special Powers of Appointment

General powers of appointment are those in which the holder of such a power is free to exercise it in favor of anyone, including the holder. A general power of appointment is one that can be exercised in favor of the holder, the holder's estate, the creditors of the holder, or the creditors of the holder's estate.

In addition to the mentioned situations, a general power of appointment is one that is not capable of being measured or limited according to the Internal Revenue Code's definition of "an ascertainable standard." Therefore, any power of appointment that is not capable of being measured by this ascertainable standard is deemed to be a general power of appointment. Internal Revenue Code Section 2041(b)(1)(A) and Treasury Regulation Section 20.2041-1(c)(2) describe those situations and powers which are capable of meeting the "ascertainable standard." All others are considered general powers of appointment if they cannot meet this ascertainable standard. Among the powers of appointment that are considered general are the following:

1. Power that can be exercised for the holder's comfort, welfare, and happiness
2. Power that can be exercised for the holder's health, maintenance, and welfare
3. Power that can be exercised in favor of the holder for the holder's happiness and well-being
4. Power that can be exercised in favor of the holder for the holder's happiness
5. Power that can be exercised in favor of the holder for the holder's comfort
6. Power that can be exercised in favor of the holder, the holder's creditors, the holder's estate, or the creditors of the holder's estate

In contrast to these special or limited powers of appointment are those which meet the definition of an ascertainable standard. These powers are capable of being measured or are restricted in some way so that they are considered limited. Among the special powers of appointment are the following:

1. Power that can be exercised in favor of the holder for support in the holder's accustomed manner of living (an ascertainable standard)
2. Power that can be exercised in favor of the holder only with the consent of the creator of the power
3. Power that can be exercised in favor of the holder for support in reasonable comfort (an ascertainable standard)
4. Power that can be exercised in favor of the holder's children only (limited to a specific class of beneficiaries)
5. Power that can be exercised only with the consent of a person who has interests similar to the holder (a condition that requires the consent of more than one individual, but only for powers created prior to October 22, 1942)
6. Power that can be exercised only with the consent of a person who has interests adverse to the holder (a condition that requires the consent of more than one individual)
7. Power that can be exercised in favor of the holder for the holder's health, education, maintenance, and support.
8. Power that can be exercised in favor of the holder for the holder's maintenance in reasonable health and reasonable comfort (capable of being measured by an ascertainable standard)
9. Power that can be exercised in favor of the holder for the holder's education (an ascertainable standard)
10. Power that can be exercised in favor of the holder for the costs of graduate or professional school for the holder (an ascertainable standard)
11. Power that can be exercised in favor of the holder for all medical expenses including expenses of convalescence for the holder (an ascertainable standard).

In addition to this list, if there is any situation in which the holder's ability to use the power is restricted in terms of when the holder can use it (e.g., the consent of other parties is needed prior to exercising it), the power is considered a special power of appointment. Only when there are no restrictions on the holder's ability to use, enjoy, or convey the property will the property subject to the power be considered a general power of appointment.

Exercises, Releases, and Lapses

When the holder of the power of appointment chooses to use it in favor of one or more beneficiaries, the holder *exercises* the power. The general effect of exercising a power of appointment is to remove the property from the holder's dominion and control. Thus, if a holder of a general power of appointment exercises the power in favor of the holder's children, the exercise of the power effectively shifts the property from the holder's dominion and control to the children. In effect, the exercise of the power is treated as a completed gift of the property to the children. As a result, the exercise of a general power of appointment removes the property subject to the power from the holder's gross estate. It does not matter that the exercise of the power occurs within 3 years of the death of the holder. The property subject to the power will be treated as an irrevocable gift and such a transfer follows the general rule that gifts made within 3 years of death are not added to the gross estate of the holder. (Only in certain limited circumstances will the property subject to the general power be added to the gross estate of the holder, for example, if the property subject to the power is a life insurance policy).

Again, it should be noted that the exercise of a general power of appointment removes the property subject to the power from the gross estate of the holder. If the power is a special power of appointment, its exercise will not cause the property to be included in the gross estate of the holder. Special powers of appointment are not included in the gross estate of the holder and the exercise of such a power will have no bearing on the estate tax liability of the holder of a special power. The exercise of a limited power of appointment may result in a taxable gift in four limited situations that will be discussed later in this chapter. When a general power of appointment is exercised it may subject the property to a possible gift tax. Since the exercise of a general power of appointment is treated as a completed gift, the property subject to the power may be subject to a gift tax liability if the value of the transferred property exceeds the amount of the annual exclusion. There is no gift tax liability when exercising a special power of appointment over property, since the holder did not exercise dominion and control over the property before exercise of the power. Therefore, the holder of a special power of appointment pays no gift tax on the exercise of the power.

A general power of appointment may also be *released*. A release of a power of appointment occurs when the holder of a power loses all control to determine who the beneficiaries of the property will be. When a general power of appointment is released, the same estate and gift tax consequences occur that occur when the general power of appointment is exercised. There are no estate or gift tax consequences to the holder of a special power of appointment when the power is released.

When a general power of appointment is not exercised within a given period of time, it *lapses*. An example of a lapsed power of appointment would be a situation in which the holder was required to exercise the power within a 12-month time period and failed to exercise it. The failure to exercise the power causes it to lapse. Generally, the lapse of a special power of appointment has no estate or gift tax consequences to the holder of the special power.

When a general power of appointment lapses, a special situation occurs regarding the estate and gift taxation of the property subject to the power. When a general power of appointment lapses, the holder of the power is subject to gift tax liability for any amount of property subject to the power in excess of $5000 or 5 percent of the value of the assets which are subject to the power, whichever amount is greater. This power is referred to as a *five and five power*. If the amount of property that lapses is less than $5000 per year or less than 5 percent of the total value of all assets subject to the power there is no gift tax liability to the holder of a general power of this type that is allowed to lapse. Since a lapse of a general power is treated as if it were a release, it will be treated as if the amount of property subject to the lapse (the greater of $5000 or 5 percent of the trust corpus) had been gifted. Thus, this property will be removed from the holder's gross estate and will reduce the holder's estate tax liability. If the holder of a general power of appointment wishes to avoid gift tax liability, the holder must permit no more than $5000 or 5 percent of the value of the assets to be treated as a lapse per year. The remainder of the property subject to the power (the 95 percent remaining after the exercise or lapse of the five and five power) is not included in the gross estate of the holder of the five and five power.

If gift tax consequences are to be avoided for the holder over an amount greater than 5 percent of the assets, then the holder must exercise a disclaimer over the power. A disclaimer over a general power of appointment will cause the property to be treated as if it had originally been transferred to someone other than the holder. In order for the disclaimer to be valid, the holder must disclaim the property before receiving any of the benefits from it. This disclaimer must also be in writing, and should specify the property that is being disclaimed. In order for the disclaimer to be considered qualified, the written disclaimer must be absolute and irrevocable. The disclaimer must be filed within 9 months from the date on which the power was created, or if the holder is incompetent, within 9 months from the date of regaining competency. Upon filing the disclaimer, the disclaimed property must pass to someone other than the holder or the spouse of the creator. Upon filing the qualified disclaimer, the holder will not be subject to a taxable gift on the value of the property transferred as a result of the disclaimer.

Taxable Exercise of a Limited Power of Appointment

In four special situations, the exercise of a special or limited power of appointment may result in a taxable gift to the holder. The exercise of a special power of appointment may result in a taxable gift when: (1) the exercise of the power is a result of a general power of appointment that was reduced to a special power of appointment, (2) the exercise of the power creates another power, (3) the limited power of appointment is exercised over the corpus of the trust in which the holder also has the right to receive and enjoy income from the property, or (4) the special power of appointment is exercised by the holder of a general power. Of these four situations, perhaps the second one deserves the greatest explanation. If a limited power of appointment can be exercised in such a manner that some portion of the property vests at a later, postponed date, the portion which is vested in another individual at a later date would be considered a general power of appointment. For example, if the grantor creates a trust in which the holder can exercise the power for the holder's children alone (a special power of appointment) but also gives one of the children the right to appoint the remainder interest in the property, the holder has converted the special power of appointment to a general power, as a result of giving one of the children the absolute right to appoint the balance of the property. In this situation, the holder will not be taxed on the portion of the property passed directly to the children; but the value of the property transferred to the child who has been given the right to appoint the balance will be treated as a general power of appointment, and this amount will be subject to a possible gift tax for the holder.

THE MARITAL DEDUCTION

An important estate tax deferral technique for the estate of a decedent spouse is the use of the marital deduction. The amount of property that is transferred to the surviving spouse is included in the gross estate of the decedent. But such property qualifies as a tax-free interest because it passes to the surviving spouse. Thus, this property will not be subject to estate tax liability in the estate of the first decedent spouse. This property must be included in the estate of the surviving spouse, however, and this acts as a means of tax deferral rather than tax avoidance. Unless the surviving spouse consumes the property or makes lifetime gifts of it to others during the spouse's lifetime, the property transferred to the surviving spouse will be taxed in the survivor's estate. The only way the surviving spouse can avoid estate tax on this property is by making a charitable bequest of this property that qualified for the charitable deduction; alternatively, if the survivor remarries, the survivor can use the marital deduction if the surviving spouse of the first marriage predeceases the spouse of the second marriage.

In order for property to qualify for the marital deduction, the property transferred must pass to the surviving spouse and to the surviving spouse alone; the property must vest absolute title, enjoyment, and benefit of the property and its income in the surviving spouse and in no one else; the surviving spouse must have a general power of appointment over the property and the power cannot vest in anyone else; and the property must be included in the gross estate of the surviving spouse. If all of these conditions apply, the property qualifies for the marital deduction.

Any property that does not meet these conditions fails to qualify for the marital deduction. For example, if the property can be divided between the spouse and another person, or if the income from such property can be divided between the spouse and others; or if someone other than the surviving spouse can exercise a general power of appointment over the property; or if anyone other than the surviving spouse can determine when the property or income can be distributed, these conditions cause the property to fail to qualify for the marital deduction.

In addition, there are other conditions under which the property will not qualify for the marital deduction. If the interest that passes to the surviving spouse can be terminated on the happening of a specified event, or with the passing of a given period of time, then the interest being transferred to the spouse is referred to as a "terminable interest." An example of terminable interest is a life income interest to the spouse that terminates on the subsequent remarriage of the surviving spouse. Another example of a terminable interest is a life income interest that terminates after 25 years. The right of the surviving spouse to live in a house that was solely owned by the decedent is also a life estate, and as such is a terminable interest.

Terminable interests do not, as a general rule, qualify for the marital deduction. Therefore, if the deceased spouse wishes to have the property qualify for the marital deduction, the surviving spouse should not be given an interest that will terminate on the occurrence of a specific event, for example, remarriage.

Though terminable interests do not qualify for the marital deduction as a general rule, there are five important exceptions where a terminable interest will qualify for the marital deduction if the property is "qualified." These five exceptions are

1. *The General Power of Appointment Exception.* This exception allows the surviving spouse to receive only the lifetime income interest from the corpus, while exercising a postmortem general power of appointment over the property for the benefit of the spouse's estate; or, it allows the spouse to exercise the power of appointment over the property in the spouse's lifetime.

2. *The Survivorship Condition Exception.* This exception allows property to qualify for the marital deduction if the only condition for receiving the property is that the spouse survives the deceased by a period of time that does not exceed 6 months. Thus, if the decedent

places a term in his will that leaves the property to the surviving spouse if the spouse outlives the decedent by 4 months, the surviving spouse will receive the property and it will qualify for the marital deduction since: (1) the time of survivorship as stated in the will did not exceed 6 months (in this case it was 4 months), and (2) the surviving spouse was, in fact, alive at the end of the 4-month period stated in the will.

3. *The Life Insurance and Annuity Settlement Exception.* This exception allows property to qualify for the marital deduction if the surviving spouse has a right to receive payment from either a life insurance company or from a commercial annuity company and, combined with this right of payment, the surviving spouse has a power of appointment in the proceeds which will pay the proceeds directly to the spouse or to the spouse's estate.

4. *The Qualified Terminable Interest Property Exception.* Perhaps the most notable exception to the terminable interest rule is the situation in which a lifetime income interest is payable to the surviving spouse yet also qualifies for the marital deduction. In order for this property to qualify, however, the executor of the decedent's estate must make an election to treat the property as "qualified" on the federal estate tax return. If this election is not made, the property fails to qualify for the marital deduction. The most common example of qualified terminable interest property is the Q-TIP trust. There may be a number of reasons why the decedent structures his or her estate so that the executor must make an election on the federal estate tax return.

   a. A decedent may not know whether his or her spouse needs income from the property. The decedent may wish to leave this decision to the executor of the estate since the decedent assumes that the executor is in a better position to determine the income needs of the surviving spouse.

   b. A decedent may be uncertain of the dollar amount of the decedent's gross estate and may wish to leave a greater portion of the decedent's estate to the surviving spouse in the form of a life income. Because the decedent does not know the precise amount of the decedent's estate tax liability, the decedent may wish to provide for the possibility of qualifying a greater amount of the estate for the marital deduction should there be significant estate tax liability when the estate is being probated.

   c. A decedent may not be in a position to determine whether the ultimate beneficiaries of the property should be the surviving spouse or other family members. If the decedent wishes to leave the property to family members, but chooses not to make the decision at the time of death, the executor can make the decision and name other family members as the ultimate beneficiaries of the property while also passing a lifetime income stream to the surviving spouse. The executor may be in a superior position to determine whose needs are greater—those of the spouse or those of other family members.

There may be other factors that need to be considered when structuring the estate plan and electing to treat the property as qualifying or nonqualifying. The primary considerations should be those of transferring the property to intended beneficiaries as well as minimizing estate tax liability.

5. *The Noncharitable Beneficiary Income Interest Exception.* This exception permits a decedent's estate to take advantage of the marital deduction in a situation where the decedent has established a charitable remainder trust and has given the surviving spouse a stream of income from the trust as the noncharitable income beneficiary. Though the interest is terminable, it is allowed to qualify for the marital deduction.

THE USE OF MARITAL AND NONMARITAL TRUSTS IN ESTATE PLANNING

An important part of planning an estate for a married client involves the use of marital and nonmarital trusts. The effective use of these trusts for the client with a sizeable estate will ensure that the decedent's property is transferred to the intended beneficiaries. It will also ensure that the decedent's estate is transferred effectively with a minimum amount of estate and gift tax.

This portion of Chapter 6 will focus on the characteristics of marital and nonmarital trusts as a part of planning an estate effectively. Then, the estate tax implications of marital and nonmarital trusts will be reviewed so that the financial planner is aware of what will happen to the decedent's tax liability if any one of these trusts is used. Finally, the financial planner will learn how these trusts can be used in conjunction with each other in order to determine how the client's estate plan can be structured most effectively.

There are four major types of trusts used in estate planning for a married client. These trusts are: (1) the marital trust, (2) the nonmarital trust, (3) the Q-TIP trust, and (4) the estate trust. The marital trust, the Q-TIP trust, and the estate trust are forms of marital transfers, while the nonmarital trust is a form of a nonmarital transfer. Each of these types of trusts will be reviewed separately.

The Marital Trust

The marital trust is sometimes referred to as "the power of appointment" trust. It is also sometimes known as the "A" trust. The marital trust consists of property transferred to the surviving spouse at the decedent's death. The surviving spouse has either a lifetime or testamentary general power of appointment over this property and can transfer it to whomever he or she wishes. The surviving spouse can use this property for his or her own needs, or can bequeath it to anyone the decedent spouse wants to leave it to under the terms of the will if the spouse only has a lifetime income interest in the property. The key characteristic of a power of appointment trust or marital trust is that the surviving spouse has postmortem control over the property in this trust.

The marital trust can be structured so that it provides a stream of income to the surviving spouse for the spouse's lifetime. Even though this trust provides income to the surviving spouse, he or she usually has the ability to invade the entire amount of the corpus of this trust for his or her needs. The income stream that is distributed to the spouse cannot be split with any other individual. The surviving spouse *must* be the only recipient of this income; though, once the income is received, the spouse is free to give the income to whomever he or she wishes. The income from this trust must be distributed at least once per year.

The property placed in the marital trust qualifies for the marital deduction in the gross estate of the decedent. Therefore, although it is included in the decedent's estate, it is not subject to estate tax. The property must be included in the gross estate of the surviving spouse because it was transferred to him or her estate-tax free as a result of qualifying for the marital deduction in the first estate. The value of this property will be included in the surviving spouse's gross estate unless it is consumed or given away by the surviving spouse in the spouse's lifetime, or made the subject of a charitable bequest.

Again, the primary feature of this trust is that the surviving spouse has postmortem control over the property. This means that when the trust terminates, the corpus and all undistributed income are passed to the surviving spouse. The spouse's will determines who receives this property when the spouse dies.

The Nonmarital Trust

The nonmarital trust is referred to as the "bypass trust" or "family trust." It is also sometimes referred to as the "B" trust. The nonmarital trust consists of property transferred to the trust at the time of the decedent's death. The primary characteristic of the nonmarital trust is that it gives the decedent postmortem control over the property. The amount of property transferred to the trust is usually an amount equal to the exemption equivalent. As a result, though the amount of property placed into this trust usually remains in the decedent's taxable estate, it does not incur any estate tax liability because the decedent's unified credit amount fully absorbs the estate tax due on the value of this property.

The nonmarital trust can be structured so that it provides a stream of income to the surviving spouse only. However, the income stream can be split among the spouse and other individuals if the decedent so chooses. Thus, a decedent could use the nonmarital trust to provide income to both the surviving spouse and children. The income from this trust would not have to be distributed annually. It could be distributed according to the terms of the trust or it could be distributed as the trustee sees fit.

While a nonmarital trust may give only the surviving spouse income for life, the income can also be distributed to the children only if the trust is so worded. If the spouse has a life interest in the income stream, it is known as a terminable interest. This means that the spouse has no postmortem control over the property; the spouse's right to receive income from the trust ends when he or she dies. The spouse has no enforceable right to determine who will receive the property after he or she dies. The surviving spouse's inability to exercise postmortem control over the trust property means that the property does not qualify for the marital deduction in the gross estate of the decedent. The property remains in the taxable estate of the decedent and may be subject to estate tax liability if it exceeds the amount of the exemption equivalent. Though the property will not qualify for the marital deduction in the estate of the decedent, it also will not be included in the surviving spouse's gross estate.

In special circumstances, the surviving spouse may be able to exercise limited rights of invasion over the corpus and income of a nonmarital trust. As long as the surviving spouse is not given the power to withdraw more than 5 percent of the corpus of a nonmarital trust, or is not given the power to withdraw more than $5000 per year (whichever is greater), the property in the nonmarital trust will not be included in the surviving spouse's gross estate (this power is known as a five and five power).

Since the surviving spouse does not have a general power of appointment over the property in this trust, the decedent exercises a postmortem control over the property. Thus, a decedent could establish a nonmarital trust to provide the surviving spouse with income for the remainder of the survivor's life and, upon the death of the survivor, the trust would terminate and the corpus and all undistributed income could be transferred to the couple's children.

If the nonmarital trust is funded in an amount equal to the exemption equivalent, the value of the trust property will remain in the decedent's estate but will not be subject to estate tax liability since the amount of estate tax payable on a trust of this amount would equal the amount of the available unified credit. A nonmarital trust is one way of ensuring that the decedent's estate takes advantage of the unified credit without overqualifying the bulk of the estate for the marital deduction.

The Q-TIP Trust

The Q-TIP trust is also referred to as the "current income interest" trust or the "C" trust. This trust is used when the decedent wishes to provide the surviving spouse with a stream of income that will be paid for life, yet also wishes to qualify the property for the marital deduction. The Q-TIP trust or "qualified terminable interest property" trust, as it is sometimes called, accomplishes this purpose.

The Q-TIP trust is generally used in situations where the decedent spouse wishes to provide the surviving spouse with a stream of income payable from the trust corpus. The Q-TIP trust is used because it allows the decedent to have postmortem control over the property when the surviving spouse dies. Thus, a Q-TIP can distribute income to the surviving spouse for his or her life yet allow the decedent to determine who receives the property when the surviving spouse dies. The property, or a portion of it, can be made to qualify for the marital deduction in the estate of the decedent (and must be included as an asset in the gross estate of the surviving spouse) even though the surviving spouse is only entitled to a life income interest. Thus, the taxable estate of the decedent can be reduced substantially by taking advantage of this trust. However, in order for such property to qualify for the marital deduction, the executor of the decedent's estate must elect to treat the property as qualifying for the marital deduction on the federal estate tax return.

It is important to note that, in order for property to be treated as Q-TIP property, the executor of the decedent's estate must make an election on the decedent's federal estate tax return. If the executor fails to check the election box on the estate tax return, the property in this trust will not be treated as Q-TIP property and will be subject to estate tax liability in the decedent's gross estate. It will be treated for tax purposes as if it were a nonmarital property, which means it will remain in the taxable estate of the decedent and could subject the decedent's estate to tax liability.

The Q-TIP trust provides a stream of income to the surviving spouse. The income stream on this trust *must* be distributed at least once annually. The income from this trust can be paid only to the surviving spouse and to no one else. The surviving spouse cannot be the recipient of the trust corpus when the trust terminates. The surviving spouse possesses no postmortem control over this property and cannot determine who will receive the property upon the death of the surviving spouse. (However, it should be noted that a surviving spouse could elect to take against the will, thereby giving up the income stream from the Q-TIP trust and taking, in its place, a fractional portion of the decedent's entire estate. To safeguard against this, the decedent needs to give a sufficient amount of other property, exclusive of the Q-TIP income, to the surviving spouse.)

The surviving spouse may be given a limited power of invasion over the corpus and income of a Q-TIP trust. This power of invasion is similar to that provided to the surviving spouse in a nonmarital trust. Thus, the surviving spouse may only withdraw the greater of $5000 or 5 percent of the trust corpus annually if the trust is structured to give the spouse this power of withdrawal. It should be noted that this power of invasion is not cumulative and is lost if not exercised in the current year. The exercise of a five and five power, if authorized by the trust, gives the surviving spouse a limited right to invade the corpus. It does *not* provide the surviving spouse with any estate tax benefits since all of the property in the trust must be included in the surviving spouse's estate.

The Estate Trust

Sometimes a client and his or her spouse have accumulated a substantial amount of wealth in their lifetimes so that the surviving spouse does not need in his or her lifetime the income or the corpus of a trust established by the decedent. In situations like this, an estate trust may be appropriate. An estate trust is a trust established by the decedent which accumulates its income rather than distributing it to the spouse. The trustee, in his or her discretion, may distribute a part of the income to the surviving spouse during the spouse's lifetime. However, the primary characteristic of the estate trust is that its income is accumulated. Upon the death of the surviving spouse, the survivor's estate exercises a general power of appointment over the corpus and undistributed income and determines who ultimately receives the property. The estate trust may be thought of as a marital trust that does not provide the surviving spouse with an income stream. Upon the death of the surviving spouse, the survivor's will determines who receives the property. Thus, the surviving spouse does exercise postmortem control over this property. Because the surviving spouse has this element of postmortem control, the property qualifies for the marital deduction in the estate of the first decedent spouse and its value must be included as an asset in the gross estate of the surviving spouse.

Whether one or more of these trusts are appropriate in a given situation depends on the client's estate planning objectives. Several of these trusts may be used in conjunction with each other in order to achieve the most efficient estate plan.

The following guidelines serve as a reminder to the financial planner, to suggest the conditions under which one or more marital or nonmarital trusts may be appropriate.

A marital trust may be appropriate when

1. the decedent does not want to restrict or control the surviving spouse's use or enjoyment of the property.
2. the decedent has confidence in the management abilities and financial expertise of the surviving spouse.
3. the decedent wants to qualify the property for the marital deduction.
4. the decedent has confidence in the ability of the surviving spouse to provide for minor children and other beneficiaries.

A nonmarital trust may be appropriate when

1. the decedent wants to provide the surviving spouse with a stream of income that terminates upon the survivor's death.
2. the decedent wants to determine who the ultimate beneficiaries of the property will be upon the death of the surviving spouse.
3. the decedent wants to fully use the amount of available unified credit for his or her estate.
4. the decedent wants to reduce estate tax liability by taking advantage of the unified credit and by preventing overqualification of property for the marital deduction in the surviving spouse's estate.

A Q-TIP trust may be appropriate when

1. the decedent wants to provide the surviving spouse with a stream of income.
2. the decedent wants to determine who the ultimate beneficiaries of the property will be upon the death of the surviving spouse.
3. the decedent wants to qualify this property or a portion of it for the marital deduction.
4. the decedent wants the surviving spouse to be the sole recipient of the income for the spouse's life.

An estate trust may be appropriate when

1. the decedent wants to qualify the property for the marital deduction.
2. the decedent wants the surviving spouse to have postmortem control over the property when the surviving spouse dies.
3. the surviving spouse does not need income or corpus during the spouse's lifetime.

4. the decedent wishes to have the income from such a trust accumulate over a period of time instead of being distributed.

If the client wishes to achieve one or more objectives that can only be accomplished by the use of more than one of these trusts, then the client may wish to structure a multiple trust combination that takes advantage of these characteristics. For example, a client would want to use a combination of the nonmarital and Q-TIP trusts when he or she

1. wishes to provide the surviving spouse with a stream of income that lasts for the life of the spouse.
2. wishes to determine who the ultimate beneficiaries of the property will be after the death of the surviving spouse.
3. wants to take advantage of both the unified credit and the marital deduction amounts in an effort to reduce estate tax liability.
4. wants to avoid giving the surviving spouse any postmortem control over any of the property.

Only by implementing this combination of the nonmarital and Q-TIP trusts can the client achieve all four objectives. The selection of an appropriate marital or nonmarital trust arrangement should always be considered in light of whether the trusts achieve the specific objectives established by the client.

One way of ensuring that the optimal combination of trusts is achieved is by placing provisions in the will that properly allocate the decedent's estate to a particular type of trust. Because most individuals do not know when they will die, it can sometimes be difficult to determine how large the nonmarital trust should be. Rather than funding such a trust with a specific dollar amount (e.g., $400,000), the client should structure the nonmarital trust in such a way that it is equal to the amount of the exemption equivalent in the year of the client's death. This will ensure that the nonmarital trust escapes any estate tax liability and also ensures that the decedent's estate fully utilizes the maximum amount of unified credit available to the estate.

The remaining portion of the estate can be allocated to either the marital trust or the Q-TIP trust, depending on the client's estate planning objectives. If it is the client's desire to leave the property outright to the surviving spouse and thereby give the spouse absolute control and enjoyment over the property, then either an outright marital transfer or a marital trust would be appropriate. Both the outright transfer and the marital trust qualify for the marital deduction and this portion of the estate (after the nonmarital portion has first been funded) escapes any estate tax liability in the client's estate.

If it is the client's desire to provide the surviving spouse with a lifetime income while also retaining postmortem control over the property, then the Q-TIP trust would be appropriate for the remainder of the estate (after the nonmarital portion of the estate has first been funded). The Q-TIP trust would allow the client to determine the ultimate beneficiary of the corpus of the Q-TIP while also providing the surviving spouse with a stream of income from the corpus for the spouse's lifetime. If elected by the executor, the Q-TIP trust qualifies for the marital deduction in the estate of the deceased client, thereby escaping any federal estate tax liability.

It should be noted that a nonmarital transfer need not be in the form of a trust. Though it is commonly used as a means of providing an income stream to the spouse or children, the transfer of property in such an arrangement can be similar to an outright marital transfer, avoiding the use of a trust arrangement. The value of the assets transferred to the beneficiaries (who would be anyone other than the surviving spouse) would be equal to the exemption equivalent. This property would still remain in the taxable estate of the client but would escape estate tax liability because of the use of the available unified credit.

Also, property that is elected to be treated as Q-TIP property need not be in the form of a trust though, for practical reasons, it is most frequently structured in this form. It is possible to give the surviving spouse a life interest in a property (such as a right to live in a residence that was solely owned by the decedent) and upon the death of the surviving spouse, title to the residence would transfer to the couple's children. As long as the executor of the first decedent spouse's estate elected to treat the property as Q-TIP property, the property would qualify for the marital deduction in the estate of the first decedent even though it is not in the form of a trust.

A summary of the various characteristics of marital and nonmarital trusts is found in Exhibit A: Marital and Nonmarital Trusts that Affect Estate Planning.

Exhibit A *MARITAL AND NONMARITAL TRUSTS THAT AFFECT ESTATE PLANNING*

	Marital Trust	Nonmarital Trust	Q-TIP Trust	Estate Trust
Also known as:	Power of appointment trust "A" Trust	Bypass trust/Family trust "B" Trust	Current beneficial interest trust "C" Trust	
Qualify in decedent's estate for marital deduction?	Yes	No	Yes, if elected by executor of decedent's estate	Yes
Provide income stream to surviving spouse?	Yes	Yes, if structured to provide income	Yes	Usually, no
Included in survivor's gross estate?	Yes	No	Yes—if elected by executor	Yes
Does surviving spouse have right to invade corpus?	Usually	Limited right to invade corpus—limited to the greater of $5000 or 5% of corpus, noncumulative, only if included in language of trust instrument	Limited right to invade corpus—limited to the greater of $5000 or 5% of corpus, noncumulative, only if included in language of trust instrument	No

Question				
Is surviving spouse ultimate beneficiary of corpus when trust terminates?	Yes, either because of a general power of appointment or because of absolute ownership of property	No	No	Yes—upon death of surviving spouse
Can income be split with another income beneficiary?	No	Yes	No	No—usually nonapplicable
Must trust distribute income annually?	Yes	No	Yes	No
Does surviving spouse have a general power of appointment over trust?	Yes	No	No	Yes—but only upon death
How is trust funded?	Usually, after nonmarital trust has first been funded	Usually, equal in amount to the exemption equivalent	Usually, after nonmarital trust has first been funded	Usually, with a corpus that permits income to accumulate
Can it be used with other trusts?	Yes—to achieve maximum estate tax savings	Yes—to achieve maximum estate tax savings	Yes—to achieve maximum estate tax savings	Yes—to provide ultimate testamentary control to surviving spouse

7

CHARITABLE GIFTING STRATEGIES

INTRODUCTION

Lifetime gifting or testamentary transfers of property to a qualified charity are two types of strategies used commonly in the estate planning of a donor's assets. Charitable gifts or charitable testamentary transfers can achieve a number of client objectives. The most common reasons for gifting or bequeathing property to a qualified charity include the following:

1. Allowing the donor the satisfaction of seeing the charity or other donee enjoy the property; or fulfilling the donative intentions of the donor either while the donor is alive or after the donor's death, for example, "$50,000 to my church, Church of the Risen Christ."

2. Lifetime gifts of appreciating property that are gifted to a qualified charity remove all future appreciation of the property from the donor's gross estate, thereby preventing the donor's estate tax liability from increasing. If a sufficient amount of property is gifted in the donor's lifetime, the property removed from the gross estate can

reduce the size of the taxable estate and can actually reduce the estate tax liability of the donor.

3. Lifetime gifts of income-producing property can reduce the income tax liability of the donor. Since the donor irrevocably parts with legal title to the property,the income produced by the gifted property is taxable income to the donee. This can be a significant reason for making lifetime gifts to the charity donee.

4. A donor can either reduce gift tax liability or avoid gift tax liability altogether by making lifetime gifts to a qualified charity. Gift tax liability can be reduced by having both spouses make a split gift of the property to the donee; in addition, the donors can avoid gift tax liability by taking advantage of the gift tax charitable deduction for gifts made to a qualified charity.

5. There are times when a donor wishes to gift or bequeath property for a very special purpose. For example, a donor may wish to ensure that a gift or bequest of property is transferred to a qualified charity for purposes of medical research or educational purposes. A donor may wish to gift or bequeath property to the donor's *alma mater,* or may direct that a specific bequest of property be left for a specific purpose, for example, "I hereby bequeath $100,000 to the Law School of Creighton University, to be used for expansion and development of the Law School Library." If the donor has a donative intent which carries a special meaning for the donor, the donor may wish to ensure that a specified recipient receive the property; for example, a diabetic donor may wish to make a gift or bequest to the American Diabetes Association for the specific purpose of educational research. A donor with arthritis may wish to make a gift to the American Arthritis Foundation in the hopes that a cure will be found for the disease. Donors may wish, for personal reasons, to leave either lifetime gifts or bequests to such organizations as: the American Cancer Society, the American Heart Association, the American Kidney Foundation, or any other qualified charity whose purpose is to find a cure for a serious disease.

If a donor wishes to reduce estate, gift, and income taxes, the donor can establish an estate plan that combines both lifetime gifts and testamentary transfers. The lifetime gifts can reduce income tax liability, while also reducing gift tax liability. Testamentary transfers to qualified charities can reduce or avoid estate tax liability. A careful examination of both types of techniques can maximize tax savings in all three areas. Before making gifts to qualified charities as part of a client's estate plan, the financial planner needs to analyze the client's financial position to determine whether the donor can afford to make a gift to a donee charity.

WHEN DONOR CAN AFFORD TO MAKE A GIFT

Whether the donor can afford to make a qualified gift to a charity depends on a number of factors that the financial planner needs to analyze. Ideally, the financial planner will gather most of the data needed during the data gathering process with the client. After this information has been analyzed, the financial planner needs to confer with the client about the feasibility of making a lifetime gift or a testamentary transfer to a qualified charity.

The factors which the financial planner needs to analyze before recommending that the client make a gift to a charity include the following:

1. What are the financial needs of the donor and the donor's spouse and beneficiaries? If the donor needs a specified amount of income for living expenses, it may be inappropriate for the donor to make a gift if such a gift would cause financial hardship to the donor or the donor's family.

2. What are the projected needs of the donor and the donor's spouse for retirement purposes? If the donor and donor's spouse need a specified sum for their retirement, a gift of property or cash may be inappropriate if it prevents the donor and donor's spouse from living comfortably in retirement.

3. Does the donor have property that he can afford to gift or bequeath and still adequately provide for the donor's spouse and other family members? It should be remembered that, in some states, a donor cannot make an unlimited gift or bequest to a charity if the donor is survived by a spouse and other family members. The *mortmain statutes* prevent a donor from making an excessive charitable bequest. Therefore, if a donor wishes to make a charitable transfer, the donor should first adequately provide for the donor, spouse, children, and other family members.

4. Does the donor need a reduction in income tax liability? If the answer is no, then the donor may wish to consider whether a gift or bequest of income-producing property is appropriate. If the donor does need an income tax reduction, the donor may wish to consider a gift of income-producing property to a qualified charity, or may wish to use some form of a split-interest gift which divides the gift into a present gift of income to a noncharitable beneficiary and a gift of the remainder interest to a qualified charity.

5. Does the donor need a reduction in estate tax liability? If the projected amount of estate tax liability is high, the donor may wish to make a

lifetime gift of property to a charity in order to reduce the size of the donor's taxable estate. If the property remains in the taxable estate of the donor, all future appreciation of the property will cause the donor's estate tax liability to increase.

6. Does the donor have sufficient liquidity in his or her estate so that all taxes and administrative expenses can be paid? If there is a liquidity problem for the estate, it may not be appropriate to make a gift of liquid property to the charity, especially if the estate will need the property (e.g., cash or cash equivalents) to pay taxes, debts, funeral expenses, administrative expenses, and attorney's fees. A donor should not make a lifetime gift to a charity if the gift would create a liquidity problem for his estate.

7. Does the donor wish to avoid gift tax liability on a gift? If the answer is yes, then the donor may wish to consider a lifetime gift to a qualified charity that qualifies for the gift tax charitable deduction. An explanation of the gift tax charitable deduction appears later in this chapter.

8. Does the donor have a specific reason for making a gift to a charity? Does the donor wish to leave property to a special organization for research or educational purposes? Does the donor wish to gift property to a church or synagogue? Does the donor wish to gift property to a humanitarian organization or for a specific charitable, scientific, educational, or cultural purpose? If the answer to any of these questions is yes, then the donor may wish to consider a gift to one of these charitable groups.

9. Would the donor be better off by not gifting the property, from a tax standpoint? For example, assuming that the property being considered for gifting had depreciated in value, so that its present fair market value is less the donor's basis in the property, the donor might be wise to keep the property, sell it at a loss, and take the capital losses on the donor's individual income tax return. This would be more advantageous for the donor then making a completed gift of the property to the charity. A gift of the property to the charity would not enable the donor to take the capital loss, whereas a sale of the property at a loss would allow the donor this income tax advantage. In addition, the donor could take the proceeds of the sale and gift them to the charity, thus still enabling the donor to take the charitable deduction as well as the capital loss in the same tax year.

In addition to these nine factors, there may be other factors that need to be considered which may affect the appropriateness of making a gift.

PROPERTY THAT IS APPROPRIATE FOR GIFTING

Once a donor has determined that he or she can afford to make a gift, the next question that must be asked is what property is the most appropriate to gift to a qualified charity? The answer to this question depends on a number of factors, including the adjusted gross income (AGI) and marginal tax bracket of the donor, the type of property owned by the donor, whether the property produces income or is nonincome-producing, and whether the donee is a public charity or a private charity. Each of these factors can affect the type of property that is contributed to a qualified charity and the amount of the charitable deduction that can be taken in a tax year.

Charitable contributions can be classified according to the following criteria:

Type of property contributed: (1) cash, (2) ordinary income property, (3) long-term capital gain property (stock, real estate), (4) tangible personal property, (a) use-related, (b) use-unrelated, and (5) future interests.

Identity of donee: (1) public charity, (2) private charity.

Adjusted gross income of donor as affecting the maximum charitable deduction: (1) 50 percent of adjusted gross income deduction, and (2) 30 percent of adjusted gross income deduction.

Each of these factors will be analyzed in light of its effect on the tax liability of the donor.

Type of Property

Generally, the type of property that is donated to a qualified charity can determine the amount of the charitable contribution that can be taken by the donor. The general rules for charitable contributions are as follows:

1. If the gift is a gift of *cash*, the donor is allowed a maximum annual charitable contribution equal to 50 percent of the donor's adjusted gross income. Thus, if a donor's adjusted gross income is $160,000 and the donor makes a cash contribution of $35,000 to a qualified *public* charity, the donor will be entitled to take a charitable deduction equal to 50 percent of the donor's adjusted gross income, or $80,000. In this case, since the amount donated to the qualified *public* charity is less than the maximum charitable deduction allowed ($80,000), the full amount of the cash contribution, or $35,000 could be deducted in the year it is gifted. If the donor's adjusted gross income is $60,000 and

the donor still makes a $35,000 cash contribution, the donor's maximum charitable contribution for the year of the gift would be $30,000 (50 percent of adjusted gross income). The remaining $5000 would be carried over into the next tax year and could be deducted on the donor's income tax return as a charitable deduction for that year.

2. Property that does not meet the definition of long-term capital gain property is classified as *ordinary income property*. Included in this category as *ordinary income property* are assets held as short-term capital assets (stock held less than 6 months prior to January 1, 1988, and stock held for less than 1 year if acquired after December 31, 1987); stock acquired in a corporate nontaxable transaction; works of art, compositions, and books and other creations given by the individual who created them; and stock in trade and inventory that would have resulted in ordinary income if sold.

Ordinary income property can sometimes be deducted by the donor in an amount equal to 50 percent of the donor's adjusted gross income. Thus, if a donor gives $50,000 worth of ordinary income property to a qualified public charity, and the donor has an adjusted gross income of $90,000, the maximum charitable contribution deduction that can be taken by the donor in the year of the gift would be $45,000; the remaining $5000 would be carried over into the year after the gift was made and would be deducted in the second year.

However, for a donor of ordinary income property, the deduction is usually limited to the donor's basis (usually the donor's cost) in the donated property if sold. Thus, if the donor makes a gift of short-term capital gain property, such as short-term stock, the donor's maximum charitable deduction will be limited to 50 percent of the donor's adjusted gross income or the donor's basis, usually its cost in the stock, whichever is less. If the donor's basis in the stock is $12,000, and the stock has a fair market value of $30,000 at the time it is donated to the qualified public charity, the donor's maximum charitable deduction will be limited to $12,000, not 50 percent of the donor's adjusted gross income of $60,000, or $30,000.

The charitable deduction is limited to the donor's cost basis in other types of ordinary income property as well. For example, if the donor makes a charitable contribution of inventory or stock in trade, and the property has a value of $35,000 at the time it is gifted but has a cost basis to the donor of $25,000, the donor's maximum charitable deduction will be the donor's basis in the property—$25,000, rather than 50 percent of the donor's adjusted gross income of $70,000,or $35,000.

Gifts of life insurance also pose a special problem for the donor. If a donor makes a gift of a life insurance policy on the donor's life to a qualified public charity, and the face amount of the policy is $50,000 but the donor's total net premiums and other consideration paid equal $14,000, the donor's maximum charitable deduction will be limited to the donor's basis (cost) in the policy: $14,000.

If, however, the value of the policy (its face amount) is less than the value of the donor's basis (total net premiums paid), the donor will be allowed to take as the maximum charitable contribution the value of the policy. Thus, if the policy had a value of $16,000 at the time it was gifted to the public charity, but the donor has paid a total of $20,000 in net premiums, the donor will be able to take a maximum charitable deduction of $16,000 rather than the value of the premiums paid to date. The Tax Reform Act of 1986 specifically retains the limitations on deductibility of an ordinary income property, such as stock, by limiting the deductibility of a gift of short-term stock (stock held less than 6 months prior to January 1, 1988, or stock held less than 1 year if acquired after December 31, 1987) to the donor's basis in the stock.

3. Property that is defined as *long-term capital gain property* is property which has been held for longer than these time periods. Included in this category are stock and real estate held long-term. For property that is classified as long-term capital gain property, the donor is entitled to take a maximum charitable contribution deduction equal to the fair market value of the property, subject to a maximum charitable contribution in one year of 30 percent of the donor's adjusted gross income. Thus, if a donor has long-term capital gain property, such as corporate stock, that has a fair market value of $30,000, and the donor's adjusted gross income is $60,000, the donor can take a maximum charitable contribution deduction of $18,000 in the year the gift is made. The remaining $12,000 can be carried over to the year after the initial gift is made, and can be deducted fully in the second year.

Prior to TRA '86, when donating long-term capital gain property, however, the donor could make an election that would result in a greater maximum charitable deduction for the year of the gift. If the donor elected to reduce the amount of gain on the donated property by 40 percent, the donor was then entitled to a maximum charitable deduction of 50 percent of the donor's adjusted gross income. This achieved a greater charitable contribution deduction for the donor than if the donor had chosen to take the deduction based on 30 percent of the donor's adjusted gross income. With the enactment of TRA '86, the attractiveness of making this selection appears to have been lost, since the donor in such situations will be limited to his or her basis in the property. However, when the amount that may be deducted is limited to the cost in the long-term capital gain property, the amount that may be deducted in any one year is 50 percent of the donor's adjusted gross income.

Assume, for example, that in 1991 a donor makes a charitable contribution of long-term capital gain property valued at $55,000 which has a cost basis of $15,000 to the donor. Assume also that the donor has an adjusted gross income of $90,000. In this situation, assuming that the donor chose to deduct the fair market value of the property, then the donor's maximum charitable contribution is 30 percent of the donor's adjusted gross income or $27,000. Thus, $27,000 is the maximum charitable deduction in the year the long-term capital gain property is gifted; the remaining $28,000 is carried over to a second year where some or all of it may be deducted, depending on the amount of the donor's adjusted gross income in the second year. But assuming that the donor's adjusted gross income remains constant at $90,000 in the second year, then the donor may take a deduction of $27,000 in the second year, and the remaining $1000 could be deducted in the third year.

Assume, however, that the donor chose to deduct only his or her cost in the property. In this situation, the donor can only take a maximum charitable deduction limited to the donor's basis in the property. In this hypothetical case, the donor has an adjusted gross income of $90,000, but could have taken a deduction up to 50 percent of the donor's adjusted gross income, or $45,000. But since the maximum deduction is limited to the donor's cost in the property, he or she can only take a maximum charitable deduction of $15,000 representing the value of the donor's basis in the property. This is a decrease in the amount of the maximum charitable deduction from $27,000 to $15,000. Thus, the donor has lost an additional $12,000 in charitable deductions in the year of the charitable contribution that would have been available if the donor had not elected to increase the AGI limit from 30 to 50 percent. By making such an election, the donor has decreased the amount of the charitable deduction in the year of the gift so that the donor has lost a means of achieving greater income tax savings. Few donors would want to intentionally lose valuable charitable deductions when the loss of these deductions means an increase in income tax liability.

4. If the gift is a gift of *tangible personal property* it is treated as a long-term capital gain property for purposes of obtaining the charitable contribution deduction. Tangible personal property includes jewelry, automobiles, art works, stamp collections, and books, but only if the art works or collections are created or produced by someone other than the grantor. The maximum charitable deduction that can be

taken by the donor of the tangible personal property depends on whether the donated property is use-related or use-unrelated to the purposes of the charitable organization.

The general rule regarding donations of use-related property to a qualified public charity is that the donor can take a maximum charitable deduction of 30 percent of the donor's adjusted gross income, and that the entire fair market value of the donated property can be deducted over a period of years. If the donated property is use-unrelated, the donor can take a maximum charitable deduction limited to the donor's basis in the property. Note that for 1991 only, contributions of use-related tangible personal property are fully deductible (the fair market value of the donated property is deductible without having to report any of the gain as a tax preference item for purposes of the alternative minimum tax).

The distinction between use-related and use-unrelated tangible personal property depends on the purpose of the charitable organization. Thus, if a donor makes a gift of a gun and rifle collection to a state historical museum, the donation would be use-related (the property donated to the charitable organization could be used directly by the charity itself). If the property donated to the charity is not related to the purpose of the charitable organization (such as a donation of a painting to a church that does not plan to exhibit the painting but intends, instead, to sell it and use the sales proceeds), then the donation is classified as use-unrelated. For purposes of obtaining a charitable contribution deduction, the distinction between a donation of use-related and use-unrelated tangible personal property can become significant, especially since the maximum charitable deduction on use-related property is normally 30 percent of the donor's adjusted gross income (subject to deducting the fair market value of the property) while the maximum charitable deduction on use-unrelated property is normally equal to the donor's basis in the property. Table 7.1 at the end of this chapter illustrates the amounts deductible, dependent on the type of property donated to a charity.

5. Future interest gifts of property to a qualified public charity ordinarily do not qualify for the charitable contribution deduction. By definition, a *future interest gift* is any gift in which the right to use or enjoy the property is deferred until some time in the future. Since there is no immediate right by the donee to use, possess, own, or enjoy the property or interest, the donee has not received the benefits of the gift and the donor has not ensured that the donee's use and enjoyment of the property have been completed in the year of the transfer. Because the rules that determine the deductibility of charitable contributions specifically state that the contribution must actually be paid in cash or other property before the close of the tax year, the

donor does not receive a charitable contribution deduction because the donee charity has not been "paid."

Thus, any gift of a future interest to a charity, such as a gift of an original Miro painting to an art museum with a stipulation that allows the donor to keep the painting until the donor's death is a gift of a future interest that does not qualify for the charitable contribution deduction.

Unless a gift of property to a charity is structured as a partial interest gift (with a present interest being gifted to one donee and the future interest being gifted to another donee), the donor will be unable to take a charitable contribution deduction. Many donors can still make a partial interest gift to a qualified charity that will qualify for a charitable contribution deduction if the donated property is transferred into some form of a charitable remainder trust. These trusts will be fully discussed later in this chapter.

Identity of the Donee

The identity of the donee can determine the maximum amount of a charitable contribution. For example, in the discussion of charitable contributions (see previous subsection, Type of Property), all of the examples used a *public* charity as the donee. Where the donee is a public charity, then the maximum annual charitable deduction is 50 percent of the donor's adjusted gross income for gifts of cash; 50 percent of the donor's adjusted gross income for gifts of ordinary income property (except where the donor is limited to the donor's basis in the property); 30 percent of the donor's adjusted gross income for long-term capital gain property (except where the donor may elect to deduct only the cost and become eligible for a 50 percent deduction based on 50 percent of the donor's adjusted gross income); the donor's basis in the property if the donor has held the property for less than 6 months prior to January 1, 1988, or for less than 1 year after December 31, 1987; 30 percent of the donor's adjusted gross income for contributions of tangible personal property to a public charity where the donated property is use-related; and the donor's basis in the property if the property is tangible personal property and is use-unrelated, with the ability to carry over any amount of the property in excess of 50 percent of the donor's adjusted gross income that is needed to match the donor's basis.

For donations of property to a *private* charity, the amount that can be deducted differs significantly. If the donee is a private charity, the maximum charitable contribution that can be taken in the year of the contribution is limited to the donor's basis in the property, if the property has appreciated in value since the date of its acquisition and the donee is a private nonoperating foundation, such as a grant-making institution.

By definition, a public charity includes any organization which is "qualified." This includes such organizations as nonprofit schools, universities, institutions of higher learning, churches, synagogues, the YMCA, the YWCA, the United Fund, the United Way, the American Red Cross, and the Boy Scouts and Girl Scouts of America. It also includes groups whose primary purpose is to assist in the discovery of a cure for a disease—organizations such as the Heart Association, the American Cancer Society, the American Diabetes Association, the Arthritis Foundation, and the Society for the Prevention of Blindness. As long as the organization has, as its primary purpose, some religious, educational, philanthropic, scientific, or literary purpose, and is intended to benefit the public at large, it most likely will meet the definition of a qualified public charity.

Note that the organization does not qualify for a charitable deduction if its purpose is to influence legislation or political ideologies. Thus, most political action committees and political action groups (e.g., Common Cause, the National Rifle Association, or any political group that hires lobbyists such as the American Dairy Association) cannot obtain a charitable deduction for donors who contribute property to such groups.

A contribution to a private charity also qualifies for the charitable contribution deduction. As long as the charity operates to provide an educational, scientific, philanthropic or humanitarian purpose, it will qualify for a charitable contribution deduction. Thus, if a private nonprofit foundation existed for the purpose of providing shelter, food, and medical services for abused women and children, the organization would qualify as a private charity and the donor would be eligible to take a charitable contribution deduction for property gifted to the organization (limited to the donor's basis in the property).

The maximum carryover period for a charitable contribution made to public charities as well as private charities is 5 years. Thus, if the donor has not been able to take the full value of the donated property as a charitable deduction within the 5-year period, the donor loses the amount of the deduction that could not be taken. This seldom occurs, however, since the 5-year time period provides most donors with ample opportunity to carryover charitable deductions that could not be taken in the year of the gift.

HOW THE TAX REFORM ACT OF 1986 AFFECTS THE MAXIMUM CHARITABLE DEDUCTION

Donors who previously made large charitable contributions to qualified charities must be especially cautious of the pitfalls that may lie dormant within the provisions of TRA '86. In particular, philanthropic clients need to be aware that certain charitable contributions of appreciated property will trigger the application of the alternative minimum tax (AMT) on the amount of gain if the donor otherwise is subject to the application of the alternative minimum tax.

Since the Tax Reform Act of 1986 eliminated the favorable tax treatment of long-term capital gains, it might appear that charitable contributions of property or cash by a donor might lose some of their attractiveness. Granted, because of a lowering in the overall income tax liability rates, a charitable contribution deduction will not provide the donor with as large a tax savings as the donor would have obtained under the old law. Nevertheless, a donor can still obtain valuable income tax, gift tax, or estate tax savings by making a charitable contribution of cash or other property as the charitable contribution for cash and ordinary income property is basically unchanged from what it was prior to TRA '86. As a result, donors should not disregard the planning opportunities provided by charitable contribution deductions.

TAX IMPLICATIONS OF GIFTING PROPERTY TO A QUALIFIED CHARITY

As stated previously, there can be significant estate, gift, and income tax implications resulting from a lifetime gift of property to a qualified charity. For a donor who gifts property that is appreciating in value, the lifetime gift removes the property and all further appreciation of it from the donor's gross estate. This can effectively "freeze" the estate tax liability in the donor's estate so as to prevent it from increasing, or it can also reduce the estate tax liability because the fair market value of the asset on the date of the gift is removed from the donor's gross estate.

A gift of property to a qualified charity can also provide the donor with significant income tax savings in the form of charitable deductions The deductions can be used to offset the donor's income tax liability, which may be fairly high. In addition, if the donated property is income-producing, the donor acquires additional income tax savings, because that income is no longer being received by the donor. Since the donor no longer receives this property, the income it produces is no longer taxable to him.

Finally, the gift of property to a qualified charity can produce significant gift tax savings for the donor. Since the gift is transferred to a qualified charity, the value of the gift is not subject to gift tax because of the gift tax charitable deduction. Thus, for a donor seeking to reduce estate, income, and gift taxes, a gift of property to a qualified charity may be appropriate to achieve these objectives.

PROPERTY AND INTERESTS THAT DO NOT QUALIFY FOR THE CHARITABLE CONTRIBUTION DEDUCTION

Certain items for which a donor may attempt to take a charitable contribution deduction are not eligible for such a deduction. In order to qualify properly for the charitable deduction, the item donated to the charity must either be cash or other property that is given in the year of the deduction. For this reason, certain items, which are considered neither cash nor property, are not deductible if "donated" to a qualified charity. Among these nondeductible items are the following:

1. **A donation of free rent or lease space:** If a donor makes a charitable contribution of free rent or leasing space to a charitable organization, this is not an income tax deductible expense to the donor. Similarly, if the donor creates a work of art that is later contributed to a qualified charity, the donor cannot deduct the lease space or studio rent for the time in which the donor created the work of art. Thus, a photographer or artist could not deduct the cost of rent for the time period in which the donated object was being created or produced. A donor is limited to a deduction that is measured by the donor's basis (usually cost) in the materials. All other expenses are nondeductible.

2. **Free use of property:** If a donor allows a qualified charity to use property belonging to the donor, for which the donor would normally charge a fee or cost, the donor cannot deduct the cost of the "free rent." For example, if a donor gives a qualified charity the free use of land or a "park area" owned by the donor, the donor cannot take this as a charitable contribution deduction even if the donor would have charged another individual for the use of the space. As a result, if a donor allows the American Cancer Society the free use of the donor's private fairground for the purpose of hosting a cancer awareness symposium, the donor cannot deduct the cost of allowing the Cancer Society to use the land free of charge.

3. **Personal and artistic services:** The donor's personal or artistic services cannot be deducted if those services were rendered in conjunction with the production of property that is donated to the charity. For example, if a sculptor creates a sculpture that is valued at $12,000, and donates it to a qualified charity, the sculptor will only be able to deduct the cost of materials used to produce the sculpture. Thus, if the donor estimates that $3,000 of materials were used, and estimates that the remaining $9,000 represents the sculptor's "artistic contribution," the donor can only deduct the cost of the materials. The value of the artistic contribution is a nondeductible expense.

4. Time: If a donor donates his or her time to produce a product or property that is later donated to a qualified charity, the donor cannot deduct the value of the time spent to produce the product. Thus, in the example of the sculpture given above, the sculptor-donor cannot deduct the value of the donor's time in producing the work of art. Thus, if the sculptor estimates that it took him 30 hours to create the work, and the sculptor would normally charge $50 per hour if the work were being produced for a noncharitable buyer, the value of the donor's time ($50 × 30 or $1,500) could not be deducted as a charitable contribution deduction, even if the donor would have charged the same fee to an interested buyer.

The conditions under which items may or may not be deducted need to be reviewed periodically by the financial planner with the client in order to avoid having the client audited or in order to avoid complications that can arise from incorrectly taking charitable deductions that are not available to the donor. These precautionary measures save both the financial planner and the client time as well as money, and can further promote a solid working relationship between the financial planner and client.

TYPES OF CHARITABLE TRANSFER TECHNIQUES

Various charitable transfer techniques are available to a donor who wishes to make a qualified charity the donee of a gift. All of these transfer techniques require that the donor make a completed irrevocable gift of the property to the qualified charity, or at least a completed irrevocable gift of a portion of the property (e.g., the income) to the charity. With some gifts, known as *partial interest gifts,* there are two donees: the qualified charity and a noncharitable beneficiary. Depending on the type of charitable transfer technique selected, either the charity or the noncharitable beneficiary can be the recipient of the income, while the remainder interest in the property is distributed to the nonincome recipient either upon the death of the noncharitable beneficiary or after a stated period of years. These types of partial interest gifts will be discussed later in this chapter.

If the selected charitable transfer technique is implemented properly, the transfer will accomplish gift tax savings for the donor through the use of the gift tax charitable deduction for the value of the property received by the charity. In addition, the selected transfer technique can generate income tax savings for the donor in the form of charitable contribution deductions as well as through the transfer of taxable income on income-producing property to the charity. Finally, if a sizeable amount of property is transferred during the donor's lifetime, the property reduces the size of the donor's gross estate and prevents further appreciation in the size of the estate thereby "freezing" the donor's estate tax liability. In addition, post-mortem transfers of property to a qualified charity are eligible for the estate tax charitable deduction and thus serve to reduce the size of the donor's taxable estate. The most commonly used types of charitable transfer techniques are featured on the following pages.

Outright Charitable Gift

This involves an irrevocable transfer of property from the donor to the qualified charity as donee. In order for the transfer to be considered effective, the donor must irrevocably part with all ownership or control of the property. If there are "strings attached" or conditions specified by the donor under which the property may be used or enjoyed by the donee, then a completed gift has not occurred. For example, if a donor makes a gift of an original Grant Wood painting to a qualified charity but specifies that the donor is allowed to keep the painting if the charity fails to endorse a philanthropic cause espoused by the donor, then a completed gift has not occurred. Further, the "gift" will not qualify for a gift tax charitable deduction, nor will it qualify for an income tax deduction in the form of the charitable contribution deduction. Finally, since the transfer is technically the retention of ownership (instead of a life estate), there will be no estate tax charitable deduction because the property fails to pass to the charity due to the unmet condition. Inclusion of the painting as an asset in the gross estate of the donor could prevent a reduction in the donor's administrative expenses and attorney's fees, since such fees are usually calculated as a percentage of the decedent's probate estate. Therefore, when a donor makes a gift of property to a qualified charity, the donor would be wise to consider an outright irrevocable transfer of the property to the charity rather than any other arrangement.

Net Gift

For a donor who would like to make a gift but who cannot afford to pay the gift tax liability on such a transfer, the donor may consider the net gifting technique. A net gift is used when the *donee* of the gifted property agrees to pay the gift tax liability on such a gift rather than having the donor pay the gift tax, as is normally done. The situations under which the net gift will be made are not frequently found, but occasionally the net gift will be used when the donor has already exhausted the total amount of available unified credit on prior lifetime gifts. In addition, the net gift technique will be used only for a noncharitable beneficiary who is a donee, since a gift to a qualified charity would not incur any gift tax liability. As a result, the only situations involving charitable donees in which the net gift technique would be used would be in situations in which a partial interest gift has been made and in which the donor would incur gift tax liability on the portion of the gift being received by the noncharitable beneficiary.

The net gift technique would be used primarily by the donor who has a liquidity problem and cannot afford to pay the gift tax on such a transfer. In most circumstances, if the donor has a severe liquidity problem and needs the property that is being contemplated as a gift, the donor would be in a better economic position by retaining ownership of the property rather than making an outright gift or net gift of the property to the donee.

However, there are certain advantages that are found by using the net gifting technique. One advantage is that the value of the gifted property is reduced, for gift tax purposes, by the amount of the gift tax paid by the donee. Thus, the value of the gift is less than its reportable fair market value at the time the gift is made, and the donee pays less gift tax than would be paid if the donor had paid the gift tax. A second advantage is that the donor can gift the property without a concern for payment of gift taxes. If the donor wishes to achieve a specific donative intent, such as seeing that a specified noncharitable beneficiary, such as a family member, receives, uses and enjoys the property in the donor's lifetime, the donor can use the net gift if the donor knows the marginal tax bracket of the donee and knows that the donee can afford to pay the gift tax liability. Since a net gift of property is a gift of a present interest, it qualifies for the gift tax annual exclusion so the gift tax liability for the donee may be minimal, especially if the donee has not used any of the unified credit available to the donee.

Gift of a Remainder Interest

Many donors wish to make a gift of property to a qualified charity when the donor owns property in which the donor has a present interest. However, there are occasions on which the donor wishes to make a gift of property to a qualified charity and the donor *has not yet received the property.* If the donor's right to receive the property is *vested,* meaning that the donor has an absolute right to receive the property at some indefinite time in the future, then the donor has a legal interest in the property yet to be received. This interest is known as a remainder interest. A common example of a remainder interest is the donor's right to receive the corpus of a trust after the lifetime income beneficiary dies.

Since the remainder interest to be received by the donor can be valued, for gift tax purposes, the property can appropriately be gifted even though the donor has not yet received it. Valuation of the remainder interest depends on a number of factors, including the life expectancy of the lifetime income recipient, the value of the property, and the projected date on which it is expected that the remainder interest will become a gift of a present interest for the donor. Based on these factors, the value of the remainder interest can be determined. As a result, a donor may wish to make a gift of a remainder interest in property to a qualified charity.

A gift of a remainder interest in property to a qualified charity ensures that the charity will receive the property on the termination of the life interest. Thus, the property is removed from the gross estate of the donor before it has actually been received. As a result, a gift of a future interest not only avoids gift tax liability if it is received by a donee charity, but also escapes estate tax liability and, if it is income-producing property, escapes income tax liability as well. Common examples of gifts of future interests in property that are gifted to qualified charities include the following: a gift of a remainder interest in the corpus of a trust, a gift of a remainder interest in a residence, and a gift of a remainder interest in stocks and bonds.

It should be noted that, since a gift of a remainder interest is a gift of a future interest, it does not qualify for the annual exclusion. However, if the gift is made to a qualified charity, it still escapes gift tax liability because of the gift tax charitable deduction. Also, it is possible for a gift of a remainder interest to qualify for both a gift tax charitable deduction and an income tax deduction where the donor is the recipient of the income stream for property in which the charity receives the future interest. Both CRATs and CRUTs are examples of such deductions.

Bargain Sale

For a donor who wishes to make a gift of property to a donee (charitable or otherwise) but who also needs a stream of income or a readily available source of liquidity, the bargain sale may be an appropriate technique. The bargain sale is a combination of both gift and sale of a specified property. The terms of the bargain sale are usually arranged so that the buying party pays less than fair market value for the property. The difference between the fair market value of the property and the price paid by the buyer is considered a gift.

For example, assume that the owner of farmland wishes to make a gift of the property to a qualified charity. Yet the landowner is cash poor and needs income from the property. If the landowner and charity could agree on terms, the landowner could sell the land to the charity at a price far below the fair market value of the land. In this case, assume the land has a fair market value of $100,000 but the landowner sells it to the charity for $50,000. The former owner of the land will receive $50,000 in proceeds, relieving him of the liquidity problem. In addition, the $50,000 "discount" on the value of the property represents a gift to the charity. Since the gift qualifies for the gift tax charitable deduction, the donor-seller will have no gift tax liability. In addition, the donor has reduced his gross estate by

$50,000 since he gave away property worth $100,000 but received only $50,000 in return.

The proper use of a bargain sale can reduce both estate and gift tax liability as well as provide the donor-seller with much needed cash. The bargain sale can also be used with noncharitable beneficiaries, but it should be noted that in such situations there could be potential gift tax liability for the portion of the sale representing the gift. Since the gift tax charitable deduction is not available for a gift to a noncharitable beneficiary, the donor could face gift tax liability if the amount representing the "gift" exceeds the amount of the annual exclusion, or if the donor has fully exhausted his or her available unified credit on prior lifetime gifts.

Charitable Stock Bailout

In situations where the owner of closely held stock wishes to make a gift of property to a qualified charity, the charitable stock bailout may be an appropriate charitable transfer technique. The charitable stock bailout works like this: Assume that the owner of stock (closely held) wishes to make a gift of property to a qualified charity. The stockholder may wish to obtain a sizeable income tax deduction in the form of a charitable contribution deduction. The stockholder can achieve this deduction by use of the charitable stock bailout. In the charitable stock bailout, the stockholder donates the property to the charity. The charity actually cannot use the stock as it is and would prefer the cash rather than the stock. Thus, the charity receives the stock but returns it to the corporation in the form of a redemption for cash. Thus, the stock is returned to the corporation, and it allows the donor-stockholder to retain corporate control when the redeemed shares return to the corporation. In addition, the charity now has the cash it wanted and the donor receives a valuable charitable contribution deduction measured by the fair market value of the donated stock.

When structuring the transaction for a charitable stock bailout, there are a number of considerations which need to be addressed in order to avoid adverse tax consequences. To qualify for a charitable contribution deduction, the stockholder and the charity cannot agree to the time or certainty of the redemption. In other words, at the time the stock is gifted to the charity there cannot be an understanding or contract (formal or informal) to redeem the stock at a specified time. If the redemption takes on the characteristics of a prearranged transaction, it tends to lose its charitable traits and may be construed as a contract to redeem, thereby disqualifying the donor from taking a charitable contribution deduction.

In addition, the donor should gift the stock to the charity and have the charity redeem the stock back through the corporation. If the corporation does not redeem the stock, a redemption of the stock directly to the shareholder would result in dividend treatment of the redeemed stock, and could result in taxable income to the donor. To preserve the estate, income and gift tax advantages of the charitable stock bailout for the donor of such stock, the recommendations listed should be followed closely if the client chooses this type of technique.

Charitable Remainder Annuity Trust (CRAT)

The charitable remainder annuity trust is the first of many featured partial interest gifts. A charitable remainder annuity trust is used in situations where the donor wishes to provide a noncharitable beneficiary (either the donor, the donor's spouse, or some third party) with a stream of income to last for a period of years, usually for the life of the income recipient or for a stated term of years. If a term of years is used, the period cannot exceed twenty years. This is also true of a charitable remainder unitrust (CRUT). At the termination of the period during which the beneficiary receives income, the remainder interest in the property passes to a qualified charity. The donor receives a present income tax deduction for the present value of the remainder interest which passes to the charity. Thus, the donor can take advantage of the income tax deduction during his lifetime, even though the remainder interest in the gifted property may not pass to the charity until after the death of the donor.

In addition to structuring the charitable remainder annuity trust to take effect during the life of the donor, such a trust can also be structured to take effect after the donor's death as a postmortem transaction. When structured as a postmortem transaction, the decedent's estate receives a valuable estate tax deduction based on the present value of the remainder interest eventually passing to the charity. For example, if a donor structures a charitable remainder annuity trust so that the donor's spouse receives a life income interest which takes effect when the donor dies, the donor's estate is entitled to receive an estate tax charitable deduction for the present value of the remainder interest that the charity will eventually receive.

In order to successfully use the charitable remainder annuity trust, the donor must comply with the following requirements:

1. The donor must make an irrevocable transfer of the property to the trust.

2. The donor can make only one initial transfer of property to the corpus; there can be no additions or increases to the corpus of the trust in later years.

3. Once the trust is established, the corpus must pay out a specified amount of income (a sum certain) each year—in a CRAT, the trust must pay a minimal amount of at least 5 percent of the initial value of

the corpus. If the trust does not generate at least enough income to meet this 5 percent requirement, the corpus must be invaded to supplement the difference. The income must be distributed to the beneficiary.

4. The amount of income payable to the trust beneficiary remains fixed once the initial payments are calculated. Thus, the amount of income payable by the trust to the beneficiary remains fixed and does not increase or decrease in succeeding years.

5. The amount of the charitable deduction that the donor can receive depends on the value of the remainder interest passing to the charity. Because the charity will eventually receive the corpus of the trust, the donor is entitled to an immediate income tax deduction for the present value of the property that passes to the charity as the remainderman. If the trust is structured to take effect upon the death of the donor, so that the donor's spouse or some other beneficiary receives the income, then the donor's estate receives an estate tax charitable deduction that is based on the present value of the charity's right to eventually receive the property.

If these requirements are complied with by the donor, he will be able to take advantage of the tax benefits associated with the use of the CRAT.

Charitable Remainder Unitrust (CRUT)

A donor may wish to make a charitable contribution of property in which a qualified charity receives the remainder interest while a noncharitable beneficiary receives the income interest. If the donor wishes to have a variable amount of income being distributed to the income beneficiary, then a charitable remainder unitrust or CRUT may be appropriate.

The CRUT operates in the same fashion as the CRAT, except that it has the following requirements:

1. The donor must make an irrevocable transfer of the property to the trust.

2. The donor can make more than one transfer of property to the trust; multiple transfers or deposits of property into the corpus of the trust are possible.

3. Once the trust is established, the corpus must pay out a specified amount of income (a fixed percentage) each year; in a CRUT, the trust must pay out a minimal amount of at least 5 percent of the annually reappraised value of the corpus. Thus, if in year one, $100,000 is placed in the corpus of the trust and the terms of the trust specify that 8 percent of the earnings must be distributed, then $8000 would be

distributed to the trust beneficiary. However, if the trust had actually earned $12,000 in year one, then the remaining undistributed $4000 would be added to the corpus of the trust and in year two, 8 percent of $104,000 or $8320 would be distributed to the trust beneficiary. Thus, if the assets in the trust are appreciating in value, this can generate an increase in income that is distributed to the trust beneficiary. As long as the undistributed earnings are added to the corpus of the trust and reappraised annually, the amount of income distributable to the beneficiary increases with each succeeding year.

It should be remembered, however, that if the value of the assets in the trust *decreases* or the corpus does not produce sufficient income, then the trust beneficiary could actually receive less income in a year subsequent to the establishment of the trust than in the original year the trust was established. This can be a serious disadvantage if the donor established the trust for the purpose of giving the beneficiary a stream of income that would serve as a hedge against inflation.

4. The amount of income produced by the trust increases with each year that the value of the corpus increases in value and this can be valuable to a trust beneficiary whose income needs increase with each succeeding year.

5. The amount of the charitable deduction that the donor receives depends on the value of the remainder interest passing to the charity. Because the charity will eventually receive the corpus of the trust, the donor is entitled to an immediate income tax deduction for the present value of the property that passes to the charity as the remainderman. If the trust is structured to take effect upon the death of the donor, so that the donor's spouse or some other beneficiary receives the income, then the donor's estate receives an estate tax charitable deduction that is based on the present value of the charity's right to eventually receive the property.

If these requirements are complied with by the donor, the donor will be able to take advantage of the tax benefits associated with the use of the CRUT.

Charitable Lead Trust

In some situations a donor may wish to provide a qualified charity with an immediate stream of income and transfer the remainder interest to a noncharitable beneficiary. If this is the case, then the charitable lead trust may be an appropriate charitable transfer technique for the donor.

The charitable lead trust is structured to provide a qualified charity with a stream of income for a stated period of years. Upon termination of the income stream to the charity, the trust terminates and the remainder interest (the corpus and any undistributed income) passes to a noncharitable beneficiary. Thus, in a charitable lead trust, the donor receives an immediate income tax deduction for the present value of the income stream received by the charity.

In order to successfully use the charitable lead trust, the donor must comply with the following requirements:

1. The donor must make an irrevocable transfer of property to the trust.
2. The income produced by the trust must be distributed to the charity. Unlike a CRAT or CRUT, the income in a charitable lead trust can be distributed to a charity for a period longer than 20 years.
3. The corpus of the trust must pass to a noncharitable beneficiary upon expiration of the lead income period. The corpus cannot be passed to a succeeding qualified charity.
4. The donor receives an immediate income tax deduction in the form of a gift to the charity. The gift is measured by the present value of the income stream being distributed to the charity. The amount of the charitable deduction is based not only on the length of time during which income is distributed to the charity, but also on the amount of property placed in the corpus. The donor receives an income tax deduction only as long as the donor is treated as the owner of the lead income for income tax purposes.

If these requirements are complied with by the donor, the donor will be able to take advantage of the tax benefits associated with the use of the charitable lead trust.

Pooled Income Fund

In certain situations a donor may wish to receive income from property transferred to a trust. If the donor wishes to receive the income from the earnings of property placed in the trust, as well as receiving a valuable gift tax deduction, he may wish to transfer assets to a charitable transfer technique known as a pooled income fund.

A pooled income fund is a trust arrangement in which the donor places property into a common trust fund. The donor's property is commingled with the property of other donors so that there is one common fund in which all deposits have been placed. Once placed into the trust, a public charity controls and manages the trust assets. After the income distribution on the trust assets terminates, the charity receives the remainder interest in the assets.

In order to successfully use the pooled income fund, the donor must comply with the following requirements:

1. The donor must make an irrevocable transfer of the property to the trust.

2. The property transferred to the trust is commingled with the property of other donors and the entire amount in the trust (pooled income fund) is managed by the charity.

3. The property transferred to the trust cannot be invested in tax-exempt securities.

4. The donor cannot be a trustee of the funds, nor can any income beneficiary be a trustee of the trust.

5. The donor retains for himself or herself or retains for the benefit of any other income beneficiary a life income interest.

6. Each beneficiary must receive a prorated share of the income from the pooled income fund and the income must be distributed on an annual basis.

7. Upon the death of the life income beneficiary, the remainder interest in the pooled income fund vests with the charity, which continues to maintain the pooled income fund.

8. The donor receives an income tax deduction for the present value of the remainder interest that is transferred to the charity. In addition, the donor receives a valuable gift tax deduction for the value of the property gifted to the charity as the remainder interest in the pooled income fund.

9. Beginning February 15, 1991, all pooled income fund instruments that continue to accept assets must establish a depreciation reserve account for any depreciable or depletable assets. In addition, the depreciation reserve amount must be determined in accordance with Generally Accepted Accounting Principles (GAAP).

If these requirements are met, the donor will be able to take advantage of the tax benefits associated with the use of the pooled income fund.

DETERMINING THE MOST APPROPRIATE CHARITABLE TRANSFER TECHNIQUE

After considering all of the characteristics of the various charitable transfer techniques, and the tax implications for each of these techniques, a financial planner may wish to consider the most appropriate charitable transfer technique. The most accurate method of determining the most appropriate charitable transfer technique for a client is the selection of a transfer technique that achieves all of his or her objectives.

If the donor wishes to receive a stream of income from the property while also qualifying the property for the gift tax charitable deduction as well as an income tax deduction, then the donor may wish to consider one of the various forms that provides the noncharitable beneficiary with a stream of income (e.g., a CRAT or a CRUT or a pooled income fund). If, however, the donor wishes to have the income beneficiary receive a variable amount of income rather than a fixed stream of income, then the CRUT is more appropriate than the CRAT.

If the donor wishes to have the charity receive a stream of income from the property and have the remainder interest pass to a noncharitable beneficiary, then the charitable lead trust is the most appropriate charitable transfer technique. If the donor wishes to remove property from the donor's gross estate while qualifying the transfer for the gift tax charitable deduction or estate tax charitable deduction, then the outright charitable gift may be the most appropriate transfer technique.

If the donor wishes to provide a stream of income to a noncharitable beneficiary but wishes to reduce current income tax liability, then the donor can use either a CRUT or a CRAT. If the income is distributed to either of them, the income will be taxed to the donor. However, the donor will receive a charitable income tax deduction that can be used to offset or reduce the tax liability that would otherwise occur on the income received.

Finally, the financial planner should always be reminded that the most appropriate charitable transfer technique is the technique which achieves the greatest number of client objectives.

Table 7.1 *CHARITABLE CONTRIBUTION DEDUCTIONS FOR GIFTED ASSETS*

Type of Property	50% Charities		Private Foundations		Other 30% Charities	
	Amt Deduct	% Limit	Amt Deduct	% Limit	Amt Deduct	% Limit
Cash	Cost	50	Cost	30	Cost	30
Ordinary income property, including life insurance, inventory, oil and gas property, Section 306 stock, market discount bonds, art work by its creator	Cost	50	Cost	30	Cost	30
Short-term capital gain property	Cost	50	Cost	30	Cost	30
Long-term capital gain property	Fair market value	30	Cost	20	Fair market value	20
Long-term capital gain property, if election is made to reduce the amount of the deduction	Cost	50	Not applicable		Not applicable	
Tangible personal property use-related	Fair market value	30	Fair market value	20	Fair market value	20
use-unrelated	Cost	50	Cost	20	Cost	20
Qualified appreciated stock	Not applicable		Fair market value	20	Not applicable	

8

POSTMORTEM PLANNING TECHNIQUES

INTRODUCTION

The proper planning of an estate often involves the use of various techniques that will reduce estate tax liability as well as transfer assets to intended beneficiaries. Though the transfer of assets occurs as a testamentary transaction, proper planning for the transfer begins while the client is still alive. These techniques, which establish a pattern of distribution for the assets of an individual at death, are referred to as postmortem planning techniques.

Postmortem planning techniques are a significant part of estate planning because they can achieve a number of client objectives, if properly utilized. Postmortem techniques can accomplish any of the following objectives:

1. A postmortem planning technique, if properly used, can reorder the distribution of a decedent's estate; this redistribution can distribute property to the surviving spouse or other heirs of the deceased, resulting in a more equitable distribution of the estate.

2. A postmortem planning technique, if properly used, can result in a lower overall amount of estate tax liability. The tax savings can be

achieved because of the optimal use of both the marital deduction and the unified credit, as well as the charitable deduction and other credits available to offset estate tax liability. In addition, further estate tax savings can occur by disclaiming certain property before it is received.

3. A postmortem planning technique, if properly used, can result in a lower amount of gift tax liability on lifetime gifts. If lifetime gifts are split between spouses, the amount of adjusted taxable gifts which form a part of the tentative tax base is smaller, and the estate pays a lower amount of estate tax as a result.

4. A postmortem planning technique, if properly used, can result in a lower amount of income tax liability. Certain elections can be made which can decrease income tax liability on income earned by the decedent prior to death and on income earned by the estate of the decedent after death. The effect of selecting these elections is to increase the amount of property which can be distributed to heirs, spouses, and other beneficiaries.

5. A postmortem planning technique, if properly used, can facilitate the transfer of property from the decedent to the intended beneficiary. This is especially true in the case of a decedent who owned a closely held business interest which may be difficult to transfer because of a liquidity problem. Certain postmortem elections can be used by the decedent's estate, such as special use valuation, Section 303 stock redemption, or using the installment method of paying estate tax, that will allow the decedent's estate to transfer the business interest to the intended beneficiary with greater ease.

6. A postmortem planning technique, if properly used, can preserve and protect certain property from creditors of the decedent's estate. For example, in many states, the homestead property and any property which qualifies as "exempt property" cannot be reached by the creditors of the decedent's estate. These post-mortem planning techniques thus serve to protect a certain amount of property for the spouse and children of the decedent.

7. A postmortem planning technique, if properly used, can result in lower probate costs and administrative expenses for the decedent's estate. For example, if a decedent dies and all of his family members and heirs can agree upon a distribution of the estate, an agreement of this nature can minimize the costs of litigation or administration of the estate. With lower administrative expenses and attorney's fees, there is a greater amount of property that can be distributed to heirs and other family members.

There may be other reasons why a decedent's estate may choose a particular postmortem planning technique. This list is not all-inclusive.

What is important about most postmortem planning techniques is that, to effectively use them in an estate plan, proper planning for use of the technique must begin during the decedent's lifetime.

It should also be noted that most postmortem planning techniques involve the use of some discretionary power. In other words, an *election* or decision must be made by someone that a particular postmortem planning technique will be used by the estate. Usually, the technique is elected by the estate's personal representative if the decedent dies without a will, by the estate's executor or by the person named in the will to serve in that capacity. It is important that the personal representative or executor actually make the election required to take advantage of the postmortem technique. If the election is not made, a court will not presume that it was the decedent's intention that the election be made, nor will a court assume that the executor intended to make the election without proper evidence of such an election. If the evidence of the election is not presented, the estate will not be granted the election and considerable estate, gift, and income tax savings could be lost. Therefore, it is extremely important that the election be made in a timely fashion and that the election comply with all legal requirements for a valid election.

There are over 25 different kinds of postmortem elections that can be used by an estate in an effort to redistribute property as well as generate estate, gift, and income tax savings. Most of these will be featured in this chapter. The characteristics of each of these postmortem planning techniques will be reviewed, as will the estate, gift, and income tax implications of the use of each of these techniques. After all postmortem planning techniques have been examined, this chapter will focus on the analytical process used to select the most appropriate postmortem planning techniques for a client's estate plan.

POSTMORTEM PLANNING TECHNIQUES

Qualified Disclaimer

As discussed earlier in Chapter 6, a qualified disclaimer may sometimes be used as a means of estate tax savings. As a postmortem planning technique, a qualified disclaimer is an invaluable technique that can reduce estate tax liability. Primarily, the qualified disclaimer can be used by the surviving spouse in situations where the estate of the first decedent has overqualified the estate for the marital deduction. Rather than waste the amount of the unified credit available to the first estate, the surviving spouse can file a qualified disclaimer over a portion of the inherited property. The amount of the disclaimed property remains in the taxable estate of the decedent and no longer qualifies for the marital deduction but is removed from the taxable estate of the surviving spouse. By keeping the property in the taxable estate of the decedent, the decedent's estate fully utilizes the amount of unified credit available to it, and there is an overall estate tax savings on the amount of estate taxes paid by *both* estates, as opposed to having the survivor's estate pay all of the estate tax.

Assume, for example, that a decedent left his surviving wife an estate valued at $1 million. If the entire amount qualified for the marital deduction, the decedent's estate would pay zero estate tax and the surviving spouse's estate would pay an estate tax of $194,000, assuming she died in 1987 or later with a total gross estate of $1.1 million ($1 million transferred to her from her late husband and $100,000 of her own property which she owned at the time of her death).

If, however, the surviving spouse filed a qualified disclaimer over $500,000 of the property received from her husband's estate, his taxable estate would be $500,000. If the wife died in 1987 or later, with a total gross estate of $600,000 ($500,000 transferred from her late husband, representing the amount that was not disclaimed and $100,000 of her own property), her estate tax liability on an estate of $600,000 would be $0. Her husband's estate would pay zero estate tax because the amount of his taxable estate, $500,000, is less than the exemption equivalent for a person dying in 1987 or a later year. If the disclaimer were filed, it would result in an overall estate tax savings of $194,000 (the difference between the $194,000 tax liability under the first arrangement and zero tax liability under the second arrangement). As a result, the qualified disclaimer can be used to achieve substantial estate tax savings.

A qualified disclaimer can also be used to transfer additional property to the surviving spouse, and thus qualify that property for the marital deduction, when the disclaimant is someone other than the surviving spouse. The effect of filing a qualified disclaimer may be that the property transfers to the surviving spouse under the residuary clause of the decedent's will. If this occurs, this property now qualifies for the marital deduction, and the estate of the decedent will pay less estate tax than it would have if the disclaimer had not been filed. This can result in greater estate tax savings than those originally established by the initial estate plan.

In order to be considered a qualified disclaimer, the disclaimer must meet all of the following requirements:

1. It must be irrevocable in nature and must be an unqualified refusal by a person to accept an interest in the property.
2. The disclaimer must be in writing.
3. The written refusal must be received by the grantor of the interest, the grantor's legal representative, or the holder to the title of the property being transferred. The refusal must be received no later than 9 months after the date on which the transfer was created, or in

the case of a minor, 9 months after the date on which the minor disclaimant reaches age 21.

4. The disclaimant must not have received any of the benefits or any interest in the property that was disclaimed. If any benefits (e.g., income from the property, the right to use and enjoy the property) have occurred, the disclaimer is null and void.

5. As a result of filing the disclaimer, the property must pass from the disclaimant to either: (a) the spouse of the decedent grantor, or (b) some person other than the disclaimant. The transfer of the property cannot be at the suggestion of or according to the preferences of the disclaimant. If the disclaimant could determine who would receive the property if the disclaimant chose to refuse it, the disclaimant would be exercising an incident of ownership over the property, thus nullifying the effect of the disclaimer.

Under certain circumstances, it is possible for an individual receiving a bequest of property to file a *partial disclaimer,* thus receiving some of the property but not all of it. This is especially appropriate in situations where the recipient wishes to enjoy some of the property or its benefits, but also wishes to take advantage of the tax savings generated by the filing of the partial disclaimer. However, in order to file a partial disclaimer the property subject to the disclaimer must be capable of partition or severance (e.g., stocks or bonds) and the disclaimer must specify the property that is being disclaimed.

The net effect of filing a qualified disclaimer is to treat the property as if it had never been received by the disclaimant. This is significant for gift tax purposes. If the disclaimant chooses to forego the use and enjoyment of the property, but fails to meet all of the qualifications for a qualified disclaimer, then the transaction will be treated as if the disclaimant has made a gift of the property to the individual who eventually receives it. Under these circumstances, the disclaimant could be subject to gift tax liability if the value of the property exceeds the amount of the annual exclusion, or if the disclaimant has already fully exhausted the amount of available unified credit on other lifetime gifts.

In some states, it is possible for the surviving spouse to file a qualified disclaimer on property held in joint tenancy with right of survivorship. As long as the surviving spouse does not participate in the use or enjoyment of the property disclaimed, the disclaimer will be regarded as qualified if it meets the state's definition of "qualified disclaimer," and if it meets the requirements of a qualified disclaimer for federal tax purposes. In one recent case[1] a federal district court held that the surviving spouse had effectively disclaimed her undivided one-half interest in certain jointly held real property, where the property had originally been acquired by the spouses in 1943, but where the disclaimer was filed within 7 months of the death of the husband in 1979. In that case, the federal district court determined that the surviving spouse's survivorship interest in the husband's property was created at the time of the husband's death and that, under applicable state law (Nebraska) she did not possess this interest prior to her husband's death. Therefore, the spouse could file a qualified disclaimer over this portion of the property and was entitled to a refund of gift taxes that had been previously paid on the transfer.

What is crucial in cases like this is the issue as to when the interest in the property being disclaimed was created. If the state law deems that the interest in the jointly held property is created at the time the joint tenancy was created, then the surviving spouse must disclaim the property within 9 months after the creation of the joint tenancy and *before* any benefits are received from the property, either directly or indirectly. If the state law deems that the interest in the jointly held property is created at the time the surviving spouse receives the decedent's undivided one-half interest in the property, then the one-half interest received as a result of the first decedent spouse's death may be effectively disclaimed within 9 months from the date of death. Because of these variations in local law, a licensed attorney should always be consulted before attempting to transfer or disclaim particular property. What may be an effective disclaimer in one state may be an ineffective transfer in another.

Disclaimer Trust

This postmortem planning technique is a consequence of disclaiming a portion of property. In a marital situation, it is sometimes possible that the surviving spouse may wish to receive income from property that the spouse also wishes to disclaim. In special situations, it is possible to do both so that the property is disclaimed but the surviving spouse receives a stream of income from the disclaimed bequest. This can be accomplished through the use of a *disclaimer trust*. This trust, which is irrevocable in nature, is established for the benefit of the surviving spouse. The trust is usually included as a clause in the decedent's will, thereby making it testamentary in nature. Should the surviving spouse decide to disclaim a portion of the bequest or all of the bequest, the bequest is transferred to the irrevocable trust and the income is paid in regular intervals to the surviving spouse. Since the spouse now has only a terminable interest in the income (which does not qualify for the marital deduction in the estate of the first decedent spouse), the disclaimed property will not be included in the gross estate of the surviving spouse.

In order for the disclaimer trust to be effective, the disclaimed bequest that forms the corpus of the trust must be irrevocably transferred to the trust. The spouse cannot retain any powers to invade the corpus or consume any portion of the corpus. In addition, the spouse may only receive the income for life, and only at those times specified in the terms of the trust agreement (e.g., once per year). If the spouse can demand income at his discretion, or if the spouse can invade the corpus to consume a greater amount of income, he will be deemed to possess incidents of ownership over the corpus and the disclaimer will fail.

Homestead Allowance

Traditionally, most states have afforded some degree of protection to the owner of a residence should he or she die with a substantial amount of debt. The "homestead allowance" has preserved the residence and adjacent land for the benefit of the surviving spouse and the decedent's minor children. The homestead is thus protected against the claims of creditors in recognition of the custom that the decedent's spouse and children should not lose their principal dwelling because of the death of the decedent. The insulation of the homestead from the claims of creditors is usually preserved when the homestead passes to the surviving spouse or the children of the decedent. Thus, the homestead is a significant means of preserving the family home for the family of the decedent.

Most state statutes define the property that qualifies for the homestead as including the dwelling house and the adjacent property. The amount of the adjacent property that qualifies for the homestead can vary from as little as half an acre in a city to 40 acres or more if located in a rural area. In urban areas, the state homestead statute may define the homestead allowance as a dollar amount (e.g., $20,000) rather than as an interest in real estate.

During the period of estate administration, the surviving spouse is entitled to live in the homestead and this right continues until probate is completed and the homestead is set off specifically for the spouse or other family member. The property qualifying for the homestead cannot be claimed by creditors and is exempt from the payment of debts and charges against the estate.

The homestead does not lose its character as a homestead even if it is transferred to a trust. Thus, where the homestead and adjacent qualifying real property have been transferred to a trust for the benefit of the spouse for life with the remainder passing to the children, the dwelling and adjacent land retain their character as a homestead and are still insulated from the claims of creditors of the decedent's estate. The definition of what constitutes a homestead will vary from state to state. Therefore, the particulars of state law will need to be consulted to determine how the homestead can be preserved. Most states do require that if the homestead is to be relied on when one spouse dies, the couple must file a homestead allowance at some time after the property is purchased. Failure to file the homestead exemption could cause the property to become subject to the claims of creditors of the decedent's estate.

Exempt Property Award

Most states have some form of laws which give the surviving spouse the right to receive certain personal property free from the claims of creditors. The property that is insulated from the claims of creditors of the decedent's estate is known as exempt property.

Most states specify the personal property that the surviving spouse is entitled to receive. This exempt property usually includes at least some of the following:

1. Vehicles used in the decedent's trade or business, along with tools of the decedent's trade
2. Particular household furnishings
3. In farming states, livestock and feed for a period of at least 6 months after the date of the decedent's death
4. Firearms and guns and rifles, up to a stated amount
5. All wearing apparel and clothing, up to a stated amount
6. Private libraries, pictures and paintings, up to a stated amount
7. An unmatured life insurance policy owned by the decedent-debtor
8. The decedent's rights in social security benefits, unemployment compensation, and veteran's benefits and disability benefits
9. Alimony, support, and separate maintenance monies due to the decedent and reasonably necessary for the support of the decedent-debtor and the dependents of the decedent
10. In the event the decedent filed a bankruptcy petition prior to death, the decedent's interest in accrued wages and state and federal tax refunds.

Since exempt property is defined as such by each state, the particular laws of each state must be examined before determining the status of personal property as either exempt or nonexempt. The exempt property award can provide the surviving spouse with invaluable protection against the claims of creditors of the decedent's estate. Property that meets the definition of exempt can be subjected to the claims of creditors at the surviving spouse's election. If the surviving spouse chooses, exempt property that is part of his share of the decedent's estate can become subject to the claims of creditors.

The effect of both the homestead allowance and the exempt property statutes are to provide the surviving spouse with a greater share of the decedent's estate than the spouse would otherwise receive. As such, both the homestead and the exempt property statutes provide considerable protection to those individuals for whom the decedent would have provided.

Election Against the Will by the Surviving Spouse

Another valuable postmortem technique that can serve to reorder the distribution of a decedent's estate is an election to take against the will by the surviving spouse. This election is provided to most surviving spouses under a state law known as "the elective share statute." According to the elective share statute, the surviving spouse is accorded a certain percentage of the decedent's estate (e.g., 50% of the estate if the decedent is not survived by living children and $33^{1}/_{3}\%$ if the decedent is survived by living children). The statute ensures that the surviving spouse will be entitled to at least the minimum proportion of the estate as determined by the statute so that, in the event the decedent leaves the surviving spouse an amount of property under the terms of the decedent's will that is less than the minimum amount guaranteed by the statute, the surviving spouse is free to file an election with the probate court, and specify that he or she is requesting a greater share of the decedent's estate than that left to him or her under the terms of the will.

If the decedent's will only left a quarter of the estate to the surviving spouse and the spouse files the election in order to gain a half of the estate, the election serves to redistribute the decedent's estate in a manner other than that prescribed by the will. As a result of this election, the additional quarter of the estate that is transferred to the spouse must come from those other beneficiaries who received the property according to the terms of the will. To satisfy the spouse's share, the other beneficiaries' shares must be reduced proportionally. This proportional reduction which occurs to satisfy the statutory requirement of guaranteeing the spouse a minimum percentage of the estate is referred to as *abatement*. Thus, an election against the will can effectively redistribute a large portion of the decedent's estate even though the decedent dies with a will.

Will Contest

A will contest, as previously discussed in Chapter 2, can also effectively redistribute a decedent's estate if it is successful. Basically, a will contest requires that an individual who would otherwise be the natural object of the decedent's love and affection be disinherited or receive a substantially smaller portion of the estate than they would ordinarily receive.

In order to be successful, the individual challenging the validity of the will or the validity of the terms of the will must be able to prove *any one* of the following:

1. That the maker of the will was not of sound mind at the time the will was drafted.

2. That the maker of the will was unduly influenced by another individual at the time the will was drafted and this undue influence had a direct impact on the way in which the maker distributed his or her property.

3. That the maker was fraudulently deceived by another individual at the time the will was drafted, and as a result of this fraud an individual was disinherited or received a reduced portion of the estate; this individual would otherwise have received a greater portion of the estate.

4. That the maker of the will suffered from an insane delusion at the time the will was drafted.

If the individual filing the will contest can prove any of these, the will provisions shall be rendered null, at worst; at best, the will contest will cause the decedent's property to be redistributed in such a fashion that the contestant will receive the same proportion of property that he or she would have received as an heir under the terms of the state's intestate succession laws. The effect of the will contest would cause the contestant to receive a share of the estate that otherwise would have gone to others. In this sense, the will contest would operate the same as a statute for a surviving spouse who elects to take against the will. Another individual's share of the estate would have to abate or be reduced in order to satisfy the contestant's share.

It is important to remember that the contestant has a heavy burden of proof in a will contest, since it is usually difficult to establish that another person was of unsound mind or suffered from an insane delusion at the time the will was drafted. Because the burden of proof is a heavy one, many individuals who file a will contest are not successful in their attempt to prove fraud, coercion, or mental instability. As a result, many contestants can spend large sums of money and several years in court trying to prove their case and find themselves unsuccessful several years later. Therefore, contestants should challenge a will only if they believe they have sufficient proof that will hold up in court.

Family Settlement Agreements

An informal means of redistributing a decedent's estate is by means of a family settlement agreement. The family settlement agreement usually provides a quick, efficient way of distributing the decedent's assets.

Shortly after the decedent's death, all family members and heirs of the deceased gather to determine how the estate should be distributed. If all family members can agree on the disposition of the estate, and if all debts, taxes, and charges against the estate are paid, the remainder of the estate can be divided among family members according to the terms of the agreement. The agreement is almost always in writing and *must* be in writing if real estate is a part of the conveyed property.

After all family members agree to the distribution of the estate in a particular fashion (the consent of *all* family members or their legal representatives is necessary), the agreement is submitted to the probate court for its subsequent approval. If the probate court determines that the terms of the agreement are unconscionable, or determines that one or more of the parties are harmed by the terms of the agreement, the court can refuse to allow the agreement to be enforced. If the court determines that the agreement equitably divides the property between family members, and determines that all debts, expenses, and taxes have been paid, the court will enter an order approving the terms of the family settlement agreement.

The family settlement agreement is advantageous because it is not time-consuming and helps to effectively reduce the amount of probate expenses and administrative costs. It can be used to prevent will contests and other delays in probate of the estate.

Election of the Q-TIP by the Executor of the Estate

A valuable postmortem planning technique that can be used to reduce the decedent's estate tax liability is the election of the Q-TIP on certain property that is terminable by nature. The executor of the decedent's estate makes an election on the federal estate tax return of the decedent; by filing this election, property which would otherwise not qualify for the marital deduction is allowed to qualify. As a result, the property is removed from the taxable estate of the decedent and reduces the decedent's estate tax liability. However, as a result of filing this election, the property must be included in the gross estate of the surviving spouse, even though the surviving spouse is only entitled to receive the income from the property for the rest of the spouse's life.

Whether the executor elects to have the property treated as qualifying for the marital deduction depends on a number of factors. The decision to treat the terminable property as Q-TIP property depends on such factors as: the size of the decedent's estate, the size of the surviving spouse's estate, the needs of the surviving spouse (whether the surviving spouse needs a stream of income from the Q-TIP property), and the needs of other family members (whether the children or other heirs of the decedent have been bequeathed any property under the terms of the decedent's will).

If the surviving spouse needs a stream of income from the property, and if the decedent wishes to bequeath the property to other family members after the surviving spouse dies and if the decedent has a need to reduce estate tax liability by qualifying an additional amount of property for the marital deduction, then the executor should qualify the property as Q-TIP property. Normally, the executor is given this choice under the terms of the decedent's will. In fact, some wills contain an express clause *requiring* the executor to make the election. Failure of the executor to make the election causes the property to remain in the taxable estate of the decedent. If this causes additional estate tax liability and increased administrative and probate costs, so that the decedent's wife, family members, and other designated beneficiaries receive a smaller portion of the estate than originally intended, the spouse and family members may bring legal action against the executor for failing to follow the express commands of the decedent.

Filing a Joint Income Tax Return

An important postmortem planning technique that can reduce income tax liability for the surviving spouse and the decedent's estate is the filing of a joint income tax return for the portion of the calendar year in which the decedent was alive. By filing a joint income tax return for that portion of the calendar year, the income tax liability can be reduced because of the lower tax liability occurring for a married couple as opposed to the tax rates imposed on a single person for an identical amount of taxable income.

If the joint return is filed for that portion of the taxable year in which the decedent was alive, the tax savings achieved by the filing of the joint return can result in a greater amount of the decedent's estate available for distribution to the spouse, children, or other designated beneficiaries. Before making this election, however, the surviving spouse should consult with the financial planner, the accountant, and the decedent's attorney to ensure that the filing of the joint return is in the best interests of the surviving spouse and other family members as well as being in the best interests of the decedent's estate.

Deduction of Medical Expenses on the Decedent's Final Income Tax Return

It is sometimes valuable for an estate to have the medical expense deductions for the decedent's last illness deducted on the final income tax return rather than on the decedent's federal estate tax return. This postmortem election can be made by the executor of the decedent's estate or by the decedent's spouse. The postmortem election may be appropriate in the following circumstances.

Where a decedent dies with a gross estate that is less than the amount of the exemption equivalent, there is no federal estate tax liability. This is also true in situations where the decedent's estate exceeds the exemption equivalent, but where the decedent has utilized both the unified credit and the marital deduction to take advantage of tax savings. In either of these situations, the marital deduction and unified credit amounts absorb all estate tax liability. As a result, when the medical expenses and expenses of the decedent's last illness are deducted on the federal estate tax return, the advantage of taking the deduction is lost since the estate has already escaped any tax liability. Because of this situation, it is preferable to deduct these expenses on the decedent's last income tax return, where these expenses may be fully deductible and result in lower income tax liability. The election to deduct these expenses can thus achieve an overall reduction in *both* income tax liability *and* estate tax liability.

The election to deduct the final medical expenses on the decedent's final income tax return can only be achieved under certain circumstances, however. If the final medical expenses are fully reimbursed through insurance or other payments, then the expenses cannot be deducted on *either* the income tax return or the estate tax return. Finally, in situations where the expenses could be deducted on *either* return, a projection of the tax liability must be calculated using both returns so that the greatest overall tax savings can be realized.

Election to Allow the Increase in the Redemption Value on EE or HH Bonds to Accrue on the Decedent's Final Income Tax Return

Another valuable postmortem planning technique that can be used to achieve greater tax savings is an election to allow the increase in the redemption value on EE or HH savings bonds to accrue on the decedent's final income tax return (Form 1040) instead of reporting it as income in respect of a decedent (Form 1041). Form 1040 would be used to report all income actually or constructively received prior to the date of the decedent's death in a particular calendar year, while income in respect of a decedent would be reported on a separate tax return. This form 1041 would be filed to report any income *earned* by the decedent prior to death but not yet *received* at the date of death. Although an election can be made to report the total increase in the value of the bonds to date in any one year prior to actual redemption, the estate or the surviving spouse (if named as personal representative or executor of the estate) can defer the reporting of the increase in the bonds until the time when the estate's final income tax return is filed.

If the bonds were owned individually by the decedent and the decedent's executor elects to report the increase in the redemption value of the bonds as of the date of death on the final income tax return (Form 1040), there is no income in respect of a decedent to be reported and there is no corresponding deduction for expenses related to the income earned in respect of the decedent on the final Form 1040.

In addition, there may be an estate tax deduction for the increase in the amount of personal income tax liability resulting from the deferral of the increase in redemption value. Finally, the beneficiary who receives the bonds as a bequest from the decedent's estate need only report as taxable income the increase in the value of the bonds after the date of the decedent's death. These considerations may make the deferral of the increase in the value of the bonds an attractive postmortem technique.

Selection of a Taxable Year for the Estate

For estates that receive income earned in respect of the decedent, the executor or personal representative of the estate has the option of selecting a taxable year for the estate. For an estate that receives considerable income that is classified as income earned in respect of a decedent (Form 1041), the structuring of a fiscal year can be important in reducing income tax liability, especially if the decedent is filing a final income tax return (Form 1040) in the same calendar year. It is advantageous for the *estate* to have a different income tax year from that of the *decedent* for income which must be reported on a final income tax return on a calendar year basis.

Examples of income earned in respect of a decedent that can be reported in a year other than the calendar year of the decedent's death include the following:

1. Compensation for services rendered by the decedent prior to death and not received by the decedent during the decedent's lifetime

2. Investment income earned by the decedent after the date of death, including dividends and interest

3. Rental income earned by the decedent's estate after the date of death

4. Periodic payments received by the estate for patent and copyright interests

5. Proceeds of an installment sale received by the decedent's estate where the sale was completed prior to the date of death

6. Partnership income earned by the partnership after the date of death and attributed to the deceased partner's respective share of the partnership

7. Income earned by an S corporation for the part of the corporation's tax year after the shareholder's death (any income earned by an S corporation and attributable to the shareholder prior to the end of the corporate tax year is not income in respect of a decedent and is reported on the decedent's final income tax return—Form 1040)

8. Back payments and delayed payments of support or alimony paid to the estate after the death of the recipient

9. Damages paid to the estate of the decedent where such damages would have been income had the decedent lived to receive them (e.g., punitive damages).

Subchapter S Election

In certain circumstances, a decedent or decedent's estate may be able to enjoy significant income tax savings by filing a Subchapter S election on corporate stock. If the corporation meets all of the requirements necessary for Subchapter S treatment, the stock will not be taxed at the regular corporate rates. Rather, the income or dividends earned by the shareholder will avoid the double taxation that is inherent in a corporate structure; that is, the dividends are taxed once to the corporation as earnings and are taxed again as ordinary personal income when received by the shareholder. If Subchapter S treatment is elected, the income will be taxed only once and the shareholder will pay the tax liability on the income as if it were partnership income. Thus, significant income tax savings can be generated by filing a Subchapter S election.

The Subchapter S election can be filed by an individual shareholder while alive or can be filed by the shareholder's estate. Filing of the Subchapter S election can be beneficial for the estate of the deceased shareholder, since the election permits the shareholder's estate to deduct corporate losses against other income and permits the transfer of investment credit directly to an individual shareholder or shareholder's estate from the corporation. If Subchapter S treatment is elected while the shareholder is alive, income tax savings can be generated by intrafamily gifts of stock which enable income-splitting to occur.

In order to qualify for Subchapter S treatment, the corporation cannot have more than 35 shareholders, and cannot have more than one class of stock. Differences in voting rights are permitted, however. If the Subchapter S election is made by the shareholder's estate, such an election requires the consent of all other shareholders. If the election was made while the shareholder was still alive, and some of the other shareholders now want to refuse to give the Subchapter S treatment at the time one of the shareholders dies, only those shareholders who previously consented to the election can now refuse to give their consent. In other words, new shareholders who acquired their interests since the time when the election was initially made are bound by the prior election unless more than 50 percent of the corporate stock is acquired by new shareholders. In the event more than 50 percent of the stock is acquired, the new shareholders are not bound by the prior election.

Conversely, a shareholder who consented to Subchapter S treatment while alive may have his or her estate refuse to consent to such treatment at the time the decedent's estate is probated. The refusal to give consent to have the decedent shareholder's stock treated as a Subchapter S corporation may stem from the fact that the decedent's individual tax rates may be higher than the corporate rates. Thus, to achieve greater income tax savings it may be advisable to have the stock taxed as conventional corporate income as opposed to being taxed as if it were partnership income. The advice of a financial planner, accountant, or tax attorney may be necessary before making this election or before refusing to make the election.

Election to Increase the Basis in Partnership Assets at the Partner's Death

For income tax purposes, a partnership does not cease upon the death of a partner even though, for business purposes, the partnership ceases to exist. For a partnership interest that is included in an individual's gross estate, the deceased partner's interest ordinarily receives a step-up in basis while the basis of the assets held by the partnership generally do not receive a step-up in basis. As a result, if a partnership asset is sold after the death of one of the partners, the gain on the appreciated partnership asset may have to be reported by the estate of the deceased partner.

To avoid this adverse estate tax implication and to avoid the adverse income tax implication for the partnership asset, a special election may be filed which allows the deceased partner to receive an increase in the basis of the partnership assets. By filing the special election, the deceased partner receives a step up in basis on the deceased's proportional share of the partnership assets. The election can only be filed by the partnership itself; the effect of filing such an election is to increase the basis of the partnership interest that is an asset in the deceased partner's gross estate.

As a result of filing the election, the deceased partner's estate has its own private basis for all purposes, including distribution of property to the estate in kind, depreciation allowances, and recognition of gain upon sale of the property by the partnership. Usually, little gain will have to be reported on sale of the partnership asset. Filing of the election causes the deceased partner's basis in the partnership, often referred to as the outside basis, to differ from the basis of the partnership in its own assets, referred to as the inside basis.

Once the election is filed by the partnership the election is normally irrevocable and can only be revoked for business reasons and only with the permission of the Internal Revenue Service. It should also be noted that an election to increase the basis of partnership assets can be disadvantageous at a later stage in the partnership. For example, if, upon the subsequent death of another partner, the fair market value of the partnership has decreased in value so that the value of the partnership has fallen below that partner's basis in the property, the filing of the election would require a downward adjustment of the deceased partner's interest to the inside basis of the partnership. Thus, the deceased partner's estate might have to report a loss on the value of the partnership assets.

Election by the Surviving Spouse to Split Gifts Made by the Decedent

A special postmortem election can be filed by the surviving spouse that can result in reduced gift tax rates as well as reduced estate tax rates for the decedent's estate. This election is known as the election by the surviving spouse to split gifts that were made by the decedent. The surviving spouse can file an election to have the gifts made by the decedent treated as if both spouses had made the gift. Thus, for a decedent who made $100,000 in taxable gifts to his son, with a resultant gift tax liability of $23,800, the election by the surviving spouse to split the gifts would result in tax liability for each spouse of $9400, for a total net savings of $5000 (the difference between $23,800 for the decedent and the combined sums of $18,800 for both spouses).

With the increase in the amount of gift tax savings, a greater portion of the decedent's estate can be transferred to family members and other beneficiaries. In addition, since there is now a decreased amount of adjusted taxable gifts that are returned to the estate to form the tentative tax base (due to the use of two annual exclusion amounts instead of only one), there is a decrease in the overall amount of tax due on the federal estate tax return as well. Thus, the election by the surviving spouse to split the decedent's lifetime gifts decreases both the amount of gift tax liability and estate tax liability and serves to distribute a greater portion of the decedent's estate to family members, beneficiaries, or heirs.

Waiver of Executor's Commissions and Fees

Often, when the surviving spouse is named as executor of the decedent's estate, it is beneficial to have him or her waive the right to receive executor's commissions or other fees associated with being a fiduciary for the decedent's estate.

If the decedent dies with a small estate or an estate that is not subject to the payment of estate tax because of the unlimited marital deduction, it is perhaps a better idea for the surviving spouse to waive the receipt of such commissions. From a tax standpoint, the surviving spouse would have to report as taxable income the money received as an executor's commission for handling the estate of the deceased. Yet, if these commissions were waived, there would be fewer administrative costs (deductible to the estate) and there would be a greater portion of the estate that could pass *estate tax free* to the surviving spouse in the form of the unlimited marital deduction.

Since the property is still being received by the surviving spouse (only in the form of the marital deduction rather than as taxable income), the intentions of the deceased are still being followed while avoiding *both* estate tax liability and income tax liability. Under these circumstances, the surviving spouse is in a better position if he or she waives the receipt of these fees and commissions. The surviving spouse may make such an election but such a decision is irrevocable once made. Before deciding whether to waive the executor's commissions and fees, the surviving spouse should consult with the financial planner, tax attorney, and accountant to determine whether such a course of action is appropriate. Such factors as the size of the decedent's estate, the size of the surviving spouse's estate, the financial needs of the spouse, the marginal tax bracket of the surviving spouse, and the financial needs of the decedent's minor dependents need to be examined before making a final determination on waiver of these fees and commissions.

Use of Alternate Valuation Date

The personal representative or executor of a decedent's estate may file an election to have the assets included in the decedent's gross estate valued at their alternate value, which is the value they have 6 months after the date of the decedent's death. Thus, the assets will be valued at the value they hold on this date rather than at their value on the date of the decedent's death. If the assets have depreciated in value since the time of the decedent's death, it may be advisable to use the value these assets had on the alternate valuation date.

There are certain conditions which must exist in a decedent's gross estate before the personal representative or executor can elect to have the assets valued using the alternate valuation method. All of the following conditions must occur before this method can be used:

1. The use of the alternate valuation date must cause a reduction in the total value of the decedent's gross estate.
2. The amount of federal tax liability must be reduced as a result of filing the election.
3. Use of the alternate valuation date must be uniform and universally applied to all assets.
4. The alternate valuation date cannot be used on assets that have a value that decreases with the mere passing of time, for example, a joint and last survivor annuity that decreases in value with each succeeding payment. Thus, if the estate includes a joint and last survivor annuity, alternate valuation cannot be used on the annuity because of the nature of the asset; since it cannot be used on this asset,

the annuity must be valued at its fair market (date of death) value while all other assets are valued at their alternate value.

Note that the alternate valuation date can only be used if it would actually decrease the amount of estate tax liability due from the estate. Thus, if an estate were valued at $1 million, it could not use the alternate valuation method if the entire estate had been left to the surviving spouse in the form of the unlimited marital deduction. Since this estate would not have had any estate tax liability in the first place, the use of the alternate valuation method for this estate would not have actually reduced the amount of estate tax liability. Therefore, it could not be used as a means of valuing the estate. As a planning consideration, the surviving spouse could disclaim a portion of the bequest so that the decedent's estate had estate tax liability; then, by use of the alternate valuation method, the tax liability could be reduced to zero. Thus, in cases where alternate valuation could save the estate a significant amount of estate tax liability, the surviving spouse may wish to disclaim a portion of the decedent's estate, thereby qualifying the estate for the use of the alternate valuation method while ensuring that others (e.g., children) receive a portion of the decedent's estate.

In certain situations, the use of the alternate valuation method may actually increase the basis in certain assets for specified purposes. Under the Internal Revenue Code provisions, if alternate valuation is used as an estate planning valuation method, the estate tax value of the property becomes the income tax basis of those assets. Assuming the estate contains depreciating property that will be permanently retained by the beneficiaries of the estate (e.g., real estate) as well as appreciating property that will be sold shortly after it is transferred to the beneficiaries (e.g., stocks and bonds), the use of alternate valuation on the estate assets will give the stocks and bonds a higher income tax basis (the estate tax value of the stocks and bonds, using alternate valuation, becomes the income tax basis of those items) and a reduced amount of income tax liability when the stocks and bonds are finally sold.

For these reasons, the executor or personal representative may wish to consider the advantages and disadvantages of using the alternate valuation method for assets included in the gross estate.

Use of Special Use Valuation

If an estate includes real property (land) that is used in farming, ranching, timberland production, or any other closely held business use, the personal representative or executor of the estate may elect to have the real property valued at a value other than its highest and best use (its customary value). The election to have the real property valued at its actual use as opposed to its highest and best use is referred to as the special use valuation.

In order to qualify for special use valuation, the estate of the decedent must meet a series of qualifications that enable the estate to take advantage of the reduced valuation. If an estate is successful in meeting these qualifications, the reported value of the real estate used in the closely held business can be reduced by as much as $750,000, with a resultant reduction in estate tax liability for the decedent's estate.

The requirements necessary for becoming eligible to elect the special use valuation include the following:

1. At least 50 percent of the adjusted value of the gross estate (the gross estate minus unpaid mortgages, liens, etc.) must consist of real property (land) and personal property (machinery, equipment, inventory) used for agricultural or business purposes.

2. At least 25 percent of the adjusted value of the gross estate must consist of land alone that is used for agricultural or business purposes.

3. The property used in the closely held business must pass from the decedent to an individual regarded to be "a qualified heir." For purposes of the Internal Revenue Code, qualified heirs include sons and daughters, parents, spouses, brothers and sisters, nieces and nephews, and grandchildren. Certain familial relations are not considered "qualified heirs," however; therefore, in order to ensure that the transferred property still allows the estate to qualify for special use valuation, the client, while alive, should consult with a financial planner, tax attorney, or accountant to ensure that eligibility is maintained.

4. The decedent or decedent's qualified heirs must be engaged in "material participation" in the closely held business. The material participation requirement must exist for at least 5 of the last 8 years prior to the death of the deceased. Thus, if the material participation requirement is met by a deceased individual, that individual's estate can use special valuation. The term "material participation" requires more than a passive role as legal title holder to the property. At a minimum, the term encompasses any one of the following activities: farming the land; assisting in the farming or developing of the land; supervising the maintenance, construction, or repair of equipment and property; managing the books and tax returns of the business; managing and directing the employment of assistants; handling major correspondence; and making decisions to plant certain crops or select certain types of livestock for grazing and breeding purposes. The Internal Revenue Service has even gone as far as accepting a

lease of cropland to a tenant farmer as an activity that meets the definition of "material participation."

5. If an election is made to qualify the property for special use valuation, all qualified heirs must agree in writing to have the special use valuation apply to the property. The election is then filed by the executor on the decedent's federal estate tax return.

6. The property must be used for a qualified use (farming, ranching, timber production, or other closely held business related purpose).

It should be noted that there can be possible disadvantages when using special use valuation. One disadvantage is that, if special use valuation is elected, the reduction in value may disqualify the estate from using the installment method of paying estate tax. Another disadvantage that may occur is the potential for recapture of all of the estate tax savings resulting from the special use valuation election. Recapture can occur if the closely held business or farm property is transferred to a nonqualified heir or unrelated buyer within 10 years of the filing date of the special use election, or if the property is no longer used for a qualified use—for example, farming, or ranching, within 10 years of the filing date of the special use election. If one of these situations occurs, so that there is a recapture of the estate tax savings that resulted from the special use valuation election, the qualified heirs are legally liable for the recapture amount. Because of this possibility, all qualified heirs are required to agree in writing to the use of special use valuation at the time it is elected for a decedent's estate. The agreement, usually drafted by an attorney, specifies the recapture consequences to the qualified heir should the property be transferred or converted within 10 years of the election.

It should also be noted that qualification for special use valuation is not automatic. Even if the estate meets all five of the requirements mentioned previously, application of special use valuation will only be permitted if there is a tax savings and a difference between the property's actual use and its highest and best use. Thus, if a closely held farm is surrounded by other farming operations engaged in the same type of farming (e.g., agricultural crops), the value of the farm at present (its actual use) also equals its highest and best use. But if the farm is located on the outskirts of a commercial development (e.g., a shopping mall), and the mall is interested in someday expanding, the highest and best use of the land is measured by the value it would have if converted to a shopping mall. At that point, there could be significant difference in values between its highest and best use as a shopping mall and its actual use as a farm. When this type of situation occurs so that the election of special use valuation could achieve an overall reduction in the includible value of the farm in the gross estate, the special use valuation will be permitted, assuming that all other qualifications have been met.

Use of the Installment Method of Paying Estate Taxes

Another valuable postmortem planning technique that can be used for estates including closely held business interests is the installment method of paying estate tax, pursuant to Internal Revenue Code Section 6166. If the estate property qualifies, the estate tax attributable to the closely held business interests can be paid in ten equal installments beginning 5 years and 9 months after the decedent's death. An additional advantage of the tax deferral is that a portion of the deferred tax (to be calculated below) pays an interest rate of 4 percent. The amount of tax that is subject to the 4 percent interest rate is the lesser of:

1. The actual tax deferred; or
2. A tax equal to the difference between $345,800 and the amount of unified credit allowed for the year of death (in 1987—$192,800); thus, if a decedent dies in 1987 or later, the amount of estate tax that would be subject to the 4 percent interest rate would be the lesser of the actual tax paid or the difference between $345,800 and $192,800 or $153,000.

In order to be eligible for the installment payment of estate tax, the value of the closely held business interest must exceed 35 percent of the value of the adjusted gross estate (the gross estate minus debts, taxes, and administrative expenses). The election to qualify for the installment method of paying estate tax can be taken as long as there is neither a disposition nor a withdrawal of 50 percent or more of the decedent's interest in the closely held business.

The obvious advantage of paying estate tax in installments is that the tax burden does not hit the estate or the executor all at once. It is even more advantageous than the payment of the estate tax in four equal installments, which is allowed by the Internal Revenue Code Section 6152(a).

A second advantage of the installment method of paying estate tax is that, generally, the executor has more time than is available for most postmortem elections in deciding to file the election. The election can be made either while the estate is being probated or can be made after the estate has been closed. The election can be made after the estate has been closed if all the beneficiaries enter into a written agreement to pay the deferred tax and interest, file the agreement to pay the deferred tax and interest, file the agreement with the executor or personal representative, file a verified closing statement, and take the income tax deduction for interest paid on the individual income tax returns of the beneficiaries. The decision to elect the installment method of paying taxes after the estate has been closed should only be made after consulting with a financial planner, a tax attorney, or an accountant.

Election of Administrative Expenses/Sale Expenses on Either Form 706 or Form 1041

Certain administrative expenses, such as the cost of arranging for the sale of estate assets through an auction or court-approved sale, can be deducted on either the federal estate tax return (Form 706) or the federal fiduciary income tax return (Form 1041). Whether the expenses are deducted on one form or the other depends on where the greatest tax savings occurs.

For example, if the decedent leaves his entire estate to the surviving spouse so that there is no estate tax liability due to the unlimited marital deduction, the value of the administrative expense deduction is wasted on the federal estate tax return. In a situation like this, the election should be made to deduct the administrative expenses on the fiduciary income tax return to achieve a reduction in the taxable income in respect of the decedent.

Where a fiduciary elects to take the deductions on Form 1041 rather than on the federal estate tax return, the fiduciary must file a statement with the return, stating in effect that the items have not been deducted from the gross estate on the federal estate tax return and that all rights to claim such deductions have been waived.

If the deductions are initially claimed on the federal estate tax return, taking the deduction on the fiduciary income tax return is not prevented so long as the deduction is not finally allowed on the federal estate tax return. Once the deduction is filed on the fiduciary income tax return, however, the item deducted cannot be converted to a deduction on the federal estate tax return. For that reason, a careful comparative analysis should be made as to where the deduction will achieve the greatest tax savings.

Certain administrative expenses, however, cannot be deducted on the fiduciary income tax return, such as expenses attributable to tax-exempt income or other nonincome tax deductible administrative expenses. Therefore, the only possible deductibility these expenses will have is on the federal estate tax return. In making a decision whether to deduct these expenses on the federal estate tax return or on the fiduciary income tax return, the executor or personal representative should first consult with a financial planner, tax attorney, or accountant.

Section 303 Stock Redemption

Section 303 of the Internal Revenue Code permits an estate containing stock to have all or a part of the stock redeemed in order to pay estate taxes, state death taxes, and administrative expenses without having the stock treated as a dividend. Thus, the stock redemption technique can save the estate a significant amount of income tax liability because of this preferential treatment. As long as the estate meets all of the eligibility requirements for Section 303, the amounts received from the redemption will be treated as gains or losses and will be recognized by the shareholder (the estate) to the extent of the difference between the fair market value of the distributed property and the basis of the redeemed stock. There should be little or no gain or loss on the transaction since, in most situations, there is a step up in basis occurring at the time of the decedent's death.

The eligibility requirements for a Section 303 stock redemption are as follows:

1. The value of all stock included in the decedent's gross estate must exceed 35 percent of the value of the decedent's adjusted gross estate (the value of the gross estate minus debts, unpaid taxes, and funeral and administrative expenses).

2. The amount of stock redeemed under a Section 303 stock redemption cannot exceed the total sum of all estate taxes, inheritance taxes, or taxes imposed by reason of the decedent's death, plus any interest accruing on these taxes, as well as any administrative expenses and funeral expenses. Note that a Section 303 stock redemption cannot be used to satisfy any debts or judgments that are not related to the death of the decedent and that existed prior to the death of the decedent.

3. The election to use a Section 303 stock redemption must be made within a time period that begins with the date of the decedent's death and ends on one of the following dates: either within 60 days after the Tax Court's final decision on a petition for a redetermination of an estate tax deficiency OR the last day of an extended payment period, if an election to file the estate tax on an installment method has been filed, OR 90 days after the expiration of the period of limitations provided for the assessment of federal estate tax.

4. The Section 303 stock redemption can only be used by those beneficiaries who actually bear the tax burden resulting from the probate of the estate. For example, if the decedent's will provides that all estate taxes are to be paid out of the residuary estate, only those beneficiaries who receive the residuary portion of the estate can utilize the Section 303 stock redemption since they are the ones who bear the ultimate tax liability. If the beneficiaries receive the stock as a part of the residuary estate, this is not a problem. However, if the decedent leaves a specific bequest of the stock to one individual, yet names the residuary beneficiaries as being obligated to pay the estate tax on stock that they did not receive, then the Section 303 stock redemption cannot be utilized by the residuary beneficiaries. If a decedent wishes

to have the estate take advantage of Section 303 stock redemption, then careful coordination is necessary to ensure that such a redemption is possible under the structure of the present estate plan; for example, the corporation must be in a position to redeem the stock. If it is not, restructuring of the estate plan is in order.

SELECTION OF THE MOST APPROPRIATE POSTMORTEM PLANNING TECHNIQUE

When a client wishes to utilize one or more postmortem estate planning techniques, the financial planner must undertake a lengthy analysis of the client's assets and estate planning objectives. Certain assets, by their very nature, will preclude the use of certain postmortem planning techniques; for example, a joint and last survivor private annuity will prevent the use of alternate valuation for that asset, while a closely held business that is unincorporated in form will not be able to take advantage of a Section 303 stock redemption.

In addition, the estate planning objectives of a client need to be examined. If the client wishes to reduce estate tax liability while controlling the distribution of the assets in a postmortem fashion, then the election of the Q-TIP should be mandated. The client's will should contain a clause expressly requiring the executor of the decedent's estate to elect the Q-TIP treatment so as to qualify the property for the marital deduction in the decedent's estate while also providing the decedent with postmortem control of the property and ensuring the surviving spouse of a lifetime stream of income from the property.

The selection of an appropriate postmortem planning technique will ultimately depend on the type of property in the decedent's estate, the identity of the individuals named as beneficiaries under the decedent's estate plan, and the overall estate tax and income tax savings that can be achieved through the use of one or more postmortem planning techniques. Ultimately, the most appropriate estate planning techniques that are of a postmortem variety will be those that achieve the greatest number of estate planning objectives while also reducing estate and income tax liability.

FOOTNOTES

1. Hoffman v. U.S., 85-2 U.S.T.C. ¶13,630 at 90,430 (1985).

9

WILL SUBSTITUTES

INTRODUCTION

On occasion, the financial planner encounters a client without a will who still wishes to implement some type of estate plan. The client's reasons for not having a will may vary: some clients are reluctant to talk about the subject of death, while others cannot agree with their spouses as to how the property should be divided when they die. Still others have had no previous contact with an attorney, and they do not know a trustworthy attorney to whom they can go to discuss the proper arrangement of their estate plans. Whatever the reasons, there are clients who would like to implement some sort of estate plan and *these clients do not have wills and do not plan on having wills executed in the immediate future*. Rather, these clients implement their estate plans through the use of *will substitutes*.

Will substitutes include various techniques that transfer some or all of a client's assets without the use of a will. These substitutes act to dispose of property in a particular manner so that the laws of intestate succession do not apply to property transferred through a will substitute. Thus, if a client wishes to transfer property to someone other than an heir or other person who would take the property under the laws of intestacy, and yet would also like to avoid having to draft a will to accomplish this purpose, the use of a will substitute may be an appropriate technique.

There are a variety of will substitutes that can be used by a client in creating an estate plan. For a long time, will substitutes were especially popular estate planning techniques because most will substitutes avoided the probate process. During the late 1960s, when the general public became increasingly aware of the costs involved in probating an estate, many clients began using will substitutes as a means of avoiding the administrative costs and time delays associated with the probate process. One will substitute, the revocable living trust, became an especially popular technique.

Since the enactment of ERTA in 1981, many of the concerns about the rising costs of probate and the expenses involved with payment of estate taxes have diminished, due largely to the increased amounts of the exemption equivalent and unified credit amounts, and the availability of the unlimited marital and charitable deductions for the decedent's estate. As a result, the concern of many individuals to reduce their estate tax liability while also avoiding probate is not as great as it used to be. Still, for the client who has a large estate (defined as an amount that exceeds the exemption equivalent for a single person, or an amount that exceeds two exemption equivalents for a married client and spouse), reducing estate taxes and probate costs remains a legitimate concern.

In addition to avoiding probate and its costs, other reasons why clients prefer to use some sort of a will substitute include the following:

1. Use of a will substitute avoids the time delays often associated with the probate of an estate. The probate process in its entirety can take anywhere from 6 months to several years before the decedent's property is distributed in the manner desired by the decedent. The use of a will substitute avoids this time delay by transferring title to the property *immediately* to another individual.

2. Use of a will substitute guarantees the grantor or owner of the property a greater degree of control or flexibility. In the case of a client who uses the revocable living trust as a will substitute, the grantor is assured of being able to determine who receives the property, in what amount, and the conditions or situations in which the beneficiary will cease to receive the property. In fact, should the grantor become dissatisfied with the operation of the trust, the abilities of the trustee, or the behavior of the beneficiary, the grantor can terminate the trust at will and revoke the entire transaction. The maker of a will can also revoke a will, but the execution formalities and revocation formalities of a will are usually more restricted, and if a revocation is attempted that does not comply with the state's requirements for a validly revoked will, the revocation is null and void and the will remains in effect. Thus, some will substitutes provide greater flexibility to the grantor.

3. Use of a will substitute can possibly transfer a decedent's interests to someone other than the surviving spouse without the possibility of either the spouse filing an election to take against the will or filing a will contest. Depending on the state of the decedent's residence, and depending on the decedent's intentions at the time the transfer was contemplated, the use of a will substitute may successfully accomplish this objective and prevent the surviving spouse from claiming any portion of the property. Of course, if the intentions of the decedent were to fraudulently disinherit his spouse, and if the parties had not entered into a prenuptial agreement in which each agreed to give up his or her survivorship rights in the property of the other spouse, then such an attempt could be successfully challenged by the surviving spouse.

4. Use of a will substitute is often a quicker, more convenient means of creating an estate plan than the use of a will. A will usually involves several consultations with the attorney, a consultation with the legal assistant or legal secretary, the search for and duplication of copies of important documents (e.g., titles to property, deeds, etc.), the return to the law office with these documents, a review of the terms of the proposed will by the attorney with the client, and the return to the law office to sign the will with the requisite number of witnesses. A will substitute, on the other hand, can be as simple as signing on a designated signature line, or completing an application form (e.g., joint tenancy bank accounts, Totten trusts, and life insurance contracts). Because of the ease and simplicity in entering into these types of will substitutes, the use of a will substitute may create an estate plan for the client who is psychologically or emotionally unprepared to have a will executed.

Despite the apparent advantage of having a will substitute as part of an estate plan, the use of a will substitute may have specific disadvantages or drawbacks with which the client may be unfamiliar. These drawbacks will be discussed as the characteristics of each type of will substitute are discussed, so that the financial planner will know when the use of a particular will substitute is appropriate and when the use of a will substitute may present hazards to the effectiveness of a client's estate plan. If the client insists on having an estate plan that does not include the use of a will, the financial planner should inform the client of the risks inherent in this type of planning.

TYPES OF WILL SUBSTITUTES

The types of will substitutes that will be discussed in this chapter are the following:

1. Forms of Property Ownership, including (a) joint tenancy with right of survivorship, and (b) tenancy by the entirety
2. Joint Tenancy Bank Accounts
3. Payable on Death (POD) Accounts/Bonds
4. Totten Trusts
5. Contracts Taking Effect at Death
6. Government Savings Bonds
7. Life Insurance Contracts
8. Deeds of Title
9. Revocable Living Trusts

The characteristics of each of these types of will substitutes will be reviewed, as well as the advantages and disadvantages of these will substitute techniques. By analyzing the advantages and disadvantages of each of these forms of will substitutes, the financial planner may be in a better situation to determine which will substitute forms are the most appropriate for the client who decides, for one reason or another, to refrain from making a will.

Forms of Property Ownership

There are several types of property ownership that act as will substitutes. The two most common forms of property ownership that act as a will substitute are joint tenancy with right of survivorship and tenancy by the entirety.

Both of these forms of property ownership have a survivorship feature that enables the legal title to the property to pass immediately to the survivor when the first joint tenant or tenant by the entirety dies. As a result, the property legally belongs to the survivor in its entirety and bypasses the probate process. A validly executed will that attempts to dispose of the property to anyone other than the surviving joint tenant or tenant by the entirety is null and void, at least for those portions of the will that attempt to make the conveyance.

Holding property in joint tenancy with right of survivorship or in tenancy by the entirety assures the first decedent that the survivor will obtain the entire property. It also is convenient and relatively inexpensive to achieve this form of ownership. Usually, it only requires that the deed of title to the property be amended so that it reads: "to X and Y, as joint tenants with right of survivorship and not as tenants in common"; or: "to X and Y, as tenants by the entirety, and not as tenants in common." It is important that the deed specifically exclude the possibility that the property could be held as tenants in common. If the deed does not do this, but merely states that the property is held as "joint tenants," some states will construe this to mean that the property is held by tenants in common rather than by joint tenants with right of survivorship or by tenants by the entirety. If the property is construed to be held in tenancy in common, it loses the advantages that were sought by the client who chose this as a will substitute, since property held as a tenant in common does not avoid the probate process and the attendant costs and time delays of probate.

One important consideration that should be weighed carefully before placing property in either of these forms of ownership is the effect that placing property in these forms of ownership will have on the decedent's taxable estate and the survivor's taxable estate. It would be relatively simple to take all of one's property holdings and place all of them in joint tenancy with right of survivorship or tenancy by the entirety with the surviving spouse. Yet, if this were to occur it is possible that the first decedent's estate would pay no estate tax while the surviving spouse's estate would pay all of the estate tax that had been deferred from the first estate as well as the estate tax due on the death of the survivor. This situation, known as *overqualification for the marital deduction,* actually results in a higher amount of estate tax being paid by the estate of the surviving spouse than if each estate paid a portion of the tax by not qualifying all of the property for the marital deduction. If the estate of the first decedent qualifies all property for the marital deduction, it does not take advantage of the unified credit amount available to it to offset estate tax liability.

In addition, since the surviving spouse usually does not remarry, the estate of the surviving spouse does not have the marital deduction available to it to offset estate tax liability. The resulting tax stems directly from the failure of the first estate to take advantage of the unified credit available to it. Therefore, a couple may wish to consider whether it is wise to place *all* of their property into either one of these forms of property ownership. This determination can usually be reached by examining the dollar amount of the estates of *both* spouses. If the entire value of both spouses' estates is less than the amount of one exemption equivalent ($600,000 in 1987 and years thereafter), then placing the property in this form of ownership may be advisable.

Still, there may be other reasons why a client may not wish to place all of his or her property into a form of joint property ownership: the decedent may wish to leave some property or bequests to other family members, or a decedent may wish to make a charitable bequest, or a decedent may need to have liquid assets or cash to pay state inheritance or estate taxes and attorney's fees when the decedent's estate files a state estate tax return. As a result, the decision to place property in joint tenancy or tenancy by the entirety needs to be weighed in light of other estate planning factors.

Finally, it should be noted that avoidance of probate does not necessarily eliminate the payment of federal estate tax or eliminate the need to file a federal estate tax return. Many clients mistakenly believe that if they avoid probate they can also avoid paying federal estate tax. This is a false assumption. For example, if a married couple held all of their property in joint tenancy with right of survivorship and the total value of all of the property equalled $1 million, all of it would avoid probate upon the death of the first spouse. It would also avoid any federal estate tax liability upon the death of the first spouse since all of the property would automatically qualify for the marital deduction because it passes automatically to the surviving spouse by right of survivorship. Yet, *upon the death of the surviving spouse,* the survivor's estate would be faced with federal estate tax liability of $345,800 before application of the unified credit amount. Even assuming that the surviving spouse dies in 1987 or later when the unified credit amount increases to $192,800, the surviving spouse's estate would still have estate tax liability of $153,000 which could have been minimized by partitioning the property so that each spouse owned a portion of it as sole owner during their lifetimes.

Joint Tenancy Bank Accounts

A very popular form of will substitute is the joint tenancy bank account. This account is usually established when a depositor and another individual agree to establish a joint account with a financial institution. The parties usually sign a uniform signature card when establishing the account. The account permits each individual to make deposits to and withdrawals from the account.

In such an account, the deposits are credited to the respective depositor as are the withdrawals. These deposits are subject to the control of the respective depositor alone; in other words, the nondepositing account holder is not free to withdraw from the account any funds that he or she did not originally deposit. Each account holder has an immediate present interest in the account; the depositor does not have to wait some indefinite period of time before being able to claim legal title to the account proceeds, nor is there a right to use or enjoy the funds that takes effect at some point in the future. Each depositor's right to use and enjoy the funds in the account vests immediately, but is usually limited to the respective portion of the account which they own, for example, 50 percent in the case of two depositors, each of whom contributed half of the account proceeds.

Joint tenancy bank accounts act as will substitutes because of the survivorship feature present in this type of account. When one of the depositors dies, the proceeds in the account become legally vested in the survivor, even though the survivor may not have originally deposited them in the account. The proceeds pass immediately to the survivor and are excluded from the probate estate of the decedent. Though the proceeds are removed from the probate estate of the deceased, the portion of the account proceeds that represents the contributions made by the decedent to the account normally will be included in the decedent's gross estate for federal estate tax purposes. Thus, the proceeds could be subject to possible federal estate tax liability in the depositor's gross estate. Of course, if the other account holder is the spouse, then one-half of the proceeds in the account will be included in the decedent's gross estate, regardless of actual contribution or deposits to the account. Though one-half of the proceeds will be included in the decedent's gross estate, the one-half interest qualifies for the marital deduction so that none of it is taxable in the decedent's gross estate. Instead, the entire amount is subject to estate tax in the survivor's estate unless spent or consumed in the survivor's lifetime.

Payable on Death (POD) Accounts/Bonds

This form of will substitute is established when an individual establishes an account with a financial institution or purchases bonds that are to be paid to a designated beneficiary in the event of the purchaser's death. The depositor has complete control over the account during life, and the person named as beneficiary of the account has no ability to make withdrawals, borrow the account proceeds, or use them as collateral when seeking a loan.

A POD account is often used by a depositor who wishes to make a gift of the proceeds to another family member, but wishes to have the transfer take effect upon the depositor's death. As a result, the account proceeds are payable to the designated beneficiary but only when the depositor dies. Because of the requirement that the beneficiary obtains the proceeds only upon the death of the depositor, the transfer is considered testamentary in nature, and is also considered a transfer taking effect at death. Therefore, although the proceeds of the account or the bonds themselves will avoid the probate process, they will be included in the gross estate of the decedent for federal estate tax purposes.

In addition, POD accounts and bonds may face other problems as well. In some states, a transfer that takes effect at death needs to be in writing and needs to comply with the formal execution requirements for drafting a will. If the POD account does not comply with the state's execution requirements, it may be considered an invalid or ineffective transfer and may be passed to the decedent's heirs according to the laws of intestate succession. In addition, a POD account that is established for a minor can pose certain problems, especially if the parent is named as depositor of the account. If the parent-depositor dies, the court will have to appoint a guardian to supervise the administration, control or custody of the account. This will cause delays and unexpected court costs that could rob this form of a will substitute of many of its advantages.

Totten Trusts

A Totten Trust is a form of a will substitute that is actually misnamed, since it is not technically a trust and the individual designated as "trustee" has no active trustee duties and does not act in a fiduciary capacity as the trustee of an active trust does.

A Totten Trust is an arrangement in which an individual establishes an account with a financial institution and names himself or herself as "trustee" of the account on behalf of one or more beneficiaries. The "trustee" of such an arrangement has the ability to withdraw any and all deposits in the account at will; the "trustee" may also make deposits, change beneficiary designations, or alter the terms of the "trust" in any other way considered legal. Unlike a joint tenancy bank account in which the beneficiary has an immediate vested right to the proceeds, or at least to that portion originally deposited by the beneficiary, the beneficiary of a Totten Trust does not have an immediate vested right to receive the proceeds, make withdrawals, or even make deposits. The beneficiary's only right to receive the proceeds occurs when the original depositor dies. Thus, this arrangement is similar to the POD account situation in that the transfer takes effect at death. Though the proceeds will avoid probate, the value of the funds in the Totten Trust will be included as an asset in the gross estate of the depositor for federal estate tax purposes. It should be noted that Totten Trusts are not recognized in all states.

Contracts Taking Effect at Death

Sometimes contracts are entered into in a decedent's lifetime which arrange for the transfer of property to a designated beneficiary when the decedent dies. These contracts may sometimes be considered will substitutes because they manage to transfer property to another individual without the use of a will and without probate administration. Several types of contracts, such as annuities and qualified retirement plan distributions, specify that the surviving spouse or other designated beneficiary, by reason of his or her survivorship, is to receive the proceeds in the event the annuitant or retired employee dies before all payments have been received. The beneficiary's right to receive the death benefits is premised on an enforceable contract and on the enforceable right of the deceased individual to receive the proceeds by reason of either transferring property or money to an insurance company in exchange for the annuity payment, or by reason of the decedent having worked and made contributions to the qualified retirement fund. In other words, for the contract to be valid and enforceable, each party to the contract (the decedent) has to provide consideration to the other party (the insurance company or the employer).

When such consideration has been exchanged and an enforceable contract has been entered into, the proceeds distributed to the beneficiary by reason of the decedent's death normally avoid probate and are distributed directly to the designated beneficiary. Such payments are often an important consideration to a decedent since the decedent assumed, while alive, that the surviving spouse and other family members needed income pending probate of the remainder of the estate, or that there would be insufficient assets for the spouse and other family members to live on during the difficult transition period when the surviving spouse attempts to "get on his feet" after the death of the first spouse.

While effective in avoiding probate, proceeds that are distributed to a beneficiary by reason of surviving the decedent are subject to inclusion in the decedent's gross estate for federal estate tax purposes. Furthermore, unless the surviving spouse specifically disclaims the right to receive these benefits prior to the decedent's death, or assigns the right to receive the payments to another individual at some point in time prior to the decedent's death, some portion of the proceeds will transfer automatically to the surviving spouse even though the surviving spouse is not named as the designated beneficiary on the contract or annuity. This is especially true of qualified retirement benefits since 1984. Therefore, a client should keep in mind that the only way a surviving spouse will be denied the benefits is if the spouse signs an agreement to waive his or her right to receive the benefits prior to the death of the decedent. If such a waiver is not signed and filed, then the surviving spouse will be entitled to all of the benefits by reason of his or her survivorship, and the individual named on the contract as the beneficiary will receive nothing. This specific feature of contracts that distributes benefits to the surviving spouse applies to all qualified retirement plans except for IRAs. Thus, a decedent could name someone other than the surviving spouse as the beneficiary of the decedent's IRA account, and this designation would be recognized as a valid will substitute.

Government Savings Bonds

For many years individuals have purchased Series "EE" and Series "H" U.S. Savings Bonds as a means of transferring property to another individual in such a way that will avoid probate. The purchaser of the bonds designates that the bonds can be payable either to A (the buyer) or B (the designated beneficiary) or the purchaser can designate that the bonds will be paid to A (the purchaser) or payable on the death of A to B (the designated beneficiary). In the first situation, should either the buyer or the beneficiary die, the bonds will be paid in their entirety to the survivor. In the second situation, the purchaser of the bonds will receive them but if the purchaser predeceases the designated beneficiary, the beneficiary receives the bonds. The bonds avoid probate, though they will be included in the gross estate of the purchaser in their entirety if the purchaser and beneficiary were not husband and wife and if the surviving beneficiary is unable to provide any contribution to the purchase price of the bonds.

Life Insurance Contracts

The death benefit proceeds payable from a life insurance policy to one or more beneficiaries are a commonly used will substitute technique. Life insurance proceeds avoid the probate process as long as the estate of the deceased or the decedent himself or herself is not named as the beneficiary of the death benefits.

The obvious advantage of using life insurance is that it provides liquidity to the estate or to the named beneficiary. It can also be used as a means of providing a bequest to one or more individuals where the decedent did not have sufficient assets to make a lifetime gift to the beneficiary.

Life insurance ordinarily gives the insured the right to designate the beneficiary; this is one of many "incidents of ownership." Other incidents of ownership include: the right to determine how the proceeds will be dispersed to beneficiaries, the right to determine the period of time over which the proceeds will be distributed, the right to borrow against the policy, the right to use the policy as collateral for a loan, and the right to alter the beneficiary designation.

If the insured is able to alter any of these provisions or is able to possess these incidents of ownership over the policy, the death benefits payable to the beneficiary will be included in the gross estate of the decedent insured, even though the benefits avoid probate and pass directly to the designated beneficiary. It is only if all of the incidents of ownership in the policy are irrevocably transferred more than 3 years prior to the death of the insured that the death benefits will be excluded from the insured's estate for federal estate tax purposes.

Because the beneficiary of a life insurance policy does not have a right to receive any benefits from the policy until the death of the insured, the provisions of the life insurance arrangement need not comply with the formal execution requirements for a will. However, most life insurance designations and contracts are in writing to ensure that the terms and conditions of payment are thoroughly understood by the insured, the beneficiary, and the issuing company.

As a final statement on life insurance, it should be noted that many individuals who choose to avoid probate attempt to establish a life insurance trust in their lifetimes. These trusts are funded with life insurance policies which pay their death benefits to the named trustee of the trust. If, as one of the powers of the trust, the trustee is authorized to use any portion of the trust proceeds to pay taxes, attorney's fees, or other related expenses on behalf of the decedent's estate, then the entire amount of the proceeds will be included in the decedent's gross estate for federal estate tax purposes. Thus, if a life insurance trust is contemplated by a client, the financial planner should review with the client the conditions under which the life insurance proceeds could be included in the decedent's gross estate even though it appears the decedent has given up all incidents of ownership over the policy.

Deeds of Title

A deed of title is a written instrument that serves as a will substitute. A deed conveys legal title in property (usually real estate or land) to a named individual known as a grantee. A deed effectively transfers title at the time it is executed, rather than when the grantor dies. As a result, a deed is usually irrevocable once it is executed, unlike a will which is capable of being revoked at any time prior to the death of its maker.

Though a deed of title transfers legal ownership of the property to the grantee immediately, at times the grantee's right to use or enjoy the property is postponed until such a time when the deed is delivered from an *escrow agent,* who holds the deed for the grantor until a given time, to the grantee. However, if the grantor of the deed retains the right to use and enjoy the property that is subject to the deed, it will be included in the grantor's gross estate for death tax purposes.

In order for the deed to be considered a valid document that conveys title of the property to the grantee, the deed must comply with the following requirements:

1. It must be in writing in order to comply with the Statute of Frauds.
2. It must contain an adequate and accurate legal description of the real property being conveyed. (This usually means that the legal description of the land must be included in the instrument, including the township, section, quarter, and county in which the property is located. If the property is located in an urban area, a street description and plot of the designated area is usually required.)
3. It must identify the grantee.
4. It must be signed by the grantor.
5. It must be delivered to the grantee or to a designated agent, sometimes referred to as an escrow agent.
6. In some states, it is possible that the deed is required to be recorded at the county recorder's office, though more often than not, there is no legal formality that the deed be recorded. The purpose of recording the deed is to give notice to any other alleged grantees that the grantee designated in the deed instrument has a first claim and legally protected right to the ownership of the property. Most states

operate under the assumption that, if there are competing claims to the same property, the deed recorded first in time takes priority over any other deed filed later. However, the specifics of recording procedures for each state should always be consulted.

The most difficult problem encountered when using a deed of title revolves around the issue of when the deed is to take effect. If the deed is to take effect immediately, there is usually no problem in determining that the transfer was effective in conveying legal title to the designated grantee. However, if the deed indicates that the transfer to title is to occur upon the death of the grantor, there may be problems with the legality of the deed since it is a testamentary transfer and must comply with the valid execution requirements for a will. If the deed fails to comply with the execution requirements for a will, the deed will be considered an invalid attempt to convey title to the property in question.

In determining when the title to the property is transferred, the intention of the grantor must be examined. If the deed attempts to convey title upon the death of the grantor, the transfer will be considered testamentary in nature and must comply with the execution requirements for a will. If, however, the deed postpones the use and enjoyment of the property until some time in the future, and the deed is irrevocably delivered to an escrow agent who holds it until a specified event occurs, such as the death of the grantor, the title to the property is considered to have transferred to the grantee at the time of delivery of the deed to the escrow agent. If this is the case, then the execution requirements for a valid will need not be followed.

In transferring legal title of property to a grantee by use of a deed, the grantor should always obtain the signature of the grantor's spouse on the deed. If the grantor's spouse does not cosign the deed, the spouse could later claim that his or her rights as survivor of the grantor were never extinguished in the property. Therefore, in order to avoid the possibility of having the surviving spouse claim a share of the transferred property, the signature of both the grantor and grantor's spouse should appear on the deed. As long as the deed complies with all other requirements for a validly executed deed, the conveyance should be valid.

Revocable Living Trust

For the client with a large estate who faces potentially large probate costs, the revocable living trust may be considered a viable will substitute that avoids probate. A revocable living trust is designed to give the grantor of such a trust the ability to alter the terms of the trust or terminate the trust completely should the grantor become dissatisfied with its terms or operation.

The revocable living trust gives the grantor the flexibility and control over the property without having the property included in the grantor's probate estate. The assets in the trust are used to benefit one or more beneficiaries who have an interest regarded as "equitable." They are able to use and enjoy the property but only at the discretion of the trustee, or according to the terms of the trust. Thus, the beneficiaries do not have legal title to the property placed in the trust.

If the grantor does not terminate the trust prior to the grantor's death, the trust corpus and all undistributed income is distributed to the designated beneficiaries and the trust terminates. The grantor can also provide that the trust will continue after his death and the income will continue to be received by the beneficiaries. In any event, if the trust continues, it becomes irrevocable in nature and can only be terminated if it violates the rule against perpetuities, or if a specified situation occurs upon which the trust terminates.

Because the trustee is the legal titleholder to the assets in the trust, the corpus of the trust is not included in the probate process and avoids being included in the grantor's probate estate. However, because the grantor has the ability to revoke the trust at any time in the grantor's lifetime, the grantor holds an incident of ownership over the property and the property will be included in the grantor's gross estate for federal estate tax purposes. Because the grantor does not make a completed gift of the property in the revocable trust, there is no federal gift tax liability for the grantor when the trust is established.

Because the revocable living trust vests an immediate enjoyment and use of the income to the beneficiaries in the grantor's lifetime, there is no requirement that the execution requirements of a valid will be followed. If the trust is structured so that the trust terminates upon the death of the grantor, the beneficiaries or other designated remaindermen receive legal title to the assets that make up the corpus at that time.

CONCLUSION

Whether any one of the will substitutes is appropriate for a client depends on a number of factors. If the client does not have a large estate and wishes to transfer assets with little legal complexity and little formality, the Totten Trust, joint bank account, government savings bonds, or contractual transfers taking effect at death may be appropriate. If the client has real property, then the joint tenancy with right of survivorship, or tenancy by the entirety may be appropriate. If the client has real estate and wishes to retain the full use and enjoyment of the property during his lifetime, the use of a deed may be appropriate since it may allow him to deliver the deed to an escrow agent who holds it until the death of the grantor. However, if the deed is not irrevocably delivered to an escrow agent, it could be construed as a transfer taking effect at the grantor's death and would be in the grantor's gross estate for federal estate tax purposes. If the client has little ability to make lifetime gifts to other family members but has a desire to leave some property to family members when he or she dies, the use of life insurance may be appropriate. Finally, if the client has a sizeable estate and would like to see family members enjoy income and use of the property while also retaining control and flexibility over the property, a revocable living trust may be appropriate.

The use of any will substitute depends on other factors as well: the effect that the selection of a particular will substitute has on the client's estate and gift tax liability, the financial needs of the client, the mental, legal, and financial competence of family members and other beneficiaries, and the types of property owned by the client (e.g., income-producing, appreciating or depreciating in value, liquid or illiquid assets, etc.). Ultimately, the form of will substitute that is considered the most appropriate is that which accomplishes the greatest number of client objectives.

10

ESTATE PLANNING FOR THE FAMILY OF A DEVELOPMENTALLY DISABLED PERSON*

INTRODUCTION

Most clients who wish to implement some type of estate plan do so with the intention of transferring assets to particular beneficiaries while minimizing estate taxes and related transfer costs. For the client whose family includes a developmentally disabled person, estate planning can become an even more intricate, if not precarious, process. Estate planning for the developmentally disabled beneficiary involves careful coordination of outright property transfers, inheritances, and public assistance benefits. If the disabled person receives too much property in the form of gifts or inheritances, the estate plan for the disabled individual as well as for other family members may be seriously impaired.

This chapter presents the most common estate planning pitfalls that occur in family situations involving a disabled person, and the ways in which these pitfalls can be avoided. It also discusses various estate planning possibilities for the client with a developmentally disabled family member. The advantages and disadvantages of each of these estate plan-

* © 1988 Institute of Certified Financial Planners. This chapter is reprinted with permission of Institute of Certified Financial Planners.

ning possibilities are presented in order that the financial planner may assist the client in the selection of estate planning techniques that provide the disabled person and his family with the greatest amount of flexibility at the least cost.

IDENTIFICATION OF ESTATE PLANNING PITFALLS

A developmentally disabled person is, by definition, an individual who suffers from any severe, chronic disability which can be attributed to a mental or physical impairment. The disability must be diagnosed before the person reaches the age of 22, and it must be an impairment that is likely to continue indefinitely.[1] If an individual meets this definition of developmental disability, he or she may qualify to receive public assistance benefits. Receipt of these benefits depends on the disabled person's financial resources, needs, and current income level. Eligibility for public assistance is not automatic, however, and a disabled individual may be barred from receiving benefits as a result of one or more estate planning pitfalls unknowingly created by his parents, other family members, or friends. It is important at the onset of any estate plan to identify these pitfalls and determine how they can be avoided.

Most estate planning pitfalls that affect the developmentally disabled person occur because parents or other relatives leave a sizeable amount of property to the disabled person under the terms of their wills. Similarly, if the parents or relatives die without a will (intestacy), the disabled person may come into a sizeable inheritance by operation of law. Also, if a will is improperly drafted without a residuary clause, so that part of the estate passes to the disabled person as a result of a partial intestacy, the disabled person may receive a sizeable, though unintentional, inheritance.

Trust documents can also be traps for the unwary. If a trust instrument is improperly drafted so that it is subsequently deemed invalid, the disabled person may receive legal title to the trust corpus rather than equitable title to the income received as beneficiary. The estate planning pitfalls created by any one of these errors can be significant.

1. If the disabled person receives too much property, the amount of property owned or inherited may prohibit the person from meeting the eligibility requirements for public assistance benefits. Since receipt of such assistance is based on financial need, restricted ownership of assets, and limited reportable income, an inheritance or gift from a family member may inadvertently cause the disabled person to become ineligible for such benefits. Because the average annual cost of providing for a developmentally disabled person averages

$30,000 per year,[2] the financial hardship caused by failing to qualify for public assistance benefits is readily apparent.

2. For those disabled individuals who initially qualify to receive public assistance benefits, the subsequent acquisition of property by gift or inheritance may not only cause the disabled person to become ineligible for further benefits but may also trigger reimbursement proceedings for present and past amounts expended on behalf of the disabled individual. Thus, the disabled person may not only lose all prospective benefits but would be required to pay back past expenses with the gifts or inheritances received. Since the cost of past expenditures can be significant, many gifts or inheritances received by a disabled person could be totally consumed by the agency seeking reimbursement. Such a procedure can be disastrous for the estate plan of the client who assumes that public assistance benefits will provide his or her disabled family member with a portion of his or her support, thereby permitting the client to pass the rest of his or her estate to other family members.

3. Should the disabled individual receive a gift or inheritance, there is the problem of properly managing or investing it. For the severely impaired or disabled individual, self-management of the asset is out of the question. Even when the disabled person suffers a mild disability, he may still have control and responsibility over the property unless a guardian or some other form of court-approved supervision is created. If no estate planning arrangements are made, the disabled individual could lose the assets through mismanagement, poor advice, fraud, or undue influence.

4. Another estate planning pitfall commonly occurs when a disabled individual attempts to make a testamentary disposition of assets. If a disabled person acquires property by gift or inheritance, it may be difficult for that person to dispose of the property by means of a will. Each state has its own requirements for the proper execution of a will, but one requirement that is common to all is that the maker of the will must have the testamentary capacity to make the will. The elements of testamentary capacity may vary slightly from state to state, but a person is generally said to have testamentary capacity when that person knows and understands the natural objects of his or her bounty, the nature and extent of his or her property, the distribution he or she desires to make of his or her property, and the nature of the instrument he or she is executing.[3] A problem frequently encountered when a disabled person executes a will is that the will may be subject to attack by those who would have taken the property under the laws of intestacy. Usually, these people challenge the will on the grounds that the disabled person lacked the testamentary capacity necessary to properly understand the

nature of the document. While the disabled person may, in fact, have been capable of understanding the document, a disabled person runs the risk of having the will challenged on this ground. For this reason, disabled individuals are discouraged from having wills prepared.

5. Another pitfall that adversely affects the client and other family members occurs when the disabled person is deemed ineligible to receive public assistance benefits. If the disabled person cannot receive public assistance benefits, it is possible that assets originally intended for other family members as part of an estate plan may have to be expended to support the disabled person. The estate plan for the entire family can be adversely affected, and it is possible that some assets may be totally consumed by the disabled person, leaving the client in a situation where other family members may receive little, if anything. When a part or all of the assets are consumed in this fashion, ademption by extinction occurs.[4]

6. A final pitfall that merits consideration is the effect that the act of disinheritance may have on the disabled person and on the family. Many clients are reluctant to disinherit a disabled family member even though disinheritance may qualify the person for public assistance. Clients fear the traumatic effect that disinheritance may have on the disabled person,[5] especially if that person can appreciate the significance of the act. Such situations must be treated delicately, and the financial planner may need to point out to the client the positive aspects of disinheriting the individual—making the individual eligible for public assistance benefits. Further reassurance can be provided to the parents or relatives of disabled persons by reminding them that total disinheritance of the disabled person can be avoided by the use of certain estate planning techniques. These techniques will be discussed further in this chapter.

THE NATURE OF GOVERNMENTAL BENEFITS

To better appreciate the estate planning pitfalls that can be avoided by optimal coordination of gifts, inheritances, and public assistance benefits, the financial planner needs to understand how governmental benefits may affect the estate plan of a client with a disabled family member. For the client with a small or medium-sized estate, reliance on public assistance benefits may be a necessity if the client wishes to distribute assets to other family members.

Governmental benefits generally fall into three categories: need-criteria benefits, benefits that are not based on need criteria, and "in-kind" benefits. The first category includes public assistance programs such as

SSI (Supplemental Security Income), Medicaid, and food stamps. The benefits of these programs are available to those who can demonstrate a financial need for such programs. A disabled person may qualify for SSI if his or her income is below a stated amount, and if his or her total asset ownership of nonexempt resources is below a stated amount. If either the income or resource amount exceeds a stated amount, the disabled person is deemed ineligible for public assistance benefits. Because the eligibility requirements are frequently subject to administrative modification, the financial planner should consult with the nearest Social Security Administration office for an updated list of items that meet the definition of "income,"[6] as well as for a list of items that are considered "exempt" resources.[7]

Special consideration must be given to the timing of property transfers or gifts made by the disabled person. If a disabled person makes gifts or transfers of property for any amount less than the fair market value of the property in an attempt to establish eligibility for SSI, the amount representing the difference between the fair market value of the property and the compensation received for the property will be treated as a resource for 30 months from the date of the disposal.[8] For this reason, the financial planner needs to assist the disabled individual or his family in timing the transfers in such a way that the disabled person retains eligibility for public assistance benefits.

The second category of governmental benefits which may be available to the disabled person can be identified as social insurance programs. The most prominent of these programs are Social Security and Medicare. Unlike public assistance programs, which are based on need and eligibility criteria, social insurance programs are funded by the insured individuals themselves. Under the Social Security program, it is possible for a disabled person to receive benefits even though the disabled person has never worked. Benefits are paid to the disabled person based on the work record of his parents. A disabled adult may receive Social Security benefits if he or she has a severe physical or mental disability that begins before the age of 22 and which keeps him or her from engaging in any substantial employment. In addition, the disabled person may be able to receive the benefits of an insured parent in an amount as high as 75 percent of the parent's average earnings. These benefits would be available to the disabled person at the time of the parent's retirement, death, or disability. Under Medicare, a public health care insurance program that pays expenses for a person who has been disabled for more than 2 years, the costs of hospitalization, medical and surgical care, and related medical care expenses are covered up to a stated dollar amount.

A third category of governmental assistance may be available in the form of "in-kind" benefits. Typically, these are goods and services rather than cash payments. One of the most prominent types of in-kind benefits available to disabled persons is the vocational rehabilitation program. Among the types of services provided to a disabled person under this program are: medical examinations to determine the nature and severity of the disability; continuous counseling to determine appropriate employment opportunities for the disabled person; vocational training at trade or technical schools, rehabilitation centers, or in the home of the disabled person; room and board, transportation, and other expenses related to job maintenance; and tuition and other expenses related to efforts to obtain a job.[9] This list is not all-inclusive and financial planners with concerns about specific vocational rehabilitation services should contact their state department of vocational rehabilitation.

TECHNIQUES TO AVOID ESTATE PLANNING PITFALLS

Once the financial planner understands the significance of coordinating the disabled person's assets with public assistance benefits, proper estate planning techniques can be applied to avoid the pitfalls previously mentioned. The characteristics of each of these techniques, as well as the advantages and disadvantages of each, are featured in this portion of the chapter.

Guardianship

A guardianship is a legal relationship in which a court-appointed person controls and manages the personal affairs of the disabled person (known as a guardianship of the person) or the financial concerns of the disabled person (known as guardianship of the estate). A guardian is not legal title holder of the disabled's property. Rather, the guardian is a fiduciary who owes a duty of loyalty and fairness to the disabled person (ward).

Guardians of the person can be appointed to make decisions of a personal nature, such as the selection of a school, expenditures for food and other necessities, and so on. Guardians of the estate are responsible for investment and management decisions related to the ward's property. It is not unusual for one individual to serve as both guardian of the person and guardian of the estate.

A guardianship can be absolute or limited in terms of the control it gives the guardian over the affairs of the ward. An absolute guardianship gives total authority to the guardian for decisions affecting the ward, including decisions of a personal nature as well as those that affect the estate. For a number of years, guardianships could only be absolute; in order for a guardian to be appointed by the court, the ward first had to be declared totally incompetent. Usually, the guardian was given control of the ward's assets or personal concerns. Today, a number of states[10] recognize the concept of a limited guardianship, a relationship in which the ward need not be considered totally incompetent before a guardian will be appointed. Limited guardianships are appropriate for a ward who is considered mildly disabled—one who can hold a job, manage a simple budget, and live independently. The guardian makes decisions for the ward on matters that require more sophisticated judgment calls, matters concerning investments, decisions related to the sale or exchange of real estate, or contractual matters. A limited guardianship may also be appropriate in medical emergency situations where the consent of an adult is sought prior to surgery or other medical treatment. If the ward cannot give informed consent for impending surgery or medical treatment, a limited guardianship may be appropriate, if not necessary, for that purpose.

While a guardianship has the advantages of providing a ward with supervision of personal concerns and assets, it also has potential disadvantages. It is generally expensive to administer. There is usually a bond requirement for the guardian, and there are the additional expenses of court filing fees, attorney's fees, and expert witness fees. Since guardians are usually required to file an annual accounting of their expenditures on behalf of the ward, this can also add to the costs of a guardianship. A guardianship can, in certain circumstances, be ineffective in terms of caring for the ward's personal and financial needs. A guardianship generally lacks flexibility and all expenditures made by a guardian on a ward's behalf must first be approved by the court. A considerable time delay may also occur when seeking court approval for expenditures and accountings. Ordinarily, a guardian has very limited investment authority with the ward's assets. Such limited investment authority may deny the guardian the opportunity to make the ward's assets as productive as they could be if given broader investment authority.

Finally, a guardianship may be disadvantageous because it requires, in most states, a legal declaration that the ward is incompetent. This usually requires a court hearing in which medical evidence of the ward's incompetence must be established. Unless the state has some form of limited guardianship statute, this is the only alternative available to the client if the guardianship is to be used. The emotional trauma that a declaration of this type may have on the ward must be considered carefully before implementation. Thus, despite its feasibility as an estate planning technique to take care of the needs of the disabled person, the guardianship has particular drawbacks that may make it less advantageous than other estate planning techniques.

Power of Attorney

A power of attorney is a written document in which a principal (the disabled person) gives authority to another (the agent) to undertake some specific act on the principal's behalf. The power of attorney document assures the principal that, in the event of a serious illness or disability, the agent can conduct the transaction on the principal's behalf.

A power of attorney document has several advantages. Unlike a guardianship, which requires a legal declaration that the disabled person is both legally and mentally incompetent, a power of attorney can be used without the stigma of a declaration of incompetency. In fact, a power of attorney can only be used on behalf of a competent person, and the use of such a device by a mildly disabled person may be more advantageous, from a time and cost perspective, than a guardianship. A power of attorney is also relatively inexpensive to administer and its form is usually quite simple. Frequently, only one document need be drafted and the agent may only exercise those powers expressly contained in the document. There are no implied powers that may be inferred from the fiduciary role that the agent undertakes, unlike some of the implied powers of a trustee. This can be an advantage for the disabled principal, since the agent cannot undertake additional powers without the consent of the principal.

Yet, the power of attorney instrument may also be disadvantageous, as an agent may undertake only those powers expressly conferred by the document. The lack of flexibility within the document may prohibit the agent from exercising a power that needs to be exercised but which cannot be because it is not one of those powers contained within the document. For example, if the document is drafted so that the agent may enter into certain contracts relating only to personal property, but the needs of the disabled principal require that his real estate holdings be liquidated, the power of attorney document is of no benefit to the disabled person. In many states,[11] the power of attorney document is referred to as being "durable," meaning that the document is binding at the time it is executed until such time as it is revoked by the disabled person, or until the time when the disabled person dies. Even if the disabled individual should later become senile or be declared mentally incompetent, the power of attorney document is still binding if it has not been revoked prior to the declaration of incompetence. This inflexibility can be disadvantageous to the disabled person should his or her financial needs change considerably after becoming incompetent.

Repositioning of Assets into Exempt Categories

A third estate planning technique that maximizes public assistance benefits while maintaining the estate plan for the rest of the family is the repositioning of assets into exempt categories. The disabled person is allowed to own these properties while still qualifying for public assistance benefits. Unfortunately, the amount and type of assets that a disabled person may own are quite restricted and this strategy may only be of limited value. It should not be thought of as an exclusive remedy for the disabled person.

Trusts

Perhaps the most effective estate planning technique used for clients with disabled family members is the trust. A trust may be considered appropriate as an estate planning technique for the disabled for a variety of reasons. First, a trustee may be selected by the client without court approval, unlike a guardianship. Second, there is no need for continuous, detailed reports when acting as a trustee, unlike the forms that must be filed by the guardian. Third, the trustee has broader investment authority and has many implied powers that are not available to the guardian. Fourth, there is no need for court approval prior to making expenditures on behalf of the disabled person, unlike the court approval needed by the guardian. Fifth, there is no need to have the disabled beneficiary declared legally or mentally incompetent, unlike an absolute guardianship. Perhaps the most compelling reason why a trust is appropriate for the disabled person is because the legal structure of a trust, if properly drafted, enables the disabled individual to retain beneficial ownership of assets while permitting the disabled beneficiary to receive public assistance benefits. This, in turn, allows the parents or other family members to distribute remaining assets to other family members as part of the overall estate plan.

There are numerous types of trusts available for the client whose family includes a developmentally disabled member. Whether a particular type of trust is appropriate depends on the estate planning objectives of the parents as well as the income, estate, and gift tax implications of each type of trust. This chapter features four types of trusts frequently used when creating an estate plan for the client with a disabled family member.

The revocable living trust.   The revocable living trust is used primarily when the grantor desires to set up a fund to benefit the disabled person but wishes, at a later time, to revoke, alter, terminate, or amend the terms of the trust agreement. Thus, this arrangement provides the grantor with the flexibility needed to accommodate the needs of the disabled person. This can be an important factor, since the health, life expectancy, or financial needs of the disabled person may change dramatically, or there may be changes in the law that affect the well-being of the disabled person.

The revocable living trust avoids probate, as well as possible gift tax consequences. Since this type of trust is subject to possible revocation by the grantor, no completed gift has occurred at the time the trust is established; thus, there is no gift tax. Unfortunately, because the grantor retains the power to revoke the trust, any income produced by it is taxable to the grantor, and the value of the trust corpus is included in the gross estate of the grantor for federal estate tax purposes. Thus, this type of trust should not be used by an individual who wishes to reduce estate and income taxes. Nevertheless, the use of a revocable living trust for the disabled person's needs may be appropriate since the disabled person does not have legal title to the assets placed in the corpus. This allows the disabled person to retain eligibility for public assistance benefits despite being the trust beneficiary.

The irrevocable living trust. An irrevocable living trust can also be used to provide a means of support to a disabled individual without disqualifying him or her from receiving public assistance benefits. Once established, the grantor of an irrevocable living trust has no power to alter, terminate, or modify the terms on which income is distributed to the disabled beneficiary. This can be a tremendous disadvantage from an estate planning perspective, particularly because the disabled person's circumstances may change drastically after the trust is established. An irrevocable living trust also avoids probate. However, unlike the revocable living trust, income from the irrevocable living trust is taxed to the beneficiary at the time of distribution, or is taxed to the trust itself, if undistributed. Also, the initial transfer of assets into the irrevocable trust is treated as a gift for gift tax purposes. Not only are there possible gift tax consequences for the grantor at the time the trust is created, but the value of the assets placed in the trust will be treated as an adjustable taxable gift and this amount will be added to the taxable estate when determining the net federal estate tax payable by the grantor's estate.

The greatest drawback of this type of trust is the lack of flexibility it provides to a client with a disabled family member. If the financial needs of the disabled person increase because of loss of eligibility for public assistance, marriage, birth of children, or other reasons, this form of trust could easily become inappropriate. Other trusts or estate planning techniques should be considered in conjunction with an irrevocable living trust if such a trust is intended as an estate planning technique for a disabled individual.

The life insurance trust. A life insurance trust can be either revocable or irrevocable, funded or unfunded,[12] and can take effect either during the grantor's lifetime or at his or her death. Frequently, the life insurance trust is structured so that the trustee is named as beneficiary of one or more life insurance policies. At the death of the grantor (who is usually the insured), the proceeds pass immediately to the trustee, who invests, supervises, and controls the management of the proceeds. The return on the investment proceeds is used to pay income to the disabled person, who is named as beneficiary of the trust.

This is a relatively inexpensive way to provide income to the disabled beneficiary; essentially, it involves the legal costs of setting up the trust plus premium payments on the policy. It is one way to assure that the disabled beneficiary receives the income from the trust proceeds while allowing the beneficiary to remain eligible for public assistance benefits.

The supplemental or Craven trust.   This trust, which is normally an irrevocable living trust, is structured to allow the disabled beneficiary to receive public assistance benefits. It is also used to prevent federal, state, or local agencies from seeking reimbursement for public assistance benefits currently being paid or previously paid to the disabled beneficiary.

This trust form differs from the "normal trust" in several respects: first, it is used to provide supplemental income to the disabled individual in addition to what the disabled person receives by means of public assistance. It is not a trust for the "general welfare, comfort, and support" of the disabled individual, as are many trusts that are subject to attack by governmental agencies seeking reimbursement. It is important that the purpose of this trust be clearly established in the language of the trust agreement itself in order to avoid possible reimbursement proceedings. The trust should also contain spendthrift provisions so that neither corpus nor income can be spent by the beneficiary before actual distribution. Such provisions should curtail any invasion of corpus or income by governmental or private creditors. To avoid possible invasion of either corpus or income by governmental creditors, the trust should be carefully worded so that the beneficiary can demand neither. As a further safeguard, the trust should prohibit the trustee from dispersing large amounts of cash to the beneficiary that would otherwise disqualify the beneficiary from receiving public assistance benefits. Instead, the trustee should be given authority to make expenditures for goods and services on the beneficiary's behalf rather than cash or cash equivalents that would jeopardize the beneficiary's eligibility.

In short, if a client wishes to use a trust to provide income to a disabled beneficiary, it is clear that the language of an "ordinary trust" cannot normally be used. To avoid the pitfalls previously discussed, a special form of trust known as the supplemental or Craven trust[13] should be used.

CONCLUSION

It should be noted that no single estate planning technique is necessarily "the best choice." Each disabled person's situation is unique, and each disabled individual has specific needs and special problems. The optimal estate plan is one that is flexible enough to accommodate changing financial needs, health, marital status, and changes in the law affecting eligibility requirements for public assistance. Flexibility and accuracy of detail are the trademarks of an efficient estate plan for the client whose family includes a developmentally disabled member.

FOOTNOTES

1. 42 U.S.C. Section 6001(5) as contained in the Developmentally Disabled Assistance and Bill of Rights Act.

2. Russell, Mark L. *Alternatives: A Family Guide to Legal and Financial Planning for the Disabled.* Evanston, IL: First Publications, Inc., 1983 at 7, 63.

3. In re Estate of Secrist, 186 N.W. 2d 665 (Iowa 1971). In general, most states have similar requirements for testamentary capacity.

4. "Ademption" is the extinction or withdrawal of a legacy by act of the testator equivalent to a revocation or indicating intention to revoke. BLACK'S LAW DICTIONARY 5th ed. at 36. The net effect of an ademption by extinction is that no assets remain to be distributed to other family members.

5. In all states but Louisiana it is possible for parents to disinherit a child. Under Louisiana state law, a portion of a deceased parent's estate must pass to the child or children.

6. The definition of "income" and the list of exclusions may be found at 42 U.S.C. Section 1382a and following sections.

7. 42 U.S.C. 1382b(a)(1) and following sections.

8. 42 U.S.C. 1382b(c)(1).

9. 29 U.S.C. Section 723(a) and (b).

10. As of this writing, most states recognize some form of limited guardianship for a mildly disabled individual. This number is expected to increase because of the flexibility that this form of guardianship provides.

11. As of this writing approximately 45 states have authorized a durable power of attorney by state statute.

12. A "funded" life insurance trust is one that contains cash or other income-producing cash equivalents that are used to pay premiums on the life of the insured. An unfunded life insurance trust is one that does not contain any assets prior to the death of the insured but serves as a receptacle for the proceeds of the policy when the insured dies.

13. The term "Craven trust" originates from the trust form written for the Craven family of Wenatchee, Wash., for their mentally disabled

daughter. A copy of the sample Craven trust document may be obtained for a nominal fee by writing the Foundation for the Handicapped, a nonprofit corporation organized under the state of Washington. Its principal place of business is 1550 West Armory Way, Seattle, Wash. 98119.

11

ESTATE PLANNING FOR THE FAMILY OF THE DEVELOPMENTALLY DISABLED PERSON:
A Case Study Approach*

INTRODUCTION

Most people who wish to implement some type of estate plan do so with the intention of transferring assets to particular beneficiaries while minimizing estate taxes and related transfer costs. For the individual who has a developmentally disabled person as a beneficiary, estate planning can be a more intricate, if not precarious process. For such an individual, estate planning for the disabled individual involves careful coordination of outright property transfers, inheritances, and public assistance benefits. If the disabled person receives too much property in the form of gifts or inheritances, the estate plans for all family members may be seriously impaired.

The second portion of this chapter uses a case study approach to identify the estate planning pitfalls that occur most often in intrafamily situations affecting the developmentally disabled person. It discusses the ways in which these pitfalls can be avoided by focusing on the various estate planning techniques that can be used to bypass these pitfalls. The

* © 1988 International Association for Financial Planning, Inc. This chapter is reprinted with permission of International Association for Financial Planning, Inc.

advantages and disadvantages of each of these techniques are presented in order that the financial planner may assist the client in the selection of an estate planning technique that provides the disabled person with the greatest amount of flexibility at the least cost.

IDENTIFICATION OF ESTATE PLANNING PITFALLS

The starting point for the development of an estate plan for a client whose family includes a developmentally disabled person begins by defining the term "developmentally disabled person." A developmentally disabled person is an individual who suffers from any severe, chronic disability which

1. is attributable to a mental or physical impairment or combination of mental and physical impairment,
2. is manifested before the person reaches the age of 22,
3. is likely to continue indefinitely,
4. results in substantial functional limitations in three or more of the following areas of major life activity: (a) self-care, (b) receptive and expressive language, (c) learning, (d) mobility, (e) self-direction, (f) capacity for independent living, and (g) economic sufficiency,
5. reflects the person's need for a combination and sequence of special, interdisciplinary, or generic care, treatment, or other services which are of lifelong or extended duration and are individually planned and coordinated.[1]

If an individual meets this definition of developmental disability, the person may qualify to receive public assistance benefits. Receipt of these benefits depends on the disabled's financial resources, needs, and current income level. Eligibility for public assistance benefits is not automatic, however, and a disabled individual may be barred from receiving benefits as a result of one or more estate planning pitfalls unknowingly created by the disabled's parents, other family members, or friends. It is important at the onset of any estate plan to identify these pitfalls and determine how they can be avoided.

Most pitfalls occur because parents or other family members leave a sizeable amount of property to the disabled person under the terms of a will. The disabled person may also inherit a large amount of property because the parents die without a will, or because the parents' wills do not contain a residuary clause, which would have passed the property to someone other than the disabled person. Similarly, an improperly drafted trust or a trust that terminates because its terms have been completed can cause the corpus to revert back to the disabled person. The estate planning pitfalls created by any one of these errors can be significant. Let us take a hypothetical couple with a disabled child to illustrate the pitfalls that can occur in this type of situation.

Client Profile

Randy and Elaine Bradley have been married for 20 years and have three children: Matthew, age 19, Steve, age 17, and Lisa, age 12. Randy, Elaine, Steve and Lisa are in good health. Matthew suffers from a developmental disability that he has had since birth. Matthew's disability is severe enough that, in the opinion of medical experts, he will be unable to live without adult supervision. Matthew plans on moving into a group home in the near future. He can hold a job that requires only simple work skills. His counselors feel that he could work well in a sheltered workshop environment. Matthew can perform simple tasks and manage his own living expenses with the assistance of his parents. Matthew will need individualized health care on a continuing basis for the rest of his life. Matthew has a life expectancy of an additional 30 to 35 years. Randy, age 46, has assets currently valued at $900,000. Elaine, age 44, has assets currently valued at $600,000. Both Randy and Elaine are employed full time, he as an electrical engineer earning $70,000 per year, and she as an assistant professor of biology at a nearby state university, earning $35,000 per year.

Estate Planning Objectives

Since Matthew will be unable to hold a job that provides him with complete financial independence, Randy would like to leave a portion of his assets outright to Matthew. Randy would like to make a lifetime gift to Matthew that would provide him with about one-third of the value of Randy's estate. This lifetime transfer would be a cash gift of $300,000. Randy believes this amount would be adequate to take care of Matthew's living expenses for the duration of his son's life. The other children would receive their one-third shares after Elaine's death. If Randy predeceases Elaine, as they both anticipate, Elaine would live on the income produced by her own property holdings as well as on the income produced by the two-thirds of Randy's estate that will eventually pass to the other children at Elaine's death. Neither Randy nor Elaine has any other relatives who are depending on them for support.

Assume that Randy implements an estate plan that leaves $300,000 as a lifetime gift to Matthew. The remaining $600,000 is placed in a testamentary nonmarital trust with life income to Elaine. At her death, the trust corpus is to be divided equally between Steve and Lisa. Assume that Randy makes the gift to Matthew in 1989. The money is placed in

Matthew's bank account, which pays 5.25 percent interest. Both Randy and Elaine advise Matthew on how to spend the money, stressing the need to conserve it for future health care and living expenses. However, Matthew is legal titleholder of the account. If Randy dies in 1991, his estate tax liability would look like this (assume a 6% rate of appreciation on the property assigned to the nonmarital trust):

$636,000	gross estate
−50,000	funeral, administrative expenses[2]
$586,000	taxable estate
+280,000	post-1976 adjusted taxable gifts[3]
$866,000	tentative tax base
293,540	tentative tax
−0	minus gift taxes paid on lifetime gifts[4]
$293,540	tax before reduction for credits
−$192,800	unified credit for 1991[5]
$100,740	net federal estate tax liability
$485,260	net estate (to be divided equally between Steve and Lisa at their mother's death)

The pitfalls created by Randy's and Elaine's estate plan can be identified as follows:

1. **Excessive Tax Liability:** Randy's federal estate tax liability could have been reduced by more effective use of the nonmarital trust and the marital deduction. In addition, he should have avoided an outright gift of the money to Matthew, as most of this gift returns to the tentative tax base and prevents his federal estate tax liability from decreasing.

2. **Inadequate Amount Gifted to Son:** Randy made a significant error in his estate plan when he assumed that the $300,000 would adequately cover Matthew's living expenses for the duration of his son's life. Assuming an annual appreciation rate of 5.25 percent on the unused portion of the gift, this sum would not be adequate to take care of Matthew's living expenses for the rest of his life. Living expenses, including health care and other related costs, currently average $30,000 per year for a disabled person.[6] Thus, assuming an appreciation rate of 5.25 percent on the unused portion of the gift and assuming a yearly cost increase of 5.25 percent for living expenses, the gift would be totally depleted in less than 11 years.[7] At that time, Matthew would be approximately 30 years old.

3. **Ineligibility for Public Assistance Benefits:** By transferring ownership of $300,000 to his disabled son, Randy has given his son so much

property that Matthew is now ineligible for public assistance benefits. This is a prime example of how a family member with good intentions can inadvertently destroy the estate plan for both the disabled person and the family member. Because eligibility for public assistance benefits is dependent on such factors as financial need and ownership of assets, almost the entire amount of the $300,000 gift would have to be expended before Matthew could attain eligibility for supplemental security income (SSI), the most prominent form of public assistance. If proper estate planning had been done, Matthew could have received public assistance benefits without depleting the $300,000.

4. Possibility of Reimbursement: Assume that Matthew becomes eligible for public assistance benefits at some time after the $300,000 gift is totally consumed. If he then subsequently acquires additional gifts or. inheritances from his mother's estate, Matthew would not only become ineligible for further public assistance benefits, but would also be required to reimburse federal, state, or local agencies for amounts previously spent on his behalf as public assistance benefits. The amounts required to be reimbursed could seriously deplete, if not totally consume, any property received by the disabled person. This possibility could seriously disrupt the estate plans of the parents for their son. Careful coordination of public assistance benefits, gifts, and inheritances could have avoided this problem.

5. Disruption of Estate Plan for Other Family Members: If the $300,000 gift were totally consumed by Matthew within 11 years from the date of the initial transfer, this could have a serious effect on the estate plan for other family members.

Assume that the $300,000 gift is totally consumed by Matthew, thereby entitling Matthew to receipt of public assistance benefits. If the amount received as public assistance is inadequate to take care of Matthew's living expenses, or if there is a waiting period before receipt of benefits, so that other means of support must be relied upon, it may be necessary to invade the nonmarital trust corpus for Matthew's support and maintenance. Thus, though the trust corpus might be appreciating on an annual basis, it may be necessary to invade it. These invasions could reduce or seriously deplete the amount of corpus remaining to be distributed to Steve and Lisa, and the amount received by each could be much less than the original one-third share intended by their parents. Under Randy's present estate plan, administrative expenses and federal estate taxes are subtracted from the property allocated to the nonmarital trust. If this amount is further reduced by invasions of the corpus in order to support Matthew, there will be even less property available for distribution to the other children.

6. Asset Management Problems: The cash gift of $300,000 to Matthew presents a significant problem: proper asset management of the gift. Matthew's disability prevents him from making proper investment and management decisions affecting the gift. Since a custodianship or guardianship has not been legally established, Matthew is presumed to be competent to manage the money. Though his parents may assume that they are free to make investment decisions for their son, this is not the case. Even though they are his parents, Randy and Elaine would first have to petition a court and be named as legal guardians before they could make investment decisions affecting Matthew's property. Under the circumstances, it is apparent that Matthew is not competent to manage the $300,000 alone. Professional expertise is needed to ensure that the proper investment decisions are made.

7. Testamentary Distribution of the Unused Gift: Since the $300,000 would be consumed by Matthew within a 11-year time period, the problem of testamentary disposition of any unconsumed portion of the gift would probably not arise. However, if Matthew were to die before the 11-year time period had expired, or if his rate of consumption was less than the amount of appreciation, there could be a portion of the gift remaining that would be included in Matthew's gross estate. There could be legal complications stemming from the testamentary disposition of the remaining portion of the gift. Specifically, if Matthew had made a will in which he left the remaining portion of the gift to someone other than those who would take under the laws of intestacy (parents, brother, and sister), those who would take the property by operation of law could challenge the will on the grounds that Matthew lacked the testamentary capacity necessary to make such a document. A costly and lengthy will contest could result if this factual pattern developed. Thus, Matthew's estate plan for the testamentary disposition of his property could be effectively destroyed.

HOW THESE ESTATE PLANNING PITFALLS CAN BE AVOIDED

A number of estate planning techniques can be utilized to solve some or all of the Bradleys' estate planning problems. A financial planner might choose to implement a guardianship for Matthew by having his parents named as guardians of his estate. The guardianship would enable Randy and Elaine to assist Matthew in managing the property. They are familiar with Matthew's health problems as well as his emotional needs and they could make decisions that are in Matthew's best interests, unlike a trustee, who may not be familiar with the disabled person's circumstances. Generally, guardianships present some significant disadvantages. They are often expensive to administer; they usually involve time delays because court approval is required before the guardian can make expenditures on the disabled person's behalf. In addition, a court hearing must first be held in which the disabled person must be declared legally incompetent; and state law may restrict the investment authority of the named guardian.

Another option that might be considered is the use of a written document called a power of attorney. The power of attorney can give both Randy and Elaine the authority to make management decisions on Matthew's behalf. Unlike the guardianship, the power of attorney document can be used without having Matthew declared legally incompetent. It is less expensive to use than a guardianship, and the powers conferred on those who act on behalf of the disabled person are limited only to those powers expressly stated in the terms of the document. But if those powers are too tightly drawn so that Randy and Elaine cannot act on Matthew's behalf if the occasion warrants it, the power of attorney might be a useless instrument. Careful wording of the instrument is necessary in order to avoid having a document that becomes obsolete in light of the disabled person's changing circumstances.

Another disadvantage might occur if Randy and Elaine live in a state that has enacted a durable power of attorney statute. If a power of attorney is "durable" it means that the power is binding until such time when the disabled person revokes it. Such an instrument might be used by a mildly disabled person, such as Matthew, who could be considered legally competent. But if Matthew were to later become incompetent without having revoked the power of attorney instrument, his parents would be restricted to the use of those powers expressly conferred upon them in the instrument. If these powers are inadequate to take care of Matthew's physical needs, a petition and court hearing for creation of a guardianship would be necessary.

Perhaps the optimal estate planning technique for a disabled person is the trust. A trust may be considered appropriate for a variety of reasons. First, a trustee may be selected by a family member without court approval, unlike a guardianship. There are fewer restrictions on investment policies and procedures than there are for a guardian of the estate. There is not a need for continuous detailed reports when acting as a trustee, unlike the forms that must be filed by the guardian. In addition, the trustee has broader investment authority and has many implied powers that are not available to the guardian. For example, a trustee may be able to invest assets in a particular investment vehicle that may draw a higher rate of return than the investment vehicle to which the guardian may be restricted by state law. Also, there is no need for court approval prior to making expenditures on the disabled person's behalf, unlike the court approval needed by the guardian.

Another reason why a trust may be more appropriate is because, unlike the guardianship, there is no need to have the disabled person declared legally or mentally incompetent. Perhaps the most compelling reason why a trust is appropriate for the disabled person is because the structure of a trust, if properly drafted, enables the disabled individual to retain beneficial and legal ownership of certain assets while permitting the disabled beneficiary to receive public assistance benefits. This, in turn, allows the parents to distribute remaining assets to other family members as part of the overall estate plan.

There are numerous types of trusts available as part of an estate plan for the family containing a disabled individual. Whether a particular type of trust is appropriate depends on the estate planning objectives of the parents or other family members, as well as the income, estate, and gift tax implications resulting from the use of each type of trust. This chapter features three types of trusts frequently used when creating an estate plan for the client with a disabled family member.

Revocable Living Trust

As with any trust arrangement, legal title to the assets placed in the corpus of the trust rests with the trustee, while beneficial or equitable title to the income passes to the disabled beneficiary. If a revocable living trust is used, the creators of the trust (usually the parents or other family members) place certain income-producing assets into the trust. The revocable living trust is used primarily when the creators desire to set up a fund to benefit the disabled person but wish, at a later time, to revoke, alter, or modify the terms of the trust. This arrangement provides the creators with the flexibility essential for accommodating the needs of the disabled person. This can be an important factor since the health or life circumstances of the disabled person may change drastically, or there may be changes in the law that affect the ability of the disabled person to receive public assistance.

The revocable living trust avoids probate, as well as possible gift tax consequences. Since this type of trust is subject to possible revocation by the creator, no completed gift has occurred at the time the trust is created. Thus, there is no gift tax. Unfortunately, because of the possibility of revocation, any income produced by the trust is taxable to the creators of the trust, and the value of the assets placed in the corpus is included in the gross estate of the creators. Thus, this type of trust should not be used by an individual who wishes to reduce income and estate taxes. Still, the use of a revocable living trust for the disabled person's needs may be appropriate since the disabled person does not have legal title to the assets in the trust, enabling him to qualify for public assistance benefits.

Irrevocable Living Trust

An irrevocable living trust can also be used to provide a means of support to a disabled person without disqualifying that person from receiving public assistance benefits. The major difference between a revocable and irrevocable living trust is that, once established, the creator of the irrevocable living trust has no power to alter, amend, or revoke the terms of the trust. This can be a tremendous disadvantage from an estate planning perspective, particularly because the disabled person's needs and circumstances may change drastically after the trust is established. An irrevocable living trust is similar to a revocable living trust in that both avoid probate and both provide the disabled beneficiary with income while maintaining public assistance eligibility. However, unlike the revocable living trust, in which income is taxed to the creator of the trust, income from the irrevocable living trust is taxed to the trust itself if undistributed, or to the disabled beneficiary, if distributed. Also, the initial transfer of assets into the corpus is treated as a gift for gift tax purposes. Not only are there gift tax consequences for the settlor of the trust at the time the trust is created, but the value of the assets placed in the trust will be treated as an adjusted taxable gift and will be added to the taxable estate when determining the net federal estate tax payable by the settlor's estate.

Perhaps the greatest drawback of this type of trust is the lack of flexibility that it provides to a client with a disabled family member. If the financial situation of the disabled person changes drastically, or if living expenses for the disabled person increase because of health problems, marriage, birth of children, or loss of eligibility for public assistance benefits, this form of trust could easily be inadequate to provide for the financial needs of the disabled person. If such a trust is utilized as part of an estate plan, it should be funded with a sizeable amount of corpus to provide the disabled beneficiary with sufficient income, if needed.

Supplemental or Craven Trust

This trust is usually structured to assist the disabled person in receiving public assistance benefits. It is also used to prevent federal, state, or local agencies from seeking reimbursement for public assistance benefits currently or previously paid to the disabled individual. This trust differs from the standard trust in several respects: first, it is structured to provide supplemental income to the disabled person in addition to what the disabled person receives by means of public assistance. Thus, it is not a trust for the "general welfare, comfort, and support" of the disabled individual, as are many of the trusts that are subject to attack by governmental agencies seeking reimbursement. It is important that the purpose of this trust be expressly stated in the language of the trust instrument in order to avoid possible reimbursement proceedings. In addition, the trust should also contain spendthrift provisions so that neither corpus nor income can be spent by the beneficiary before actual distribution. Such provisions should curtail any invasion of corpus or income by governmental or private creditors. An additional safeguard is to structure the trust in such a way that the beneficiary can demand neither corpus nor income. The trust should prohibit the trustee from dispersing large amounts of cash or other property to the beneficiary that would cause disqualification for public assistance benefits. Instead, the trustee should be given authority to make expenditures for goods and services on the beneficiary's behalf. Ordinarily, receipt of goods and services will not jeopardize the beneficiary's eligibility for public assistance benefits.

In summary, if the client wishes to use a trust to provide income to a disabled beneficiary, it is clear that the language of a standard trust form is inappropriate and cannot be used. Rather, to avoid the pitfalls previously discussed, a special trust form known as supplemental or Craven trust should be used.[8]

Assume that Randy implements the Craven trust in 1989 as part of his estate plan and funds it with the $300,000 instead of providing Matthew with an outright gift of that amount. Assume also that Randy makes maximum use of the marital deduction for Elaine and the exemption equivalent amount for the other children. Since the amount transferred to the Craven trust is an irrevocable gift, it will be treated as a gift for tax purposes. Assuming the same set of facts as presented earlier, with an additional assumption that Randy leaves Elaine $318,000 worth of property (one-half of his gross estate) qualifying for the marital deduction, Randy's federal estate tax liability would look like this if he died in 1991:

$636,000	gross estate
−50,000	funeral, administrative expenses
318,000	marital deduction amount (in 1991)
268,000	taxable estate (less than the exemption equivalent for 1991—passes to Steve and Lisa in equal shares)
+280,000	post-1976 adjusted taxable gift (Craven trust property)
$548,000	tentative tax base
173,560	tentative tax
−0	gift taxes paid on lifetime gifts
$173,560	tax before reduction for credits

| $-192,800$ | unified credit for 1991 |
| $\$\quad\quad 0$ | net federal estate tax liability (arises from inclusion of adjusted taxable gift to taxable estate) |

By using the Craven trust, Randy has eliminated any federal estate tax liability; in addition, the income received by Matthew as trust beneficiary can supplement the public assistance benefits for which he is now eligible. The possibility of consuming the total amount of $300,000 is also averted. Since the Craven trust is strictly supplemental in nature, neither Randy nor Matthew has to worry about the possibility of reimbursement proceedings. Also, proper management of the money ceases to be a problem and the possibility of a will contest or other testamentary dispute over an unconsumed amount of the property gifted to Matthew is avoided. Finally, the use of the Craven trust ensures that the value of the nonmarital trust assets will remain intact for Steve and Lisa at their mother's death.

CONCLUSION

It should be noted that no single estate planning technique is necessarily "the best choice." Each disabled person's situation is unique and each disabled individual's particular needs and problems must be met. The optimal estate plan is one that is flexible enough to accommodate the disabled's changing financial needs, health, marital status, and changes in the law that affect the disabled's eligibility status for public assistance.

FOOTNOTES

1. 42 U.S.C. Section 6001(5) as contained in the Developmentally Disabled Assistance and Bill of Rights Act.
2. These expenses would be paid by the trust, thereby reducing the amount available for distribution to Steve and Lisa at Elaine's death.
3. Randy and Elaine elect to make a split gift of the $300,000, (using two annual exclusions or $20,000) resulting in an adjusted taxable gift of $280,000.
4. The unified credit amount of $192,800 in 1991 would have eliminated any actual gift tax liability.
5. When adjusted taxable gifts are added to the taxable estate, the full amount of the available unified credit is restored. For purposes of simplifying the hypothetical case, the state death tax credit is ignored, as are credits for foreign taxes and credits on prior transfers.

6. Russell, Mark. *Alternatives: A Family Guide to Legal and Financial Planning for the Disabled.* Evanston, IL: First Publications, Inc., 1983 at 7, 63.

Gift Year	Value Remaining	Consumption Rate (5.25% per year)	Appreciation on Unused Gift (5.25% per year)	Balance at End of Year
1	$300,000	$30,000	$15,750	$285,750
2	285,750	31,575	15,002	269,177
3	269,177	33,233	14,132	250,076
4	250,076	34,978	13,129	228,227
5	228,227	36,814	11,982	203,395
6	203,395	38,747	10,678	175,326
7	175,326	40,781	9,205	143,750
8	143,750	42,922	7,547	108,375
9	108,375	45,175	5,690	68,890
10	68,890	47,547	3,617	24,960
11	24,690	50,043	1,310	-0-

8. The term "Craven trust" originates from the trust form used for the Craven family of Wenatchee, Wash., for their mentally disabled daughter. A copy of the model Craven trust instrument may be obtained for a nominal fee by writing the Foundation for the Handicapped, a nonprofit corporation organized under the state of Washington. Its principal place of business is 1550 West Armory Way, Seattle, Wash. 98119.

Appendix A

*FEDERAL UNIFIED TRANSFER TAX RATE AND TABLES**

RATE TABLE

Estate and Gift Tax Rates for U.S. Citizens and Residents

If the amount is:	The tentative tax is:
Not over $10,000	18 percent of such amount.
Over $10,000 but not over $20,000	$1,800, plus 20 percent of the excess of such amount over $10,000.
Over $20,000 but not over $40,000	$3,800, plus 22 percent of the excess of such amount over $20,000.
Over $40,000 but not over $60,000	$8,200, plus 24 percent of the excess of such amount over $40,000.
Over $60,000 but not over $80,000	$13,000, plus 26 percent of the excess of such amount over $60,000.
Over $80,000 but not over $100,000	$18,200, plus 28 percent of the excess of such amount over $80,000.
Over $100,000 but not over $150,000	$23,800, plus 30 percent of the excess of such amount over $100,000.

* © Zaritsky, *Estate and Gift Tax Guide,* Prentice-Hall, Inc., 1985. This appendix is reprinted with permission of Prentice-Hall, Inc.

If the amount is:	The tentative tax is:
Over $150,000 but not over $250,000	$38,800, plus 32 percent of the excess of such amount over $150,000.
Over $250,000 but not over $500,000	$70,800, plus 34 percent of the excess of such amount over $250,000.
Over $500,000 but not over $750,000	$155,800 plus 37 percent of the excess of such amount over $500,000.
Over $750,000 but not over $1,000,000 ..	$248,300, plus 39 percent of the excess of such amount over $750,000.
Over $1,000,000 but not over $1,250,000	$345,800, plus 41 percent of the excess of such amount over $1,000,000.
Over $1,250,000 but not over $1,500,000	$448,300, plus 43 percent of the excess of such amount over $1,250,000.
Over $1,500,000 but not over $2,000,000	$555,800, plus 45 percent of the excess of such amount over $1,500,000.
Over $2,000,000 but not over $2,500,000	$780,800, plus 49 percent of the excess of such amount over $2,000,000.

For decedents dying and gifts made in 1982

Over $250,000 but not over $3,000,000 ..	$1,025,800, plus 53% of the excess over $2,500,000.
Over $3,000,000 but not over $3,500,000	$1,290,800, plus 57% of the excess over $3,000,000.
Over $3,500,000 but not over $4,000,000	$1,575,800, plus 61% of the excess over $3,500,000.
Over $4,000,000	$1,880,800, plus 65% of the excess over $4,000,000.

For decedents dying and gifts made in 1983

Over $2,500,000 but not over $3,000,000	$1,025,800, plus 53% of the excess over $2,500,000.
Over $3,000,000 but not over $3,500,000	$1,290,800, plus 57% of the excess over $3,000,000.
Over $3,500,000	$1,575,800, plus 60% of the excess over $3,500,000.

Estate and Gift Tax Guide

For decedents dying and gifts made in 1984, 1985, 1986, and 1987

Over $2,500,000 but not over $3,000,000	$1,025,800, plus 53% of the excess over $2,500,000.
Over $3,000,000	$1,290,800, plus 55% of the excess over $3,000,000.

For decedents dying and gifts made in 1988 through 1992

Over $3,000,000	$1,290,800, plus 55 percent of the excess of such amount over $3,000,000.

UNIFIED CREDIT

Unified Estate and Gift Tax Credit for U.S. Citizens and Residents

Year	Unified Credit	Exemption Equivalent
1977	$ 30,000	$120,667
1978	34,000	134,000
1979	38,000	147,333
1980	42,500	161,563
1981	47,000	175,625
1982	62,800	225,000
1983	79,300	275,000
1984	96,300	325,000
1985	121,800	400,000
1986	155,800	500,000
1987 and thereafter	192,800	600,000

Note: The allowable unified credit is reduced by an amount equal to 20% of the amount allowed as a prior law specific exemption for gifts made after September 8, 1976 and before January 1, 1977. There is no reduction if the specific exemption was used for gifts made before September 9, 1976. Also for gift tax purposes, only $6000 of the unified credit was available for gifts made after December 31, 1976 and before July 1, 1977.

Phaseout of Unified Credit on Large Estates After the Tax Revenue Act of 1987

For transfers after December 31, 1987, the '87 Act phases out the benefit of the graduated rates and the unified credit. A 5 percent surtax is applied to taxable transfers in excess of $10 million. The rate adjustment for estates and for gifts made after December 31, 1987, and before December 31, 1992, occurs for cumulative taxable transfers between $10 million and $21,040,000. Once the maximum adjustment applies, the 55 percent rate becomes the rate of taxation. After December 31, 1992, the maximum rate of taxation becomes 50 percent.

Example

John Q. Public dies in 1988 with a taxable estate of $14 million. His estate tax is computed as follows:

Tax on first $3 million of transfer	$1,290,800
Tax on remaining $11 million at 55%	6,050,000
New surtax (5% of $4 million)	200,000
Total taxes before unified credit	$7,540,800
Less unified credit	192,800
Tax Due	$7,348,000

ACTUARIAL TABLES

Table S (6.0 to 15.8%)

The following tables present the valuation factors for the present value of a single life annuity, life estate, and remainder interest for a charitable remainder annuity transaction. These tables are for charitable remainder annuity trusts with interest rates ranging from 6 to 15.8 percent, though the tables in Publication 1457 are printed and contain the tables for interest rates ranging from a low of 2.2 percent to a high of 26 percent. The tables have been in use since May 1, 1989.

To calculate the present value of a remainder interest in a charitable remainder annuity trust transaction, use the following steps.

First, determine the fair market value of the property transferred to the charitable remainder annuity trust.

Second, ensure that the correct valuation table has been used by applying the appropriate table, based on the interest rate selected for the income payout on the charitable remainder annuity trust.

Third, determine the age of the income recipient (column 1) (the holder of the life estate) of the charitable remainder annuity trust.

Fourth, select the appropriate remainder factor (column 4) for the fair market value of the property.

Fifth, subtract the appropriate remainder factor from the whole number 1 to arrive at the life estate factor.

Sixth, divide the life estate factor by the applicable interest rate to determine the present annuity factor.

Seventh, multiply the present annuity factor by the annuity amount received annually. The product of this amount is the present value of the annuity received by the income beneficiary for life.

Eighth, subtract the present value of the annuity from the fair market value of the property transferred to the CRAT. The difference is the amount of the charitable contribution deduction.

Note that tables for determining the present values of joint and survivor charitable remainder annuity trusts are found in Publication 1457 at Table R(2).

Table S(6.0) SINGLE LIFE, 6.0 PERCENT, BASED ON LIFE TABLE 80CNSMT
SHOWING THE PRESENT WORTH OF AN ANNUITY, OF A LIFE ESTATE,
AND OF A REMAINDER INTEREST

Age	Annuity	Life Estate	Remainder	Age	Annuity	Life Estate	Remainder
(1)	(2)	(3)	(4)	(1)	(2)	(3)	(4)
0	16.0427	.96256	.03744	55	11.5878	.69527	.30473
1	16.2159	.97295	.02705	56	11.3904	.68342	.31658
2	16.2044	.97227	.02773	57	11.1880	.67128	.32872
3	16.1875	.97125	.02875	58	10.9810	.65886	.34114
4	16.1670	.97002	.02998	59	10.7696	.64617	.35383
5	16.1438	.96863	.03137	60	10.5543	.63326	.36674
6	16.1185	.96711	.03289	61	10.3358	.62015	.37985
7	16.0912	.96547	.03453	62	10.1144	.60686	.39314
8	16.0617	.96370	.03630	63	9.8904	.59342	.40658
9	16.0298	.96179	.03821	64	9.6635	.57981	.42019
10	15.9954	.95973	.04027	65	9.4331	.56599	.43401
11	15.9583	.95750	.04250	66	9.1987	.55192	.44808
12	15.9190	.95514	.04486	67	8.9604	.53762	.46238
13	15.8782	.95269	.04731	68	8.7182	.52309	.47691
14	15.8370	.95022	.04978	69	8.4733	.50840	.49160
15	15.7958	.94775	.05225	70	8.2265	.49359	.50641
16	15.7547	.94528	.05472	71	7.9789	.47874	.52126
17	15.7135	.94281	.05719	72	7.7305	.46383	.53617
18	15.6718	.94031	.05969	73	7.4811	.44887	.55113
19	15.6289	.93774	.06226	74	7.2300	.43380	.56620
20	15.5847	.93508	.06492	75	6.9766	.41860	.58140
21	15.5392	.93235	.06765	76	6.7207	.40324	.59676
22	15.4919	.92951	.07049	77	6.4628	.38777	.61223
23	15.4425	.92655	.07345	78	6.2041	.37225	.62775
24	15.3902	.92341	.07659	79	5.9466	.35679	.64321
25	15.3348	.92009	.07991	80	5.6919	.34151	.65849
26	15.2757	.91654	.08346	81	5.4424	.32655	.67345
27	15.2127	.91276	.08724	82	5.1993	.31196	.68804
28	15.1458	.90875	.09125	83	4.9635	.29781	.70219
29	15.0748	.90449	.09551	84	4.7347	.28408	.71592
30	14.9997	.89998	.10002	85	4.5120	.27072	.72928
31	14.9199	.89520	.10480	86	4.2973	.25784	.74216
32	14.8358	.89015	.10985	87	4.0930	.24558	.75442
33	14.7469	.88481	.11519	88	3.8979	.23388	.76612
34	14.6533	.87920	.12080	89	3.7088	.22253	.77747
35	14.5550	.87330	.12670	90	3.5239	.21143	.78857
36	14.4521	.86713	.13287	91	3.3455	.20073	.79927
37	14.3445	.86067	.13933	92	3.1778	.19067	.80933
38	14.2322	.85393	.14607	93	3.0224	.18135	.81865
39	14.1150	.84690	.15310	94	2.8805	.17283	.82717
40	13.9928	.83957	.16043	95	2.7526	.16516	.83484
41	13.8657	.83194	.16806	96	2.6392	.15835	.84165
42	13.7338	.82403	.17597	97	2.5364	.15218	.84782
43	13.5973	.81584	.18416	98	2.4438	.14663	.85337
44	13.4558	.80735	.19265	99	2.3583	.14150	.85850
45	13.3093	.79856	.20144	100	2.2788	.13673	.86327
46	13.1579	.78947	.21053	101	2.2029	.13217	.86783
47	13.0015	.78009	.21991	102	2.1238	.12743	.87257
48	12.8405	.77043	.22957	103	2.0399	.12240	.87760
49	12.6752	.76051	.23949	104	1.9468	.11681	.88319
50	12.5056	.75034	.24966	105	1.8323	.10994	.89006
51	12.3317	.73990	.26010	106	1.6694	.10017	.89983
52	12.1528	.72917	.27083	107	1.4370	.08622	.91378
53	11.9690	.71814	.28186	108	1.0649	.06389	.93611
54	11.7807	.70684	.29316	109	0.4717	.02830	.97170

Table S(6.2) *SINGLE LIFE, 6.2 PERCENT, BASED ON LIFE TABLE 80CNSMT SHOWING THE PRESENT WORTH OF AN ANNUITY, OF A LIFE ESTATE, AND OF A REMAINDER INTEREST*

Age	Annuity	Life Estate	Remainder	Age	Annuity	Life Estate	Remainder
(1)	(2)	(3)	(4)	(1)	(2)	(3)	(4)
0	15.5589	.96465	.03535	55	11.3681	.70482	.29518
1	15.7280	:97514	.02486	56	11.1783	.69305	.30695
2	15.7182	.97453	.02547	57	10.9836	.68098	.31902
3	15.7033	.97360	.02640	58	10.7842	.66862	.33138
4	15.6849	.97247	.02753	59	10.5803	.65598	.34402
5	15.6640	.97117	.02883	60	10.3726	.64310	.35690
6	15.6410	.96974	.03026	61	10.1615	.63001	.36999
7	15.6162	.96820	.03180	62	9.9475	.61675	.38325
8	15.5893	.96653	.03347	63	9.7308	.60331	.39669
9	15.5600	.96472	.03528	64	9.5111	.58969	.41031
10	15.5285	.96277	.03723	65	9.2878	.57584	.42416
11	15.4944	.96065	.03935	66	9.0604	.56175	.43825
12	15.4581	.95840	.04160	67	8.8290	.54740	.45260
13	15.4204	.95606	.04394	68	8.5936	.53280	.46720
14	15.3824	.95371	.04629	69	8.3554	.51803	.48197
15	15.3445	.95136	.04864	70	8.1151	.50314	.49686
16	15.3067	.94901	.05099	71	7.8738	.48818	.51182
17	15.2689	.94667	.05333	72	7.6315	.47315	.52685
18	15.2306	.94430	.05570	73	7.3881	.45806	.54194
19	15.1913	.94186	.05814	74	7.1429	.44286	.55714
20	15.1507	.93935	.06065	75	6.8951	.42750	.57250
21	15.1089	.93675	.06325	76	6.6446	.41197	.58803
22	15.0654	.93406	.06594	77	6.3921	.39631	.60369
23	15.0200	.93124	.06876	78	6.1384	.38058	.61942
24	14.9719	.92826	.07174	79	5.8858	.36492	.63508
25	14.9208	.92509	.07491	80	5.6357	.34941	.65059
26	14.8662	.92170	.07830	81	5.3905	.33421	.66579
27	14.8077	.91808	.08192	82	5.1515	.31939	.68061
28	14.7457	.91423	.08577	83	4.9195	.30501	.69499
29	14.6797	.91014	.08986	84	4.6942	.29104	.70896
30	14.6097	.90580	.09420	85	4.4748	.27744	.72256
31	14.5353	.90119	.09881	86	4.2631	.26431	.73569
32	14.4566	.89631	.10369	87	4.0616	.25182	.74818
33	14.3733	.89115	.10885	88	3.8692	.23989	.76011
34	14.2856	.88570	.11430	89	3.6824	.22831	.77169
35	14.1932	.87998	.12002	90	3.4997	.21698	.78302
36	14.0964	.87398	.12602	91	3.3234	.20605	.79395
37	13.9951	.86770	.13230	92	3.1575	.19577	.80423
38	12.8892	.86113	.13887	93	3.0038	.18623	.81377
39	13.7785	.85427	.14573	94	2.8633	.17753	.82247
40	13.6630	.84710	.15290	95	2.7367	.16967	.83033
41	13.5426	.83964	.16036	96	2.6244	.16271	.83729
42	13.4177	.83190	.16810	97	2.5225	.15639	.84361
43	13.2881	.82386	.17614	98	2.4308	.15071	.84929
44	13.1537	.81553	.18447	99	2.3461	.14546	.85454
45	13.0144	.80690	.19310	100	2.2674	.14058	.85942
46	12.8703	.79796	.20204	101	2.1922	.13592	.86408
47	12.7213	.78872	.21128	102	2.1139	.13106	.86894
48	12.5677	.77920	.22080	103	2.0309	.12592	.87408
49	12.4099	.76941	.23059	104	1.9387	.12020	.87980
50	12.2479	.75937	.24063	105	1.8252	.11316	.88684
51	12.0815	.74905	.25095	106	1.6637	.10315	.89685
52	11.9102	.73843	.26157	107	1.4327	.08883	.91117
53	11.7340	.72751	.27249	108	1.0623	.06586	.93414
54	11.5533	.71631	.28369	109	0.4708	.02919	.97081

Table S(6.4) *SINGLE LIFE, 6.4 PERCENT, BASED ON LIFE TABLE 80CNSMT*
SHOWING THE PRESENT WORTH OF AN ANNUITY, OF A LIFE ESTATE,
AND OF A REMAINDER INTEREST

Age	Annuity	Life Estate	Remainder	Age	Annuity	Life Estate	Remainder
(1)	(2)	(3)	(4)	(1)	(2)	(3)	(4)
0	15.1017	.96651	.03349	55	11.1554	.71395	.28605
1	15.2669	.97708	.02292	56	10.9729	.70226	.29774
2	15.2586	.97655	.02345	57	10.7855	.69027	.30973
3	15.2454	.97571	.02429	58	10.5933	.67797	.32203
4	15.2289	.97465	.02535	59	10.3967	.66539	.33461
5	15.2099	.97344	.02656	60	10.1962	.65255	.34745
6	15.1891	.97210	.02790	61	9.9922	.63950	.36050
7	15.1665	.97065	.02935	62	9.7853	.62626	.37374
8	15.1419	.96908	.03092	63	9.5755	.61283	.38717
9	15.1151	.96737	.03263	64	9.3627	.59922	.40078
10	15.0861	.96551	.03449	65	9.1463	.58536	.41464
11	15.0546	.96350	.03650	66	8.9256	.57124	.42876
12	15.0211	.96135	.03865	67	8.7008	.55685	.44315
13	14.9863	.95912	.04088	68	8.4720	.54221	.45779
14	14.9512	.95688	.04312	69	8.2402	.52737	.47263
15	14.9162	.95464	.04536	70	8.0062	.51240	.48760
16	14.8814	.95241	.04759	71	7.7711	.49735	.50265
17	14.8466	.95018	.04982	72	7.5347	.48222	.51778
18	14.8115	.94793	.05207	73	7.2972	.46702	.53298
19	14.7753	.94562	.05438	74	7.0575	.45168	.54832
20	14.7380	.94323	.05677	75	6.8153	.43618	.56382
21	14.6996	.94078	.05922	76	6.5701	.42049	.57951
22	14.6597	.93822	.06178	77	6.3227	.40465	.59535
23	14.6179	.93554	.06446	78	6.0740	.38874	.61126
24	14.5736	.93271	.06729	79	5.8260	.37287	.62713
25	14.5263	.92969	.07031	80	5.5805	.35715	.64285
26	14.4758	.92645	.07355	81	5.3395	.34173	.65827
27	14.4216	.92298	.07702	82	5.1044	.32668	.67332
28	14.3639	.91929	.08071	83	4.8761	.31207	.68793
29	14.3025	.91536	.08464	84	4.6543	.29787	.70213
30	14.2372	.91118	.08882	85	4.4381	.28404	.71596
31	14.1677	.90673	.09327	86	4.2295	.27069	.72931
32	14.0942	.90203	.09797	87	4.0307	.25796	.74204
33	14.0161	.89703	.10297	88	3.8408	.24581	.75419
34	13.9337	.89176	.10824	89	3.6564	.23401	.76599
35	13.8468	.88620	.11380	90	3.4758	.22245	.77755
36	13.7558	.88037	.11963	91	3.3015	.21130	.78870
37	13.6603	.87426	.12574	92	3.1375	.20080	.79920
38	13.5603	.86786	.13214	93	2.9853	.19106	.80894
39	13.4557	.86117	.13883	94	2.8463	.18216	.81784
40	13.3464	.85417	.14583	95	2.7209	.17414	.82586
41	13.2324	.84688	.15312	96	2.6097	.16702	.83298
42	13.1139	.83929	.16071	97	2.5088	.16056	.83944
43	12.9909	.83142	.16858	98	2.4179	.15475	.84525
44	12.8632	.82325	.17675	99	2.3340	.14938	.85062
45	12.7307	.81476	.18524	100	2.2561	.14439	.85561
46	12.5934	.80598	.19402	101	2.1817	.13963	.86037
47	12.4514	.79689	.20311	102	2.1041	.13466	.86534
48	12.3048	.78751	.21249	103	2.0219	.12940	.87060
49	12.1540	.77786	.22214	104	1.9306	.12356	.87644
50	11.9991	.76794	.23206	105	1.8182	.11637	.88363
51	11.8398	.75775	.24225	106	1.6579	.10611	.89389
52	11.6757	.74725	.25275	107	1.4284	.09142	.90858
53	11.5068	.73643	.26357	108	1.0598	.06783	.93217
54	11.3334	.72534	.27466	109	0.4699	.03008	.96992

Table S(6.6)   *SINGLE LIFE, 6.6 PERCENT, BASED ON LIFE TABLE 80CNSMT*
SHOWING THE PRESENT WORTH OF AN ANNUITY, OF A LIFE ESTATE,
AND OF A REMAINDER INTEREST

Age	Annuity	Life Estate	Remainder	Age	Annuity	Life Estate	Remainder
(1)	(2)	(3)	(4)	(1)	(2)	(3)	(4)
0	14.6692	.96817	.03183	55	10.9495	.72266	.27734
1	14.8305	.97881	.02119	56	10.7738	.71107	.28893
2	14.8236	.97836	.02164	57	10.5934	.69916	.30084
3	14.8119	.97759	.02241	58	10.4082	.68694	.31306
4	14.7971	.97661	.02339	59	10.2184	.67442	.32558
5	14.7799	.97547	.02453	60	10.0248	.66164	.33836
6	14.7610	.97422	.02578	61	9.8277	.64863	.35137
7	14.7403	.97286	.02714	62	9.6275	.63542	.36458
8	14.7178	.97137	.02863	63	9.4245	.62201	.37799
9	14.6932	.96975	.03025	64	9.2183	.60841	.39159
10	14.6665	.96799	.03201	65	9.0084	.59455	.40545
11	14.6374	.96607	.03393	66	8.7942	.58042	.41958
12	14.6064	.96402	.03598	67	8.5758	.56601	.43399
13	14.5741	.96189	.03811	68	8.3533	.55132	.44868
14	14.5416	.95975	.04025	69	8.1278	.53643	.46357
15	14.5093	.95762	.04238	70	7.8999	.52139	.47861
16	14.4772	.95549	.04451	71	7.6706	.50626	.49374
17	14.4451	.95338	.04662	72	7.4401	.49104	.50896
18	14.4128	.95125	.04875	73	7.2081	.47574	.52426
19	14.3796	.94905	.05095	74	6.9740	.46028	.53972
20	14.3453	.94679	.05321	75	6.7370	.44464	.55536
21	14.3100	.94446	.05554	76	6.4970	.42880	.57120
22	14.2732	.94203	.05797	77	6.2546	.41280	.58720
23	14.2347	.93949	.06051	78	6.0107	.39671	.60329
24	14.1938	.93679	.06321	79	5.7674	.38065	.61935
25	14.1502	.93391	.06609	80	5.5262	.36473	.63527
26	14.1034	.93082	.06918	81	5.2894	.34910	.65090
27	14.0531	.92750	.07250	82	5.0581	.33384	.66616
28	13.9995	.92397	.07603	83	4.8335	.31901	.68099
29	13.9422	.92019	.07981	84	4.6150	.30459	.69541
30	13.8813	.91617	.08383	85	4.4020	.39053	.70947
31	13.8164	.91188	.08812	86	4.1963	.27695	.72305
32	13.7475	.90733	.09267	87	4.0002	.26401	.73599
33	13.6742	.90250	.09750	88	3.8128	.25164	.74836
34	13.5968	.89739	.10261	89	3.6307	.23963	.76037
35	13.5151	.89200	.10800	90	3.4523	.22785	.77215
36	13.4294	.88634	.11366	91	3.2799	.21648	.78352
37	13.3393	.88039	.11961	92	3.1177	.20577	.79423
38	13.2449	.87416	.12584	93	2.9671	.19583	.80417
39	13.1459	.86763	.13237	94	2.8295	.18675	.81325
40	13.0425	.86080	.13920	95	2.7053	.17855	.82145
41	12.9344	.85367	.14633	96	2.5952	.17128	.82872
42	12.8220	.84625	.15375	97	2.4952	.16468	.83532
43	12.7051	.83854	.16146	98	2.4052	.15874	.84126
44	12.5837	.83052	.16948	99	2.3221	.15326	.84674
45	12.4575	.82220	.17780	100	2.2449	.14816	.85184
46	12.3267	.81356	.18644	101	2.1712	.14330	.85670
47	12.1912	.80462	.19538	102	2.0944	.13823	.86177
48	12.0512	.79538	.20462	103	2.0130	.13286	.86714
49	11.9071	.78587	.21413	104	1.9226	.12689	.87311
50	11.7589	.77609	.22391	105	1.8112	.11954	.88046
51	11.6064	.76602	.23398	106	1.6522	.10905	.89095
52	11.4491	.75564	.24436	107	1.4242	.09400	.90600
53	11.2870	.74495	.25505	108	1.0572	.06978	.93022
54	11.1205	.73396	.26604	109	0.4690	.03096	.96904

Age	Annuity	Life Estate	Remainder	Age	Annuity	Life Estate	Remainder
(1)	(2)	(3)	(4)	(1)	(2)	(3)	(4)
0	14.2596	.96965	.03035	55	10.7500	.73100	.26900
1	14.4172	.98037	.01963	56	10.5809	.71950	.28050
2	14.4114	.97998	.02002	57	10.4071	.70768	.29232
3	14.4011	.97927	.02073	58	10.2285	.69554	.30446
4	14.3877	.97837	.02163	59	10.0454	.68309	.31691
5	14.3721	.97731	.02269	60	9.8583	.67037	.32963
6	14.3549	.97613	.02387	61	9.6677	.65741	.34259
7	14.3360	.97485	.02515	62	9.4741	.64424	.35576
8	14.3153	.97344	.02656	63	9.2774	.63087	.36913
9	14.2927	.97190	.02810	64	9.0777	.61728	.38272
10	14.2681	.97023	.02977	65	8.8741	.60344	.39656
11	14.2411	.96840	.03160	66	8.6662	.58930	.41070
12	14.2124	.96644	.03356	67	8.4539	.57487	.42513
13	14.1824	.96440	.03560	68	8.2375	.56015	.43985
14	14.1523	.96236	.03764	69	8.0179	.54522	.45478
15	14.1224	.96032	.03968	70	7.7959	.53012	.46988
16	14.0927	.95830	.04170	71	7.5724	.51492	.48508
17	14.0632	.95630	.04370	72	7.3474	.49962	.50038
18	14.0334	.95427	.04573	73	7.1209	.48422	.51578
19	14.0028	.95219	.04781	74	6.8921	.46866	.53134
20	13.9712	.95004	.04996	75	6.6603	.45290	.54710
21	13.9387	.94783	.05217	76	6.4253	.43692	.56308
22	13.9048	.94553	.05447	77	6.1878	.42077	.57923
23	13.8694	.94312	.05688	78	5.9486	.40451	.59549
24	13.8316	.94055	.05945	79	5.7097	.38826	.61174
25	13.7913	.93781	.06219	80	5.4728	.37215	.62785
26	13.7479	.93485	.06515	81	5.2400	.35632	.64368
27	13.7012	.93168	.06832	82	5.0126	.34086	.65914
28	13.6513	.92829	.07171	83	4.7915	.32582	.67418
29	13.5979	.92466	.07534	84	4.5763	.31119	.68881
30	13.5410	.92079	.07921	85	4.3664	.29692	.70308
31	13.4802	.91665	.08335	86	4.1635	.28312	.71688
32	13.4156	.91226	.08774	87	3.9701	.26997	.73003
33	13.3469	.90759	.09241	88	3.7851	.25739	.74261
34	13.2741	.90264	.09736	89	3.6053	.24516	.75484
35	13.1972	.89741	.10259	90	3.4290	.23317	.76683
36	13.1163	.89191	.10809	91	3.2586	.22158	.77842
37	13.0313	.88613	.11387	92	3.0981	.21067	.78933
38	12.9421	.88006	.11994	93	2.9491	.20054	.79946
39	12.8485	.87370	.12630	94	2.8128	.19127	.80873
40	12.7504	.86703	.13297	95	2.6898	.18291	.81709
41	12.6479	.86006	.13994	96	2.5808	.17549	.82451
42	12.5412	.85280	.14720	97	2.4818	.16876	.83124
43	12.4301	.84525	.15475	98	2.3926	.16270	.83730
44	12.3145	.83739	.16261	99	2.3103	.15710	.84290
45	12.1944	.82922	.17078	100	2.2338	.15190	.84810
46	12.0697	.82074	.17926	101	2.1608	.14694	.85306
47	11.9403	.81194	.18806	102	2.0848	.14177	.85823
48	11.8065	.80284	.19716	103	2.0042	.13629	.86371
49	11.6687	.79347	.20653	104	1.9147	.13020	.86980
50	11.5269	.78383	.21617	105	1.8043	.12269	.87731
51	11.3808	.77390	.22610	106	1.6465	.11196	.88804
52	11.2300	.76364	.23636	107	1.4200	.09656	.90344
53	11.0744	.75306	.24694	108	1.0547	.07172	.92828
54	10.9145	.74218	.25782	109	0.4682	.03184	.96816

Table S(7.0) *SINGLE LIFE, 7.0 PERCENT, BASED ON LIFE TABLE 80CNSMT*
SHOWING THE PRESENT WORTH OF AN ANNUITY, OF A LIFE ESTATE,
AND OF A REMAINDER INTEREST

Age	Annuity	Life Estate	Remainder	Age	Annuity	Life Estate	Remainder
(1)	(2)	(3)	(4)	(1)	(2)	(3)	(4)
0	13.8711	.97098	.02902	55	10.5567	.73897	.26103
1	14.0251	.98176	.01824	56	10.3940	.72758	.27242
2	14.0204	.98143	.01857	57	10.2264	.71585	.28415
3	14.0112	.98079	.01921	58	10.0541	.70379	.29621
4	13.9992	.97995	.02005	59	9.8773	.69141	.30859
5	13.9851	.97895	.02105	60	9.6966	.67876	.32124
6	13.9693	.97785	.02215	61	9.5123	.66586	.33414
7	13.9520	.97664	.02336	62	9.3248	.65274	.34726
8	13.9330	.97531	.02469	63	9.1344	.63940	.36060
9	13.9122	.97385	.02615	64	8.9407	.62585	.37415
10	13.8894	.97226	.02774	65	8.7431	.61202	.38798
11	13.8644	.97051	.02949	66	8.5413	.59789	.40211
12	13.8377	.96864	.03136	67	8.3350	.58345	.41655
13	13.8098	.96669	.03331	68	8.1244	.56871	.43129
14	13.7819	.96473	.03527	69	7.9107	.55375	.44625
15	13.7542	.96279	.03721	70	7.6943	.53860	.46140
16	13.7267	.96087	.03913	71	7.4763	.52334	.47666
17	13.6994	.95896	.04104	72	7.2568	.50797	.49203
18	13.6719	.95704	.04296	73	7.0356	.49249	.50751
19	13.6437	.95506	.04494	74	6.8119	.47683	.52317
20	13.6146	.95302	.04698	75	6.5851	.46096	.53904
21	13.5846	.95093	.04907	76	6.3550	.44485	.55515
22	13.5534	.94874	.05126	77	6.1222	.42856	.57144
23	13.5207	.94645	.05355	78	5.8876	.41213	.58787
24	13.4858	.94401	.05599	79	5.6531	.39572	.60428
25	13.4485	.94139	.05861	80	5.4203	.37942	.62058
26	13.4082	.93858	.06142	81	5.1915	.36341	.63659
27	13.3648	.93554	.06446	82	4.9678	.34774	.65226
28	13.3183	.93228	.06772	83	4.7501	.33251	.66749
29	13.2685	.92880	.07120	84	4.5382	.31767	.68233
30	13.2154	.92508	.07492	85	4.3313	.30319	.69681
31	13.1584	.92109	.07891	86	4.1313	.28919	.71081
32	13.0979	.91685	.08315	87	3.9404	.27583	.72417
33	13.0333	.91233	.08767	88	3.7578	.26305	.73695
34	12.9648	.90754	.09246	89	3.5803	.25062	.74938
35	12.8923	.90246	.09754	90	3.4060	.23842	.76158
36	12.8160	.89712	.10288	91	3.2375	.22663	.77337
37	12.7357	.89150	.10850	92	3.0787	.21551	.78449
38	12.6513	.88559	.11441	93	2.9313	.20519	.79481
39	12.5626	.87939	.12061	94	2.7964	.19575	.80425
40	12.4697	.87288	.12712	95	2.6746	.18722	.81278
41	12.3724	.86607	.13393	96	2.5666	.17966	.82034
42	12.2710	.85897	.14103	97	2.4685	.17279	.82721
43	12.1654	.85158	.14842	98	2.3801	.16661	.83339
44	12.0553	.84387	.15613	99	2.2986	.16090	.83910
45	11.9408	.83586	.16414	100	2.2229	.15560	.84440
46	11.8218	.82753	.17247	101	2.1506	.15054	.84946
47	11.6982	.81888	.18112	102	2.0753	.14527	.85473
48	11.5704	.80993	.19007	103	1.9954	.13968	.86032
49	11.4386	.80070	.19930	104	1.9068	.13347	.86653
50	11.3027	.79119	.20881	105	1.7974	.12582	.87418
51	11.1627	.78139	.21861	106	1.6409	.11486	.88514
52	11.0181	.77126	.22874	107	1.4158	.09911	.90089
53	10.8687	.76081	.23919	108	1.0522	.07366	.92634
54	10.7149	.75005	.24995	109	0.4673	.03271	.96729

Table S(7.2) SINGLE LIFE, 7.2 PERCENT, BASED ON LIFE TABLE 80CNSMT
SHOWING THE PRESENT WORTH OF AN ANNUITY, OF A LIFE ESTATE,
AND OF A REMAINDER INTEREST

Age	Annuity	Life Estate	Remainder	Age	Annuity	Life Estate	Remainder
(1)	(2)	(3)	(4)	(1)	(2)	(3)	(4)
0	13.5024	.97217	.02783	55	10.3694	.74659	.25341
1	13.6529	.98301	.01699	56	10.2126	.73531	.26469
2	13.6491	.98273	.01727	57	10.0511	.72368	.27632
3	13.6410	.98215	.01785	58	9.8848	.71171	.28829
4	13.6301	.98137	.01863	59	9.7141	.69941	.30059
5	13.6172	.98044	.01956	60	9.5394	.68683	.31317
6	13.6028	.97940	.02060	61	9.3610	.67399	.32601
7	13.5870	.97826	.02174	62	9.1796	.66093	.33907
8	13.5695	.97700	.02300	63	8.9950	.64764	.35236
9	13.5502	.97562	.02438	64	8.8072	.63412	.36588
10	13.5291	.97410	.02590	65	8.6155	.62032	.37968
11	13.5059	.97243	.02757	66	8.4194	.60620	.39380
12	13.4810	.97064	.02936	67	8.2189	.59176	.40824
13	13.4551	.96877	.03123	68	8.0140	.57701	.42299
14	13.4291	.96689	.03311	69	7.8058	.56202	.43798
15	13.4033	.96504	.03496	70	7.5950	.54684	.45316
16	13.3779	.96321	.03679	71	7.3824	.53153	.46847
17	13.3526	.96139	.03861	72	7.1681	.51610	.48390
18	13.3273	.95956	.04044	73	6.9520	.50054	.49946
19	13.3012	.95769	.04231	74	6.7333	.48480	.51520
20	13.2744	.95576	.04424	75	6.5114	.46882	.53118
21	13.2467	.95377	.04623	76	6.2861	.45260	.54740
22	13.2179	.95169	.04831	77	6.0579	.43617	.56383
23	13.1877	.94952	.05048	78	5.8277	.41960	.58040
24	13.1555	.94719	.05281	79	5.5975	.40302	.59698
25	13.1209	.94470	.05530	80	5.3688	.38655	.61345
26	13.0835	.94201	.05799	81	5.1438	.37035	.62965
27	13.0431	.93910	.06090	82	4.9237	.35450	.64550
28	12.9998	.93598	.06402	83	4.7094	.33908	.66092
29	12.9533	.93264	.06736	84	4.5006	.32405	.67595
30	12.9035	.92905	.07095	85	4.2968	.30937	.69063
31	12.8502	.92521	.07479	86	4.0995	.29516	.70484
32	12.7933	.92112	.07888	87	3.9112	.28161	.71839
33	12.7326	.91675	.08325	88	3.7309	.26863	.73137
34	12.6681	.91210	.08790	89	3.5555	.25600	.74400
35	12.5997	.90718	.09282	90	3.3833	.24360	.75640
36	12.5277	.90200	.09800	91	3.2167	.23160	.76840
37	12.4518	.89653	.10347	92	3.0596	.22029	.77971
38	12.3719	.89078	.10922	93	2.9136	.20978	.79022
39	12.2879	.88473	.11527	94	2.7801	.20017	.79983
40	12.1997	.87838	.12162	95	2.6595	.19148	.80852
41	12.1073	.87173	.12827	96	2.5525	.18378	.81622
42	12.0109	.86478	.13522	97	2.4553	.17678	.82322
43	11.9104	.85755	.14245	98	2.3678	.17048	.82952
44	11.8055	.85000	.15000	99	2.2870	.16466	.83534
45	11.6963	.84213	.15787	100	2.2120	.15926	.84074
46	11.5827	.83396	.16604	101	2.1404	.15411	.84589
47	11.4647	.82546	.17454	102	2.0658	.14874	.85126
48	11.3424	.81665	.18335	103	1.9868	.14305	.85695
49	11.2162	.80756	.19244	104	1.8989	.13672	.86328
50	11.0861	.79820	.20180	105	1.7906	.12892	.87108
51	10.9518	.78853	.21147	106	1.6353	.11774	.88226
52	10.8130	.77853	.22147	107	1.4117	.10164	.89836
53	10.6695	.76820	.23180	108	1.0497	.07558	.92442
54	10.5216	.75756	.24244	109	0.4664	.03358	.96642

Age	Annuity	Life Estate	Remainder	Age	Annuity	Life Estate	Remainder
(1)	(2)	(3)	(4)	(1)	(2)	(3)	(4)
0	13.1519	.97324	.02676	55	10.1877	.75389	.24611
1	13.2990	.98413	.01587	56	10.0367	.74272	.25728
2	13.2960	.98391	.01609	57	9.8809	.73119	.26881
3	13.2889	.98338	.01662	58	9.7204	.71931	.28069
4	13.2791	.98265	.01735	59	9.5554	.70710	.29290
5	13.2673	.98178	.01822	60	9.3865	.69460	.30540
6	13.2541	.98081	.01919	61	9.2139	.68183	.31817
7	13.2396	.97973	.02027	62	9.0382	.66883	.33117
8	13.2235	.97854	.02146	63	8.8593	.65559	.34441
9	13.2056	.97722	.02278	64	8.6772	.64211	.35789
10	13.1860	·97577	.02423	65	8.4911	.62834	.37166
11	13.1645	.97417	.02583	66	8.3006	.61424	.38576
12	13.1413	.97245	.02755	67	8.1056	.59981	.40019
13	13.1170	.97066	.02934	68	7.9062	.58506	.41494
14	13.0928	.96887	.03113	69	7.7034	.57005	.42995
15	13.0689	.96710	.03290	70	7.4978	.55484	.44516
16	13.0452	.96534	.03466	71	7.2904	.53949	.46051
17	13.0218	.96362	.03638	72	7.0812	.52401	.47599
18	12.9984	.96188	.03812	73	6.8701	.50839	.49161
19	12.9743	.96010	.03990	74	6.6563	.49256	.50744
20	12.9495	.95827	.04173	75	6.4391	.47649	.52351
21	12.9240	.95638	.04362	76	6.2184	.46016	.53984
22	12.8974	.95441	.04559	77	5.9947	.44361	.55639
23	12.8695	.95234	.04766	78	5.7689	.42690	.57310
24	12.8396	.95013	.04987	79	5.5428	.41017	.58983
25	12.8076	.94776	.05224	80	5.3181	.39354	.60646
26	12.7728	.94519	.05481	81	5.0968	.37717	.62283
27	12.7352	.94241	.05759	82	4.8803	.36114	.63886
28	12.6948	.93941	.06059	83	4.6693	.34553	.65447
29	12.6513	.93620	.06380	84	4.4637	.33031	.66969
30	12.6048	.93275	.06725	85	4.2627	.31544	.68456
31	12.5547	.92905	.07095	86	4.0681	.30104	.69896
32	12.5013	.92509	.07491	87	3.8823	.28729	.71271
33	12.4441	.92087	.07913	88	3.7043	.27412	.72588
34	12.3834	.91637	.08363	89	3.5311	.26130	.73870
35	12.3188	.91159	.08841	90	3.3609	.24871	.75129
36	12.2508	.90656	.09344	91	3.1961	.23651	.76349
37	12.1790	.90124	.09876	92	3.0407	.22501	.77499
38	12.1033	.89564	.10436	93	2.8962	.21432	.78568
39	12.0236	.88975	.11025	94	2.7640	.20453	.79547
40	11.9399	.88356	.11644	95	2.6445	.19569	.80431
41	11.8521	.87706	.12294	96	2.5385	.18785	.81215
42	11.7604	.87027	.12973	97	2.4422	.18073	.81927
43	11.6646	.86318	.13682	98	2.3556	.17431	.82569
44	11.5647	.85579	.14421	99	2.2755	.16839	.83161
45	11.4605	.84808	.15192	100	2.2012	.16289	.83711
46	11.3520	.84005	.15995	101	2.1303	.15764	.84236
47	11.2391	.83170	.16830	102	2.0564	.15218	.84782
48	11.1221	.82304	.17696	103	1.9781	.14638	.85362
49	11.0013	.81409	.18591	104	1.8912	.13995	.86005
50	10.8765	.80486	.19514	105	1.7838	.13200	.86800
51	10.7478	.79534	.20466	106	1.6297	.12060	.87940
52	10.6144	.78547	.21453	107	1.4075	.10416	.89584
53	10.4765	.77526	.22474	108	1.0473	.07750	.92250
54	10.3343	.76474	.23526	109	0.4655	.03445	.96555

Table S(7.6) *SINGLE LIFE, 7.6 PERCENT, BASED ON LIFE TABLE 80CNSMT
SHOWING THE PRESENT WORTH OF AN ANNUITY, OF A LIFE ESTATE,
AND OF A REMAINDER INTEREST*

Age	Annuity	Life Estate	Remainder	Age	Annuity	Life Estate	Remainder
(1)	(2)	(3)	(4)	(1)	(2)	(3)	(4)
0	12.8185	.97421	.02579	55	10.0116	.76088	.23912
1	12.9624	.98514	.01486	56	9.8660	.74981	.25019
2	12.9600	.98496	.01504	57	9.7157	.73839	.26161
3	12.9537	.98448	.01552	58	9.5607	.72661	.27339
4	12.9449	.98381	.01619	59	9.4013	.71450	.28550
5	12.9342	.98300	.01700	60	9.2378	.70208	.29792
6	12.9221	.98208	.01792	61	9.0708	.68938	.31062
7	12.9087	.98106	.01894	62	8.9005	.67644	.32356
8	12.8938	.97993	.02007	63	8.7272	.66326	.33674
9	12.8773	.97867	.02133	64	8.5505	.64984	.35016
10	12.8590	.97729	.02271	65	8.3698	.63610	.36390
11	12.8389	.97576	.02424	66	8.1846	.62203	.37797
12	12.8172	.97411	.02589	67	7.9950	.60762	.39238
13	12.7946	.97239	.02761	68	7.8009	.59287	.40713
14	12.7720	.97067	.02933	69	7.6033	.57785	.42215
15	12.7497	.96897	.03103	70	7.4028	.56262	.43738
16	12.7277	.96730	.03270	71	7.2005	.54724	.45276
17	12.7060	.96566	.03434	72	6.9962	.53171	.46829
18	12.6843	.96401	.03599	73	6.7899	.51603	.48397
19	12.6620	.96231	.03769	74	6.5808	.50014	.49986
20	12.6391	.96057	.03943	75	6.3682	.48399	.51601
21	12.6155	.95878	.04122	76	6.1520	.46755	.53245
22	12.5909	.95691	.04309	77	5.9327	.45088	.54912
23	12.5651	.95495	.04505	78	5.7111	.43404	.56596
24	12.5375	.95285	.04715	79	5.4891	.41717	.58283
25	12.5077	.95059	.04941	80	5.2682	.40039	.59961
26	12.4754	.94813	.05187	81	5.0507	.38385	.61615
27	12.4403	.94546	.05454	82	4.8375	.36765	.63235
28	12.4026	.94260	.05740	83	4.6298	.35187	.64813
29	12.3619	.93951	.06049	84	4.4272	.33647	.66353
30	12.3183	.93619	.06381	85	4.2291	.32141	.67859
31	12.2713	.93262	.06738	86	4.0372	.30682	.69318
32	12.2211	.92880	.07120	87	3.8538	.29289	.70711
33	12.1672	.92471	.07529	88	3.6781	.27954	.72046
34	12.1099	.92036	.07964	89	3.5070	.26653	.73347
35	12.0490	.91572	.08428	90	3.3388	.25375	.74625
36	11.9847	.91083	.08917	91	3.1758	.24136	.75864
37	11.9166	.90567	.09433	92	3.0220	.22967	.77033
38	11.8449	.90022	.09978	93	2.8790	.21880	.78120
39	11.7694	.89447	.10553	94	2.7481	.20885	.79115
40	11.6898	.88843	.11157	95	2.6297	.19986	.80014
41	11.6063	.88208	.11792	96	2.5247	.19188	.80812
42	11.5190	.87544	.12456	97	2.4293	.18463	.81537
43	11.4278	.86851	.13149	98	2.3435	.17810	.82190
44	11.3324	.86127	.13873	99	2.2642	.17208	.82792
45	11.2329	.85370	.14630	100	2.1905	.16648	.83352
46	11.1293	.84582	.15418	101	2.1203	.16114	.83886
47	11.0213	.83762	.16238	102	2.0471	.15558	.84442
48	10.9093	.82910	.17090	103	1.9696	.14969	.85031
49	10.7935	.82030	.17970	104	1.8835	.14314	.85686
50	10.6739	.81121	.18879	105	1.7771	.13506	.86494
51	10.5503	.80182	.19818	106	1.6242	.12344	.87656
52	10.4222	.79209	.20791	107	1.4034	.10666	.89334
53	10.2896	.78201	.21799	108	1.0448	.07940	.92060
54	10.1528	.77161	.22839	109	0.4647	.03532	.96468

Table S(7.8) *SINGLE LIFE, 7.8 PERCENT, BASED ON LIFE TABLE 80CNSMT*
SHOWING THE PRESENT WORTH OF AN ANNUITY, OF A LIFE ESTATE,
AND OF A REMAINDER INTEREST

Age	Annuity	Life Estate	Remainder	Age	Annuity	Life Estate	Remainder
(1)	(2)	(3)	(4)	(1)	(2)	(3)	(4)
0	12.5010	.97508	.02492	55	9.8407	.76757	.23243
1	12.6417	.98605	.01395	56	9.7003	.75662	.24338
2	12.6400	.98592	.01408	57	9.5552	.74531	.25469
3	12.6344	.98549	.01451	58	9.4055	.73363	.26637
4	12.6264	.98486	.01514	59	9.2514	.72161	.27839
5	12.6166	.98410	.01590	60	9.0933	.70927	.29073
6	12.6055	.98323	.01677	61	8.9315	.69666	.30334
7	12.5931	.98227	.01773	62	8.7665	.68379	.31621
8	12.5794	.98119	.01881	63	8.5984	.67067	.32933
9	12.5640	.98000	.02000	64	8.4269	.65730	.34270
10	12.5471	.97867	.02133	65	8.2514	.64361	.35639
11	12.5283	.97721	.02279	66	8.0715	.62957	.37043
12	12.5080	.97562	.02438	67	7.8869	.61518	.38482
13	12.4868	.97397	.02603	68	7.6979	.60044	.39956
14	12.4656	.97232	.02768	69	7.5054	.58542	.41458
15	12.4448	.97070	.02930	70	7.3099	.57017	.42983
16	12.4243	.96910	.03090	71	7.1124	.55477	.44523
17	12.4042	.96753	.03247	72	6.9129	.53921	.46079
18	12.3841	.96596	.03404	73	6.7113	.52348	.47652
19	12.3634	.96435	.03565	74	6.5067	.50753	.49247
20	12.3422	.96269	.03731	75	6.2987	.49130	.50870
21	12.3204	.96099	.03901	76	6.0869	.47478	.52522
22	12.2976	.95922	.04078	77	5.8718	.45800	.54200
23	12.2738	.95735	.04265	78	5.6543	.44104	.55896
24	12.2481	.95535	.04465	79	5.4363	.42403	.57597
25	12.2205	.95320	.04680	80	5.2192	.40710	.59290
26	12.1904	.95085	.04915	81	5.0052	.39041	.60959
27	12.1577	.94830	.05170	82	4.7955	.37405	.62595
28	12.1224	.94555	.05445	83	4.5909	.35809	.64191
29	12.0844	.94258	.05742	84	4.3913	.34252	.65748
30	12.0435	.93939	.06061	85	4.1960	.32729	.67271
31	11.9993	.93595	.06405	86	4.0066	.31252	.68748
32	11.9520	.93226	.06774	87	3.8257	.29841	.70159
33	11.9013	.92830	.07170	88	3.6522	.28488	.71512
34	11.8472	.92408	.07592	89	3.4832	.27169	.72831
35	11.7896	.91959	.08041	90	3.3169	.25872	.74128
36	11.7287	.91484	.08516	91	3.1557	.24615	.75385
37	11.6643	.90982	.09018	92	3.0036	.23428	.76572
38	11.5963	.90451	.09549	93	2.8620	.22323	.77677
39	11.5245	.89891	.10109	94	2.7323	.21312	.78688
40	11.4489	.89302	.10698	95	2.6151	.20398	.79602
41	11.3695	.88682	.11318	96	2.5111	.19586	.80414
42	11.2863	.88033	.11967	97	2.4166	.18849	.81151
43	11.1993	.87355	.12645	98	2.3315	.18185	.81815
44	11.1083	.86645	.13355	99	2.2529	.17573	.82427
45	11.0133	.85904	.14096	100	2.1799	.17003	.82997
46	10.9141	.85130	.14870	101	2.1104	.16461	.83539
47	10.8108	.84324	.15676	102	2.0379	.15896	.84104
48	10.7035	.83487	.16513	103	1.9611	.15297	.84703
49	10.5925	.82621	.17379	104	1.8758	.14631	.85369
50	10.4777	.81726	.18274	105	1.7704	.13809	.86191
51	10.3591	.80801	.19199	106	1.6187	.12626	.87374
52	10.2360	.79841	.20159	107	1.3993	.10915	.89085
53	10.1084	.78846	.21154	108	1.0423	.08130	.91870
54	9.9767	.77819	.22181	109	0.4638	.03618	.96382

Age	Annuity	Life Estate	Remainder	Age	Annuity	Life Estate	Remainder
(1)	(2)	(3)	(4)	(1)	(2)	(3)	(4)
0	12.1984	.97587	.02413	55	9.6749	.77399	.22601
1	12.3360	.98688	.01312	56	9.5394	.76315	.23685
2	12.3348	.98679	.01321	57	9.3994	.75195	.24805
3	12.3299	.98639	.01361	58	9.2547	.74038	.25962
4	12.3227	.98582	.01418	59	9.1056	.72845	.27155
5	12.3137	.98510	.01490	60	8.9526	.71621	.28379
6	12.3035	.98428	.01572	61	8.7959	.70367	.29633
7	12.2921	.98336	.01664	62	8.6360	.69088	.30912
8	12.2793	.98234	.01766	63	8.4729	.67783	.32217
9	12.2650	.98120	.01880	64	8.3064	.66452	.33548
10	12.2492	.97994	.02006	65	8.1360	.65088	.34912
11	12.2316	.97853	.02147	66	7.9610	.63688	.36312
12	12.2126	.97701	.02299	67	7.7814	.62251	.37749
13	12.1927	.97542	.02458	68	7.5974	.60779	.39221
14	12.1729	.97383	.02617	69	7.4097	.59278	.40722
15	12.1534	.97227	.02773	70	7.2190	.57752	.42248
16	12.1343	.97074	.02926	71	7.0263	.56210	.43790
17	12.1156	.96925	.03075	72	6.8314	.54651	.45349
18	12.0969	.96775	.03225	73	6.6343	.53074	.46926
19	12.0778	.96622	.03378	74	6.4342	.51473	.48527
20	12.0581	.96465	.03535	75	6.2305	.49844	.50156
21	12.0379	.96303	.03697	76	6.0229	.48183	.51817
22	12.0168	.96135	.03865	77	5.8120	.46496	.53504
23	11.9947	.95958	.04042	78	5.5986	.44788	.55212
24	11.9709	.95767	.04233	79	5.3844	.43075	.56925
25	11.9452	.95562	.04438	80	5.1710	.41368	.58632
26	11.9172	.95338	.04662	81	4.9605	.39684	.60316
27	11.8867	.95094	.04906	82	4.7541	.38032	.61968
28	11.8537	.94830	.05170	83	4.5526	.36421	.63579
29	11.8180	.94544	.05456	84	4.3559	.34847	.65153
30	11.7796	.94237	.05763	85	4.1633	.33307	.66693
31	11.7381	.93905	.06095	86	3.9766	.31812	.68188
32	11.6936	.93549	.06451	87	3.7980	.30384	.69616
33	11.6458	.93166	.06834	88	3.6267	.29014	.70986
34	11.5947	.92757	.07243	89	3.4597	.27677	.72323
35	11.5402	.92321	.07679	90	3.2953	.26362	.73638
36	11.4825	.91860	.08140	91	3.1359	.25087	.74913
37	11.4214	.91372	.08628	92	2.9853	.23882	.76118
38	11.3569	.90855	.09145	93	2.8451	.22761	.77239
39	11.2887	.90310	.09690	94	2.7167	.21734	.78266
40	11.2168	.89734	.10266	95	2.6006	.20805	.79195
41	11.1411	.89129	.10871	96	2.4976	.19981	.80019
42	11.0618	.88495	.11505	97	2.4039	.19231	.80769
43	10.9789	.87831	.12169	98	2.3196	.18557	.81443
44	10.8920	.87136	.12864	99	2.2417	.17934	.82066
45	10.8011	.86409	.13591	100	2.1694	.17356	.82644
46	10.7063	.85650	.14350	101	2.1005	.16804	.83196
47	10.6073	.84859	.15141	102	2.0288	.16230	.83770
48	10.5045	.84036	.15964	103	1.9527	.15622	.84378
49	10.3980	.83184	.16816	104	1.8682	.14946	.85054
50	10.2879	.82303	.17697	105	1.7638	.14110	.85890
51	10.1739	.81391	.18609	106	1.6132	.12906	.87094
52	10.0556	.80444	.19556	107	1.3952	.11162	.88838
53	9.9328	.79463	.20537	108	1.0399	.08319	.91681
54	9.8060	.78448	.21552	109	0.4630	.03704	.96296

Table S(8.2) SINGLE LIFE, 8.2 PERCENT, BASED ON LIFE TABLE 80CNSMT
SHOWING THE PRESENT WORTH OF AN ANNUITY, OF A LIFE ESTATE,
AND OF A REMAINDER INTEREST

Age	Annuity	Life Estate	Remainder	Age	Annuity	Life Estate	Remainder
(1)	(2)	(3)	(4)	(1)	(2)	(3)	(4)
0	11.9096	.97659	.02341	55	9.5139	.78014	.21986
1	12.0442	.98763	.01237	56	9.3832	.76942	.23058
2	12.0435	.98757	.01243	57	9.2479	.75833	.24167
3	12.0392	.98722	.01278	58	9.1081	.74686	.25314
4	12.0327	.98668	.01332	59	8.9638	.73503	.26497
5	12.0245	.98600	.01400	60	8.8156	.72288	.27712
6	12.0150	.98523	.01477	61	8.6639	.71044	.28956
7	12.0045	.98437	.01563	62	8.5088	.69772	.30228
8	11.9926	.98340	.01660	63	8.3506	.68475	.31525
9	11.9793	.98230	.01770	64	8.1890	.67149	.32851
10	11.9645	.98109	.01891	65	8.0233	.65791	.34209
11	11.9480	.97974	.02026	66	7.8531	.64396	.35604
12	11.9302	.97827	.02173	67	7.6784	.62963	.37037
13	11.9115	.97674	.02326	68	7.4991	.61492	.38508
14	11.8929	.97522	.02478	69	7.3161	.59992	.40008
15	11.8747	.97372	.02628	70	7.1301	.58467	.41533
16	11.8568	.97226	.02774	71	6.9419	.56924	.43076
17	11.8394	.97083	.02917	72	6.7515	.55362	.44638
18	11.8220	.96941	.03059	73	6.5588	.53782	.46218
19	11.8042	.96795	.03205	74	6.3630	.52177	.47823
20	11.7860	.96645	.03355	75	6.1636	.50541	.49459
21	11.7673	.96491	.03509	76	5.9602	.48873	.51127
22	11.7477	.96331	.03669	77	5.7533	.47177	.52823
23	11.7272	.96163	.03837	78	5.5437	.45459	.54541
24	11.7051	.95982	.04018	79	5.3333	.43733	.56267
25	11.6812	.95786	.04214	80	5.1236	.42013	.57987
26	11.6551	.95572	.04428	81	4.9165	.40315	.59685
27	11.6266	.95338	.04662	82	4.7133	.38649	.61351
28	11.5957	.95085	.04915	83	4.5149	.37022	.62978
29	11.5623	.94811	.05189	84	4.3211	.35433	.64567
30	11.5262	.94515	.05485	85	4.1312	.33875	.66125
31	11.4871	.94195	.05805	86	3.9469	.32364	.67636
32	11.4452	.93851	.06149	87	3.7706	.30919	.69081
33	11.4000	.93480	.06520	88	3.6015	.29532	.70468
34	11.3517	.93084	.06916	89	3.4365	.28179	.71821
35	11.3002	.92661	.07339	90	3.2740	.26847	.73153
36	11.2455	.92213	.07787	91	3.1163	.25553	.74447
37	11.1876	.91738	.08262	92	2.9672	.24331	.75669
38	11.1263	.91235	.08765	93	2.8285	.23193	.76807
39	11.0614	.90704	.09296	94	2.7013	.22151	.77849
40	10.9930	.90142	.09858	95	2.5863	.21208	.78792
41	10.9209	.89551	.10449	96	2.4842	.20370	.79630
42	10.8453	.88931	.11069	97	2.3914	.19609	.80391
43	10.7661	.88282	.11718	98	2.3078	.18924	.81076
44	10.6831	.87601	.12399	99	2.2307	.18291	.81709
45	10.5962	.86889	.13111	100	2.1591	.17704	.82296
46	10.5054	.86144	.13856	101	2.0908	.17145	.82855
47	10.4106	.85367	.14633	102	2.0197	.16562	.83438
48	10.3120	.84558	.15442	103	1.9444	.15944	.84056
49	10.2098	.83720	.16280	104	1.8607	.15257	.84743
50	10.1040	.82853	.17147	105	1.7572	.14409	.85591
51	9.9945	.81955	.18045	106	1.6078	.13184	.86816
52	9.8807	.81021	.18979	107	1.3912	.11408	.88592
53	9.7625	.80053	.19947	108	1.0375	.08507	.91493
54	9.6403	.79050	.20950	109	0.4621	.03789	.96211

Table S(8.4) *SINGLE LIFE, 8.4 PERCENT, BASED ON LIFE TABLE 80CNSMT*
SHOWING THE PRESENT WORTH OF AN ANNUITY, OF A LIFE ESTATE,
AND OF A REMAINDER INTEREST

Age	Annuity	Life Estate	Remainder	Age	Annuity	Life Estate	Remainder
(1)	(2)	(3)	(4)	(1)	(2)	(3)	(4)
0	11.6338	.97724	.02276	55	9.3575	.78603	.21397
1	11.7655	.98830	.01170	56	9.2314	.77543	.22457
2	11.7653	.98828	.01172	57	9.1007	.76446	.23554
3	11.7615	.98797	.01203	58	8.9655	.75310	.24690
4	11.7556	.98747	.01253	59	8.8259	.74137	.25863
5	11.7480	.98683	.01317	60	8.6824	.72932	.27068
6	11.7393	.98610	.01390	61	8.5352	.71696	.28304
7	11.7295	.98528	.01472	62	8.3849	.70433	.29567
8	11.7185	.98436	.01564	63	8.2313	.69143	.30857
9	11.7061	.98331	.01669	64	8.0743	.67824	.32176
10	11.6923	.98215	.01785	65	7.9133	.66472	.33528
11	11.6768	.98085	.01915	66	7.7478	.65082	.34918
12	11.6600	.97944	.02056	67	7.5777	.63653	.36347
13	11.6424	.97796	.02204	68	7.4030	.62185	.37815
14	11.6249	.97649	.02351	69	7.2246	.60687	.39313
15	11.6078	.97505	.02495	70	7.0431	.59162	.40838
16	11.5911	.97365	.02635	71	6.8593	.57618	.42382
17	11.5748	.97228	.02772	72	6.6733	.56055	.43945
18	11.5587	.97093	.02907	73	6.4848	.54473	.45527
19	11.5421	.96954	.03046	74	6.2933	.52863	.47137
20	11.5252	.96812	.03188	75	6.0979	.51223	.48777
21	11.5078	.96666	.03334	76	5.8986	.49548	.50452
22	11.4897	.96513	.03487	77	5.6956	.47843	.52157
23	11.4707	.96354	.03646	78	5.4899	.46115	.53885
24	11.4501	.96181	.03819	79	5.2832	.44379	.55621
25	11.4279	.95994	.04006	80	5.0769	.42646	.57354
26	11.4035	.95790	.04210	81	4.8732	.40935	.59065
27	11.3769	.95566	.04434	82	4.6731	.39254	.60746
28	11.3479	.95323	.04677	83	4.4777	.37613	.62387
29	11.3166	.95059	.04941	84	4.2867	.36008	.63992
30	11.2826	.94774	.05226	85	4.0994	.34435	.65565
31	11.2458	.94465	.05535	86	3.9176	.32908	.67092
32	11.2063	.94133	.05867	87	3.7436	.31446	.68554
33	11.1636	.93774	.06226	88	3.5766	.30043	.69957
34	11.1179	.93391	.06609	89	3.4135	.28674	.71326
35	11.0691	.92980	.07020	90	3.2529	.27324	.72676
36	11.0173	.92545	.07455	91	3.0969	.26014	.73986
37	10.9622	.92083	.07917	92	2.9494	.24775	.75225
38	10.9040	.91593	.08407	93	2.8120	.23621	.76379
39	10.8423	.91075	.08925	94	2.6860	.22563	.77437
40	10.7771	.90528	.09472	95	2.5721	.21606	.78394
41	10.7083	.89950	.10050	96	2.4710	.20756	.79244
42	10.6362	.89344	.10656	97	2.3790	.19984	.80016
43	10.5605	.88709	.11291	98	2.2962	.19288	.80712
44	10.4812	.88042	.11958	99	2.2197	.18646	.81354
45	10.3981	.87344	.12656	100	2.1488	.18050	.81950
46	10.3111	.86613	.13387	101	2.0811	.17482	.82518
47	10.2202	.85850	.14150	102	2.0107	.16890	.83110
48	10.1256	.85055	.14945	103	1.9361	.16263	.83737
49	10.0275	.84231	.15769	104	1.8532	.15567	.84433
50	9.9259	.83378	.16622	105	1.7506	.14705	.85295
51	9.8206	.82493	.17507	106	1.6024	.13460	.86540
52	9.7111	.81573	.18427	107	1.3872	.11652	.88348
53	9.5973	.80617	.19383	108	1.0350	.08694	.91306
54	9.4795	.79628	.20372	109	0.4613	.03875	.96125

Table S(8.6) *SINGLE LIFE, 8.6 PERCENT, BASED ON LIFE TABLE 80CNSMT
SHOWING THE PRESENT WORTH OF AN ANNUITY, OF A LIFE ESTATE,
AND OF A REMAINDER INTEREST*

Age	Annuity	Life Estate	Remainder	Age	Annuity	Life Estate	Remainder
(1)	(2)	(3)	(4)	(1)	(2)	(3)	(4)
0	11.3701	.97783	.02217	55	9.2057	.79169	.20831
1	11.4991	.98892	.01108	56	9.0839	.78121	.21879
2	11.4992	.98893	.01107	57	8.9575	.77035	.22965
3	11.4959	.98865	.01135	58	8.8268	.75910	.24090
4	11.4905	.98818	.01182	59	8.6916	.74748	.25252
5	11.4836	.98759	.01241	60	8.5526	.73552	.26448
6	11.4755	.98690	.01310	61	8.4100	.72326	.27674
7	11.4664	.98611	.01389	62	8.2641	.71071	.28929
8	11.4562	.98523	.01477	63	8.1150	.69789	.30211
9	11.4446	.98423	.01577	64	7.9625	.68478	.31522
10	11.4316	.98312	.01688	65	7.8060	.67132	.32868
11	11.4170	.98186	.01814	66	7.6450	.65747	.34253
12	11.4012	.98050	.01950	67	7.4793	.64322	.35678
13	11.3846	.97908	.02092	68	7.3091	.62858	.37142
14	11.3681	.97766	.02234	69	7.1351	.61362	.38638
15	11.3521	.97628	.02372	70	6.9579	.59838	.40162
16	11.3364	.97493	.02507	71	6.7785	.58295	.41705
17	11.3212	.97363	.02637	72	6.5966	.56731	.43269
18	11.3062	.97233	.02767	73	6.4123	.55146	.44854
19	11.2908	.97101	.02899	74	6.2248	.53534	.46466
20	11.2751	.96965	.03035	75	6.0335	.51888	.48112
21	11.2589	.96827	.03173	76	5.8381	.50207	.49793
22	11.2421	.96682	.03318	77	5.6389	.48495	.51505
23	11.2244	.96530	.03470	78	5.4370	.46758	.53242
24	11.2053	.96366	.03634	79	5.2338	.45011	.54989
25	11.1846	.96188	.03812	80	5.0310	.43267	.56733
26	11.1619	.95992	.04008	81	4.8306	.41543	.58457
27	11.1369	.95777	.04223	82	4.6336	.39849	.60151
28	11.1098	.95544	.04456	83	4.4411	.38194	.61806
29	11.0803	.95291	.04709	84	4.2528	.36574	.63426
30	11.0484	.95016	.04984	85	4.0681	.34986	.65014
31	11.0137	.94718	.05282	86	3.8887	.33443	.66557
32	10.9764	.94397	.05603	87	3.7170	.31966	.68034
33	10.9360	.94050	.05950	88	3.5520	.30547	.69453
34	10.8928	.93678	.06322	89	3.3909	.29162	.70838
35	10.8465	.93280	.06720	90	3.2320	.27796	.72204
36	10.7973	.92857	.07143	91	3.0777	.26468	.73532
37	10.7450	.92407	.07593	92	2.9317	.25213	.74787
38	10.6896	.91931	.08069	93	2.7957	.24043	.75957
39	10.6309	.91426	.08574	94	2.6710	.22970	.77030
40	10.5688	.90891	.09109	95	2.5581	.21999	.78001
41	10.5032	.90327	.09673	96	2.4578	.21137	.78863
42	10.4343	.89735	.10265	97	2.3667	.20354	.79646
43	10.3620	.89113	.10887	98	2.2846	.19648	.80352
44	10.2861	.88460	.11540	99	2.2089	.18996	.81004
45	10.2065	.87776	.12224	100	2.1385	.18391	.81609
46	10.1232	.87059	.12941	101	2.0716	.17815	.82185
47	10.0360	.86310	.13690	102	2.0018	.17215	.82785
48	9.9452	.85529	.14471	103	1.9279	.16580	.83420
49	9.8510	.84719	.15281	104	1.8457	.15873	.84127
50	9.7533	.83879	.16121	105	1.7441	.14999	.85001
51	9.6520	.83007	.16993	106	1.5970	.13734	.86266
52	9.5466	.82101	.17899	107	1.3832	.11895	.88105
53	9.4370	.81158	.18842	108	1.0326	.08881	.91119
54	9.3234	.80181	.19819	109	0.4604	.03959	.96041

Table S(8.8) *SINGLE LIFE, 8.8 PERCENT, BASED ON LIFE TABLE 80CNSMT
SHOWING THE PRESENT WORTH OF AN ANNUITY, OF A LIFE ESTATE,
AND OF A REMAINDER INTEREST*

Age	Annuity	Life Estate	Remainder	Age	Annuity	Life Estate	Remainder
(1)	(2)	(3)	(4)	(1)	(2)	(3)	(4)
0	11.1178	.97837	.02163	55	9.0582	.79712	.20288
1	11.2441	.98948	.01052	56	8.9405	.78676	.21324
2	11.2446	.98952	.01048	57	8.8183	.77601	.22399
3	11.2417	.98927	.01073	58	8.6918	.76488	.23512
4	11.2368	.98884	.01116	59	8.5609	.75336	.24664
5	11.2304	.98828	.01172	60	8.4262	.74151	.25849
6	11.2230	.98762	.01238	61	8.2879	.72933	.27067
7	11.2145	.98688	.01312	62	8.1463	.71688	.28312
8	11.2050	.98604	.01396	63	8.0016	.70414	.29586
9	11.1941	.98508	.01492	64	7.8534	.69110	.30890
10	11.1819	.98401	.01599	65	7.7012	.67771	.32229
11	11.1682	.98280	.01720	66	7.5445	.66391	.33609
12	11.1532	.98148	.01852	67	7.3831	.64972	.35028
13	11.1376	.98011	.01989	68	7.2172	.63511	.36489
14	11.1220	.97874	.02126	69	7.0475	.62018	.37982
15	11.1069	.97741	.02259	70	6.8745	.60496	.39504
16	11.0922	.97612	.02388	71	6.6992	.58953	.41047
17	11.0780	.97487	.02513	72	6.5215	.57389	.42611
18	11.0640	.97363	.02637	73	6.3412	.55803	.44197
19	11.0496	.97237	.02763	74	6.1577	.54188	.45812
20	11.0350	.97108	.02892	75	5.9703	.52538	.47462
21	11.0200	.96976	.03024	76	5.7786	.50852	.49148
22	11.0043	.96838	.03162	77	5.5833	.49133	.50867
23	10.9879	.96694	.03306	78	5.3849	.47387	.52613
24	10.9702	.96537	.03463	79	5.1853	.45631	.54369
25	10.9509	.96367	.03633	80	4.9858	.43875	.56125
26	10.9296	.96180	.03820	81	4.7886	.42140	.57860
27	10.9062	.95975	.04025	82	4.5947	.40433	.59567
28	10.8808	.95751	.04249	83	4.4050	.38764	.61236
29	10.8531	.95507	.04493	84	4.2194	.37131	.62869
30	10.8230	.95243	.04757	85	4.0373	.35528	.64472
31	10.7903	.94955	.05045	86	3.8602	.33970	.66030
32	10.7550	.94644	.05356	87	3.6907	.32478	.67522
33	10.7169	.94308	.05692	88	3.5277	.31044	.68956
34	10.6759	.93948	.06052	89	3.3685	.29643	.70357
35	10.6320	.93561	.06439	90	3.2115	.28261	.71739
36	10.5853	.93150	.06850	91	3.0588	.26917	.73083
37	10.5356	.92713	.07287	92	2.9143	.25646	.74354
38	10.4828	.92249	.07751	93	2.7796	.24460	.75540
39	10.4269	.91757	.08243	94	2.6560	.23373	.76627
40	10.3676	.91235	.08765	95	2.5442	.22389	.77611
41	10.3050	.90684	.09316	96	2.4449	.21515	.78485
42	10.2392	.90105	.09895	97	2.3546	.20720	.79280
43	10.1701	.89497	.10503	98	2.2732	.20004	.79996
44	10.0974	.88857	.11143	99	2.1981	.19343	.80657
45	10.0212	.88186	.11814	100	2.1284	.18730	.81270
46	9.9413	.87484	.12516	101	2.0621	.18146	.81854
47	9.8577	.86748	.13252	102	1.9930	.17538	.82462
48	9.7705	.85980	.14020	103	1.9197	.16894	.83106
49	9.6800	.85184	.14816	104	1.8384	.16178	.83822
50	9.5860	.84357	.15643	105	1.7376	.15291	.84709
51	9.4885	.83499	.16501	106	1.5917	.14007	.85993
52	9.3870	.82606	.17394	107	1.3792	.12137	.87863
53	9.2813	.81676	.18324	108	1.0302	.09066	.90934
54	9.1718	.80712	.19288	109	0.4596	.04044	.95956

Table S(9.0) SINGLE LIFE, 9.0 PERCENT, BASED ON LIFE TABLE 80CNSMT
SHOWING THE PRESENT WORTH OF AN ANNUITY, OF A LIFE ESTATE,
AND OF A REMAINDER INTEREST

Age	Annuity	Life Estate	Remainder	Age	Annuity	Life Estate	Remainder
(1)	(2)	(3)	(4)	(1)	(2)	(3)	(4)
0	10.8762	.97886	.02114	55	8.9148	.80233	.19767
1	11.0000	.99000	.01000	56	8.8011	.79209	.20791
2	11.0007	.99006	.00994	57	8.6829	.78146	.21854
3	10.9982	.98984	.01016	58	8.5604	.77044	.22956
4	10.9938	.98944	.01056	59	8.4337	.75903	.24097
5	10.9879	.98891	.01109	60	8.3031	.74728	.25272
6	10.9810	.98829	.01171	61	8.1689	.73520	.26480
7	10.9731	.98758	.01242	62	8.0315	.72283	.27717
8	10.9642	.98678	.01322	63	7.8909	.71018	.28982
9	10.9540	.98586	.01414	64	7.7469	.69722	.30278
10	10.9425	.98483	.01517	65	7.5988	.68390	.31610
11	10.9296	.98366	.01634	66	7.4463	.67017	.32983
12	10.9154	.98239	.01761	67	7.2891	.65602	.34398
13	10.9006	.98105	.01895	68	7.1273	.64146	.35854
14	10.8859	.97973	.02027	69	6.9618	.62656	.37344
15	10.8717	.97845	.02155	70	6.7929	.61136	.38864
16	10.8579	.97721	.02279	71	6.6216	.59595	.40405
17	10.8446	.97601	.02399	72	6.4479	.58031	.41969
18	10.8315	.97483	.02517	73	6.2715	.56444	.43556
19	10.8181	.97363	.02637	74	6.0918	.54827	.45173
20	10.8044	.97240	.02760	75	5.9082	.53174	.46826
21	10.7904	.97114	.02886	76	5.7203	.51483	.48517
22	10.7759	.96983	.03017	77	5.5286	.49757	.50243
23	10.7606	.96846	.03154	78	5.3338	.48004	.51996
24	10.7441	.96697	.03303	79	5.1376	.46238	.53762
25	10.7261	.96535	.03465	80	4.9414	.44473	.55527
26	10.7062	.96356	.03644	81	4.7473	.42726	.57274
27	10.6843	.96159	.03841	82	4.5563	.41007	.58993
28	10.6604	.95944	.04056	83	4.3695	.39325	.60675
29	10.6343	.95709	.04291	84	4.1865	.37679	.62321
30	10.6060	.95454	.04546	85	4.0068	.36062	.63938
31	10.5751	.95176	.04824	86	3.8321	.34489	.65511
32	10.5418	.94876	.05124	87	3.6647	.32982	.67018
33	10.5057	.94551	.05449	88	3.5038	.31534	.68466
34	10.4668	.94201	.05799	89	3.3464	.30118	.69882
35	10.4251	.93826	.06174	90	3.1911	.28720	.71280
36	10.3807	.93427	.06573	91	3.0401	.27360	.72640
37	10.3335	.93001	.06999	92	2.8970	.26073	.73927
38	10.2832	.92549	.07451	93	2.7637	.24873	.75127
39	10.2299	.92069	.07931	94	2.6413	.23771	.76229
40	10.1734	.91560	.08440	95	2.5304	.22774	.77226
41	10.1136	.91022	.08978	96	2.4320	.21888	.78112
42	10.0506	.90456	.09544	97	2.3425	.21083	.78917
43	9.9845	.89860	.10140	98	2.2619	.20357	.79643
44	9.9149	.89234	.10766	99	2.1875	.19687	.80313
45	9.8419	.88577	.11423	100	2.1184	.19066	.80934
46	9.7652	.87887	.12113	101	2.0527	.18474	.81526
47	9.6850	.87165	.12835	102	1.9842	.17858	.82142
48	9.6012	.86411	.13589	103	1.9116	.17205	.82795
49	9.5142	.85627	.14373	104	1.8310	.16479	.83521
50	9.4238	.84814	.15186	105	1.7312	.15581	.84419
51	9.3299	.83970	.16030	106	1.5864	.14277	.85723
52	9.2321	.83089	.16911	107	1.3752	.12377	.87623
53	9.1302	.82172	.17828	108	1.0278	.09251	.90749
54	9.0245	.81221	.18779	109	0.4587	.04128	.95872

Age	Annuity	Life Estate	Remainder	Age	Annuity	Life Estate	Remainder
(1)	(2)	(3)	(4)	(1)	(2)	(3)	(4)
0	10.6447	.97931	.02069	55	8.7754	.80734	.19266
1	10.7660	.99047	.00953	56	8.6655	.79722	.20278
2	10.7669	.99056	.00944	57	8.5512	.78671	.21329
3	10.7648	.99036	.00964	58	8.4326	.77580	.22420
4	10.7607	.98999	.01001	59	8.3097	.76450	.23550
5	10.7553	.98949	.01051	60	8.1831	.75284	.24716
6	10.7489	.98890	.01110	61	8.0529	.74087	.25913
7	10.7416	.98822	.01178	62	7.9195	.72859	.27141
8	10.7332	.98746	.01254	63	7.7829	.71603	.28397
9	10.7236	.98658	.01342	64	7.6429	.70315	.29685
10	10.7128	.98558	.01442	65	6.4989	.68990	.31010
11	10.7006	.98445	.01555	66	7.3503	.67623	.32377
12	10.6872	.98322	.01678	67	7.1972	.66214	.33786
13	10.6732	.98193	.01807	68	7.0394	.64763	.25237
14	10.6593	.98065	.01935	69	6.8779	.63276	.36724
15	10.6458	.97942	.02058	70	6.7130	.61759	.38241
16	10.6328	.97822	.02178	71	6.5456	.60220	.39780
17	10.6204	.97707	.02293	72	6.3757	.58656	.41344
18	10.6081	.97594	.02406	73	6.2032	.57069	.42931
19	10.5956	.97479	.02521	74	6.0272	.55451	.44549
20	10.5828	.97362	.02638	75	5.8473	.53795	.46205
21	10.5698	.97242	.02758	76	5.6630	.52100	.47900
22	10.5563	.97118	.02882	77	5.4748	.50368	.49632
23	10.5421	.96987	.03013	78	5.2835	.48608	.51392
24	10.5267	.96845	.03155	79	5.0906	.46834	.53166
25	10.5098	.96691	.03309	80	4.8977	.45059	.54941
26	10.4912	.96519	.03481	81	4.7066	.43301	.56699
27	10.4707	.96330	.03670	82	4.5186	.41571	.58429
28	10.4482	.96124	.03876	83	4.3345	.39877	.60123
29	10.4237	.95898	.04102	84	4.1541	.38217	.61783
30	10.3970	.95652	.04348	85	3.9768	.36587	.63413
31	10.3678	.95384	.04616	86	3.8044	.35000	.65000
32	10.3363	.95094	.04906	87	3.6391	.33480	.66520
33	10.3020	.94779	.05221	88	3.4801	.32017	.67983
34	10.2652	.94440	.05560	89	3.3246	.30586	.69414
35	10.2256	.94075	.05925	90	3.1710	.29173	.70827
36	10.1834	.93687	.06313	91	3.0215	.27798	.72202
37	10.1384	.93273	.06727	92	2.8800	.26496	.73504
38	10.0905	.92833	.07167	93	2.7479	.25281	.74719
39	10.0396	.92365	.07635	94	2.6266	.24165	.75835
40	9.9856	.91868	.08132	95	2.5168	.23155	.76845
41	9.9285	.91342	.08658	96	2.4193	.22258	.77742
42	9.8683	.90788	.09212	97	2.3306	.21441	.78559
43	9.8050	.90206	.09794	98	2.2507	.20706	.79294
44	9.7383	.89593	.10407	99	2.1769	.20028	.79972
45	9.6683	.88948	.11052	100	2.1085	.19398	.80602
46	9.5947	.88272	.11728	101	2.0433	.18799	.81201
47	9.5176	.87562	.12438	102	1.9755	.18174	.81826
48	9.4371	.86821	.13179	103	1.9036	.17513	.82487
49	9.3534	.86051	.13949	104	1.8238	.16779	.83221
50	9.2664	.85251	.14749	105	1.7248	.15868	.84132
51	9.1760	.84420	.15580	106	1.5811	.14546	.85454
52	9.0817	.83552	.16448	107	1.3713	.12616	.87384
53	8.9834	.82648	.17352	108	1.0255	.09434	.90566
54	8.8814	.81709	.18291	109	0.4579	.04212	.95788

Table S(9.4) *SINGLE LIFE, 9.4 PERCENT, BASED ON LIFE TABLE 80CNSMT*
SHOWING THE PRESENT WORTH OF AN ANNUITY, OF A LIFE ESTATE,
AND OF A REMAINDER INTEREST

Age	Annuity	Life Estate	Remainder	Age	Annuity	Life Estate	Remainder
(1)	(2)	(3)	(4)	(1)	(2)	(3)	(4)
0	10.4226	.97973	.02027	55	8.6399	.81215	.18785
1	10.5415	.99090	.00910	56	8.5335	.80215	.19785
2	10.5427	.99101	.00899	57	8.4229	.79176	.20824
3	10.5408	.99084	.00916	58	8.3081	.78096	.21904
4	10.5372	.99049	.00951	59	8.1890	.76977	.23023
5	10.5321	.99002	.00998	60	8.0662	.75822	.24178
6	10.5262	.98946	.01054	61	7.9398	.74634	.25366
7	10.5193	.98882	.01118	62	7.8102	.73416	.26584
8	10.5115	.98808	.01192	63	7.6775	.72168	.27832
9	10.5025	.98724	.01276	64	7.5414	.70889	.29111
10	10.4923	.98628	.01372	65	7.4012	.69571	.30429
11	10.4807	.98519	.01481	66	7.2566	.68212	.31788
12	10.4680	.98399	.01601	67	7.1073	.66809	.33191
13	10.4547	.98274	.01726	68	6.9534	.65362	.34638
14	10.4415	.98150	.01850	69	6.7957	.63880	.36120
15	10.4288	.98031	.01969	70	6.6347	.62366	.37634
16	10.4166	.07916	.02084	71	6.4711	.60829	.39171
17	10.4049	.97806	.02194	72	6.3050	.59267	.40733
18	10.3934	.97698	.02302	73	6.1361	.57679	.42321
19	10.3817	.97588	.02412	74	5.9638	.56060	.43940
20	10.3698	.97476	.02524	75	5.7875	.54402	.45598
21	10.3576	.97362	.02638	76	5.6067	.52703	.47297
22	10.3450	.97243	.02757	77	5.4220	.50967	.49033
23	10.3318	.97119	.02881	78	5.2340	.49200	.50800
24	10.3174	.96984	.03016	79	5.0444	.47418	.52582
25	10.3017	.96836	.03164	80	4.8546	.45634	.54366
26	10.2842	.96672	.03328	81	4.6666	.43866	.56134
27	10.2650	.96491	.03509	82	4.4814	.42125	.57875
28	10.2438	.96292	.03708	83	4.2999	.40419	.59581
29	10.2207	.96075	.03925	84	4.1221	.38747	.61253
30	10.1955	.95838	.04162	85	3.9472	.37104	.62896
31	10.1680	.95579	.04421	86	3.7770	.35504	.64496
32	10.1381	.95298	.04702	87	3.6138	.33969	.66031
33	10.1056	.94993	.05007	88	3.4567	.32493	.67507
34	10.0706	.94664	.05336	89	3.3030	.31048	.68952
35	10.0330	.94310	.05690	90	3.1511	.29621	.70379
36	9.9928	.93932	.06068	91	3.0032	.28230	.71770
37	9.9499	.93530	.06470	92	2.8631	.26913	.73087
38	9.9043	.93101	.06899	93	2.7323	.25683	.74317
39	9.8557	.92644	.07356	94	2.6122	.24554	.75446
40	9.8042	.92159	.07841	95	2.5034	.23532	.76468
41	9.7495	.91645	.08355	96	2.4067	.22623	.77377
42	9.6919	.91104	.08896	97	2.3188	.21797	.78203
43	9.6313	.90534	.09466	98	2.2396	.21052	.78948
44	9.5674	.89933	.10067	99	2.1664	.20365	.79635
45	9.5001	.89301	.10699	100	2.0986	.19727	.80273
46	9.4295	.88638	.11362	101	2.0341	.19120	.80880
47	9.3555	.87941	.12059	102	1.9669	.18488	.81512
48	9.2780	.87213	.12787	103	1.8956	.17819	.82181
49	9.1975	.86456	.13544	104	1.8165	.17076	.82924
50	9.1137	.85669	.14331	105	1.7185	.16154	.83846
51	9.0266	.84850	.15150	106	1.5758	.14813	.85187
52	8.9357	.83996	.16004	107	1.3673	.12853	.87147
53	8.8408	.83104	.16896	108	1.0231	.09617	.90383
54	8.7423	.82178	.17822	109	0.4570	.04296	.95704

Table S(9.6) *SINGLE LIFE, 9.6 PERCENT, BASED ON LIFE TABLE 80CNSMT SHOWING THE PRESENT WORTH OF AN ANNUITY, OF A LIFE ESTATE, AND OF A REMAINDER INTEREST*

Age	Annuity	Life Estate	Remainder	Age	Annuity	Life Estate	Remainder
(1)	(2)	(3)	(4)	(1)	(2)	(3)	(4)
0	10.2095	.98011	.01989	55	8.5081	.81678	.18322
1	10.3260	.99129	.00871	56	8.4052	.80690	.19310
2	10.3274	.99143	.00857	57	8.2981	.79662	.20338
3	10.3258	.99128	.00872	58	8.1868	.78593	.21407
4	10.3225	.99096	.00904	59	8.0714	.77485	.22515
5	10.3178	.99051	.00949	60	7.9522	.76341	.23659
6	10.3123	.98998	.01002	61	7.8295	.75163	.24837
7	10.3059	.98936	.01064	62	7.7036	.73955	.26045
8	10.2985	.98866	.01134	63	7.5746	.72716	.27284
9	10.2900	.98784	.01216	64	7.4422	.71445	.28555
10	10.2804	.98692	.01308	65	7.3058	.70135	.29865
11	10.2694	.98586	.01414	66	7.1649	.68783	.31217
12	10.2574	.98471	.01529	67	7.0194	.67386	.32614
13	10.2447	.98349	.01651	68	6.8693	.65945	.34055
14	10.2322	.98229	.01771	69	6.7153	.64467	.35533
15	10.2202	.98114	.01886	70	6.5580	.62957	.37043
16	10.2086	.98003	.01997	71	6.3981	.61422	.38578
17	10.1976	.97897	.02103	72	6.2356	.59862	.40138
18	10.1868	.97793	.02207	73	6.0703	.58275	.41725
19	10.1758	.97688	.02312	74	5.9016	.56655	.43345
20	10.1647	.97581	.02419	75	5.7287	.54996	.45004
21	10.1534	.97473	.02527	76	5.5514	.53294	.46706
22	10.1416	.97360	.02640	77	5.3701	.51553	.48447
23	10.1293	.97241	.02759	78	5.1854	.49780	.50220
24	10.1159	.97112	.02888	79	4.9990	.47991	.52009
25	10.1012	.96971	.03029	80	4.8123	.46198	.53802
26	10.0848	.96814	.03186	81	4.6271	.44421	.55579
27	10.0667	.96640	.03360	82	4.4447	.42669	.57331
28	10.0468	.96450	.03550	83	4.2659	.40953	.59047
29	10.0250	.96240	.03760	84	4.0905	.39269	.60731
30	10.0013	.96012	.03988	85	3.9180	.37613	.62387
31	9.9752	.95762	.04238	86	3.7500	.36000	.64000
32	9.9469	.95490	.04510	87	3.5888	.34452	.65548
33	9.9161	.95194	.04806	88	3.4336	.32963	.67037
34	9.8828	.94875	.05125	89	3.2817	.31505	.68495
35	9.8470	.94531	.05469	90	3.1315	.30062	.69938
36	9.8088	.94164	.05836	91	2.9851	.28657	.71343
37	9.7679	.93772	.06228	92	2.8464	.27326	.72674
38	9.7244	.93354	.06646	93	2.7169	.26082	.73918
39	9.6780	.92908	.07092	94	2.5979	.24939	.75061
40	9.6287	.92435	.07565	95	2.4900	.23904	.76096
41	9.5764	.91933	.08067	96	2.3943	.22985	.77015
42	9.5212	.91404	.08596	97	2.3071	.22148	.77852
43	9.4631	.90846	.09154	98	2.2286	.21394	.78606
44	9.4018	.90257	.09743	99	2.1561	.20698	.79302
45	9.3373	.89638	.10362	100	2.0889	.20053	.79947
46	9.2695	.88987	.11013	101	2.0249	.19439	.85061
47	9.1982	.88303	.11697	102	1.9583	.18800	.81200
48	9.1237	.87588	.12412	103	1.8877	.18122	.81878
49	9.0462	.86843	.13157	104	1.8094	.17370	.82630
50	8.9655	.86069	.13931	105	1.7122	.16437	.83563
51	8.8815	.85263	.14737	106	1.5706	.15078	.84922
52	8.7938	.84421	.15579	107	1.3634	.13089	.86911
53	8.7023	.83542	.16458	108	1.0207	.09799	.90201
54	8.6071	.82628	.17372	109	0.4562	.04380	.95620

Table S(9.8) *SINGLE LIFE, 9.8 PERCENT, BASED ON LIFE TABLE 80CNSMT
SHOWING THE PRESENT WORTH OF AN ANNUITY, OF A LIFE ESTATE,
AND OF A REMAINDER INTEREST*

Age	Annuity	Life Estate	Remainder	Age	Annuity	Life Estate	Remainder
(1)	(2)	(3)	(4)	(1)	(2)	(3)	(4)
0	10.0047	.98046	.01954	55	8.3798	.82122	.17878
1	10.1190	.99166	.00834	56	8.2802	.81146	.18854
2	10.1205	.99181	.00819	57	8.1765	.80130	.19870
3	10.1192	.99168	.00832	58	8.0687	.79073	.20927
4	10.1162	.99138	.00862	59	7.9567	.77976	.22024
5	10.1119	.99096	.00904	60	7.8410	.76842	.23158
6	10.1067	.99046	.00954	61	7.7219	.75675	.24325
7	10.1007	.98987	.01013	62	7.5996	.74476	.25524
8	10.0938	.98919	.01081	63	7.4741	.73246	.26754
9	10.0858	.98841	.01159	64	7.3453	.71984	.28016
10	10.0767	.98751	.01249	65	7.2125	.70683	.29317
11	10.0662	.98649	.01351	66	7.0753	.69337	.30663
12	10.0548	.98537	.01463	67	6.9334	.67947	.32053
13	10.0427	.98418	.01582	68	6.7869	.66512	.33488
14	10.0308	.98302	.01698	69	6.6366	.65039	.34961
15	10.0194	.98190	.01810	70	6.4829	.63532	.36468
16	10.0085	.98083	.01917	71	6.3266	.62000	.38000
17	9.9981	.97982	.02018	72	6.1676	.60442	.39558
18	9.9880	.97882	.02118	73	6.0058	.58857	.41143
19	9.9777	.97782	.02218	74	5.8405	.57237	.42763
20	9.9673	.97680	.02320	75	5.6710	.55576	.44424
21	9.9567	.97576	.02424	76	5.4971	.53871	.46129
22	9.9458	.97468	.02532	77	5.3190	.52127	.47873
23	9.9342	.97356	.02644	78	5.1376	.50348	.49652
24	9.9217	.97233	.02767	79	4.9543	.48552	.51448
25	9.9080	.97098	.02902	80	4.7706	.46752	.53248
26	9.8926	.96948	.03052	81	4.5883	.44965	.55035
27	9.8756	.96781	.03219	82	4.4086	.43204	.56796
28	9.8569	.96597	.03403	83	4.2324	.41477	.58523
29	9.8363	.96396	.03604	84	4.0594	.39782	.60218
30	9.8138	.96175	.03825	85	3.8892	.38114	.61886
31	9.7891	.95933	.04067	86	3.7233	.36489	.63511
32	9.7623	.95671	.04329	87	3.5641	.34929	.65071
33	9.7330	.95384	.04616	88	3.4108	.33426	.66574
34	9.7014	.95074	.04926	89	3.2607	.31955	.68045
35	9.6673	.94740	.05260	90	3.1121	.30498	.69502
36	9.6309	.94383	.05617	91	2.9673	.29079	.70921
37	9.5919	.94001	.05999	92	2.8299	.27733	.72267
38	9.5503	.93593	.06407	93	2.7016	.26476	.73524
39	9.5060	.93159	.06841	94	2.5837	.25320	.74680
40	9.4589	.92697	.07303	95	2.4769	.24273	.75727
41	9.4088	.92206	.07794	96	2.3819	.23343	.76657
42	9.3559	.91688	.08312	97	2.2955	.22496	.77504
43	9.3002	.91142	.08858	98	2.2177	.21733	.78267
44	9.2414	.90566	.09434	99	2.1458	.21029	.78971
45	9.1794	.89958	.10042	100	2.0792	.20376	.79624
46	9.1142	.89320	.10680	101	2.0158	.19755	.80245
47	9.0457	.88648	.11352	102	1.9498	.19108	.80892
48	8.9740	.87945	.12055	103	1.8799	.18423	.81577
49	8.8993	.87213	.12787	104	1.8023	.17662	.82338
50	8.8216	.86452	.13548	105	1.7059	.16718	.83282
51	8.7406	.85658	.14342	106	1.5655	.15341	.84659
52	8.6560	.84828	.15172	107	1.3596	.13324	.86676
53	8.5675	.83962	.16038	108	1.0184	.09980	.90020
54	8.4755	.83060	.16940	109	0.4554	.04463	.95537

Table S(10.0) *SINGLE LIFE, 10.0 PERCENT, BASED ON LIFE TABLE 80CNSMT SHOWING THE PRESENT WORTH OF AN ANNUITY, OF A LIFE ESTATE, AND OF A REMAINDER INTEREST*

Age	Annuity	Life Estate	Remainder	Age	Annuity	Life Estate	Remainder
(1)	(2)	(3)	(4)	(1)	(2)	(3)	(4)
0	9.8078	.98078	.01922	55	8.2550	.82550	.17450
1	9.9199	.99199	.00801	56	8.1586	.81586	.18414
2	9.9216	.99216	.00784	57	8.0581	.80581	.19419
3	9.9205	.99205	.00795	58	7.9536	.79536	.20464
4	9.9178	.99178	.00822	59	7.8449	.78449	.21551
5	9.9138	.99138	.00862	60	7.7326	.77326	.22674
6	9.9090	.99090	.00910	61	7.6169	.76169	.23831
7	9.9034	.99034	.00966	62	7.4980	.74980	.25020
8	9.8969	.98969	.01031	63	7.3760	.73760	.26240
9	9.8893	.98893	.01107	64	7.2507	.72507	.27493
10	9.8806	.98806	.01194	65	7.1213	.71213	.28787
11	9.8707	.98707	.01293	66	6.9876	.69876	.30124
12	9.8598	.98598	.01402	67	6.8492	.68492	.31508
13	9.8483	.98483	.01517	68	6.7063	.67063	.32937
14	9.8370	.98370	.01630	69	6.5595	.65595	.34405
15	9.8262	.98262	.01738	70	6.4093	.64093	.35907
16	9.8158	.98158	.01842	71	6.2564	.62564	.37436
17	9.8060	.98060	.01940	72	6.1009	.61009	.38991
18	9.7965	.97965	.02035	73	5.9425	.59425	.40575
19	9.7869	.97869	.02131	74	5.7805	.57805	.42195
20	9.7771	.97771	.02229	75	5.6144	.56144	.43856
21	9.7672	.97672	.02328	76	5.4437	.54437	.45563
22	9.7570	.97570	.02430	77	5.2689	.52689	.47311
23	9.7462	.97462	.02538	78	5.0906	.50906	.49094
24	9.7345	.97345	.02655	79	4.9103	.49103	.50897
25	9.7216	.97216	.02784	80	4.7295	.47295	.52705
26	9.7072	.97072	.02928	81	4.5501	.45501	.54499
27	9.6912	.96912	.03088	82	4.3730	.43730	.56270
28	9.6736	.96736	.03264	83	4.1993	.41993	.58007
29	9.6542	.96542	.03458	84	4.0287	.40287	.59713
30	9.6329	.96329	.03671	85	3.8608	.38608	.61392
31	9.6095	.96095	.03905	86	3.6970	.36970	.63030
32	9.5840	.95840	.04160	87	3.5398	.35398	.64602
33	9.5562	.95562	.04438	88	3.3883	.33883	.66117
34	9.5262	.95262	.04738	89	3.2399	.32399	.67601
35	9.4937	.94937	.05063	90	3.0929	.30929	.69071
36	9.4589	.94589	.05411	91	2.9496	.29496	.70504
37	9.4217	.94217	.05783	92	2.8136	.28136	.71864
38	9.3820	.93820	.06180	93	2.6865	.26865	.73135
39	9.3396	.93396	.06604	94	2.5697	.25697	.74303
40	9.2945	.92945	.07055	95	2.4638	.24638	.75362
41	9.2465	.92465	.07535	96	2.3697	.23697	.76303
42	9.1959	.91959	.08041	97	2.2840	.22840	.77160
43	9.1424	.91424	.08576	98	2.2069	.22069	.77931
44	9.0859	.90859	.09141	99	2.1356	.21356	.78644
45	9.0264	.90264	.09736	100	2.0696	.20696	.79304
46	8.9637	.89637	.10363	101	2.0068	.20068	.79932
47	8.8978	.88978	.11022	102	1.9414	.19414	.80586
48	8.8287	.88287	.11713	103	1.8721	.18721	.81279
49	8.7567	.87567	.12433	104	1.7952	.17952	.82048
50	8.6818	.86818	.13182	105	1.6997	.16997	.83003
51	8.6037	.86037	.13963	106	1.5603	.15603	.84397
52	8.5220	.85220	.14780	107	1.3557	.13557	.86443
53	8.4365	.84365	.15635	108	1.0160	.10160	.89840
54	8.3476	.83476	.16524	109	0.4545	.04545	.95455

Table S(10.2) *SINGLE LIFE, 10.2 PERCENT, BASED ON LIFE TABLE 80CNSMT SHOWING THE PRESENT WORTH OF AN ANNUITY, OF A LIFE ESTATE, AND OF A REMAINDER INTEREST*

Age	Annuity	Life Estate	Remainder	Age	Annuity	Life Estate	Remainder
(1)	(2)	(3)	(4)	(1)	(2)	(3)	(4)
0	9.6185	.98109	.01891	55	8.1335	.82961	.17039
1	9.7284	.99230	.00770	56	8.0401	.82009	.17991
2	9.7303	.99249	.00751	57	7.9428	.81016	.18984
3	9.7294	.99240	.00760	58	7.8414	.79982	.20018
4	9.7269	.99214	.00786	59	7.7359	.78907	.21093
5	9.7232	.99176	.00824	60	7.6269	.77794	.22206
6	9.7187	.99131	.00869	61	7.5144	.76647	.23353
7	9.7134	.99077	.00923	62	7.3989	.75468	.24532
8	9.7073	.99014	.00986	63	7.2802	.74258	.25742
9	9.7001	.98941	.01059	64	7.1582	.73013	.26987
10	9.6919	.98858	.01142	65	7.0322	.71729	.28271
11	9.6825	.98761	.01239	66	6.9018	.70399	.29601
12	9.6720	.98655	.01345	67	6.7669	.69022	.30978
13	9.6611	.98543	.01457	68	6.6274	.67599	.32401
14	9.6503	.98433	.01567	69	6.4840	.66137	.33863
15	9.6400	.98328	.01672	70	6.3372	.64639	.35361
16	9.6302	.98228	.01772	71	6.1877	.63114	.36886
17	9.6210	.98134	.01866	72	6.0354	.61561	.38439
18	9.6120	.98042	.01958	73	5.8803	.59979	.40021
19	9.6029	.97950	.02050	74	5.7216	.58361	.41639
20	9.5938	.97857	.02143	75	5.5587	.56699	.43301
21	9.5845	.97762	.02238	76	5.3912	.54991	.45009
22	9.5749	.97664	.02336	77	5.2195	.53239	.46761
23	9.5649	.97562	.02438	78	5.0443	.51452	.48548
24	9.5539	.97450	.02550	79	4.8670	.49644	.50356
25	9.5419	.97327	.02673	80	4.6891	.47829	.52171
26	9.5284	.97189	.02811	81	4.5124	.46026	.53974
27	9.5133	.97035	.02965	82	4.3379	.44247	.55753
28	9.4966	.96866	.03134	83	4.1667	.42500	.57500
29	9.4783	.96678	.03322	84	3.9985	.40784	.59216
30	9.4581	.96473	.03527	85	3.8327	.39094	.60906
31	9.4360	.96247	.03753	86	3.6710	.37445	.62555
32	9.4118	.96000	.04000	87	3.5157	.35861	.64139
33	9.3854	.95731	.04269	88	3.3661	.34334	.65666
34	9.3567	.95439	.04561	89	3.2193	.32837	.67163
35	9.3258	.95123	.04877	90	3.0739	.31354	.68646
36	9.2926	.94785	.05215	91	2.9321	.29907	.70093
37	9.2571	.94422	.05578	92	2.7974	.28534	.71466
38	9.2191	.94035	.05965	93	2.6715	.27250	.72750
39	9.1786	.93621	.06379	94	2.5558	.26069	.73931
40	9.1353	.93180	.06820	95	2.4509	.24999	.75001
41	9.0894	.92712	.07288	96	2.3576	.24047	.75953
42	9.0408	.92216	.07784	97	2.2727	.23181	.76819
43	8.9894	.91692	.08308	98	2.1962	.22401	.77599
44	8.9352	.91139	.08861	99	2.1256	.21681	.78319
45	8.8780	.90555	.09445	100	2.0601	.21013	.78987
46	8.8177	.89940	.10060	101	1.9978	.20378	.79622
47	8.7542	.89293	.10707	102	1.9330	.19717	.80283
48	8.6876	.88614	.11386	103	1.8644	.19017	.80983
49	8.6183	.87906	.12094	104	1.7882	.18240	.81760
50	8.5460	.87169	.12831	105	1.6936	.17274	.82726
51	8.4706	.86400	.13600	106	1.5552	.15863	.84137
52	8.3917	.85595	.14405	107	1.3518	.13789	.86211
53	8.3091	.84753	.15247	108	1.0137	.10340	.89660
54	8.2231	.83876	.16124	109	0.4537	.04628	.95372

Table S(10.4) *SINGLE LIFE, 10.4 PERCENT, BASED ON LIFE TABLE 80CNSMT SHOWING THE PRESENT WORTH OF AN ANNUITY, OF A LIFE ESTATE, AND OF A REMAINDER INTEREST*

Age	Annuity	Life Estate	Remainder	Age	Annuity	Life Estate	Remainder
(1)	(2)	(3)	(4)	(1)	(2)	(3)	(4)
0	9.4362	.98136	.01864	55	8.0152	.83358	.16642
1	9.5441	.99259	.00741	56	7.9247	.82417	.17583
2	9.5461	.99279	.00721	57	7.8304	.81436	.18564
3	9.5454	.99272	.00728	58	7.7320	.80413	.19587
4	9.5431	.99248	.00752	59	7.6297	.79348	.20652
5	9.5396	.99212	.00788	60	7.5237	.78247	.21753
6	9.5354	.99168	.00832	61	7.4144	.77110	.22890
7	9.5305	.99117	.00883	62	7.3020	.75941	.24059
8	9.5247	.99057	.00943	63	7.1865	.74740	.25260
9	9.5179	.98986	.01014	64	7.0678	.73505	.26495
10	9.5101	.98905	.01095	65	6.9451	.72229	.27771
11	9.5011	.98811	.01189	66	6.8180	.70907	.29093
12	9.4911	.98708	.01292	67	6.6863	.69538	.30462
13	9.4807	.98599	.01401	68	6.5501	.68121	.31879
14	9.4704	.98492	.01508	69	6.4100	.66664	.33336
15	9.4606	.98390	.01610	70	6.2665	.65171	.34829
16	9.4513	.98293	.01707	71	6.1202	.63651	.36349
17	9.4425	.98202	.01798	72	5.9712	.62101	.37899
18	9.4341	.98114	.01886	73	5.8193	.60521	.39479
19	9.4255	.98026	.01974	74	5.6638	.58904	.41096
20	9.4170	.97936	.02064	75	5.5040	.57242	.42758
21	9.4083	.97846	.02154	76	5.3397	.55533	.44467
22	9.3993	.97753	.02247	77	5.1710	.53779	.46221
23	9.3899	.97655	.02345	78	4.9988	.51987	.48013
24	9.3797	.97549	.02451	79	4.8244	.50174	.49826
25	9.3684	.97431	.02569	80	4.6493	.48353	.51647
26	9.3556	.97299	.02701	81	4.4753	.46543	.53457
27	9.3414	.97151	.02849	82	4.3034	.44755	.55245
28	9.3257	.96987	.03013	83	4.1346	.42999	.57001
29	9.3084	.96807	.03193	84	3.9686	.41274	.58726
30	9.2893	.96609	.03391	85	3.8050	.39572	.60428
31	9.2683	.96390	.03610	86	3.6454	.37912	.62088
32	9.2453	.96151	.03849	87	3.4920	.36317	.63683
33	9.2201	.95889	.04111	88	3.3441	.34779	.65221
34	9.1929	.95606	.04394	89	3.1990	.33270	.66730
35	9.1633	.95298	.04702	90	3.0552	.31774	.68226
36	9.1317	.94969	.05031	91	2.9148	.30314	.69686
37	9.0977	.94616	.05384	92	2.7815	.28927	.71073
38	9.0614	.94239	.05761	93	2.6568	.27630	.72370
39	9.0226	.93835	.06165	94	2.5421	.26438	.73562
40	8.9812	.93404	.06596	95	2.4381	.25356	.74644
41	8.9371	.92946	.07054	96	2.3456	.24394	.75606
42	8.8904	.92461	.07539	97	2.2614	.23519	.76481
43	8.8411	.91948	.08052	98	2.1856	.22730	.77270
44	8.7890	.91406	.08594	99	2.1156	.22002	.77998
45	8.7340	.90833	.09167	100	2.0507	.21327	.78673
46	8.6759	.90230	.09770	101	1.9890	.20685	.79315
47	8.6148	.89594	.10406	102	1.9247	.20017	.79983
48	8.5507	.88927	.11073	103	1.8567	.19310	.80690
49	8.4837	.88231	.11769	104	1.7812	.18525	.81475
50	8.4140	.87506	.12494	105	1.6874	.17549	.82451
51	8.3412	.86749	.13251	106	1.5501	.16121	.83879
52	8.2650	.85956	.14044	107	1.3480	.14019	.85981
53	8.1851	.85125	.14875	108	1.0114	.10519	.89481
54	8.1019	.84260	.15740	109	0.4529	.04710	.95290

Table S(10.6) SINGLE LIFE, 10.6 PERCENT, BASED ON LIFE TABLE 80CNSMT SHOWING THE PRESENT WORTH OF AN ANNUITY, OF A LIFE ESTATE, AND OF A REMAINDER INTEREST

Age	Annuity	Life Estate	Remainder	Age	Annuity	Life Estate	Remainder
(1)	(2)	(3)	(4)	(1)	(2)	(3)	(4)
0	9.2606	.98162	.01838	55	7.8999	.83739	.16261
1	9.3665	.99285	.00715	56	7.8123	.82810	.17190
2	9.3686	.99307	.00693	57	7.7208	.81840	.18160
3	9.3681	.99301	.00699	58	7.6253	.80828	.19172
4	9.3660	.99279	.00721	59	7.5260	.79775	.20225
5	9.3628	.99245	.00755	60	7.4230	.78684	.21316
6	9.3588	.99204	.00796	61	7.3168	.77558	.22442
7	9.3542	.99154	.00846	62	7.2074	.76399	.23601
8	9.3487	.99096	.00904	63	7.0950	.75207	.24793
9	9.3423	.99028	.00972	64	6.9794	.73981	.26019
10	9.3349	.98949	.01051	65	6.8598	.72714	.27286
11	9.3262	.98858	.01142	66	6.7359	.71400	.28600
12	9.3167	.98757	.01243	67	6.6074	.70039	.29961
13	9.3067	.98651	.01349	68	6.4744	.68629	.31371
14	9.2969	.98547	.01453	69	6.3375	.67178	.32822
15	9.2875	.98448	.01552	70	6.1972	.65690	.34310
16	9.2787	.98354	.01646	71	6.0541	.64174	.35826
17	9.2704	.98266	.01734	72	5.9083	.62627	.37373
18	9.2624	.98182	.01818	73	5.7595	.61050	.38950
19	9.2544	.98097	.01903	74	5.6070	.59435	.40565
20	9.2463	.98011	.01989	75	5.4503	.57774	.42226
21	9.2382	.97925	.02075	76	5.2890	.56063	.43937
22	9.2298	.97836	.02164	77	5.1233	.54307	.45693
23	9.2210	.97743	.02257	78	4.9540	.52512	.47488
24	9.2114	.97641	.02359	79	4.7825	.50694	.49306
25	9.2008	.97528	.02472	80	4.6101	.48867	.51133
26	9.1888	.97402	.02598	81	4.4387	.47050	.52950
27	9.1754	.97259	.02741	82	4.2693	.45255	.54745
28	9.1606	.97102	.02898	83	4.1029	.43490	.56510
29	9.1441	.96928	.03072	84	3.9392	.41755	.58245
30	9.1261	.96736	.03264	85	3.7777	.40044	.59956
31	9.1061	.96525	.03475	86	3.6201	.38373	.61627
32	9.0843	.96293	.03707	87	3.4686	.36767	.63233
33	9.0603	.96039	.03961	88	3.3224	.35217	.64783
34	9.0343	.95764	.04236	89	3.1789	.33696	.66304
35	9.0061	.95465	.04535	90	3.0366	.32188	.67812
36	8.9759	.95144	.04856	91	2.8977	.30715	.69285
37	8.9434	.94800	.05200	92	2.7656	.29316	.70684
38	8.9087	.94432	.05568	93	2.6421	.28006	.71994
39	8.8715	.94038	.05962	94	2.5285	.26802	.73198
40	8.8318	.93617	.06383	95	2.4254	.25709	.74291
41	8.7895	.93168	.06832	96	2.3337	.24738	.75262
42	8.7447	.92694	.07306	97	2.2503	.23853	.76147
43	8.6973	.92192	.07808	98	2.1751	.23056	.76944
44	8.6472	.91660	.08340	99	2.1057	.22320	.77680
45	8.5942	.91099	.08901	100	2.0413	.21638	.78362
46	8.5383	.90506	.09494	101	1.9802	.20990	.79010
47	8.4794	.89881	.10119	102	1.9165	.20315	.79685
48	8.4176	.89226	.10774	103	1.8491	.19601	.80399
49	8.3530	.88542	.11458	104	1.7743	.18808	.81192
50	8.2857	.87828	.12172	105	1.6813	.17822	.82178
51	8.2154	.87083	.12917	106	1.5450	.16377	.83623
52	8.1417	.86302	.13698	107	1.3442	.14249	.85751
53	8.0645	.85483	.14517	108	1.0091	.10696	.89304
54	7.9839	.84630	.15370	109	0.4521	.04792	.95208

Table S(10.8) *SINGLE LIFE, 10.8 PERCENT, BASED ON LIFE TABLE 80CNSMT SHOWING THE PRESENT WORTH OF AN ANNUITY, OF A LIFE ESTATE, AND OF A REMAINDER INTEREST*

Age	Annuity	Life Estate	Remainder	Age	Annuity	Life Estate	Remainder
(1)	(2)	(3)	(4)	(1)	(2)	(3)	(4)
0	9.0913	.98186	.01814	55	7.7877	.84107	.15893
1	9.1954	.99310	.00690	56	7.7027	.83189	.16811
2	9.1975	.99333	.00667	57	7.6140	.82231	.17769
3	9.1971	.99329	.00671	58	7.5213	.81230	.18770
4	9.1952	.99308	.00692	59	7.4248	.80188	.19812
5	9.1922	.99276	.00724	60	7.3248	.79107	.20893
6	9.1885	.99236	.00764	61	7.2214	.77991	.22009
7	9.1842	.99189	.00811	62	7.1150	.76842	.23158
8	9.1790	.99133	.00867	63	7.0056	.75661	.24339
9	9.1729	.99067	.00933	64	6.8930	.74444	.25556
10	9.1658	.98991	.01009	65	6.7764	.73185	.26815
11	9.1576	.98902	.01098	66	6.6555	.71880	.28120
12	9.1485	.98803	.01197	67	6.5302	.70526	.29474
13	9.1388	.98700	.01300	68	6.4003	.69123	.30877
14	9.1295	.98598	.01402	69	6.2665	.67678	.32322
15	9.1205	.98502	.01498	70	6.1292	.66196	.33804
16	9.1121	.98411	.01589	71	5.9893	.64684	.35316
17	9.1043	.98326	.01674	72	5.8465	.63142	.36858
18	9.0967	.98245	.01755	73	5.7007	.61568	.38432
19	9.0891	.98163	.01837	74	5.5513	.59954	.40046
20	9.0815	.98081	.01919	75	5.3975	.58294	.41706
21	9.0739	.97998	.02002	76	5.2392	.56583	.43417
22	9.0660	.97913	.02087	77	5.0764	.54825	.45175
23	9.0578	.97824	.02176	78	4.9099	.53027	.46973
24	9.0488	.97727	.02273	79	4.7412	.51205	.48795
25	9.0388	.97619	.02381	80	4.5715	.49372	.50628
26	9.0276	.97498	.02502	81	4.4027	.47549	.52451
27	9.0149	.97361	.02639	82	4.2357	.45746	.54254
28	9.0009	.97210	.02790	83	4.0716	.43974	.56026
29	8.9854	.97042	.02958	84	3.9101	.42230	.57770
30	8.9682	.96857	.03143	85	3.7508	.40508	.59492
31	8.9492	.96652	.03348	86	3.5951	.38827	.61173
32	8.9285	.96427	.03573	87	3.4454	.37210	.62790
33	8.9056	.96181	.03189	88	3.3009	.35650	.64350
34	8.8808	.95913	.04087	89	3.1591	.34118	.65882
35	8.8539	.95622	.04378	90	3.0183	.32598	.67402
36	8.8250	.95310	.04690	91	2.8808	.31112	.68888
37	8.7940	.94975	.05025	92	2.7500	.29700	.70300
38	8.7607	.94615	.05385	93	2.6276	.28378	.71622
39	8.7250	.94230	.05770	94	2.5150	.27162	.72838
40	8.6869	.93819	.06181	95	2.4128	.26059	.73941
41	8.6463	.93380	.06620	96	2.3220	.25077	.74923
42	8.6033	.92915	.07085	97	2.2392	.24184	.75816
43	8.5578	.92424	.07576	98	2.1647	.23379	.76621
44	8.5095	.91903	.08097	99	2.0958	.22635	.77365
45	8.4585	.91352	.08648	100	2.0321	.21946	.78054
46	8.4047	.90770	.09230	101	1.9715	.21292	.78708
47	8.3479	.90157	.09843	102	1.9084	.20610	.79390
48	8.2882	.89513	.10487	103	1.8416	.19889	.80111
49	8.2259	.88840	.11160	104	1.7675	.19088	.80912
50	8.1609	.88138	.11862	105	1.6753	.18093	.81907
51	8.0930	.87404	.12596	106	1.5400	.16632	.83368
52	8.0217	.86634	.13366	107	1.3404	.14477	.85523
53	7.9470	.85828	.14172	108	1.0068	.10873	.89127
54	7.8691	.84986	.15014	109	0.4513	.04874	.95126

Table S(11.0) *SINGLE LIFE, 11.0 PERCENT, BASED ON LIFE TABLE 80CNSMT SHOWING THE PRESENT WORTH OF AN ANNUITY, OF A LIFE ESTATE, AND OF A REMAINDER INTEREST*

Age	Annuity	Life Estate	Remainder	Age	Annuity	Life Estate	Remainder
(1)	(2)	(3)	(4)	(1)	(2)	(3)	(4)
0	8.9281	.98209	.01791	55	7.6783	.84461	.15539
1	9.0302	.99333	.00667	56	7.5959	.83555	.16445
2	9.0325	.99357	.00643	57	7.5098	.82608	.17392
3	9.0322	.99354	.00646	58	7.4198	.81618	.18382
4	9.0305	.99335	.00665	59	7.3260	.80586	.19414
5	9.0277	.99305	.00695	60	7.2288	.79517	.20483
6	9.0242	.99267	.00733	61	7.1283	.78411	.21589
7	9.0201	.99221	.00779	62	7.0247	.77272	.22728
8	9.0152	.99167	.00833	63	6.9182	.76100	.23900
9	9.0094	.99103	.00897	64	6.8084	.74893	.25107
10	9.0027	.99029	.00971	65	6.6948	.73643	.26357
11	8.9948	.98943	.01057	66	6.5769	.72346	.27654
12	8.9860	.98846	.01154	67	6.4545	.71000	.29000
13	8.9768	.98745	.01255	68	6.3276	.69604	.30396
14	8.9678	.98646	.01354	69	6.1969	.68165	.31835
15	8.9593	.98552	.01448	70	6.0626	.66689	.33311
16	8.9513	.98464	.01536	71	5.9256	.65182	.34818
17	8.9438	.98382	.01618	72	5.7858	.63644	.36356
18	8.9367	.98303	.01697	73	5.6430	.62073	.37927
19	8.9295	.98225	.01775	74	5.4965	.60462	.39538
20	8.9224	.98146	.01854	75	5.3457	.58802	.41198
21	8.9152	.98067	.01933	76	5.1902	.57092	.42908
22	8.9078	.97986	.02014	77	5.0303	.55333	.44667
23	8.9001	.97901	.02099	78	4.8666	.53532	.46468
24	8.8917	.97808	.02192	79	4.7006	.51706	.48294
25	8.8823	.97705	.02295	80	4.5335	.49868	.50132
26	8.8717	.97589	.02411	81	4.3672	.48039	.51961
27	8.8597	.97457	.02543	82	4.2026	.46229	.53771
28	8.8465	.97311	.02689	83	4.0408	.44449	.55551
29	8.8317	.97149	.02851	84	3.8815	.42696	.57304
30	8.8155	.96970	.03030	85	3.7242	.40966	.59034
31	8.7974	.96772	.03228	86	3.5704	.39275	.60725
32	8.7777	.96554	.03446	87	3.4225	.37648	.62352
33	8.7559	.96315	.03685	88	3.2797	.36077	.63923
34	8.7322	.96054	.03946	89	3.1395	.34534	.65466
35	8.7065	.95771	.04229	90	3.0002	.33002	.66998
36	8.6788	.95467	.04533	91	2.8640	.31504	.68496
37	8.6491	.95140	.04860	92	2.7345	.30080	.69920
38	8.6172	.94789	.05211	93	2.6133	.28746	.71254
39	8.5830	.94413	.05587	94	2.5017	.27519	.72481
40	8.5465	.94011	.05989	95	2.4004	.26405	.73595
41	8.5075	.93582	.06418	96	2.3103	.25414	.74586
42	8.4661	.93127	.06873	97	2.2283	.24511	.75489
43	8.4233	.92645	.07355	98	2.1544	.23698	.76302
44	8.3759	.92135	.07865	99	2.0861	.22947	.77053
45	8.3268	.91594	.08406	100	2.0229	.22252	.77748
46	8.2748	.91023	.08977	101	1.9628	.21591	.78409
47	8.2201	.90421	.09579	102	1.9003	.20903	.79097
48	8.1625	.89787	.10213	103	1.8341	.20175	.79825
49	8.1023	.89126	.10874	104	1.7606	.19367	.80633
50	8.0395	.88435	.11565	105	1.6693	.18362	.81638
51	7.9739	.87712	.12288	106	1.5350	.16885	.83115
52	7.9049	.86954	.13046	107	1.3367	.14703	.85297
53	7.8326	.86159	.13841	108	1.0045	.11050	.88950
54	7.7571	.85329	.14671	109	0.4505	.04955	.95045

Age	Annuity	Life Estate	Remainder	Age	Annuity	Life Estate	Remainder
(1)	(2)	(3)	(4)	(1)	(2)	(3)	(4)
0	8.7705	.98230	.01770	55	7.5716	.84802	.15198
1	8.8709	.99354	.00646	56	7.4918	.83908	.16092
2	8.8732	.99380	.00620	57	7.4082	.82971	.17029
3	8.8730	.99378	.00622	58	7.3208	.81993	.18007
4	8.8715	.99361	.00639	59	7.2296	.80972	.19028
5	8.8689	.99332	.00668	60	7.1351	.79913	.20087
6	8.8656	.99295	.00705	61	7.0373	.78818	.21182
7	8.8617	.99251	.00749	62	6.9365	.77689	.22311
8	8.8571	.99199	.00801	63	6.8327	.76527	.23473
9	8.8516	.99137	.00863	64	6.7258	.75329	.24671
10	8.8451	.99065	.00935	65	6.6150	.74088	.25912
11	8.8376	.98981	.01019	66	6.5000	.72800	.27200
12	8.8292	.98887	.01113	67	6.3805	.71461	.28539
13	8.8203	.98788	.01212	68	6.2565	.70073	.29927
14	8.8117	.98691	.01309	69	6.1286	.68641	.31359
15	8.8035	.98600	.01400	70	5.9973	.67170	.32830
16	8.7959	.98514	.01486	71	5.8632	.65668	.34332
17	8.7888	.98434	.01566	72	5.7263	.64134	.35866
18	8.7820	.98359	.10641	73	5.5863	.62567	.37433
19	8.7753	.98283	.01717	74	5.4427	.60958	.39042
20	8.7685	.98207	.01793	75	5.2947	.59301	.40699
21	8.7618	.98132	.01868	76	5.1420	.57590	.42410
22	8.7548	.98054	.01946	77	4.9849	.55830	.44170
23	8.7476	.97973	.02027	78	4.8239	.54028	.45972
24	8.7397	.97885	.02115	79	4.6606	.52198	.47802
25	8.7309	.97786	.02214	80	4.4960	.50356	.49644
26	8.7209	.97674	.02326	81	4.3322	.48521	.51479
27	8.7096	.97548	.02452	82	4.1700	.46704	.53296
28	8.6970	.97407	.02593	83	4.0104	.44917	.55083
29	8.6831	.97250	.02750	84	3.8532	.43156	.56844
30	8.6676	.97077	.02923	85	3.6979	.41417	.58583
31	8.6504	.96885	.03115	86	3.5461	.39716	.60284
32	8.6316	.96674	.03326	87	3.3999	.38079	.61921
33	8.6109	.96442	.03558	88	3.2588	.36498	.63502
34	8.5882	.96188	.03812	89	3.1201	.34945	.65055
35	8.5636	.95913	.04087	90	2.9823	.33401	.66599
36	8.5372	.95616	.04384	91	2.8475	.31892	.68108
37	8.5087	.95297	.04703	92	2.7192	.30455	.69545
38	8.4781	.94955	.05045	93	2.5991	.29110	.70890
39	8.4453	.94588	.05412	94	2.4885	.27871	.72129
40	8.4102	.94194	.05806	95	2.3881	.26747	.73253
41	8.3727	.93774	.06226	96	2.2988	.25747	.74253
42	8.3329	.93329	.06671	97	2.2174	.24835	.75165
43	8.2908	.92857	.07143	98	2.1442	.24014	.75986
44	8.2461	.92356	.07644	99	2.0765	.23256	.76744
45	8.1987	.91826	.08174	100	2.0138	.22554	.77446
46	8.1487	.91265	.08735	101	1.9542	.21887	.78113
47	8.0958	.90673	.09327	102	1.8922	.21193	.78807
48	8.0402	.90051	.09949	103	1.8267	.20459	.79541
49	7.9821	.89400	.10600	104	1.7539	.19643	.80357
50	7.9214	.88720	.11280	105	1.6633	.18629	.81371
51	7.8579	.88009	.11991	106	1.5301	.17137	.82863
52	7.7912	.87262	.12738	107	1.3329	.14929	.85071
53	7.7212	.86478	.13522	108	1.0022	.11225	.88775
54	7.6481	.85659	.14341	109	0.4496	.05036	.94964

Age	Annuity	Life Estate	Remainder	Age	Annuity	Life Estate	Remainder
(1)	(2)	(3)	(4)	(1)	(2)	(3)	(4)
0	8.6184	.98250	.01750	55	7.4677	.85132	.14868
1	8.7170	.99374	.00626	56	7.3902	.84248	.15752
2	8.7193	.99400	.00600	57	7.3090	.83323	.16677
3	8.7193	.99400	.00600	58	7.2241	.82355	.17645
4	8.7179	.99384	.00616	59	7.1355	.81345	.18655
5	8.7155	.99357	.00643	60	7.0436	.80297	.19703
6	8.7124	.99322	.00678	61	6.9484	.79212	.20788
7	8.7087	.99280	.00720	62	6.8502	.78093	.21907
8	8.7043	.99229	.00771	63	6.7492	.76940	.23060
9	8.6991	.99169	.00831	64	6.6449	.75752	.24248
10	8.6929	.99099	.00901	65	6.5369	.74520	.25480
11	8.6857	.99017	.00983	66	6.4246	.73240	.26760
12	8.6776	.98925	.01075	67	6.3079	.71910	.28090
13	8.6691	.98828	.01172	68	6.1867	.70529	.29471
14	8.6608	.98733	.01267	69	6.0617	.69104	.30896
15	8.6530	.98644	.01356	70	5.9332	.67639	.32361
16	8.6457	.98561	.01439	71	5.8020	.66142	.33858
17	8.6389	.98484	.01516	72	5.6678	.64613	.35387
18	8.6325	.98410	.01590	73	5.5307	.63050	.36950
19	8.6261	.98338	.01662	74	5.3898	.61444	.38556
20	8.6197	.98265	.01735	75	5.2446	.59788	.40212
21	8.6134	.98193	.01807	76	5.0946	.58079	.41921
22	8.6069	.98118	.01882	77	4.9402	.56318	.43682
23	8.6001	.98041	.01959	78	4.7819	.54514	.45486
24	8.5927	.97956	.02044	79	4.6212	.52681	.47319
25	8.5844	.97862	.02138	80	4.4592	.50834	.49166
26	8.5749	.97754	.02246	81	4.2977	.48994	.51006
27	8.5643	.97633	.02367	82	4.1379	.47172	.52828
28	8.5524	.97497	.02503	83	3.9805	.45377	.54623
29	8.5391	.97346	.02654	84	3.8253	.43609	.56391
30	8.5244	.97179	.02821	85	3.6720	.41861	.58139
31	8.5081	.96992	.03008	86	3.5220	.40151	.59849
32	8.4901	.96787	.03213	87	3.3776	.38505	.61495
33	8.4703	.96562	.03438	88	3.2381	.36914	.63086
34	8.4487	.96315	.03685	89	3.1009	.35350	.64650
35	8.4251	.96047	.03953	90	2.9645	.33796	.66204
36	8.3998	.95758	.04242	91	2.8311	.32275	.67725
37	8.3725	.95447	.04553	92	2.7041	.30827	.69173
38	8.3432	.95112	.04888	93	2.5851	.29470	.70530
39	8.3117	.94753	.05247	94	2.4755	.28220	.71780
40	8.2780	.94369	.05631	95	2.3759	.27086	.72914
41	8.2419	.93958	.06042	96	2.2874	.26076	.73924
42	8.2036	.93521	.06479	97	2.2067	.25156	.74844
43	8.1630	.93059	.06941	98	2.1340	.24328	.75672
44	8.1200	.92568	.07432	99	2.0669	.23563	.76437
45	8.0743	.92047	.07953	100	2.0047	.22854	.77146
46	8.0261	.91497	.08503	101	1.9457	.22181	.77819
47	7.9750	.90915	.09085	102	1.8843	.21481	.78519
48	7.9213	.90303	.09697	103	1.8193	.20740	.79260
49	7.8652	.89663	.10337	104	1.7471	.19917	.88083
50	7.8065	.88994	.11006	105	1.6574	.18894	.88106
51	7.7451	.88294	.11706	106	1.5251	.17386	.82614
52	7.6805	.87558	.12442	107	1.3292	.15153	.84847
53	7.6127	.86785	.13215	108	1.0000	.11399	.88601
54	7.5418	.85977	.14023	109	0.4488	.05117	.94883

Table S(11.6) SINGLE LIFE, 11.6 PERCENT, BASED ON LIFE TABLE
80CNSMT SHOWING THE PRESENT WORTH OF AN ANNUITY, OF A LIFE
ESTATE, AND OF A REMAINDER INTEREST

Age	Annuity	Life Estate	Remainder	Age	Annuity	Life Estate	Remainder
(1)	(2)	(3)	(4)	(1)	(2)	(3)	(4)
0	8.4714	.98268	.01732	55	7.3663	.85449	.14551
1	8.5683	.99392	.00608	56	7.2911	.84577	.15423
2	8.5707	.99420	.00580	57	7.2123	.83662	.16338
3	8.5708	.99421	.00579	58	7.1298	.82705	.17295
4	8.5695	.99406	.00594	59	7.0436	.81706	.18294
5	8.5672	.99380	.00620	60	6.9541	.80668	.19332
6	8.5644	.99346	.00654	61	6.8615	.79593	.20407
7	8.5609	.99306	.00694	62	6.7659	.78485	.21515
8	8.5567	.99257	.00743	63	6.6674	.77342	.22658
9	8.5516	.99199	.00801	64	6.5658	.76163	.23837
10	8.5457	.99131	.00869	65	6.4604	.74941	.25059
11	8.5388	.99050	.00950	66	6.3508	.73669	.26331
12	8.5310	.98960	.01040	67	6.2368	.72347	.27653
13	8.5228	.98865	.01135	68	6.1184	.70973	.29027
14	8.5149	.98773	.01227	69	5.9961	.69555	.30445
15	8.5074	.98686	.01314	70	5.8704	.68097	.31903
16	8.5004	.98604	.01396	71	5.7419	.66606	.33394
17	8.4939	.98530	.01470	72	5.6104	.65081	.34919
18	8.4879	.98459	.01541	73	5.4760	.63522	.36478
19	8.4818	.98389	.01611	74	5.3379	.61919	.38081
20	8.4758	.98319	.01681	75	5.1953	.60266	.39734
21	8.4698	.98250	.01750	76	5.0480	.58557	.41443
22	8.4637	.98179	.01821	77	4.8963	.56797	.43203
23	8.4573	.98105	.01895	78	4.7406	.54991	.45009
24	8.4503	.98024	.01976	79	4.5824	.53155	.46845
25	8.4425	.97933	.02067	80	4.4228	.51305	.48695
26	8.4336	.97830	.02170	81	4.2637	.49459	.50541
27	8.4235	.97713	.02287	82	4.1061	.47631	.52369
28	8.4122	.97582	.02418	83	3.9509	.45830	.54170
29	8.3997	.97436	.02564	84	3.7978	.44055	.55945
30	8.3857	.97274	.02726	85	3.6464	.42298	.57702
31	8.3701	.97093	.02907	86	3.4983	.40580	.59420
32	8.3530	.96895	.03105	87	3.3556	.38924	.61076
33	8.3341	.96675	.03325	88	3.2176	.37325	.62675
34	8.3134	.96435	.03565	89	3.0820	.35751	.64249
35	8.2908	.96174	.03826	90	2.9470	.34186	.65814
36	8.2666	.95892	.04108	91	2.8149	.32653	.67347
37	8.2404	.95589	.04411	92	2.6891	.31194	.68806
38	8.2122	.95262	.04738	93	2.5712	.29826	.70174
39	8.1820	.94911	.05089	94	2.4625	.28566	.71434
40	8.1496	.94535	.05465	95	2.3639	.27421	.72579
41	8.1149	.94132	.05868	96	2.2761	.26402	.73598
42	8.0780	.93705	.06295	97	2.1961	.25474	.74526
43	8.0389	.93252	.06748	98	2.1240	.24638	.75362
44	7.9974	.92770	.07230	99	2.0574	.23866	.76134
45	7.9534	.92259	.07741	100	1.9958	.23151	.76849
46	7.9068	.91719	.08281	101	1.9373	.22472	.77528
47	7.8575	.91147	.08853	102	1.8764	.21766	.78234
48	7.8056	.90545	.09455	103	1.8120	.21019	.78981
49	7.7513	.89916	.10084	104	1.7405	.20190	.79810
50	7.6946	.89257	.10743	105	1.6515	.19157	.80843
51	7.6351	.88568	.11432	106	1.5202	.17634	.82366
52	7.5726	.87843	.12157	107	1.3255	.15376	.84624
53	7.5069	.87081	.12919	108	0.9977	.11573	.88427
54	7.4382	.86283	.13717	109	0.4480	.05197	.94803

Table S(11.8) SINGLE LIFE, 11.8 PERCENT, BASED ON LIFE TABLE
80CNSMT SHOWING THE PRESENT WORTH OF AN ANNUITY, OF A LIFE
ESTATE, AND OF A REMAINDER INTEREST

Age	Annuity	Life Estate	Remainder	Age	Annuity	Life Estate	Remainder
(1)	(2)	(3)	(4)	(1)	(2)	(3)	(4)
0	8.3293	.98285	.01715	55	7.2674	.85756	.14244
1	8.4246	.99410	.00590	56	7.1944	.84894	.15106
2	8.4270	.99438	.00562	57	7.1178	.83990	.16010
3	8.4272	.99440	.00560	58	7.0376	.83044	.16956
4	8.4260	.99427	.00573	59	6.9539	.82055	.17945
5	8.4239	.99402	.00598	60	6.8668	.81028	.18972
6	8.4212	.99370	.00630	61	6.7766	.79963	.20037
7	8.4179	.99331	.00669	62	6.6834	.78865	.21135
8	8.4139	.99284	.00716	63	6.5874	.77732	.22268
9	8.4091	.99227	.00773	64	6.4883	.76562	.23438
10	8.4034	.99160	.00840	65	6.3855	.75349	.24651
11	8.3967	.99082	.00918	66	6.2785	.74087	.25913
12	8.3893	.98993	.01007	67	6.1672	.72773	.27227
13	8.3814	.98900	.01100	68	6.0514	.71407	.28593
14	8.3737	.98810	.01190	69	5.9318	.69995	.30005
15	8.3665	.98725	.01275	70	5.8087	.68543	.31457
16	8.3598	.98646	.01354	71	5.6829	.67058	.32942
17	8.3537	.98573	.01427	72	5.5541	.65539	.34461
18	8.3479	.98505	.01495	73	5.4223	.63984	.36016
19	8.3421	.98437	.01563	74	5.2868	.62384	.37616
20	8.3364	.98370	.01630	75	5.1469	.60733	.39267
21	8.3308	.98304	.01696	76	5.0022	.59026	.40974
22	8.3251	.98236	.01764	77	4.8530	.57266	.42734
23	8.3191	.98165	.01835	78	4.6999	.55459	.44541
24	8.3125	.98087	.01913	79	4.5441	.53621	.46379
25	8.3051	.98001	.01999	80	4.3870	.51767	.48233
26	8.2967	.97902	.02098	81	4.2303	.49917	.50083
27	8.2872	.97789	.02211	82	4.0749	.48083	.51917
28	8.2765	.97662	.02338	83	3.9217	.46276	.53724
29	8.2645	.97521	.02479	84	3.7707	.44494	.55506
30	8.2512	.97365	.02635	85	3.6212	.42730	.57270
31	8.2364	.97189	.02811	86	3.4748	.41003	.58997
32	8.2200	.96996	.03004	87	3.3338	.39339	.60661
33	8.2019	.96783	.03217	88	3.1974	.37730	.62270
34	8.1821	.96549	.03451	89	3.0632	.36146	.63854
35	8.1605	.96294	.03706	90	2.9297	.34570	.65430
36	8.1373	.96020	.03980	91	2.7989	.33027	.66973
37	8.1122	.95724	.04276	92	2.6743	.31556	.68444
38	8.0851	.95405	.04595	93	2.5574	.30178	.69822
39	8.0561	.95061	.04939	94	2.4497	.28907	.71093
40	8.0249	.94693	.05307	95	2.3519	.27753	.72247
41	7.9915	.94299	.05701	96	2.2649	.26725	.73275
42	7.9560	.93881	.06119	97	2.1855	.25789	.74211
43	7.9183	.93436	.06564	98	2.1140	.24946	.75054
44	7.8783	.92964	.07036	99	2.0480	.24167	.75833
45	7.8358	.92462	.07538	100	1.9869	.23445	.76555
46	7.7908	.91932	.08068	101	1.9289	.22761	.77239
47	7.7432	.91370	.08630	102	1.8685	.22049	.77951
48	7.6930	.90778	.09222	103	1.8047	.21295	.78705
49	7.6405	.90158	.09842	104	1.7339	.20459	.79541
50	7.5856	.89510	.10490	105	1.6456	.19418	.80582
51	7.5281	.88831	.11169	106	1.5153	.17881	.82119
52	7.4675	.88117	.11883	107	1.3218	.15597	.84403
53	7.4039	.87365	.12635	108	0.9954	.11746	.88254
54	7.3372	.86579	.13421	109	0.4472	.05277	.94723

Table S(12.0) SINGLE LIFE, 12.0 PERCENT, BASED ON LIFE TABLE
80CNSMT SHOWING THE PRESENT WORTH OF AN ANNUITY, OF A LIFE
ESTATE, AND OF A REMAINDER INTEREST

Age	Annuity	Life Estate	Remainder	Age	Annuity	Life Estate	Remainder
(1)	(2)	(3)	(4)	(1)	(2)	(3)	(4)
0	8.1918	.98302	.01698	55	7.1710	.86052	.13948
1	8.2855	.99426	.00574	56	7.1001	.85201	.14799
2	8.2880	.99456	.00544	57	7.0256	.84308	.15692
3	8.2882	.99459	.00541	58	6.9477	.83372	.16628
4	8.2872	.99446	.00554	59	6.8661	.82394	.17606
5	8.2852	.99422	.00578	60	6.7814	.81376	.18624
6	8.2826	.99392	.00608	61	6.6935	.80322	.19678
7	8.2795	.99354	.00646	62	6.6028	.79233	.20767
8	8.2757	.99308	.00692	63	6.5092	.78110	.21890
9	8.2711	.99253	.00747	64	6.4125	.76950	.23050
10	8.2657	.99188	.00812	65	6.3122	.75746	.24254
11	8.2593	.99111	.00889	66	6.2077	.74493	.25507
12	8.2521	.99025	.00975	67	6.0989	.73187	.26813
13	8.2445	.98933	.01067	68	5.9857	.71829	.28171
14	8.2371	.98845	.01155	69	5.8687	.70424	.29576
15	8.2301	.98762	.01238	70	5.7482	.68979	.31021
16	8.2237	.98685	.01315	71	5.6250	.67500	.32500
17	8.2179	.98614	.01386	72	5.4988	.65985	.34015
18	8.2123	.98548	.01452	73	5.3696	.64435	.35565
19	8.2069	.98483	.01517	74	5.2366	.62839	.37161
20	8.2015	.98418	.01582	75	5.0993	.61191	.38809
21	8.1962	.98354	.01646	76	4.9571	.59486	.40514
22	8.1908	.98289	.01711	77	4.8105	.57726	.42274
23	8.1851	.98222	.01778	78	4.6598	.55918	.44082
24	8.1790	.98147	.01853	79	4.5065	.54078	.45922
25	8.1720	.98064	.01936	80	4.3517	.52221	.47779
26	8.1641	.97969	.02031	81	4.1972	.50367	.49633
27	8.1550	.97860	.02140	82	4.0440	.48528	.51472
28	8.1449	.97738	.02262	83	3.8929	.46715	.53285
29	8.1335	.97602	.02398	84	3.7438	.44926	.55074
30	8.1208	.97450	.02550	85	3.5962	.43155	.56845
31	8.1067	.97280	.02720	86	3.4516	.41420	.58580
32	8.0911	.97093	.02907	87	3.3123	.39747	.60253
33	8.0738	.96885	.03115	88	3.1775	.38129	.61871
34	8.0548	.96658	.03342	89	3.0447	.36537	.63463
35	8.0341	.96409	.03591	90	2.9126	.34951	.65049
36	8.0118	.96141	.03859	91	2.7830	.33396	.66604
37	7.9877	.95852	.04148	92	2.6596	.31915	.68085
38	7.9617	.95540	.04460	93	2.5438	.30526	.69474
39	7.9337	.95205	.04795	94	2.4371	.29245	.70755
40	7.9037	.94845	.05155	95	2.3401	.28081	.71919
41	7.8716	.94459	.05541	96	2.2538	.27045	.72955
42	7.8374	.94048	.05952	97	2.1751	.26101	.73899
43	7.8010	.93613	.06387	98	2.1042	.25250	.74750
44	7.7624	.93149	.06851	99	2.0387	.24465	.75535
45	7.7214	.92657	.07343	100	1.9781	.23737	.72623
46	7.6779	.92135	.07865	101	1.9206	.23047	.76953
47	7.6319	.91583	.08417	102	1.8608	.22329	.77671
48	7.5834	.91001	.08999	103	1.7975	.21570	.78430
49	7.5326	.90391	.09609	104	1.7273	.20727	.79273
50	7.4794	.89753	.10247	105	1.6398	.19678	.80322
51	7.4237	.89085	.10915	106	1.5105	.18126	.81874
52	7.3651	.88381	.11619	107	1.3182	.15818	.84182
53	7.3033	.87640	.12360	108	0.9932	.11919	.88081
54	7.2387	.86864	.13136	109	0.4464	.05357	.94643

Table S(12.2) SINGLE LIFE, 12.2 PERCENT, BASED ON LIFE TABLE
80CNSMT SHOWING THE PRESENT WORTH OF AN ANNUITY, OF A LIFE
ESTATE, AND OF A REMAINDER INTEREST

Age	Annuity	Life Estate	Remainder	Age	Annuity	Life Estate	Remainder
(1)	(2)	(3)	(4)	(1)	(2)	(3)	(4)
0	8.0588	.98317	.01683	55	7.0768	.86337	.13663
1	8.1509	.99441	.00559	56	7.0079	.85497	.14503
2	8.1534	.99472	.00528	57	6.9356	.84615	.15385
3	8.1537	.99476	.00524	58	6.8598	.83689	.16311
4	8.1528	.99464	.00536	59	6.7804	.82721	.17279
5	8.1510	.99442	.00558	60	6.6979	.81714	.18286
6	8.1485	.99412	.00588	61	6.6123	.80670	.19330
7	8.1456	.99376	.00624	62	6.5239	.79591	.20409
8	8.1419	.99332	.00668	63	6.4326	.78478	.21522
9	8.1375	.99278	.00722	64	6.3383	.77328	.22672
10	8.1323	.99215	.00785	65	6.2404	.76133	.23867
11	8.1262	.99139	.00861	66	6.1384	.74888	.25112
12	8.1192	.99054	.00946	67	6.0320	.73591	.26409
13	8.1119	.98965	.01035	68	5.9213	.72240	.27760
14	8.1048	.98878	.01122	69	5.8068	.70843	.29157
15	8.0981	.98797	.01203	70	5.6889	.69404	.30596
16	8.0919	.98721	.01279	71	5.5681	.67931	.32069
17	8.0863	.98653	.01347	72	5.4445	.66422	.33578
18	8.0811	.98589	.01411	73	5.3178	.64877	.35123
19	8.0759	.98526	.01474	74	5.1873	.63285	.36715
20	8.0708	.98463	.01537	75	5.0524	.61640	.38360
21	8.0657	.98402	.01598	76	4.9128	.59936	.40064
22	8.0606	.98340	.01660	77	4.7686	.58177	.41823
23	8.0553	.98275	.01725	78	4.6204	.56368	.43632
24	8.0495	.98204	.01796	79	4.4694	.54527	.45473
25	8.0430	.98124	.01876	80	4.3170	.52667	.47333
26	8.0355	.98033	.01967	81	4.1647	.50809	.49191
27	8.0269	.97928	.02072	82	4.0136	.48966	.51034
28	8.0172	.97810	.02190	83	3.8646	.47148	.52852
29	8.0064	.97678	.02322	84	3.7174	.45352	.54648
30	7.9944	.97531	.02469	85	3.5716	.43574	.56426
31	7.9808	.97366	.02634	86	3.4287	.41831	.58169
32	7.9659	.97184	.02816	87	3.2910	.40150	.59850
33	7.9494	.96982	.03018	88	3.1577	.38524	.61476
34	7.9312	.96761	.03239	89	3.0264	.36922	.63078
35	7.9113	.96518	.03482	90	2.8956	.35326	.64674
36	7.8899	.96257	.03743	91	2.7673	.33762	.66238
37	7.8667	.95974	.04026	92	2.6451	.32270	.67730
38	7.8418	.95670	.04330	93	2.5303	.30870	.69130
39	7.8149	.95342	.04658	94	2.4245	.29579	.70421
40	7.7860	.94989	.05011	95	2.3284	.28406	.71594
41	7.7550	.94611	.05389	96	2.2428	.27362	.72638
42	7.7220	.94209	.05791	97	2.1647	.26410	.73590
43	7.6870	.93781	.06219	98	2.0944	.25552	.74448
44	7.6497	.93327	.06673	99	2.0295	.24760	.75240
45	7.6101	.92843	.07157	100	1.9694	.24026	.75974
46	7.5681	.92331	.07669	101	1.9124	.23331	.76669
47	7.5236	.91788	.08212	102	1.8530	.22607	.77393
48	7.4767	.91216	.08784	103	1.7903	.21842	.78158
49	7.4275	.90616	.09384	104	1.7207	.20993	.79007
50	7.3760	.89987	.10013	105	1.6340	.19935	.80065
51	7.3220	.89329	.10671	106	1.5056	.18369	.81631
52	7.2652	.88635	.11365	107	1.3145	.16037	.83963
53	7.2053	.87905	.12095	108	0.9910	.12090	.87910
54	7.1426	.87140	.12860	109	0.4456	.05437	.94563

Table S(12.4) SINGLE LIFE, 12.4 PERCENT, BASED ON LIFE TABLE
80CNSMT SHOWING THE PRESENT WORTH OF AN ANNUITY, OF A LIFE
ESTATE, AND OF A REMAINDER INTEREST

Age	Annuity	Life Estate	Remainder	Age	Annuity	Life Estate	Remainder
(1)	(2)	(3)	(4)	(1)	(2)	(3)	(4)
0	7.9300	.98331	.01669	55	6.9850	.86614	.13386
1	8.0206	.99456	.00544	56	6.9180	.85783	.14217
2	8.0231	.99487	.00513	57	6.8477	.84911	.15089
3	8.0235	.99492	.00508	58	6.7739	.83996	.16004
4	8.0227	.99481	.00519	59	6.6967	.83039	.16961
5	8.0210	.99460	.00540	60	6.6163	.82042	.17958
6	8.0187	.99431	.00569	61	6.5329	.81008	.18992
7	8.0158	.99396	.00604	62	6.4467	.79939	.20061
8	8.0124	.99354	.00646	63	6.3577	.78835	.21165
9	8.0082	.99301	.00699	64	6.2657	.77694	.22306
10	8.0032	.99239	.00761	65	6.1701	.76509	.23491
11	7.9972	.99165	.00835	66	6.0704	.75273	.24727
12	7.9905	.99082	.00918	67	5.9664	.73984	.26016
13	7.9834	.98994	.01006	68	5.8582	.72641	.27359
14	7.9765	.98909	.01091	69	5.7461	.71252	.28748
15	7.9701	.98829	.01171	70	5.6306	.69819	.30181
16	7.9642	.98756	.01244	71	5.5123	.68352	.31648
17	7.9588	.98689	.01311	72	5.3911	.66849	.33151
18	7.9538	.98627	.01373	73	5.2668	.65309	.34691
19	7.9489	.98566	.01434	74	5.1388	.63721	.36279
20	7.9440	.98506	.01494	75	5.0064	.62079	.37921
21	7.9393	.98447	.01553	76	4.8691	.60377	.39623
22	7.9345	.98387	.01613	77	4.7274	.58619	.41381
23	7.9295	.98326	.01674	78	4.5815	.56811	.43189
24	7.9240	.98258	.01742	79	4.4329	.54968	.45032
25	7.9178	.98181	.01819	80	4.2827	.53106	.46894
26	7.9107	.98093	.01907	81	4.1326	.51245	.48755
27	7.9026	.97992	.02008	82	3.9836	.49397	.50603
28	7.8934	.97878	.02122	83	3.8366	.47573	.52427
29	7.8831	.97751	.02249	84	3.6913	.45772	.54228
30	7.8716	.97608	.02392	85	3.5473	.43987	.56013
31	7.8587	.97448	.02552	86	3.4061	.42236	.57764
32	7.8444	.97271	.02729	87	3.2700	.40548	.59452
33	7.8286	.97074	.02926	88	3.1382	.38914	.61086
34	7.8112	.96858	.03142	89	3.0083	.37303	.62697
35	7.7921	.96622	.03378	90	2.8788	.35698	.64302
36	7.7715	.96367	.03633	91	2.7518	.34123	.65877
37	7.7493	.96091	.03909	92	2.6307	.32621	.67379
38	7.7253	.95793	.04207	93	2.5170	.31211	.68789
39	7.6994	.95472	.04528	94	2.4121	.29910	.70090
40	7.6715	.95127	.04873	95	2.3167	.28728	.71272
41	7.6417	.94756	.05244	96	2.2319	.27675	.72325
42	7.6099	.94362	.05638	97	2.1545	.26715	.73285
43	7.5760	.93943	.06057	98	2.0847	.25851	.74149
44	7.5401	.93497	.06503	99	2.0203	.25052	.74948
45	7.5018	.93022	.06978	100	1.9607	.24313	.75687
46	7.4612	.92519	.07481	101	1.9042	.23612	.76388
47	7.4181	.91985	.08015	102	1.8454	.22883	.77117
48	7.3727	.91422	.08578	103	1.7832	.22112	.77888
49	7.3251	.90831	.09169	104	1.7143	.21257	.78743
50	7.2752	.90213	.09787	105	1.6283	.20191	.79809
51	7.2229	.89564	.10436	106	1.5009	.18611	.81389
52	7.1678	.88880	.11120	107	1.3109	.16255	.83745
53	7.1097	.88160	.11840	108	0.9888	.12261	.87739
54	7.0488	.87405	.12595	109	.04448	.05516	.94484

Table S(12.6) *SINGLE LIFE, 12.6 PERCENT, BASED ON LIFE TABLE 80CNSMT SHOWING THE PRESENT WORTH OF AN ANNUITY, OF A LIFE ESTATE, AND OF A REMAINDER INTEREST*

Age	Annuity	Life Estate	Remainder	Age	Annuity	Life Estate	Remainder
(1)	(2)	(3)	(4)	(1)	(2)	(3)	(4)
0	7.8052	.98345	.01655	55	6.8953	.86880	.13120
1	7.8944	.99469	.00531	56	6.8302	.86060	.13940
2	7.8969	.99501	.00499	57	6.7618	.85199	.14801
3	7.8974	.99507	.00493	58	6.6900	.84294	.15706
4	7.8966	.99497	.00503	59	6.6148	.83346	.16654
5	7.8950	.99477	.00523	60	6.5365	.82360	.17640
6	7.8928	.99450	.00550	61	6.4552	.81335	.18665
7	7.8901	.99416	.00584	62	6.3711	.80276	.19724
8	7.8869	.99374	.00626	63	6.2843	.79182	.20818
9	7.8828	.99323	.00677	64	6.1945	.78051	.21949
10	7.8780	.99263	.00737	65	6.1012	.76875	.23125
11	7.8723	.99190	.00810	66	6.0038	.75647	.24353
12	7.8658	.99109	.00891	67	5.9021	.74367	.25633
13	7.8589	.99022	.00978	68	5.7962	.73032	.26968
14	7.8523	.98939	.01061	69	5.6865	.71650	.28350
15	7.8461	.98860	.01140	70	5.5734	.70225	.29775
16	7.8404	.98789	.01211	71	5.4575	.68764	.31236
17	7.8352	.98724	.01276	72	5.3386	.67267	.32733
18	7.8304	.98664	.01336	73	5.2168	.65731	.34269
19	7.8257	.98604	.01396	74	5.0911	.64148	.35852
20	7.8211	.98546	.01454	75	4.9611	.62509	.37491
21	7.8166	.98490	.01510	76	4.8262	.60810	.39190
22	7.8121	.98432	.01568	77	4.6868	.59053	.40947
23	7.8074	.98373	.01627	78	4.5433	.57245	.42755
24	7.8022	.98308	.01692	79	4.3969	.55401	.44599
25	7.7964	.98235	.01765	80	4.2489	.53537	.46463
26	7.7897	.98150	.01850	81	4.1010	.51672	.48328
27	7.7819	.98052	.01948	82	3.9540	.49821	.50179
28	7.7732	.97943	.02057	83	3.8089	.47992	.52008
29	7.7634	.97819	.02181	84	3.6655	.46185	.53815
30	7.7525	.97681	.02319	85	3.5233	.44394	.55606
31	7.7401	.97525	.02475	86	3.3838	.42636	.57364
32	7.7265	.97353	.02647	87	3.2492	.40940	.59060
33	7.7113	.97162	.02838	88	3.1189	.39298	.60702
34	7.6946	.96952	.03048	89	2.9904	.37679	.62321
35	7.6763	.96721	.03279	90	2.8623	.36065	.63935
36	7.6565	.96472	.03528	91	2.7365	.34480	.65520
37	7.6351	.96202	.03798	92	2.6165	.32968	.67032
38	7.6120	.95911	.04089	93	2.5038	.31548	.68452
39	7.5870	.95597	.04403	94	2.3998	.30238	.69762
40	7.5602	.95259	.04741	95	2.3052	.29046	.70954
41	7.5314	.94896	.05104	96	2.2211	.27986	.72014
42	7.5007	.94509	.05491	97	2.1443	.27018	.72982
43	7.4681	.94098	.05902	98	2.0751	.26147	.73853
44	7.4333	.93660	.06340	99	2.0113	.25342	.74658
45	7.3963	.93194	.06806	100	1.9521	.24597	.75403
46	7.3570	.92699	.07301	101	1.8961	.23891	.76109
47	7.3154	.92174	.07826	102	1.8378	.23156	.76844
48	7.2714	.91620	.08380	103	1.7762	.22380	.77620
49	7.2253	.91039	.08961	104	1.7078	.21518	.78482
50	7.1770	.90430	.09570	105	1.6226	.20444	.79556
51	7.1263	.89791	.10209	106	1.4961	.18851	.81149
52	7.0728	.89117	.10883	107	1.3073	.16471	.83529
53	7.0164	.88407	.11593	108	0.9866	.12431	.87569
54	6.9573	.87662	.12338	109	0.4440	.05595	.94405

Table S(12.8) *SINGLE LIFE, 12.8 PERCENT, BASED ON LIFE TABLE 80CNSMT SHOWING THE PRESENT WORTH OF AN ANNUITY, OF A LIFE ESTATE, AND OF A REMAINDER INTEREST*

Age	Annuity	Life Estate	Remainder	Age	Annuity	Life Estate	Remainder
(1)	(2)	(3)	(4)	(1)	(2)	(3)	(4)
0	7.6842	.98358	.01642	55	6.8077	.87138	.12862
1	7.7720	.99482	.00518	56	6.7444	.86328	.13672
2	7.7746	.99515	.00485	57	6.6779	.85477	.14523
3	7.7751	.99521	.00479	58	6.6080	.84582	.15418
4	7.7744	.99512	.00488	59	6.5347	.83645	.16355
5	7.7729	.99493	.00507	60	6.4584	·82668	.17332
6	7.7708	.99467	.00533	61	6.3792	.81653	.18347
7	7.7683	.99434	.00566	62	6.2972	.80604	.19396
8	7.7651	.99394	.00606	63	6.2125	.79520	.20480
9	7.7613	.99344	.00656	64	6.1248	.78398	.21602
10	7.7566	.99285	.00715	65	6.0336	.77231	·22769
11	7.7511	.99214	.00786	66	5.9385	.76012	.23988
12	7.7448	.99134	.00866	67	5.8391	.74740	.25260
13	7.7382	.99049	.00951	68	5.7354	.73414	.26586
14	7.7317	.98966	.01034	69	5.6281	.72039	.27961
15	7.7258	.98890	.01110	70	5.5173	.70621	.29379
16	7.7203	.98819	.01181	71	5.4037	.69167	.30833
17	7.7153	.98756	.01244	72	5.2871	.67675	.32325
18	7.7108	.98698	.01302	73	5.1676	.66145	.33855
19	7.7063	.98641	.01359	74	5.0442	.64566	.35434
20	7.7019	.98585	.01415	75	4.9165	.62931	.37069
21	7.6977	.98530	.01470	76	4.7840	.61235	.38765
22	7.6934	.98475	.01525	77	4.6468	.59477	.40521
23	7.6890	.98419	.01581	78	4.5056	.57671	.42329
24	7.6841	.98356	.01644	79	4.3615	.55827	.44173
25	7.6786	.98286	.01714	80	4.2157	.53960	.46040
26	7.6722	.98204	.01796	81	4.0698	.52093	.47907
27	7.6648	.98110	.01890	82	3.9248	.50238	.49762
28	7.6565	.98004	.01996	83	3.7816	.48405	.51595
29	7.6472	.97884	.02116	84	3.6400	.46593	.53407
30	7.6367	.97750	.02250	85	3.4996	.44795	.55205
31	7.6249	.97599	.02401	86	3.3617	.43030	.56970
32	7.6119	.97432	.02568	87	3.2287	.41327	.58673
33	7.5973	.97245	.02755	88	3.0998	.39678	.60322
34	7.5813	.97040	.02960	89	2.9727	.38050	.61950
35	7.5637	.96815	.03185	90	2.8459	.36427	.63573
36	7.5447	.96572	.03428	91	2.7213	.34833	.65167
37	7.5241	.96308	.03692	92	2.6024	.33311	.66689
38	7.5018	.96023	.03977	93	2.4907	.31881	.68119
39	7.4778	.95716	.04284	94	2.3876	.30562	.69438
40	7.4519	.95385	.04615	95	2.2939	.29361	.70639
41	7.4241	.95029	.04971	96	2.2104	.28293	.71707
42	7.3945	.94650	.05350	97	2.1342	.27318	.72682
43	7.3630	.94246	.05754	98	2.0656	.26440	.73560
44	7.3294	.93816	.06184	99	2.0023	.25629	.74371
45	7.2936	.93358	.06642	100	1.9436	.24879	.75121
46	7.2556	.92872	.07128	101	1.8881	.24167	.75833
47	7.2153	.92355	.07645	102	1.8303	.23427	.76573
48	7.1727	.91810	.08190	103	1.7692	.22645	.77355
49	7.1280	.91238	.08762	104	1.7014	.21778	.78222
50	7.0811	.90639	.09361	105	1.6169	.20696	.79304
51	7.0320	.90009	.09991	106	1.4913	.19089	.80911
52	6.9801	.89345	.10655	107	1.3037	.16687	.83313
53	6.9254	.88645	.11355	108	0.9843	.12600	.87400
54	6.8679	.87910	.12090	109	0.4433	.05674	.94326

Table S(13.0) SINGLE LIFE, 13.0 PERCENT, BASED ON LIFE TABLE
80CNSMT SHOWING THE PRESENT WORTH OF AN ANNUITY, OF A LIFE
ESTATE, AND OF A REMAINDER INTEREST

Age	Annuity	Life Estate	Remainder	Age	Annuity	Life Estate	Remainder
(1)	(2)	(3)	(4)	(1)	(2)	(3)	(4)
0	7.5670	.98370	.01630	55	6.7221	.87387	.12613
1	7.6534	.99494	.00506	56	6.6606	.86587	.13413
2	7.6559	.99527	.00473	57	6.5958	.85746	.14254
3	7.6565	.99535	.00465	58	6.5278	.84861	.15139
4	7.6559	.99527	.00473	59	6.4564	.83934	.16066
5	7.6545	.99508	.00492	60	6.3821	.82967	.17033
6	7.6525	.99483	.00517	61	6.3048	.81962	.18038
7	7.6501	.99451	.00549	62	6.2248	.80922	.19078
8	7.6471	.99412	.00588	63	6.1421	.79848	.20152
9	7.6434	.99364	.00636	64	6.0565	.78735	.21265
10	7.6389	.99306	.00694	65	5.9675	.77577	.22423
11	7.6336	.99236	.00764	66	5.8744	.76368	.23632
12	7.6275	.99157	.00843	67	5.7773	.75104	.24896
13	7.6210	.99073	.00927	68	5.6758	.73786	.26214
14	7.6148	.98993	.01007	69	5.5707	.72419	.27581
15	7.6090	.98918	.01082	70	5.4621	.71008	.28992
16	7.6038	.98849	.01151	71	5.3508	.69560	.30440
17	7.5990	.98787	.01213	72	5.2365	.68075	.31925
18	7.5946	.98730	.01270	73	5.1192	.66550	.33450
19	7.5904	.98675	.01325	74	4.9981	.64976	.35024
20	7.5862	.98621	.01379	75	4.8727	.63344	.36656
21	7.5822	.98568	.01432	76	4.7424	.61651	.38349
22	7.5781	.98515	.01485	77	4.6075	.59897	.40103
23	7.5740	.98461	.01539	78	4.4685	.58090	.41910
24	7.5693	.98401	.01599	79	4.3265	.56245	.43755
25	7.5641	.98334	.01666	80	4.1829	.54377	.45623
26	7.5581	.98255	.01745	81	4.0390	.52507	.47493
27	7.5511	.98164	.01836	82	3.8960	.50649	.49351
28	7.5432	.98062	.01938	83	3.7547	.48811	.51189
29	7.5343	.97946	.02054	84	3.6149	.46994	.53006
30	7.5243	.97816	.02184	85	3.4762	.45190	.54810
31	7.5130	.97669	.02331	86	3.3400	.43419	.56581
32	7.5005	.97506	.02494	87	3.2084	.41709	.58291
33	7.4865	.97325	.02675	88	3.0810	.40053	.59947
34	7.4711	.97125	.02875	89	2.9552	.38417	.61583
35	7.4542	.96905	.03095	90	2.8296	.36785	.63215
36	7.4360	.96667	.03333	91	2.7063	.35181	.64819
37	7.4161	.96409	.03591	92	2.5885	.33650	.66350
38	7.3947	.96131	.03869	93	2.4778	.32211	.67789
39	7.3715	.95830	.04170	94	2.3756	.30882	.69118
40	7.3466	.95505	.04495	95	2.2826	.29674	.70326
41	7.3197	.95156	.04844	96	2.1998	.28597	.71403
42	7.2911	.94784	.05216	97	2.1243	.27615	.72385
43	7.2606	.94388	.05612	98	2.0562	.26731	.73269
44	7.2282	.93966	.06034	99	1.9934	.25914	.74086
45	7.1935	.93516	.06484	100	1.9352	.25158	.74842
46	7.1568	.93038	.06962	101	1.8801	.24441	.75559
47	7.1177	.92530	.07470	102	1.8228	.23696	.76304
48	7.0764	.91994	.08006	103	1.7622	.22909	.77091
49	7.0331	.91430	.08570	104	1.6951	.22036	.77964
50	7.9877	.90840	.09160	105	1.6113	.20946	.79054
51	6.9400	.90220	.09780	106	1.4866	.19326	.80674
52	6.8896	.89565	.10435	107	1.3001	.16901	.83099
53	6.8365	.88874	.11126	108	0.9822	.12768	.87232
54	6.7807	.88149	.11851	109	0.4425	.05752	.94248

Table S(13.2) *SINGLE LIFE, 13.2 PERCENT, BASED ON LIFE TABLE 80CNSMT SHOWING THE PRESENT WORTH OF AN ANNUITY, OF A LIFE ESTATE, AND OF A REMAINDER INTEREST*

Age	Annuity	Life Estate	Remainder	Age	Annuity	Life Estate	Remainder
(1)	(2)	(3)	(4)	(1)	(2)	(3)	(4)
0	7.4532	.98382	.01618	55	6.6385	.87628	.12372
1	7.5383	.99506	.00494	56	6.5787	.86838	.13162
2	7.5408	.99539	.00461	57	6.5156	.86006	.13994
3	7.5415	.99547	.00453	58	6.4494	.85132	.14868
4	7.5409	.99540	.00460	59	6.3798	.84214	.15786
5	7.5396	.99523	.00477	60	6.3073	.83257	.16743
6	7.5378	.99498	.00502	61	6.2320	.82262	.17738
7	7.5354	.99468	.00532	62	6.1539	.81232	.18768
8	7.5326	.99430	.00570	63	6.0732	.80167	.19833
9	7.5290	.99383	.00617	64	5.9897	.79063	.20937
10	7.5247	.99326	.00674	65	5.9026	.77915	.22085
11	7.5195	.99257	.00743	66	5.8117	.76714	.23286
12	7.5136	.99180	.00820	67	5.7166	.75459	.24541
13	7.5074	.99097	.00903	68	5.6173	.74149	.25851
14	7.5013	.99018	.00982	69	5.5144	.72789	.27211
15	7.4958	.98944	.01056	70	5.4080	.71386	.28614
16	7.4906	.98877	.01123	71	5.2988	.69945	.30055
17	7.4861	.98816	.01184	72	5.1868	.68465	.31535
18	7.4819	.98761	.01239	73	5.0717	.66946	.33054
19	7.4778	.98707	.01293	74	4.9528	.65377	.34623
20	7.4739	.98655	.01345	75	4.8295	.63750	.36250
21	7.4700	.98604	.01396	76	4.7014	.62059	.37941
22	7.4662	.98554	.01446	77	4.5688	.60308	.39692
23	7.4623	.98502	.01498	78	4.4319	.58501	.41499
24	7.4579	.98444	.01556	79	4.2921	.56656	.43344
25	7.4530	.98379	.01621	80	4.1505	.54787	.45213
26	7.4473	.98304	.01696	81	4.0087	.52915	.47085
27	7.4406	.98216	.01784	82	3.8676	.51053	.48947
28	7.4331	.98117	.01883	83	3.7282	.49212	.50788
29	7.4246	.98004	.01996	84	3.5901	.47390	.52610
30	7.4150	.97878	.02122	85	3.4531	.45580	.54420
31	7.4042	.97736	.02264	86	3.3184	.43803	.56197
32	7.3922	.97577	.02423	87	3.1884	.42087	.57913
33	7.3788	.97400	.02600	88	3.0623	.40423	.59577
34	7.3640	.97205	.02795	89	2.9379	.38780	.61220
35	7.3478	.96991	.03009	90	2.8136	.37139	.62861
36	7.3302	.96758	.03242	91	2.6914	.35526	.64474
37	7.3111	.96506	.03494	92	2.5747	.33986	.66014
38	7.2904	.96233	.03767	93	2.4650	.32537	.67463
39	7.2681	.95939	.04061	94	2.3636	.31200	.68800
40	7.2440	.95621	.04379	95	2.2714	.29983	.70017
41	7.2181	.95279	.04721	96	2.1893	.28899	.71101
42	7.1904	.94914	.05086	97	2.1144	.27910	.72090
43	7.1610	.94525	.05475	98	2.0469	.27019	.72981
44	7.1296	.94110	.05890	99	1.9845	.26195	.73805
45	7.0961	.93668	.06332	100	1.9268	.25434	.74566
46	7.0604	.93198	.06802	101	1.8722	.24713	.75287
47	7.0226	.92698	.07302	102	1.8153	.23963	.76037
48	6.9826	.92170	.07830	103	1.7553	.23170	.76830
49	6.9406	.91616	.08384	104	1.6887	.22291	.77709
50	6.8965	.91034	.08966	105	1.6057	.21195	.78805
51	6.8502	.90423	.09577	106	1.4819	.19562	.80438
52	6.8013	.89778	.10222	107	1.2965	.17114	.82886
53	6.7497	.89096	.10904	108	0.9800	.12936	.87064
54	6.6955	.88381	.11619	109	0.4417	.05830	.94170

Age	Annuity	Life Estate	Remainder	Age	Annuity	Life Estate	Remainder
(1)	(2)	(3)	(4)	(1)	(2)	(3)	(4)
0	7.3428	.98393	.01607	55	6.5568	.87862	.12138
1	7.4266	.99516	.00484	56	6.4986	.87081	.12919
2	7.4291	.99551	.00449	57	6.4372	.86259	.13741
3	7.4298	.99559	.00441	58	6.3727	.85394	.14606
4	7.4293	.99553	.00447	59	6.3049	.84486	.15514
5	7.4281	.99536	.00464	60	6.2342	.83538	.16462
6	7.4263	.99513	.00487	61	6.1607	.82553	.17447
7	7.4241	.99483	.00517	62	6.0845	.81533	.18467
8	7.4214	.99446	.00554	63	6.0057	.80477	.19523
9	7.4179	.99400	.00600	64	5.9241	.79383	.20617
10	7.4138	.99345	.00655	65	5.8391	.78243	.21757
11	7.4088	.99277	.00723	66	5.7501	.77052	.22948
12	7.4031	.99201	.00799	67	5.6571	.75805	.24195
13	7.3970	.99120	.00880	68	5.5599	.74503	.25497
14	7.3912	.99042	.00958	69	5.4591	.73151	.26849
15	7.3857	.98969	.01031	70	5.3548	.71755	.28245
16	7.3808	.98903	.01097	71	5.2478	.70321	.29679
17	7.3764	.98844	.01156	72	5.1379	.68848	.31152
18	7.3724	.98790	.01210	73	5.0249	.67334	.32666
19	7.3685	.98738	.01262	74	4.9082	.65770	.34230
20	7.3647	.98687	.01313	75	4.7871	.64147	.35853
21	7.3611	.98639	.01361	76	4.6612	.62460	.37540
22	7.3575	.98590	.01410	77	4.5306	.60710	.39290
23	7.3538	.98540	.01460	78	4.3959	.58905	.41095
24	7.3496	.98485	.01515	79	4.2582	.57060	.42940
25	7.3450	.98423	.01577	80	4.1186	.55189	.44811
26	7.3395	.98350	.01650	81	3.9788	.53316	.46684
27	7.3332	.98265	.01735	82	3.8396	.51451	.48549
28	7.3261	.98169	.01831	83	3.7019	.49606	.50394
29	7.3179	.98060	.01940	84	3.5656	.47779	.52221
30	7.3088	.97938	.02062	85	3.4302	·45965	.54035
31	7.2984	.97799	.02201	86	3.2971	.44182	.55818
32	7.2869	.97645	.02355	87	3.1686	.42459	.57541
33	7.2741	.97472	.02528	88	3.0439	.40788	.59212
34	7.2598	.97282	.02718	89	2.9207	.39138	.60862
35	7.2442	.97072	.02928	90	2.7977	.37489	.62511
36	7.2273	.96845	.03155	91	2.6767	.35867	.64133
37	7.2089	.96599	·03401	92	2.5610	.34318	.65682
38	7.1889	.96332	.03668	93	2.4523	.32860	.67140
39	7.1674	.96043	.03957	94	2.3518	.31514	.68486
40	7.1441	.95731	.04269	95	2.2603	.30288	.69712
41	7.1191	.95396	.04604	96	2.1789	.29197	.70803
42	7.0924	.95038	.04962	97	2.1046	.28201	.71799
43	7.0639	.94656	.05344	98	2.0376	.27304	.72696
44	7.0335	.94248	.05752	99	1.9757	.26475	.73525
45	7.0010	.93814	.06186	100	1.9185	.25708	.74292
46	6.9665	.93351	.06649	101	1.8643	.24982	.75018
47	6.9298	.92860	.07140	102	1.8080	.24227	.75773
48	6.8911	.92340	.07660	103	1.7485	.23429	.76571
49	6.8503	.91794	.08206	104	1.6825	.22545	.77455
50	6.8076	.91221	.08779	105	1.6001	.21441	·78559
51	6.7626	.90619	.09381	106	1.4773	.19796	.80204
52	6.7151	.89983	.10017	107	1.2930	.17326	.82674
53	6.6650	.89311	.10689	108	0.9778	.13103	.86897
54	6.6123	.88604	.11396	109	0.4409	.05908	.94092

Table S(13.6) *SINGLE LIFE, 13.6 PERCENT, BASED ON LIFE TABLE 80CNSMT SHOWING THE PRESENT WORTH OF AN ANNUITY, OF A LIFE ESTATE, AND OF A REMAINDER INTEREST*

Age	Annuity	Life Estate	Remainder	Age	Annuity	Life Estate	Remainder
(1)	(2)	(3)	(4)	(1)	(2)	(3)	(4)
0	7.2356	.98404	.01596	55	6.4770	.88088	.11912
1	7.3181	.99527	.00473	56	6.4203	.87317	.12683
2	7.3207	.99561	.00439	57	6.3606	.86504	.13496
3	7.3214	.99571	.00429	58	6.2977	.85648	.14352
4	7.3210	.99565	.00435	59	6.2316	.84750	.15250
5	7.3198	.99549	.00451	60	6.1626	.83812	.16188
6	7.3181	.99527	.00473	61	6.0909	.82836	.17164
7	7.3160	.99498	.00502	62	6.0166	.81825	.18175
8	7.3134	.99462	.00538	63	5.9396	.80779	.19221
9	7.3101	.99417	.00583	64	5.8599	.79694	.20306
10	7.3061	.99363	.00637	65	5.7767	.78563	.21437
11	7.3012	.99296	.00704	66	5.6898	.77381	.22619
12	7.2957	.99221	.00779	67	5.5998	.76143	.23857
13	7.2898	.99141	.00859	68	5.5036	.74849	.25151
14	7.2841	.99064	.00936	69	5.4048	.73505	.26495
15	7.2789	.98993	.01007	70	5.3026	.72116	.27884
16	7.2741	.98928	.01072	71	5.1977	.70688	.29312
17	7.2699	.98870	.01130	72	5.0898	.69222	.30778
18	7.2660	.98818	.01182	73	4.9789	.67714	.32286
19	7.2623	.98767	.01233	74	4.8643	.66155	.33845
20	7.2587	.98718	.01282	75	4.7453	.64536	.35464
21	7.2552	.98671	.01329	76	4.6215	.62852	.37148
22	7.2518	.98625	.01375	77	4.4930	.61105	.38895
23	7.2483	.98577	.01423	78	4.3604	.59302	.40698
24	7.2444	.98524	.01476	79	4.2248	.57457	.42543
25	7.2400	.98464	.01536	80	4.0872	.55586	.44414
26	7.2348	.98394	.01606	81	3.9493	.53710	.46290
27	7.2288	.98312	.01688	82	3.8120	.51843	.48157
28	7.2220	.98219	.01781	83	3.6761	.49994	.50006
29	7.2142	.98113	.01887	84	3.5414	.48164	.51836
30	7.2055	.97994	.02006	85	3.4077	.46344	.53656
31	7.1956	.97860	.02140	86	3.2761	.44555	.55445
32	7.1845	.97709	.02291	87	3.1490	.42826	.57174
33	7.1721	.97541	.02459	88	3.0257	.41149	.58851
34	7.1585	.97355	.02645	89	2.9038	.39492	.60508
35	7.1434	.97150	.02850	90	2.7820	.37835	.62165
36	7.1271	.96928	.03072	91	2.6621	.36205	.63795
37	7.1093	.96687	.03313	92	2.5475	.34646	.65354
38	7.0901	.96426	.03574	93	2.4397	.33180	.66820
39	7.0693	.96143	.03857	94	2.3401	.31825	.68175
40	7.0468	.95837	.04163	95	2.2494	.30591	.69409
41	7.0226	.95508	.04492	96	2.1686	.29493	.70507
42	6.9968	.95156	.04844	97	2.0948	.28490	.71510
43	6.9692	.94782	.05218	98	2.0284	.27586	.72414
44	6.9398	.94381	.05619	99	1.9670	.26752	.73248
45	6.9084	.93954	.06046	100	1.9103	.25980	.74020
46	6.8750	.93499	.06501	101	1.8566	.25249	.74751
47	6.8394	.93016	.06984	102	1.8007	.24489	.75511
48	6.8018	.92504	.07496	103	1.7417	.23687	.76313
49	6.7622	.91966	.08034	104	1.6763	.22797	.77203
50	6.7207	.91402	.08598	105	1.5946	.21686	.78314
51	6.6771	.90808	.09192	106	1.4727	.20028	.79972
52	6.6309	.90181	.09819	107	1.2895	.17537	.82463
53	6.5822	.89518	.10482	108	0.9756	.13269	.86731
54	6.5309	.88821	.11179	109	0.4401	.05986	.94014

Table S(13.8) *SINGLE LIFE, 13.8 PERCENT, BASED ON LIFE TABLE 80CNSMT SHOWING THE PRESENT WORTH OF AN ANNUITY, OF A LIFE ESTATE, AND OF A REMAINDER INTEREST*

Age	Annuity	Life Estate	Remainder	Age	Annuity	Life Estate	Remainder
(1)	(2)	(3)	(4)	(1)	(2)	(3)	(4)
0	7.1315	.98414	.01586	55	6.3990	.88306	.11694
1	7.2128	.99536	,00464	56	6.3438	.87544	.12456
2	7.2153	.99572	.00428	57	6.2856	.86741	.13259
3	7.2160	.99581	.00419	58	6.2243	.85895	.14105
4	7.2157	.99577	.00423	59	6.1599	.85006	.14994
5	7.2146	.99561	.00439	60	6.0926	.84078	.15922
6	7.2130	.99540	.00460	61	6.0225	.83111	.16889
7	7.2110	.99512	.00488	62	5.9500	.82109	.17891
8	7.2085	.99477	.00523	63	5.8748	.81072	.18928
9	7.2053	.99433	.00567	64	5.7969	.79997	.20003
10	7.2014	.99380	.00620	65	5.7156	.78875	.21125
11	7.1967	.99314	.00686	66	5.6305	.77701	.22299
12	7.1913	.99240	.00760	67	5.5415	.76472	.23528
13	7.1856	.99161	.00839	68	5.4483	.75186	.24814
14	7.1801	.99086	.00914	69	5.3515	.73850	.26150
15	7.1750	.99015	.00985	70	5.2513	.72468	.27532
16	7.1704	.98952	.01048	71	5.1484	.71048	.28952
17	7.1663	.98896	.01104	72	5.0426	.69588	.30412
18	7.1626	.98845	.01155	73	4.9337	.68086	.31914
19	7.1591	.98795	.01205	74	4.8212	.66532	.33468
20	7.1556	.98748	.01252	75	4.7042	.64918	.35082
21	7.1523	.98702	.01298	76	4.5824	.63238	.36762
22	7.1491	.98657	.01343	77	4.4560	.61493	.38507
23	7.1458	.98612	.01388	78	4.3254	.59691	.40309
24	7.1421	.98561	.01439	79	4.1918	.57847	.42153
25	7.1379	.98503	·01497	80	4.0562	.55975	.44025
26	7.1330	.98435	.01565	81	3.9202	.54098	.45902
27	7.1273	.98356	.01644	82	3.7847	.52228	.47772
28	7.1207	.98266	.01734	83	3.6505	.50377	.49623
29	7.1133	.98164	.01836	84	3.5176	.48542	.51458
30	7.1050	.98048	.01952	85	3.3854	.46718	.53282
31	7.0954	.97917	.02083	86	3.2553	.44924	.55076
32	7.0848	.97771	.02229	87	3.1296	.43189	.56811
33	7.0729	.97607	.02393	88	3.0076	.41506	.58494
34	7.0598	.97425	.02575	89	2.8870	.39841	.60159
35	7.0453	.97225	.02775	90	2.7664	.38177	.61823
36	7.0296	.97008	.02992	91	2.6477	.36538	.63462
37	7.0124	.96772	.03228	92	2.5341	.34971	.65029
38	6.9939	.96516	.03484	93	2.4272	.33496	.66504
39	6.9738	.96238	.03762	94	2.3285	.32133	.67867
40	6.9521	.95939	.04061	95	2.2385	.30891	.69109
41	6.9287	.95616	.04384	96	2.1584	.29785	.70215
42	6.9037	.95271	.04729	97	2.0852	.28776	.71224
43	6.8770	.94902	.05098	98	2.0193	.27866	.72134
44	6.8485	.94509	.05491	99	1.9584	.27026	.72974
45	6.8180	.94089	.05911	100	1.9021	.26249	.73751
46	6.7856	.93642	.06358	101	1.8488	.25514	.74486
47	6.7511	.93166	.06834	102	1.7934	.24749	.75251
48	6.7146	.92662	.07338	103	1.7349	.23942	.76058
49	6.6762	.92132	.07868	104	1.6701	.23047	.76953
50	6.6360	.91576	.08424	105	1.5891	.21929	.78071
51	6.5936	.90991	.09009	106	1.4680	.20259	.79741
52	6.5487	.90372	.09628	107	1.2860	.17746	.82254
53	6.5013	.89718	.10282	108	0.9735	.13434	.86566
54	6.4515	.89030	.10970	109	0.4394	.06063	.93937

Table S(14.0)   *SINGLE LIFE, 14.0 PERCENT, BASED ON LIFE TABLE 80CNSMT SHOWING THE PRESENT WORTH OF AN ANNUITY, OF A LIFE ESTATE, AND OF A REMAINDER INTEREST*

Age	Annuity	Life Estate	Remainder	Age	Annuity	Life Estate	Remainder
(1)	(2)	(3)	(4)	(1)	(2)	(3)	(4)
0	7.0303	.98424	.01576	55	6.3227	.88518	.11482
1	7.1104	.99546	.00454	56	6.2689	.87765	.12235
2	7.1129	.99581	.00419	57	6.2122	.86971	.13029
3	7.1137	.99592	.00408	58	6.1525	.86134	.13866
4	7.1134	.99588	.00412	59	6.0896	.85255	.14745
5	7.1124	.99573	.00427	60	6.0240	.84336	.15664
6	7.1109	.99552	.00448	61	5.9556	.83378	.16622
7	7.1089	.99525	.00475	62	5.8847	.82386	.17614
8	7.1065	.99491	.00509	63	5.8113	.81358	.18642
9	7.1034	.99448	.00552	64	5.7351	.80292	.19708
10	7.0997	.99396	.00604	65	5.6557	.79179	.20821
11	7.0951	.99332	.00668	66	5.5724	.78014	.21986
12	7.0899	.99259	.00741	67	5.4853	.76794	.23206
13	7.0843	.99181	.00819	68	5.3940	.75516	.24484
14	7.0790	.99106	.00894	69	5.2991	.74188	.25812
15	7.0741	.99037	.00963	70	5.2009	.72813	.27187
16	7.0696	.98975	.01025	71	5.1000	.71400	.28600
17	7.0657	.98919	.01081	72	4.9961	.69946	.30054
18	7.0621	.98870	.01130	73	4.8893	.68450	.31550
19	7.0587	.98822	.01178	74	4.7787	.66902	.33098
20	7.0554	.98776	.01224	75	4.6637	.65292	.34708
21	7.0523	.98732	.01268	76	4.5440	.63616	.36384
22	7.0492	.98688	.01312	77	4.4196	.61874	.38126
23	7.0460	.98645	.01355	78	4.2910	.60074	.39926
24	7.0426	.98596	.01404	79	4.1593	.58230	.41770
25	7.0386	.98540	.01460	80	4.0256	.56358	.43642
26	7.0339	.98475	.01525	81	3.8914	.54480	.45520
27	7.0285	.98399	.01601	82	3.7577	.52608	.47392
28	7.0222	.98311	.01689	83	3.6253	.50754	.49246
29	7.0151	.98212	.01788	84	3.4940	.48916	.51084
30	7.0071	.98100	.01900	85	3.3633	.47087	.52913
31	6.9980	.97972	.02028	86	3.2348	.45287	.54713
32	6.9878	.97830	.02170	87	3.1105	.43547	.56453
33	6.9764	.97669	.02331	88	2.9898	.41858	.58142
34	6.9637	.97492	.02508	89	2.8705	.40187	.59813
35	6.9497	.97296	.02704	90	2.7510	.38515	.61485
36	6.9346	.97084	.02916	91	2.6334	.36868	.63132
37	6.9180	.96853	.03147	92	2.5209	.35292	.64708
38	6.9001	.96602	.03398	93	2.4149	.33809	.66191
39	6.8807	.96330	.03670	94	2.3170	.32437	.67563
40	6.8597	.96036	.03964	95	2.2277	.31188	.68812
41	6.8371	.95719	.04281	96	2.1482	.30075	.69925
42	6.8129	.95380	.04620	97	2.0757	.29059	.70941
43	6.7870	.95019	.04981	98	2.0103	.28144	.71856
44	6.7594	.94632	.05368	99	1.9499	.27298	.72702
45	6.7299	.94219	.05781	100	1.8940	.26516	.73484
46	6.6985	.93779	.06221	101	1.8412	.25777	.74223
47	6.6650	.93310	.06690	102	1.7862	.25007	.74993
48	6.6296	.92814	.07186	103	1.7282	.24195	.75805
49	6.5923	.92292	.07708	104	1.6639	.23295	.76705
50	6.5532	.91744	.08256	105	1.5836	.22171	.77829
51	6.5120	.91168	.08832	106	1.4635	.20489	.79511
52	6.4684	.90558	.09442	107	1.2825	.17955	.82045
53	6.4223	.89912	.10088	108	0.9713	.13599	.86401
54	6.3738	.89233	.10767	109	0.4386	.06140	.93860

Age	Annuity	Life Estate	Remainder	Age	Annuity	Life Estate	Remainder
(1)	(2)	(3)	(4)	(1)	(2)	(3)	(4)
0	6.9319	.98433	.01567	55	6.2481	.88723	.11277
1	7.0109	.99554	.00446	56	6.1957	.87979	.12021
2	7.0134	.99590	.00410	57	6.1404	.87194	.12806
3	7.0142	.99601	.00399	58	6.0822	.86367	.13633
4	7.0139	.99598	.00402	59	6.0209	.85496	.14504
5	7.0130	.99584	.00416	60	5.9568	.84586	.15414
6	7.0116	.99564	.00436	61	5.8900	.83638	.16362
7	7.0097	.99538	.00462	62	5.8208	.82655	.17345
8	7.0074	.99505	.00495	63	5.7490	.81636	.18364
9	7.0044	.99463	.00537	64	5.6746	.80579	.19421
10	7.0008	.99411	.00589	65	5.5969	.79476	.20524
11	6.9963	.99348	.00652	66	5.5154	.78319	.21681
12	6.9913	.99276	.00724	67	5.4301	.77107	.22893
13	6.9859	.99199	.00801	68	5.3407	.75838	.24162
14	6.9807	.99126	.00874	69	5.2477	.74517	.25483
15	6.9759	.99058	.00942	70	5.1514	.73150	.26850
16	6.9716	.98996	.01004	71	5.0524	.71744	.28256
17	6.9678	.98942	.01058	72	4.9505	.70297	.29703
18	6.9643	.98894	.01106	73	4.8455	.68807	.31193
19	6.9610	.98847	.01153	74	4.7369	.67264	.32736
20	6.9579	.98802	.01198	75	4.6239	.65659	.34341
21	6.9549	.98760	.01240	76	4.5061	.63987	.36013
22	6.9520	.98718	.01282	77	4.3837	.62249	.37751
23	6.9490	.98676	.01324	78	4.2570	.60450	.39550
24	6.9457	.98629	.01371	79	4.1273	.58607	.41393
25	6.9420	.98576	.01424	80	3.9954	.56735	.43265
26	6.9375	.98513	.01487	81	3.8631	.54856	.45144
27	6.9323	.98439	.01561	82	3.7311	.52982	.47018
28	6.9264	.98354	.01646	83	3.6004	.51126	.48874
29	6.9196	.98258	.01742	84	3.4707	.49284	.50716
30	6.9119	.98149	.01851	85	3.3416	.47451	.52549
31	6.9031	.98024	.01976	86	3.2145	.45646	.54354
32	6.8933	.97886	.02114	87	3.0916	.43900	.56100
33	6.8823	.97729	.02271	88	2.9722	.42205	.57795
34	6.8701	.97556	.02444	89	2.8541	.40528	.59472
35	6.8566	.97364	.02636	90	2.7358	.38849	.61151
36	6.8420	.97157	.02843	91	2.6193	.37194	.62806
37	6.8261	.96930	.03070	92	2.5077	.35610	.64390
38	6.8088	.96684	.03316	93	2.4027	.34119	.65881
39	6.7900	.96418	.03582	94	2.3056	.32739	.67261
40	6.7697	.96129	.03871	95	2.2171	.31482	.68518
41	6.7478	.95818	.04182	96	2.1382	.30363	.69637
42	6.7243	.95486	.04514	97	2.0662	.29340	.70660
43	6.6993	.95130	.04870	98	2.0013	.28419	.71581
44	6.6725	.94750	.05250	99	1.9414	.27568	.72432
45	6.6439	.94344	.05656	100	1.8860	.26781	.73219
46	6.6134	.93911	.06089	101	1.8336	.26037	.73963
47	6.5809	.93449	.06551	102	1.7791	.25263	.74737
48	6.5465	.92961	.07039	103	1.7215	.24446	.75554
49	6.5103	.92447	.07553	104	1.6578	.23541	.76459
50	6.4723	.91907	.08093	105	1.5782	.22410	.77590
51	6.4323	.91338	.08662	106	1.4589	.20717	.79283
52	6.3899	.90737	.09263	107	1.2790	.18162	.81838
53	6.3450	.90100	.09900	108	0.9692	.13763	.86237
54	6.2978	.89429	.10571	109	0.4378	.06217	.93783

Table S(14.4) *SINGLE LIFE, 14.4 PERCENT, BASED ON LIFE TABLE 80CNSMT SHOWING THE PRESENT WORTH OF AN ANNUITY, OF A LIFE ESTATE, AND OF A REMAINDER INTEREST*

Age	Annuity	Life Estate	Remainder	Age	Annuity	Life Estate	Remainder
(1)	(2)	(3)	(4)	(1)	(2)	(3)	(4)
0	6.8362	.98442	.01558	55	6.1751	.88922	.11078
1	6.9141	.99563	.00437	56	6.1241	.88187	.11813
2	6.9166	.99599	.00401	57	6.0702	.87411	.12589
3	6.9174	.99611	.00389	58	6.0134	.86592	.13408
4	6.9172	.99608	.00392	59	5.9535	.85731	.14269
5	6.9163	.99595	.00405	60	5.8910	.84830	.15170
6	6.9150	.99575	.00425	61	5.8258	.83891	.16109
7	6.9132	.99550	.00450	62	5.7581	.82917	.17083
8	6.9109	.99518	.00482	63	5.6880	.81907	.18093
9	6.9081	.99476	.00524	64	5.6152	.80859	.19141
10	6.9046	.99426	.00574	65	5.5392	.79765	.20235
11	6.9003	.99364	.00636	66	5.4595	.78617	.21383
12	6.8953	.99293	.00707	67	5.3759	.77413	.22587
13	6.8901	.99217	.00783	68	5.2883	.76152	.23848
14	6.8850	.99144	.00856	69	5.1972	.74839	.25161
15	6.8804	.99077	.00923	70	5.1028	.73480	.26520
16	6.8762	.99017	.00983	71	5.0056	.72081	.27919
17	6.8725	.98964	.01036	72	4.9056	.70640	.29360
18	6.8692	.98916	.01084	73	4.8025	.69156	.30844
19	6.8660	.98871	.01129	74	4.6958	.67619	.32381
20	6.8630	.98827	.01173	75	4.5847	.66019	.33981
21	6.8602	.98787	.01213	76	4.4688	.64351	.35649
22	6.8574	.98746	.01254	77	4.3483	.62616	.37384
23	6.8546	.98706	.01294	78	4.2236	.60820	.39180
24	6.8515	.98661	.01339	79	4.0957	.58978	.41022
25	6.8479	.98610	.01390	80	3.9657	.57106	.42894
26	6.8437	.98549	.01451	81	3.8352	.55226	.44774
27	6.8387	.98477	.01523	82	3.7049	.53351	.46649
28	6.8330	.98395	.01605	83	3.5758	.51492	.48508
29	6.8265	.98302	.01698	84	3.4477	.49647	.50353
30	6.8191	.98196	.01804	85	3.3201	.47810	.52190
31	6.8107	.98074	.01926	86	3.1945	.46000	.54000
32	6.8013	.97939	.02061	87	3.0729	.44249	.55751
33	6.7907	.97786	.02214	88	2.9548	.42549	.57451
34	6.7790	.97617	.02383	89	2.8379	.40865	.59135
35	6.7660	.97430	.02570	90	2.7207	.39179	.60821
36	6.7518	.97226	.02774	91	2.6053	.37516	.62484
37	6.7364	.97005	.02995	92	2.4948	.35924	.64076
38	6.7197	.96764	.03236	93	2.3906	.34425	.65575
39	6.7015	.96502	.03498	94	2.2943	.33038	.66962
40	6.6819	.96219	.03781	95	2.2065	.31774	.68226
41	6.6607	.95914	.04086	96	2.1283	.30647	.69353
42	6.6380	.95587	.04413	97	2.0568	.29618	.70382
43	6.6137	.95238	.04762	98	1.9925	.28691	.71309
44	6.5878	.94864	.05136	99	1.9330	.27835	.72165
45	6.5600	.94464	.05536	100	1.8780	.27043	.72957
46	6.5304	.94038	.05962	101	1.8260	.26295	.73705
47	6.4989	.93584	.06416	102	1.7720	.25516	.74484
48	6.4655	.93103	.06897	103	1.7149	.24695	.75305
49	6.4303	.92596	.07404	104	1.6518	.23786	.76214
50	6.3933	.92064	.07936	105	1.5728	.22648	.77352
51	6.3544	.91503	.08497	106	1.4544	.20943	.79057
52	6.3132	.90910	.09090	107	1.2756	.18368	.81632
53	6.2695	.90281	.09719	108	0.9671	.13926	.86074
54	6.2236	.89619	.10381	109	0.4371	.06294	.93706

Table S(14.6) SINGLE LIFE, 14.6 PERCENT, BASED ON LIFE TABLE
80CNSMT SHOWING THE PRESENT WORTH OF AN ANNUITY, OF A LIFE
ESTATE, AND OF A REMAINDER INTEREST

Age	Annuity	Life Estate	Remainder	Age	Annuity	Life Estate	Remainder
(1)	(2)	(3)	(4)	(1)	(2)	(3)	(4)
0	6.7432	.98450	.01550	55	6.1037	.89114	.10886
1	6.8199	.99571	.00429	56	6.0540	.88388	.11612
2	6.8224	.99608	.00392	57	6.0014	.87621	.12379
3	6.8233	.99620	.00380	58	5.9460	.86811	.13189
4	6.8231	.99617	.00383	59	5.8876	.85959	.14041
5	6.8222	.99605	.00395	60	5.8265	.85067	.14933
6	6.8210	.99586	.00414	61	5.7628	.84137	.15863
7	6.8193	.99561	.00439	62	5.6967	.83172	.16828
8	6.8171	.99530	.00470	63	5.6282	.82171	.17829
9	6.8144	.99490	.00510	64	5.5570	.81132	.18868
10	6.8110	.99440	.00560	65	5.4826	.80046	.19954
11	6.8068	.99379	.00621	66	5.4046	.78907	.21093
12	6.8020	.99309	.00691	67	5.3228	.77712	.22288
13	6.7968	.99234	.00766	68	5.2369	.76459	.23541
14	6.7919	.99162	.00838	69	5.1475	.75154	.24846
15	6.7874	.99096	.00904	70	5.0549	.73802	.26198
16	6.7833	.99037	.00963	71	4.9596	.72410	.27590
17	6.7798	.98985	.01015	72	4.8614	.70976	.29024
18	6.7766	.98938	.01062	73	4.7602	.69499	.30501
19	6.7735	.98894	.01106	74	4.6553	.67967	.32033
20	6.7707	.98852	.01148	75	4.5461	.66373	.33627
21	6.7680	.98812	.01188	76	4.4321	.64709	.35291
22	6.7653	.98773	.01227	77	4.3135	.62977	.37023
23	6.7626	.98735	.01265	78	4.1906	.61183	.38817
24	6.7597	.98691	.01309	79	4.0646	.59343	.40657
25	6.7563	.98642	.01358	80	3.9364	.57471	.42529
26	6.7523	.98583	.01417	81	3.8076	.55590	.44410
27	6.7475	.98514	.01486	82	3.6790	.53714	.46286
28	6.7421	.98434	.01566	83	3.5515	.51852	.48148
29	6.7359	.98343	.01657	84	3.4250	.50004	.49996
30	6.7288	.98240	.01760	85	3.2989	.48163	.51837
31	6.7207	.98122	.01878	86	3.1746	.46350	.53650
32	6.7117	.97990	.02010	87	3.0544	.44594	.55406
33	6.7014	.97841	.02159	88	2.9375	.42888	.57112
34	6.6901	.97675	.02325	89	2.8218	.41198	.58802
35	6.6775	.97492	.02508	90	2.7058	.39505	.60495
36	6.6639	.97293	.02707	91	2.5915	.37835	.62165
37	6.6490	.97076	.02924	92	2.4819	.36236	.63764
38	6.6329	.96840	.03160	93	2.3787	.34728	.65272
39	6.6153	.96583	.03417	94	2.2831	.33333	.66667
40	6.5963	.96305	.03695	95	2.1960	.32062	.67938
41	6.5757	.96005	.03995	96	2.1184	.30929	.69071
42	6.5537	.95684	.04316	97	2.0475	.29894	.70106
43	6.5302	.95341	.04659	98	1.9837	.28961	.71039
44	6.5050	.94974	.05026	99	1.9247	.28100	.71900
45	6.4781	.94580	.05420	100	1.8701	.27304	.72696
46	6.4494	.94161	.05839	101	1.8186	.26551	.73449
47	6.4187	.93713	.06287	102	1.7649	.25768	.74232
48	6.3863	.93239	.06761	103	1.7084	.24942	.75058
49	6.3521	.92740	.07260	104	1.6458	.24028	.75972
50	6.3161	.92216	.07784	105	1.5674	.22885	.77115
51	6.2783	.91663	.08337	106	1.4499	.21168	.78832
52	6.2382	.91077	.08923	107	1.2721	.18573	.81427
53	6.1957	.90457	.09543	108	0.9650	.14088	.85912
54	6.1509	.89803	.10197	109	0.4363	.06370	.93630

Table S(14.8) *SINGLE LIFE, 14.8 PERCENT, BASED ON LIFE TABLE 80CNSMT SHOWING THE PRESENT WORTH OF AN ANNUITY, OF A LIFE ESTATE, AND OF A REMAINDER INTEREST*

Age	Annuity	Life Estate	Remainder	Age	Annuity	Life Estate	Remainder
(1)	(2)	(3)	(4)	(1)	(2)	(3)	(4)
0	6.6526	.98458	.01542	55	6.0339	.89301	.10699
1	6.7283	.99578	.00422	56	5.9854	.88584	.11416
2	6.7308	.99615	.00385	57	5.9341	.87825	.12175
3	6.7316	.99628	.00372	58	5.8800	.87024	.12976
4	6.7315	.99626	.00374	59	5.8230	.86181	.13819
5	6.7307	.99614	.00386	60	5.7633	.85297	.14703
6	6.7295	.99596	.00404	61	5.7011	.84376	.15624
7	6.7279	.99572	.00428	62	5.6365	.83420	.16580
8	6.7258	.99542	.00458	63	5.5695	.82428	.17572
9	6.7231	.99502	.00498	64	5.4999	.81398	.18602
10	6.7198	.99453	.00547	65	5.4271	.80321	.19679
11	6.7158	.99393	.00607	66	5.3507	.79191	.20809
12	6.7111	.99324	.00676	67	5.2705	.78004	.21996
13	6.7061	.99250	.00750	68	5.1864	.76759	.23241
14	6.7013	.99179	.00821	69	5.0988	.75462	.24538
15	6.6969	.99114	.00886	70	5.0079	.74117	.25883
16	6.6929	.99055	.00945	71	4.9144	.72733	.27267
17	6.6895	.99004	.00996	72	4.8179	.71306	.28694
18	6.6864	.98959	.01041	73	4.7185	.69834	.30166
19	6.6835	.98916	.01084	74	4.6155	.68309	.31691
20	6.6807	.98875	.01125	75	4.5081	.66719	.33281
21	6.6781	.98836	.01164	76	4.3959	.65060	.34940
22	6.6756	.98799	.01201	77	4.2791	.63331	.36669
23	6.6731	.98762	.01238	78	4.1581	.61540	.38460
24	6.6703	.98720	.01280	79	4.0339	.59701	.40299
25	6.6671	.98673	.01327	80	3.9074	.57830	.42170
26	6.6632	.98616	.01384	81	3.7803	.55949	.44051
27	6.6587	.98549	.01451	82	3.6535	.54071	.45929
28	6.6535	.98472	.01528	83	3.5276	.52208	.47792
29	6.6475	.98383	.01617	84	3.4025	.50357	.49643
30	6.6408	.98283	.01717	85	3.2779	.48513	.51487
31	6.6330	.98168	.01832	86	3.1551	.46695	.53305
32	6.6243	.98039	.01961	87	3.0361	.44934	.55066
33	6.6144	.97893	.02107	88	2.9205	.43223	.56777
34	6.6035	.97731	.02269	89	2.8059	.41528	.58472
35	6.5914	.97552	.02448	90	2.6911	.39828	.60172
36	6.5782	.97357	.02643	91	2.5777	.38151	.61849
37	6.5638	.97144	.02856	92	2.4692	.36544	.63456
38	6.5482	.96913	.03087	93	2.3668	.35029	.64971
39	6.5311	.96661	.03339	94	2.2720	.33626	.66374
40	6.5127	.96388	.03612	95	2.1856	.32348	.67652
41	6.4928	.96094	.03906	96	2.1087	.31208	.68792
42	6.4715	.95778	.04222	97	2.0383	.30167	.69833
43	6.4487	.95441	.04559	98	1.9749	.29229	.70771
44	6.4243	.95079	.04921	99	1.9164	.28362	.71638
45	6.3981	.94692	.05308	100	1.8623	.27562	.72438
46	6.3702	94279	.05721	101	1.8111	.26805	.73195
47	6.3404	.93838	.06162	102	1.7580	.26018	.73982
48	6.3089	.93371	.06629	103	1.7019	.25188	.74812
49	6.2756	.92879	.07121	104	1.6398	.24269	.75731
50	6.2407	.92362	.07638	105	1.5621	.23119	.76881
51	6.2039	.91817	.08183	106	1.4454	.21392	.78608
52	6.1648	.91239	.08761	107	1.2687	.18777	.81223
53	6.1234	.90627	.09373	108	0.9628	.14250	.85750
54	6.0798	.89982	.10018	109	0.4355	.06446	.93554

Table S(15.0) *SINGLE LIFE, 15.0 PERCENT, BASED ON LIFE TABLE 80CNSMT SHOWING THE PRESENT WORTH OF AN ANNUITY, OF A LIFE ESTATE, AND OF A REMAINDER INTEREST*

Age	Annuity	Life Estate	Remainder	Age	Annuity	Life Estate	Remainder
(1)	(2)	(3)	(4)	(1)	(2)	(3)	(4)
0	6.5644	.98466	.01534	55	5.9655	.89482	.10518
1	6.6390	.99585	.00415	56	5.9182	.88773	.11227
2	6.6415	.99623	.00377	57	5.8682	.88023	.11977
3	6.6424	.99636	.00364	58	5.8154	.87231	.12769
4	6.6423	.99635	.00365	59	5.7597	.86396	.13604
5	6.6416	.99623	.00377	60	5.7014	.85522	.14478
6	6.6404	.99606	.00394	61	5.6406	.84609	.15391
7	6.6389	.99583	.00417	62	5.5775	.83662	.16338
8	6.6369	.99553	.00447	63	5.5119	.82679	.17321
9	6.6343	.99514	.00486	64	5.4438	.81657	.18343
10	6.6311	.99466	.00534	65	5.3726	.80589	.19411
11	6.6271	.99407	.00593	66	5.2978	.79467	.20533
12	6.6226	.99338	.00662	67	5.2193	.78289	.21711
13	6.6177	.99265	.00735	68	5.1368	.77052	.22948
14	6.6130	.99195	.00805	69	5.0509	.75763	.24237
15	6.6087	.99131	.00869	70	4.9617	.74426	.25574
16	6.6049	.99073	.00927	71	4.8699	.73048	.26952
17	6.6016	.99023	.00977	72	4.7752	.71628	.28372
18	6.5986	.98979	.01021	73	4.6776	.70163	.29837
19	6.5958	.98937	.01063	74	4.5762	.68644	.31356
20	6.5931	.98897	.01103	75	4.4706	.67059	.32941
21	6.5906	.98860	.01140	76	4.3603	.65404	.34596
22	6.5882	.98824	.01176	77	4.2453	.63679	.36321
23	6.5859	.98788	.01212	78	4.1260	.61891	.38109
24	6.5832	.98748	.01252	79	4.0036	.60054	.39946
25	6.5801	.98702	.01298	80	3.8789	.58183	.41817
26	6.5765	.98647	.01353	81	3.7535	.56302	.43698
27	6.5722	.98582	.01418	82	3.6282	.54423	.45577
28	6.5672	.98508	.01492	83	3.5039	.52558	.47442
29	6.5614	.98422	.01578	84	3.3803	.50705	.49295
30	6.5549	.98324	.01676	85	3.2571	.48857	.51143
31	6.5474	.98212	.01788	86	3.1357	.47035	.52965
32	6.5391	.98086	.01914	87	3.0180	.45270	.54730
33	6.5296	.97944	.02056	88	2.9036	.43554	.56446
34	6.5190	.97785	.02215	89	2.7902	.41853	.58147
35	6.5073	.97610	.02390	90	2.6765	.40147	.59853
36	6.4946	.97419	.02581	91	2.5642	.38463	.61537
37	6.4807	.97210	.02790	92	2.4565	.36848	.63152
38	6.4655	.96983	.03017	93	2.3550	.35326	.64674
39	6.4490	.96736	.03264	94	2.2611	.33916	.66084
40	6.4312	.96468	.03532	95	2.1754	.32630	.67370
41	6.4119	.96178	.03822	96	2.0990	.31485	.68515
42	6.3912	.95868	.04132	97	2.0292	.30438	.69562
43	6.3691	.95536	.04464	98	1.9663	.29494	.70506
44	6.3454	.95181	.04819	99	1.9082	.28623	.71377
45	6.3200	.94800	.05200	100	1.8545	.27817	.72183
46	6.2929	.94393	.05607	101	1.8038	.27057	.72943
47	6.2640	.93959	.06041	102	1.7510	.26265	.73735
48	6.2333	.93499	.06501	103	1.6954	.25431	.74569
49	6.2009	.93014	.06986	104	1.6338	.24508	.75492
50	6.1669	.92504	.07496	105	1.5568	.23352	.76648
51	6.1311	.91967	.08033	106	1.4410	.21614	.78386
52	6.0931	.91396	.08604	107	1.2653	.18980	.81020
53	6.0528	.90792	.09208	108	0.9607	.14411	.85589
54	6.0103	.90155	.09845	109	0.4348	.06522	.93478

Table S(15.2) *SINGLE LIFE, 15.2 PERCENT, BASED ON LIFE TABLE 80CNSMT SHOWING THE PRESENT WORTH OF AN ANNUITY, OF A LIFE ESTATE, AND OF A REMAINDER INTEREST*

Age	Annuity	Life Estate	Remainder	Age	Annuity	Life Estate	Remainder
(1)	(2)	(3)	(4)	(1)	(2)	(3)	(4)
0	6.4785	.98474	.01526	55	5.8986	.89658	.10342
1	6.5521	.99592	.00408	56	5.8525	.88957	.11043
2	6.5546	.99630	.00370	57	5.8037	.88216	.11784
3	6.5555	.99644	.00356	58	5.7521	.87432	.12568
4	6.5555	.99643	.00357	59	5.6977	.86605	.13395
5	6.5547	.99632	.00368	60	5.6408	.85740	.14260
6	6.5536	.99615	.00385	61	5.5813	.84836	.15164
7	6.5522	.99593	.00407	62	5.5196	.83897	.16103
8	6.5502	.99564	.00436	63	5.4555	.82923	.17077
9	6.5477	.99526	.00474	64	5.3888	.81910	.18090
10	6.5446	.99479	.00521	65	5.3191	.80850	.19150
11	6.5408	.99420	.00580	66	5.2459	.79737	.20263
12	6.5363	.99352	.00648	67	5.1689	.78567	.21433
13	6.5316	.99280	.00720	68	5.0881	.77339	.22661
14	6.5270	.99211	.00789	69	5.0038	.76057	.23943
15	6.5229	.99147	.00853	70	4.9163	.74728	.25272
16	6.5191	.99091	.00909	71	4.8261	.73357	.26643
17	6.5159	.99042	.00958	72	4.7332	.71944	.28056
18	6.5130	.98998	.01002	73	4.6372	.70486	.29514
19	6.5103	.98957	.01043	74	4.5376	.68972	.31028
20	6.5078	.98918	.01082	75	4.4338	.67393	.32607
21	6.5054	.98882	.01118	76	4.3252	.65743	.34257
22	6.5031	.98847	.01153	77	4.2119	.64022	.35978
23	6.5008	.98813	.01187	78	4.0944	.62235	.37765
24	6.4983	.98774	.01226	79	3.9737	.60400	.39600
25	6.4954	.98730	.01270	80	3.8507	.58531	.41469
26	6.4919	.98677	.01323	81	3.7270	.56650	.43350
27	6.4878	.98614	.01386	82	3.6033	.54770	.45230
28	6.4830	.98542	.01458	83	3.4805	.52904	.47096
29	6.4775	.98458	.01542	84	3.3584	.51048	.48952
30	6.4713	.98363	.01637	85	3.2367	.49197	.50803
31	6.4641	.98254	.01746	86	3.1165	.47371	.52629
32	6.4560	.98131	.01869	87	3.0001	.45602	.54398
33	6.4468	.97992	.02008	88	2.8869	.43881	.56119
34	6.4366	.97837	.02163	89	2.7747	.42175	.57825
35	6.4253	.97665	.02335	90	2.6620	.40463	.59537
36	6.4130	.97478	.02522	91	2.5507	.38771	.61229
37	6.3995	.97273	.02727	92	2.4441	.37150	.62850
38	6.3849	.97050	.02950	93	2.3434	.35620	.64380
39	6.3689	.96808	.03192	94	2.2502	.34203	.65797
40	6.3516	.96545	.03455	95	2.1652	.32911	.67089
41	6.3329	.96260	.03740	96	2.0894	.31759	.68241
42	6.3128	.95955	.04045	97	2.0201	.30706	.69294
43	6.2914	.95629	.04371	98	1.9577	.29757	.70243
44	6.2683	.95279	.04721	99	1.9001	.28881	.71119
45	6.2437	.94904	.05096	100	1.8468	.28071	.71929
46	6.2173	.94504	.05496	101	1.7965	.27306	.72694
47	6.1892	.94076	.05924	102	1.7441	.26511	.73489
48	6.1594	.93622	.06378	103	1.6890	.25673	.74327
49	6.1279	.93144	.06856	104	1.6279	.24745	.75255
50	6.0948	.92641	.07359	105	1.5516	.23584	.76416
51	6.0599	.92111	.07889	106	1.4365	.21835	.78165
52	6.0229	.91548	.08452	107	1.2619	.19181	.80819
53	5.9837	.90952	.09048	108	0.9587	.14572	.85428
54	5.9423	.90322	.09678	109	0.4340	.06597	.93403

Table S(15.4) SINGLE LIFE, 15.4 PERCENT, BASED ON LIFE TABLE 80CNSMT SHOWING THE PRESENT WORTH OF AN ANNUITY, OF A LIFE ESTATE, AND OF A REMAINDER INTEREST

Age	Annuity	Life Estate	Remainder	Age	Annuity	Life Estate	Remainder
(1)	(2)	(3)	(4)	(1)	(2)	(3)	(4)
0	6.3949	.98481	.01519	55	5.8330	.89829	.10171
1	6.4675	.99599	.00401	56	5.7881	.89136	.10864
2	6.4700	.99637	.00363	57	5.7404	.88403	.11597
3	6.4708	.99651	.00349	58	5.6901	.87627	.12373
4	6.4708	.99651	.00349	59	5.6370	.86809	.13191
5	6.4702	.99640	.00360	60	5.5813	.85952	.14048
6	6.4691	.99624	.00376	61	5.5232	.85057	.14943
7	6.4677	.99602	.00398	62	5.4628	.84127	.15873
8	6.4658	.99574	.00426	63	5.4001	.83161	.16839
9	6.4634	.99537	.00463	64	5.3348	.82157	.17843
10	6.4604	.99490	.00510	65	5.2666	.81106	.18894
11	6.4567	.99433	.00567	66	5.1949	.80001	.19999
12	6.4523	.99366	.00634	67	5.1194	.78839	.21161
13	6.4477	.99294	.00706	68	5.0402	.77619	.22381
14	6.4432	.99226	.00774	69	4.9575	.76345	.23655
15	6.4392	.99163	.00837	70	4.8716	.75023	.24977
16	6.4355	.99107	.00893	71	4.7831	.73660	.26340
17	6.4324	.99059	.00941	72	4.6918	.72254	.27746
18	6.4296	.99016	.00984	73	4.5975	.70802	.29198
19	6.4270	.98976	.01024	74	4.4996	.69294	.30706
20	6.4246	.98938	.01062	75	4.3974	.67721	.32279
21	6.4223	.98903	.01097	76	4.2906	.66075	.33925
22	6.4201	.98870	.01130	77	4.1791	.64358	.35642
23	6.4180	.98837	.01163	78	4.0633	.62575	.37425
24	6.4156	.98800	.01200	79	3.9443	.60742	.39258
25	6.4128	.98757	.01243	80	3.8229	.58873	.41127
26	6.4095	.98706	.01294	81	3.7008	.56992	.43008
27	6.4055	.98645	.01355	82	3.5787	.55112	.44888
28	6.4009	.98574	.01426	83	3.4574	.53244	.46756
29	6.3957	.98493	.01507	84	3.3368	.51387	.48613
30	6.3896	.98401	.01599	85	3.2164	.49533	.50467
31	6.3827	.98294	.01706	86	3.0976	.47703	.52297
32	6.3749	.98174	.01826	87	2.9824	.45930	.54070
33	6.3661	.98038	.01962	88	2.8704	.44204	.55796
34	6.3562	.97886	.02114	89	2.7593	.42493	.57507
35	6.3453	.97718	.02282	90	2.6477	.40775	.59225
36	6.3334	.97534	.02466	91	2.5374	.39077	.60923
37	6.3203	.97333	.02667	92	2.4317	.37448	.62552
38	6.3062	.97115	.02885	93	2.3319	.35911	.64089
39	6.2907	.96877	.03123	94	2.2394	.34487	.65513
40	6.2739	.96618	.03382	95	2.1551	.33188	.66812
41	6.2558	.96339	.03661	96	2.0799	.32030	.67970
42	6.2363	.96039	.03961	97	2.0111	.30972	.69028
43	6.2154	.95718	.04282	98	1.9492	.30018	.69982
44	6.1931	.95374	.04626	99	1.8920	.29137	.70863
45	6.1691	.95004	.04996	100	1.8391	.28322	.71678
46	6.1435	.94610	.05390	101	1.7892	.27554	.72446
47	6.1161	.94189	.05811	102	1.7373	.26754	.73246
48	6.0871	.93741	.06259	103	1.6826	.25912	.74088
49	6.0565	.93270	.06730	104	1.6221	.24980	.75020
50	6.0243	.92774	.07226	105	1.5463	.23814	.76186
51	5.9903	.92251	.07749	106	1.4321	.22055	.77945
52	5.9543	.91696	.08304	107	1.2586	.19382	.80618
53	5.9160	.91107	.08893	108	0.9566	.14731	.85269
54	5.8757	.90485	.09515	109	0.4333	.06672	.93328

Table S(15.6) SINGLE LIFE, 15.6 PERCENT, BASED ON LIFE TABLE 80CNSMT SHOWING THE PRESENT WORTH OF AN ANNUITY, OF A LIFE ESTATE, AND OF A REMAINDER INTEREST

Age	Annuity	Life Estate	Remainder	Age	Annuity	Life Estate	Remainder
(1)	(2)	(3)	(4)	(1)	(2)	(3)	(4)
0	6.3133	.98488	.01512	55	5.7689	.89994	.10006
1	6.3850	.99605	.00395	56	5.7250	.89310	.10690
2	6.3874	.99644	.00356	57	5.6785	.88584	.11416
3	6.3883	.99658	.00342	58	5.6293	.87817	.12183
4	6.3883	.99658	.00342	59	5.5774	.87007	.12993
5	6.3877	.99648	.00352	60	5.5230	.86158	.13842
6	6.3867	.99633	.00367	61	5.4661	.85272	.14728
7	6.3854	.99612	.00388	62	5.4071	.84350	.15650
8	6.3836	.99584	.00416	63	5.3457	.83393	.16607
9	6.3812	.99547	.00453	64	5.2819	.82397	.17603
10	6.3783	.99502	.00498	65	5.2150	.81355	.18645
11	6.3747	.99445	.00555	66	5.1448	.80258	.19742
12	6.3704	.99379	.00621	67	5.0708	.79105	.20895
13	6.3659	.99308	.00692	68	4.9931	.77892	.22108
14	6.3616	.99240	.00760	69	4.9120	.76627	.23373
15	6.3576	.99178	.00822	70	4.8277	.75312	.24688
16	6.3540	.99123	.00877	71	4.7408	.73956	.26044
17	6.3510	.99076	.00924	72	4.6511	.72557	.27443
18	6.3483	.99034	.00966	73	4.5584	.71112	.28888
19	6.3458	.98994	.01006	74	4.4622	.69610	.30390
20	6.3434	.98957	.01043	75	4.3617	.68042	.31958
21	6.3413	.98924	.01076	76	4.2565	.66401	.33599
22	6.3392	.98891	.01109	77	4.1467	.64688	.35312
23	6.3371	.98859	.01141	78	4.0326	.62908	.37092
24	6.3349	.98824	.01176	79	3.9152	.61077	.38923
25	6.3322	.98783	.01217	80	3.7955	.59210	.40790
26	6.3291	.98733	.01267	81	3.6750	.57330	.42670
27	6.3253	.98674	.01326	82	3.5544	.55449	.44551
28	6.3209	.98606	.01394	83	3.4346	.53580	.46420
29	6.3158	.98527	.01473	84	3.3154	.51720	.48280
30	6.3100	.98436	.01564	85	3.1964	.49864	.50136
31	6.3033	.98332	.01668	86	3.0789	.48031	.51969
32	6.2958	.98215	.01785	87	2.9650	.46253	.53747
33	6.2873	.98082	.01918	88	2.8541	.44524	.55476
34	6.2778	.97933	.02067	89	2.7441	.42807	.57193
35	6.2672	.97768	.02232	90	2.6335	.41083	.58917
36	6.2557	.97589	.02411	91	2.5243	.39379	.60621
37	6.2431	.97392	.02608	92	2.4194	.33743	.62257
38	6.2293	.97177	.02823	93	2.3205	.36199	.63801
39	6.2143	.96943	.03057	94	2.2288	.34769	.65231
40	6.1980	.96689	.03311	95	2.1451	.33463	.66537
41	6.1804	.96414	.03586	96	2.0704	.32299	.67701
42	6.1615	.96120	.03880	97	2.0022	.31235	.68765
43	6.1413	.95804	.04196	98	1.9408	.30276	.69724
44	6.1195	.95465	.04535	99	1.8840	.29390	.70610
45	6.0962	.95101	.04899	100	1.8315	.28572	.71428
46	6.0713	.94713	.05287	101	1.7820	.27799	.72201
47	6.0447	.94298	.05702	102	1.7305	.26996	.73004
48	6.0165	.93857	.06143	103	1.6763	.26150	.73850
49	5.9867	.93392	.06608	104	1.6163	.25214	.74786
50	5.9553	.92903	.07097	105	1.5412	.24042	.75958
51	5.9222	.92387	.07613	106	1.4277	.22273	.77727
52	5.8871	.91839	.08161	107	1.2552	.19581	.80419
53	5.8498	.91257	.08743	108	0.9545	.14890	.85110
54	5.8104	.90643	.09357	109	0.4325	.06747	.93253

Table S(15.8) *SINGLE LIFE, 15.8 PERCENT, BASED ON LIFE TABLE 80CNSMT SHOWING THE PRESENT WORTH OF AN ANNUITY, OF A LIFE ESTATE, AND OF A REMAINDER INTEREST*

Age	Annuity	Life Estate	Remainder	Age	Annuity	Life Estate	Remainder
(1)	(2)	(3)	(4)	(1)	(2)	(3)	(4)
0	6.2338	.98495	.01505	55	5.7060	.90155	.09845
1	6.3045	.99611	.00389	56	5.6632	.89478	.10522
2	6.3070	.99650	.00350	57	5.6178	.88761	.11239
3	6.3079	.99665	.00335	58	5.5697	.88002	.11998
4	6.3079	.99665	.00335	59	5.5190	.87200	.12800
5	6.3073	.99656	.00344	60	5.4658	.86359	.13641
6	6.3064	.99641	.00359	61	5.4102	.85481	.14519
7	6.3051	.99620	.00380	62	5.3524	.84568	.15432
8	6.3034	.99593	.00407	63	5.2924	.83619	.16381
9	6.3011	.99557	.00443	64	5.2299	.82632	.17368
10	6.2983	.99512	.00488	65	5.1644	.81598	.18402
11	6.2947	.99456	.00544	66	5.0956	.80510	.19490
12	6.2906	.99391	.00609	67	5.0231	.79365	.20635
13	6.2861	.99321	.00679	68	4.9468	.78160	.21840
14	6.2819	.99254	.00746	69	4.8672	.76902	.23098
15	6.2780	.99193	.00807	70	4.7845	.75595	.24405
16	6.2746	.99138	.00862	71	4.6992	.74247	.25753
17	6.2716	.99092	.00908	72	4.6110	.72854	.27146
18	6.2690	.99051	.00949	73	4.5200	.71416	.28584
19	6.2666	.99012	.00988	74	4.4253	.69920	.30080
20	6.2643	.98976	.01024	75	4.3264	.68358	.31642
21	6.2622	.98943	.01057	76	4.2229	.66722	.33278
22	6.2602	.98912	.01088	77	4.1147	.65013	.34987
23	6.2583	.98881	.01119	78	4.0023	.63236	.36764
24	6.2561	.98847	.01153	79	3.8865	.61407	.38593
25	6.2536	.98807	.01193	80	3.7685	.59542	.40458
26	6.2506	.98760	.01240	81	3.6495	.57662	.42338
27	6.2470	.98702	.01298	82	3.5304	.55781	.44219
28	6.2428	.98636	.01364	83	3.4121	.53911	.46089
29	6.2379	.98559	.01441	84	3.2943	.52050	.47950
30	6.2323	.98471	.01529	85	3.1766	.50190	.49810
31	6.2259	.98369	.01631	86	3.0604	.48354	.51646
32	6.2186	.98255	.01745	87	2.9477	.46573	.53427
33	6.2104	.98124	.01876	88	2.8379	.44839	.55161
34	6.2012	.97979	.02021	89	2.7290	.43118	.56882
35	6.1910	.97817	.02183	90	2.6195	.41389	.58611
36	6.1798	.97641	.02359	91	2.5112	.39678	.60322
37	6.1676	.97448	.02552	92	2.4073	.38035	.61965
38	6.1542	.97237	.02763	93	2.3092	.36485	.63515
39	6.1397	.97007	.02993	94	2.2182	.35047	.64953
40	6.1239	.96758	.03242	95	2.1351	.33735	.66265
41	6.1068	.96487	.03513	96	2.0611	.32565	.67435
42	6.0884	.96197	.03803	97	1.9934	.31496	.68504
43	6.0688	.95887	.04113	98	1.9324	.30532	.69468
44	6.0477	.95553	.04447	99	1.8760	.29642	.70358
45	6.0250	.95195	.04805	100	1.8240	.28819	.71181
46	6.0008	.94812	.05188	101	1.7749	.28043	.71957
47	5.9749	.94403	.05597	102	1.7238	.27236	.72764
48	5.9474	.93968	.06032	103	1.6700	.26386	.73614
49	5.9183	.93510	.06490	104	1.6105	.25446	.74554
50	5.8878	.93027	.06973	105	1.5360	.24269	.75731
51	5.8556	.92518	.07482	106	1.4234	.22490	.77510
52	5.8213	.91977	.08023	107	1.2519	.19780	.80220
53	5.7850	.91402	.08598	108	0.9524	.15048	.84952
54	5.7466	.90796	.09204	109	0.4318	.06822	.93178

Table U(1) (4.2 to 26% Adjusted Payout Rate)

The following tables present the valuation factors for the present value of the remainder interest in a single life unitrust, based on the age of the income beneficiary of the unitrust. Adjusted payout rates range from a low of 4.2 percent to a high of 26 percent. The tables have been in use since May 1, 1989.

To calculate the present value of the remainder interest in a charitable remainder unitrust transaction, use the following steps.

First, determine the fair market value of the property transferred to the charitable remainder unitrust.

Second, ensure that the correct valuation table has been used by applying the appropriate adjusted payout factor, based on the adjusted payout rate used for the unitrust.

Third, determine the age of the income recipient of the charitable remainder unitrust.

Fourth, multiply the fair market value of the property transferred to the trust by the appropriate remainder factor (based on the age of the trust income recipient).

Example

John Donor, age 65, establishes a charitable remainder unitrust and funds it with $100,000 in assets. The terms of the trust provide John with income from the trust for life. The first income distribution will occur one year after the trust has been in operation. At this time, the trust provides an adjusted payout rate of 6 percent.

To determine the amount that constitutes a charitable contribution deduction for John, multiply the fair market value of the assets in trust ($100,000) by the appropriate valuation factor for a 65 year old with an adjusted payout rate of 6 percent. This factor is .41544. Thus, the present value of the remainder interest in the property transferred to the trust is $41,544. This represents John's charitable contribution deduction.

Note that the tables for determining the present values of joint and survivor charitable remainder unitrusts are found in Publication 1458 at Table U(2).

Table U(1)   *BASED ON LIFE TABLE 80CNSMT UNITRUST SINGLE LIFE REMAINDER FACTORS ADJUSTED PAYOUT RATE*

Age	4.2%	4.4%	4.6%	4.8%	5.0%	5.2%	5.4%	5.6%	5.8%	6.0%
0	.06797	.06181	.05645	.05177	.04768	.04410	.04096	.03820	.03578	.03364
1	.05881	.05243	.04686	.04199	.03773	.03400	.03072	.02784	.02531	.02308
2	.06049	.05394	.04821	.04319	.03880	.03494	.03155	.02856	.02593	.02361
3	.06252	.05579	.04990	.04473	.04020	.03621	.03270	.02961	.02688	.02446
4	.06479	.05788	.05182	.04650	.04183	.03771	.03408	.03087	.02804	.02553
5	.06724	.06016	.05393	.04845	.04363	.03937	.03562	.03230	.02936	.02675
6	.06984	.06257	.05618	.05054	.04557	.04117	.03729	.03385	.03080	.02809
7	.07259	.06513	.05856	.05276	.04764	.04310	.03909	.03552	.03236	.02954
8	.07548	.06784	.06109	.05513	.04985	.04517	.04102	.03733	.03405	.03113
9	.07854	.07071	.06378	.05765	.05221	.04738	.04310	.03928	.03588	.03285
10	.08176	.07374	.06663	.06033	.05473	.04976	.04533	.04138	.03786	.03471
11	.08517	.07695	.06966	.06319	.05743	.05230	.04772	.04364	.04000	.03673
12	.08872	.08031	.07284	.06619	.06026	.05498	.05026	.04604	.04227	.03889
13	.09238	.08378	.07612	.06929	.06320	.05776	.05289	.04853	.04463	.04113
14	.09608	.08728	.07943	.07243	.06616	.06056	.05554	.05104	.04701	.04338
15	.09981	.09081	.08276	.07557	.06914	.06337	.05820	.05356	.04938	.04563
16	.10356	.09435	.08612	.07874	.07213	.06619	.06086	.05607	.05176	.04787
17	.10733	.09792	.08949	.08192	.07513	.06902	.06353	.05858	.05413	.05010
18	.11117	.10155	.09291	.08515	.07817	.07189	.06623	.06113	.05652	.05236
19	.11509	.10526	.09642	.08847	.08130	.07484	.06901	.06375	.05899	.05469
20	.11913	.10908	.10003	.09188	.08452	.07788	.07188	.06645	.06154	.05708
21	.12326	.11300	.10375	.09539	.08784	.08101	.07483	.06923	.06416	.05955
22	.12753	.11705	.10758	.09902	.09127	.08426	.07789	.07212	.06688	.06212
23	.13195	.12125	.11156	.10279	.09484	.08763	.08109	.07514	.06973	.06481
24	.13655	.12563	.11573	.10675	.09860	.09119	.08446	.07833	.07274	.06766
25	.14136	.13022	.12010	.11091	.10255	.09495	.08802	.08171	.07595	.07069
26	.14640	.13504	.12471	.11530	.10674	.09893	.09181	.08531	.07937	.07394
27	.15169	.14011	.12956	.11994	.11117	.10316	.09584	.08915	.08302	.07742
28	.15721	.14542	.13465	.12482	.11583	.10762	.10010	.09322	.08691	.08112
29	.16299	.15097	.13999	.12994	.12075	.11233	.10461	.09753	.09104	.08507
30	.16901	.15678	.14559	.13533	.12592	.11729	.10937	.10210	.09541	.08926
31	.17531	.16287	.15146	.14099	.13137	.12254	.11441	.10694	.10006	.09372
32	.18186	.16921	.15759	.14691	.13709	.12804 .	.11972	.11205	.10497	.09844
33	.18869	.17584	.16401	.15312	.14309	.13384	.12531	.11744	.11017	.10345
34	.19578	.18273	.17070	.15961	.14937	.13992	.13119	.12312	.11565	.10874
35	.20315	.18990	.17767	.16637	.15593	.14628	.13735	.12908	.12142	.11431
36	.21076	.19732	.18490	.17340	.16276	.15291	.14377	.13531	.12745	.12016
37	.21863	.20501	.19239	.18071	.16987	.15982	.15049	.14182	.13377	.12628
38	.22676	.21296	.20016	.18828	.17725	.16701	.15748	.14862	.14037	.13269
39	.23515	.22118	.20820	.19614	.18492	.17448	.16476	.15571	.14727	.13940
40	.24379	.22967	.21652	.20428	.19288	.18225	.17234	.16310	.15447	.14641
41	.25270	.23842	.22511	.21270	.20112	.19031	.18021	.17078	.16197	.15372
42	.26184	.24742	.23395	.22137	.20962	.19864	.18836	.17875	.16975	.16132
43	.27123	.25666	.24305	.23031	.21840	.20724	.19679	.18700	.17782	.16921
44	.28085	.26616	.25241	.23952	.22745	.21613	.20551	.19554	.18618	.17739
45	.29072	.27591	.26203	.24901	.23678	.22530	.21452	.20438	.19485	.18589
46	.30082	.28591	.27191	.25875	.24639	.23476	.22381	.21352	.20382	.19468
47	.31116	.29616	.28204	.26877	.25626	.24449	.23340	.22295	.21309	.20379
48	.32171	.30663	.29241	.27902	.26640	.25449	.24326	.23265	.22264	.21318
49	.33245	.31730	.30300	.28950	.27676	.26473	.25336	.24262	.23246	.22285
50	.34338	.32816	.31379	.30020	.28735	.27521	.26371	.25283	.24253	.23277
51	.35449	.33923	.32479	.31112	.29818	.28593	.27431	.26331	.25287	.24297
52	.36582	.35053	.33603	.32230	.30927	.29692	.28520	.27408	.26352	.25349
53	.37736	.36205	.34751	.33372	.32063	.30819	.29637	.28514	.27446	.26431
54	.38909	.37376	.35921	.34537	.33221	.31970	.30780	.29647	.28569	.27542

Table U(1) (continued)

Age	4.2%	4.4%	4.6%	4.8%	5.0%	5.2%	5.4%	5.6%	5.8%	6.0%
55	.40099	.38568	.37111	.35724	.34404	.33146	.31949	.30807	.29719	.28681
56	.41308	.39779	.38322	.36934	.35610	.34348	.33143	.31994	.30898	.29851
57	.42536	.41011	.39555	.38167	.36841	.35575	.34366	.33210	.32106	.31051
58	.43781	.42262	.40810	.39422	.38096	.36828	.35615	.34454	.33344	.32281
59	.45043	.43530	.42083	.40698	.39373	.38104	.36888	.35724	.34609	.33540
60	.46318	.44813	.43372	.41992	.40668	.39400	.38183	.37017	.35898	.34824
61	.47602	.46107	.44674	.43299	.41979	.40713	.39497	.38329	.37207	.36129
62	.48893	.47410	.45986	.44617	.43303	.42039	.40825	.39657	.38534	.37454
63	.50190	.48720	.47306	.45946	.44638	.43379	.42168	.41001	.39878	.38796
64	.51494	.50038	.48636	.47286	.45986	.44733	.43526	.42362	.41240	.40158
65	.52808	.51368	.49980	.48641	.47350	.46104	.44903	.43743	.42624	.41544
66	.54134	.52711	.51338	.50013	.48733	.47496	.46302	.45148	.44033	.42956
67	.55471	.54068	.52712	.51401	.50134	.48908	.47723	.46577	.45467	.44394
68	.56820	.55437	.54100	.52805	.51552	.50339	.49165	.48027	.46925	.45858
69	.58172	.56812	.55495	.54219	.52982	.51783	.50620	.49494	.48401	.47341
70	.59526	.58190	.56894	.55637	.54417	.53234	.52086	.50971	.49889	.48838
71	.60874	.59564	.58291	.57055	.55854	.54687	.53554	.52453	.51382	.50342
72	.62218	.60934	.59685	.58471	.57291	.56143	.55026	.53939	.52882	.51854
73	.63557	.62301	.61078	.59887	.58728	.57600	.56501	.55431	.54389	.53373
74	.64896	.63669	.62472	.61307	.60171	.59064	.57985	.56932	.55906	.54906
75	.66237	.65040	.63872	.62733	.61622	.60538	.59480	.58447	.57439	.56455
76	.67581	.66416	.65279	.64168	.63083	.62023	.60988	.59977	.58989	.58023
77	.68925	.67793	.66688	.65606	.64550	.63516	.62506	.61517	.60551	.59605
78	.70263	.69166	.68093	.67044	.66016	.65010	.64026	.63062	.62119	.61195
79	.71585	.70525	.69486	.68468	.67471	.66495	.65538	.64600	.63681	.62780
80	.72885	.71860	.70856	.69872	.68906	.67959	.67031	.66120	.65227	.64350
81	.74150	.73162	.72193	.71242	.70308	.69392	.68492	.67609	.66742	.65890
82	.75376	.74425	.73490	.72572	.71671	.70785	.69915	.69059	.68219	.67393
83	.76559	.75643	.74744	.73859	.72989	.72134	.71293	.70466	.69652	.68852
84	.77700	.76821	.75955	.75104	.74266	.73441	.72629	.71831	.71044	.70270
85	.78805	.77961	.77130	.76311	.75505	.74711	.73929	.73158	.72399	.71652
86	.79866	.79056	.78258	.77472	.76697	.75933	.75180	.74438	.73707	.72985
87	.80870	.80094	.79329	.78574	.77829	.77095	.76370	.75656	.74951	.74255
88	.81825	.81081	.80348	.79623	.78908	.78202	.77506	.76818	.76139	.75469
89	.82746	.82035	.81332	.80638	.79952	.79275	.78606	.77945	.77292	.76647
90	.83643	.82963	.82291	.81627	.80971	.80322	.79681	.79047	.78420	.77801
91	.84503	.83854	.83212	.82578	.81950	.81330	.80716	.80109	.79509	.78915
92	.85308	.84689	.84076	.83470	.82870	.82276	.81689	.81107	.80532	.79963
93	.86052	.85460	.84875	.84295	.83721	.83152	.82590	.82033	.81481	.80935
94	.86729	.86163	.85602	.85046	.84496	.83951	.83412	.82877	.82348	.81823
95	.87338	.86795	.86257	.85723	.85195	.84672	.84153	.83639	.83129	.82624
96	.87877	.87354	.86836	.86323	.85814	.85309	.84809	.84313	.83822	.83334
97	.88365	.87861	.87362	.86867	.86375	.85888	.85405	.84926	.84450	.83979
98	.88805	.88318	.87835	.87356	.86880	.86409	.85941	.85477	.85016	.84559
99	.89210	.88739	.88271	.87807	.87347	.86890	.86436	.85986	.85539	.85095
100	.89588	.89131	.88678	.88227	.87780	.87337	.86896	.86459	.86024	.85593
101	.89949	.89506	.89066	.88629	.88195	.87764	.87336	.86911	.86488	.86069
102	.90325	.89897	.89471	.89047	.88627	.88209	.87794	.87381	.86971	.86564
103	.90724	.90311	.89900	.89491	.89085	.88681	.88279	.87880	.87484	.87089
104	.91167	.90770	.90376	.89983	.89593	.89205	.88819	.88435	.88053	.87673
105	.91708	.91333	.90959	.90587	.90217	.89848	.89481	.89116	.88752	.88391
106	.92470	.92126	.91782	.91440	.91100	.90760	.90422	.90085	.89749	.89414
107	.93545	.93246	.92948	.92650	.92353	.92057	.91762	.91467	.91173	.90880
108	.95239	.95016	.94792	.94569	.94346	.94123	.93900	.93678	.93456	.93234
109	.97900	.97800	.97700	.97600	.97500	.97400	.97300	.97200	.97100	.97000

Table U(1) effective 5-1-89.

Table U(1)　*BASED ON LIFE TABLE 80CNSMT UNITRUST SINGLE LIFE REMAINDER FACTORS ADJUSTED PAYOUT RATE*

Age	6.2%	6.4%	6.6%	6.8%	7.0%	7.2%	7.4%	7.6%	7.8%	8.0%
0	.03176	.03009	.02861	.02730	.02613	.02509	.02416	.02333	.02258	.02191
1	.02110	.01936	.01781	.01644	.01522	.01413	.01316	.01229	.01150	.01080
2	.02156	.01974	.01812	.01669	.01541	.01427	.01325	.01234	.01152	.01078
3	.02233	.02043	.01875	.01725	.01591	.01471	.01364	.01268	.01182	.01105
4	.02330	.02132	.01956	.01800	.01660	.01535	.01422	.01322	.01231	.01149
5	.02443	.02237	.02054	.01890	.01743	.01612	.01494	.01389	.01293	.01208
6	.02568	.02353	.02162	.01990	.01837	.01700	.01576	.01465	.01365	.01275
7	.02704	.02480	.02280	.02102	.01941	.01798	.01668	.01552	.01446	.01351
8	.02852	.02619	.02411	.02224	.02057	.01906	.01770	.01648	.01537	.01437
9	.03014	.02772	.02554	.02360	.02184	.02027	.01885	.01756	.01640	.01535
10	.03190	.02938	.02711	.02508	.02325	.02160	.02012	.01877	.01755	.01645
11	.03381	.03119	.02883	.02672	.02481	.02308	.02153	.02012	.01884	.01768
12	.03585	.03313	.03068	.02847	.02648	.02468	.02305	.02157	.02023	.01902
13	.03798	.03515	.03260	.03030	.02822	.02635	.02464	.02310	.02170	.02042
14	.04012	.03718	.03453	.03213	.02997	.02801	.02623	.02462	.02315	.02181
15	.04225	.03919	.03644	.03395	.03169	.02965	.02779	.02611	.02457	.02317
16	.04436	.04120	.03833	.03574	.03339	.03126	.02932	.02756	.02595	.02449
17	.04647	.04319	.04021	.03752	.03507	.03285	.03082	.02898	.02730	.02577
18	.04860	.04519	.04210	.03930	.03675	.03443	.03232	.03040	.02864	.02703
19	.05079	.04725	.04404	.04113	.03847	.03606	.03386	.03185	.03001	.02833
20	.05304	.04938	.04604	.04301	.04025	.03773	.03543	.03333	.03141	.02965
21	.05537	.05157	.04811	.04495	.04208	.03945	.03705	.03486	.03285	.03101
22	.05779	.05385	.05025	.04698	.04398	.04125	.03874	.03645	.03435	.03242
23	.06032	.05623	.05250	.04910	.04598	.04313	.04052	.03812	.03592	.03390
24	.06302	.05878	.05491	.05136	.04812	.04515	.04242	.03992	.03762	.03550
25	.06589	.06150	.05748	.05380	.05042	.04733	.04448	.04187	.03946	.03725
26	.06897	.06442	.06025	.05643	.05292	.04969	.04673	.04400	.04148	.03916
27	.07228	.06757	.06325	.05928	.05563	.05227	.04917	.04632	.04369	.04126
28	.07582	.07094	.06646	.06234	.05854	.05504	.05182	.04884	.04609	.04355
29	.07958	.07454	.06990	.06562	.06167	.05804	.05468	.05157	.04870	.04604
30	.08360	.07838	.07357	.06913	.06504	.06125	.05775	.05452	.05152	.04874
31	.08788	.08249	.07751	.07291	.06866	.06472	.06108	.05771	.05457	.05167
32	.09242	.08685	.08170	.07694	.07252	.06844	.06465	.06113	.05786	.05483
33	.09724	.09149	.08617	.08124	.07666	.07242	.06848	.06482	.06141	.05824
34	.10234	.09641	.09091	.08581	.08107	.07667	.07257	.06876	.06521	.06191
35	.10773	.10161	.09594	.09066	.08575	.08119	.07694	.07298	.06928	.06583
36	.11338	.10708	.10122	.09577	.09070	.08597	.08156	.07744	.07360	.07001
37	.11932	.11283	.10680	.10117	.09592	.09102	.08645	.08217	.07818	.07444
38	.12554	.11887	.11265	.10685	.10142	.09636	.09162	.08719	.08304	.07915
39	.13206	.12521	.11880	.11282	.10722	.10198	.09708	.09249	.08818	.08414
40	.13888	.13184	.12526	.11909	.11332	.10791	.10284	.09808	.09361	.08942
41	.14601	.13878	.13201	.12567	.11972	.11414	.10890	.10398	.09935	.09499
42	.15342	.14601	.13906	.13254	.12641	.12066	.11525	.11016	.10537	.10086
43	.16112	.15353	.14640	.13970	.13340	.12747	.12189	.11663	.11168	.10701
44	.16913	.16136	.15406	.14718	.14070	.13460	.12885	.12342	.11830	.11347
45	.17745	.16951	.16202	.15497	.14832	.14204	.13612	.13053	.12525	.12025
46	.18608	.17796	.17030	.16308	.15625	.14981	.14372	.13796	.13251	.12735
47	.19501	.18673	.17890	.17150	.16451	.15790	.15164	.14571	.14010	.13478
48	.20425	.19579	.18780	.18024	.17308	.16630	.15987	.15378	.14800	.14252
49	.21375	.20514	.19698	.18926	.18193	.17499	.16840	.16214	.15620	.15056
50	.22352	.21476	.20644	.19856	.19107	.18396	.17721	.17080	.16470	.15890
51	.23358	.22467	.21620	.20816	.20051	.19325	.18634	.17976	.17350	.16755
52	.24396	.23490	.22628	.21809	.21030	.20288	.19581	.18908	.18267	.17655
53	.25465	.24545	.23670	.22836	.22042	.21285	.20563	.19875	.19218	.18592
54	.26563	.25631	.24742	.23895	.23086	.22315	.21579	.20876	.20204	.19562

Table U(1) *(continued)*

Age	6.2%	6.4%	6.6%	6.8%	7.0%	7.2%	7.4%	7.6%	7.8%	8.0%
55	.27692	.26747	.25846	.24986	.24164	.23379	.22628	.21911	.21225	.20568
56	.28850	.27895	.26982	.26109	.25275	.24476	.23712	.22981	.22281	.21611
57	.30041	.29076	.28152	.27267	.26421	.25610	.24833	.24089	.23376	.22691
58	.31263	.30288	.29355	.28460	.27602	.26780	.25991	.25234	.24508	.23811
59	.32515	.31532	.30590	.29685	.28817	.27984	.27184	.26416	.25677	.24968
60	.33793	.32803	.31853	.30940	.30062	.29219	.28409	.27630	.26880	.26159
61	.35093	.34098	.33141	.32220	.31335	.30483	.29663	.28873	.28113	.27381
62	.36414	.35414	.34451	.33524	.32631	.31771	.30942	.30144	.29374	.28631
63	.37754	.36750	.35783	.34850	.33951	.33084	.32247	.31440	.30661	.29910
64	.39115	.38108	.37137	.36200	.35296	.34422	.33579	.32765	.31978	.31217
65	.40500	.39493	.38519	.37579	.36670	.35792	.34943	.34122	.33328	.32560
66	.41914	.40906	.39932	.38990	.38079	.37197	.36343	.35517	.34717	.33943
67	.43355	.42350	.41376	.40434	.39521	.38636	.37780	.36950	.36145	.35365
68	.44824	.43822	.42851	.41909	.40996	.40111	.39252	.38419	.37611	.36827
69	.46313	.45316	.44348	.43409	.42498	.41613	.40754	.39919	.39109	.38322
70	.47818	.46827	.45864	.44929	.44020	.43137	.42279	.41445	.40634	.39845
71	.49331	.48348	.47391	.46461	.45557	.44677	.43821	.42988	.42177	.41388
72	.50853	.49879	.48930	.48007	.47108	.46233	.45380	.44550	.43741	.42952
73	.52384	.51421	.50482	.49566	.48674	.47805	.46957	.46130	.45324	.44538
74	.53930	.52979	.52050	.51145	.50261	.49399	.48557	.47736	.46934	.46152
75	.55495	.54557	.53641	.52747	.51873	.51020	.50187	.49372	.48577	.47799
76	.57079	.56157	.55256	.54374	.53513	.52670	.51847	.51041	.50253	.49483
77	.58680	.57775	.56890	.56024	.55176	.54346	.53534	.52739	.51960	.51198
78	.60291	.59405	.58537	.57687	.56855	.56040	.55241	.54458	.53691	.52940
79	.61898	.61032	.60184	.59353	.58537	.57738	.56954	.56185	.55431	.54691
80	.63491	.62647	.61819	.61007	.60210	.59428	.58660	.57907	.57167	.56441
81	.65054	.64234	.63427	.62636	.61858	.61094	.60344	.59606	.58882	.58170
82	.66582	.65784	.65000	.64229	.63472	.62727	.61994	.61274	.60566	.59870
83	.68065	.67291	.66530	.65781	.65044	.64319	.63605	.62903	.62212	.61532
84	.69508	.68758	.68020	.67293	.66577	.65872	.65178	.64495	.63821	.63158
85	.70915	.70190	.69475	.68770	.68076	.67392	.66718	.66054	.65399	.64754
86	.72274	.71573	.70882	.70200	.69528	.68865	.68212	.67567	.66931	.66304
87	.73569	.72892	.72224	.71565	.70915	.70273	.69639	.69014	.68397	.67788
88	.74807	.74154	.73509	.72872	.72243	.71622	.71009	.70403	.69805	.69214
89	.76010	.75381	.74759	.74144	.73537	.72937	.72344	.71758	.71179	.70607
90	.77189	.76584	.75985	.75394	.74809	.74230	.73659	.73093	.72534	.71981
91	.78327	.77746	.77171	.76603	.76040	.75484	.74933	.74388	.73850	.73316
92	.79399	.78841	.78289	.77743	.77202	.76667	.76137	.75613	.75093	.74579
93	.80394	.79858	.79328	.78803	.78283	.77768	.77258	.76753	.76252	.75757
94	.81303	.80788	.80278	.79773	.79272	.78776	.78284	.77797	.77315	.76837
95	.82124	.81628	.81163	.80649	.80166	.79687	.79213	.78742	.78276	.77814
96	.82851	.82372	.81897	.81426	.80959	.80496	.80036	.79581	.79129	.78682
97	.83512	.83048	.82588	.82132	.81679	.81230	.80785	.80343	.79905	.79471
98	.84106	.83656	.83210	.82767	.82328	.81892	.81459	.81030	.80604	.80181
99	.84655	.84218	.83785	.83354	.82927	.82503	.82082	.81664	.81249	.80837
100	.85165	.84740	.84318	.83899	.83483	.83070	.82660	.82252	.81848	.81446
101	.85652	.85238	.84827	.84419	.84013	.83611	.83210	.82813	.82418	.82026
102	.86159	.85757	.85358	.84960	.84566	.84174	.83784	.83397	.83012	.82630
103	.86697	.86307	.85920	.85535	.85152	.84771	.84392	.84016	.83642	.83270
104	.87295	.86919	.86544	.86172	.85802	.85434	.85068	.84704	.84341	.83981
105	.88030	.87672	.87315	.86959	.86605	.86253	.85903	.85554	.85207	.84861
106	.89081	.88749	.88418	.88088	.87760	.87433	.87106	.86782	.86458	.86135
107	.90588	.90296	.90005	.89715	.89425	.89137	.88849	.88561	.88275	.87989
108	.93013	.92791	.92570	.92350	.92129	.91909	.91689	.91469	.91250	.91031
109	.96900	.96800	.96700	.96600	.96500	.96400	.96300	.96200	.96100	.96000

Table U(1)   BASED ON LIFE TABLE 80CNSMT UNITRUST SINGLE LIFE REMAINDER FACTORS ADJUSTED PAYOUT RATE

Age	8.2%	8.4%	8.6%	8.8%	9.0%	9.2%	9.4%	9.6%	9.8%	10.0%
0	.02130	.02075	.02025	.01980	.01939	.01901	.01867	.01835	.01806	.01779
1	.01017	.00960	.00908	.00861	.00819	.00780	.00745	.00712	.00683	.00655
2	.01011	.00951	.00897	.00848	.00803	.00762	.00725	.00690	.00659	.00630
3	.01035	.00971	.00914	.00862	.00815	.00771	.00732	.00696	.00663	.00632
4	.01076	.01009	.00948	.00894	.00843	.00798	.00756	.00718	.00683	.00650
5	.01130	.01059	.00996	.00938	.00885	.00836	.00792	.00752	.00714	.00680
6	.01193	.01119	.01051	.00990	.00934	.00883	.00836	.00793	.00754	.00717
7	.01265	.01187	.01116	.01051	.00992	.00938	.00888	.00842	.00800	.00762
8	.01347	.01264	.01189	.01121	.01058	.01001	.00948	.00900	.00856	.00815
9	.01440	.01353	.01274	.01201	.01135	.01075	.01019	.00968	.00921	.00877
10	.01544	.01453	.01369	.01293	.01223	.01159	.01101	.01046	.00997	.00950
11	.01662	.01566	.01478	.01398	.01324	.01257	.01195	.01137	.01085	.01036
12	.01791	.01690	.01597	.01513	.01435	.01364	.01298	.01238	.01182	.01131
13	.01926	.01820	.01722	.01634	.01552	.01477	.01408	.01344	.01285	.01231
14	.02059	.01948	.01846	.01752	.01667	.01588	.01515	.01448	.01386	.01328
15	.02189	.02072	.01965	.01867	.01777	.01694	.01617	.10547	.01481	.01421
16	.02315	.02192	.02080	.01977	.01882	.01795	.01714	.01640	.01572	.01508
17	.02436	.02308	.02190	.02082	.01982	.01891	.01806	.01728	.01656	.01589
18	.02556	.02422	.02298	.02184	.02080	.01983	.01894	.01812	.01736	.01665
19	.02679	.02537	.02408	.02288	.02178	.02077	.01983	.01897	.01817	.01742
20	.02804	.02656	.02519	.02394	.02278	.02172	.02073	.01982	.01898	.01819
21	.02932	.02776	.02633	.02501	.02380	.02268	.02164	.02068	.01979	.01896
22	.03065	.02902	.02751	.02613	.02485	.02367	.02258	.02157	.02063	.01976
23	.03204	.03033	.02876	.02730	.02595	.02471	.02356	.02249	.02150	.02058
24	.03356	.03176	.03010	.02857	.02716	.02585	.02463	.02351	.02246	.02149
25	.03520	.03332	.03158	.02997	.02848	.02710	.02582	.02463	.02352	.02249
26	.03702	.03504	.03321	.03152	.02995	.02850	.02714	.02589	.02472	.02363
27	.03902	.03695	.03502	.03324	.03159	.03006	.02863	.02730	.02607	.02492
28	.04120	.03902	.03700	.03513	.03339	.03178	.03027	.02887	.02757	.02635
29	.04358	.04129	.03917	.03720	.03537	.03367	.03208	.03061	.02923	.02794
30	.04616	.04376	.04154	.03947	.03754	.03575	.03408	.03251	.03106	.02969
31	.04897	.04646	.04413	.04195	.03993	.03804	.03627	.03463	.03309	.03165
32	.05200	.04938	.04693	.04465	.04252	.04053	.03867	.03693	.03531	.03378
33	.05529	.05254	.04998	.04758	.04534	.04325	.04130	.03946	.03775	.03614
34	.05883	.05595	.05326	.05075	.04840	.04620	.04414	.04221	.04040	.03870
35	.06262	.05961	.05680	.05417	.05170	.04939	.04723	.04520	.04329	.04149
36	.06665	.06351	.06057	.05781	.05523	.05280	.05053	.04839	.04638	.04449
37	.07094	.06766	.06459	.06171	.05900	.05646	.05407	.05182	.04971	.04771
38	.07550	.07208	.06888	.06586	.06303	.06037	.05786	.05550	.05327	.05118
39	.08034	.07678	.07344	.07029	.06733	.06454	.06191	.05943	.05709	.05489
40	.08547	.08177	.07828	.07499	.07190	.06898	.06623	.06363	.06118	.05886
41	.09090	.08704	.08341	.07998	.07675	.07371	.07083	.06811	.06553	.06310
42	.09661	.09260	.08882	.08525	.08188	.07870	.07569	.07284	.07015	.06760
43	.10260	.09844	.09451	.09080	.08729	.08397	.08083	.07785	.07503	.07236
44	.10891	.10459	.10051	.09666	.09300	.08954	.08626	.08316	.08021	.07741
45	.11553	.11106	.10683	.10282	.09902	.09542	.09201	.08876	.08568	.08276
46	.12247	.11784	.11346	.10930	.10536	.10161	.09806	.09468	.09146	.08841
47	.12974	.12496	.12042	.11611	.11202	.10813	.10443	.10091	.09756	.09438
48	.13732	.13238	.12769	.12323	.11899	.11495	.11111	.10745	.10397	.10065
49	.14520	.14011	.13526	.13064	.12625	.12207	.11809	.11429	.11066	.10721
50	.15338	.14812	.14312	.13836	.13381	.12948	.12535	.12141	.11765	.11405
51	.16187	.15646	.15130	.14639	.14169	.13721	.13294	.12885	.12495	.12121
52	.17072	.16516	.15985	.15478	.14993	.14531	.14088	.13665	.13261	.12873
53	.17993	.17422	.16876	.16353	.15854	.15377	.14920	.14482	.14064	.13662
54	.18949	.18362	.17801	.17264	.16750	.16258	.15787	.15335	.14902	.14486

Table U(1)   (continued)

Age	8.2%	8.4%	8.6%	8.8%	9.0%	9.2%	9.4%	9.6%	9.8%	10.0%
55	.19940	.19339	.18763	.18212	.17683	.17176	.16690	.16224	.15777	.15348
56	.20968	.20353	.19762	.19196	.18654	.18132	.17632	.17152	.16691	.16247
57	.22035	.21406	.20802	.20222	.19665	.19129	.18615	.18121	.17646	.17189
58	.23142	.22499	.21881	.21287	.20717	.20168	.19640	.19132	.18643	.18172
59	.24286	.23630	.23000	.22393	.21809	.21247	.20705	.20184	.19682	.19198
60	.25465	.24797	.24154	.23534	.22938	.22363	.21808	.21274	.20759	.20262
61	.26676	.25996	.25341	.24710	.24101	.23513	.22946	.22399	.21871	.21361
62	.27916	.27225	.26559	.25916	.25295	.24695	.24117	.23557	.23017	.22495
63	.29184	.28483	.27806	.27152	.26520	.25909	.25319	.24748	.24196	.23661
64	.30483	.29772	.29085	.28421	.27779	.27157	.26555	.25973	.25409	.24863
65	.31817	.31098	.30402	.29729	.29076	.28444	.27832	.27240	.26665	.26108
66	.33192	.32466	.31762	.31079	.30418	.29777	.29155	.28552	.27968	.27400
67	.34609	.33876	.33164	.32474	.31805	.31156	.30525	.29913	.29319	.28742
68	.36066	.35328	.34610	.33914	.33238	.32581	.31943	.31323	.30720	.30134
69	.37558	.36815	.36093	.35391	.34709	.34045	.33400	.32773	.32163	.31569
70	.39078	.38332	.37606	.36900	.36213	.35545	.34894	.34260	.33643	.33042
71	.40620	.39872	.39144	.38435	.37744	.37071	.36415	.35776	.35153	.34547
72	.42184	.41435	.40706	.39994	.39301	.38625	.37965	.37322	.36694	.36082
73	.43771	.43023	.42293	.41581	.40886	.40207	.39545	.38899	.38267	.37651
74	.45387	.44641	.43912	.43201	.42505	.41826	.41163	.40514	.39881	.39261
75	.47039	.46296	.45570	.44861	.44167	.43488	.42824	.42175	.41541	.40920
76	.48729	.47991	.47269	.46563	.45872	.45196	.44534	.43886	.43251	.42630
77	.50452	.49722	.49006	.48305	.47619	.46946	.46287	.45642	.45009	.44389
78	.52203	.51481	.50773	.50079	.49399	.48732	.48078	.47437	.46808	.46191
79	.53966	.53254	.52556	.51870	.51198	.50538	.49891	.49255	.48632	.48019
80	.55728	.55028	.54340	.53665	.53002	.52351	.51712	.51083	.50466	.49860
81	.57471	.56784	.56109	.55445	.54792	.54151	.53521	.52901	.52292	.51692
82	.59186	.58512	.57850	.57199	.56558	.55927	.55307	.54697	.54097	.53506
83	.60863	.60204	.59556	.58918	.58289	.57671	.57062	.56462	.55872	.55290
84	.62505	.61862	.61228	.60604	.59989	.59383	.58786	.58198	.57618	.57047
85	.64118	.63491	.62873	.62263	.61663	.61070	.60486	.59911	.59343	.58783
86	.65685	.65075	.64473	.63879	.63294	.62716	.62145	.61583	.61027	.60479
87	.67187	.66594	.66008	.65430	.64859	.64296	.63739	.63190	.62647	.62112
88	.68631	.68054	.67485	.66923	.66367	.65818	.65276	.64740	.64211	.63688
89	.70042	.69483	.68930	.68384	.67845	.67311	.66784	.66262	.65747	.65237
90	.71434	.70894	.70359	.69830	.69307	.68790	.68278	.67772	.67271	.66775
91	.72789	.72266	.71750	.71239	.70733	.70232	.69736	.69246	.68760	.68280
92	.74070	.73567	.73068	.72574	.72085	.71601	.71121	.70647	.70176	.69711
93	.75266	.74780	.74298	.73821	.73348	.72880	.72417	.71957	.71502	.71051
94	.76363	.75893	.75428	.74967	.74510	.74057	.73608	.73163	.72722	.72285
95	.77356	.76901	.76451	.76005	.75562	.75123	.74688	.74257	.73829	.73405
96	.78237	.77797	.77360	.76927	.76497	.76071	.75648	.75229	.74813	.74401
97	.79039	.78612	.78187	.77766	.77348	.76934	.76523	.76115	.75710	.75308
98	.79762	.79345	.78932	.78522	.78115	.77711	.77310	.76913	.76518	.76126
99	.80429	.80023	.79620	.79220	.78823	.78429	.78038	.77649	.77264	.76881
100	.81047	.80651	.80258	.79867	.79479	.79094	.78712	.78332	.77955	.77580
101	.81636	.81249	.80865	.80483	.80104	.79727	.79352	.78981	.78611	.78244
102	.82250	.81872	.81497	.81124	.80754	.80386	.80020	.79656	.79295	.78936
103	.82900	.82532	.82167	.81804	.81442	.81083	.80726	.80371	.80018	.79667
104	.83622	.83266	.82911	.82558	.82207	.81858	.81510	.81165	.80821	.80479
105	.84517	.84174	.83833	.83494	.83156	.82819	.82485	.82151	.81820	.81489
106	.85814	.85494	.85175	.84857	.84540	.84225	.83911	.83598	.83286	.82975
107	.87704	.87420	.87136	.86853	.86571	.86290	.86009	.85729	.85450	.85171
108	.90812	.90593	.90375	.90156	.89939	.89721	.89504	.89286	.89070	.88853
109	.95900	.95800	.95700	.95600	.95500	.95400	.95300	.95200	.95100	.95000

Table U(1) BASED ON LIFE TABLE 80CNSMT UNITRUST SINGLE LIFE
REMAINDER FACTORS ADJUSTED PAYOUT RATE

Age	10.2%	10.4%	10.6%	10.8%	11.0%	11.2%	11.4%	11.6%	11.8%	12.0%
0	.01754	.01731	.01710	.01690	.01671	.01654	.01638	.01622	.01608	.01594
1	.00630	.00607	.00585	.00565	.00547	.00530	.00514	.00499	.00485	.00472
2	.00604	.00579	.00557	.00536	.00516	.00498	.00481	.00465	.00451	.00437
3	.00604	.00578	.00554	.00532	.00511	.00492	.00474	.00458	.00442	.00427
4	.00621	.00593	.00568	.00544	.00522	.00502	.00483	.00465	.00448	.00433
5	.00648	.00619	.00592	.00567	.00544	.00522	.00502	.00483	.00465	.00449
6	.00684	.00653	.00624	.00597	.00572	.00549	.00528	.00507	.00489	.00471
7	.00726	.00693	.00663	.00634	.00608	.00583	.00560	.00539	.00518	.00499
8	.00777	.00742	.00709	.00679	.00651	.00624	.00600	.00577	.00555	.00535
9	.00837	.00800	.00765	.00733	.00703	.00675	.00649	.00625	.00602	.00580
10	.00908	.00868	.00832	.00797	.00765	.00736	.00708	.00682	.00657	.00634
11	.00991	.00949	.00910	.00874	.00840	.00808	.00779	.00751	.00725	.00700
12	.01083	.01039	.00997	.00959	.00923	.00890	.00858	.00829	.00801	.00775
13	.01181	.01134	.01090	.01049	.01012	.00976	.00943	.00912	.00883	.00855
14	.01275	.01226	.01180	.01137	.01097	.01060	.01025	.00992	.00961	.00932
15	.01365	.01313	.01264	.01219	.01177	.01138	.01101	.01066	.01034	.01003
16	.01449	.01394	.01343	.01295	.01251	.01209	.01171	.01134	.01100	.01068
17	.01526	.01469	.01415	.01365	.01318	.01274	.01233	.01195	.01159	.01125
18	.01600	.01539	.01482	.01430	.01380	.01334	.01291	.01251	.01213	.01177
19	.01673	.01609	.01550	.01494	.01442	.01393	.01348	.01305	.01265	.01227
20	.01747	.01679	.01616	.01557	.01502	.01451	.01403	.01358	.01316	.01276
21	.01820	.01748	.01682	.01620	.01562	.01508	.01457	.01409	.01365	.01323
22	.01895	.01819	.01749	.01683	.01622	.01565	.01511	.01461	.01414	.01369
23	.01972	.01893	.01818	.01749	.01684	.01624	.01567	.01514	.01464	.01417
24	.02058	.01974	.01895	.01822	.01753	.01689	.01629	.01572	.01519	.01469
25	.02154	.02064	.01981	.01903	.01830	.01762	.01698	.01638	.01582	.01529
26	.02262	.02167	.02079	.01996	.01919	.01847	.01779	.01715	.01655	.01599
27	.02385	.02284	.02191	.02103	.02021	.01944	.01872	.01804	.01740	.01680
28	.02521	.02415	.02316	.02222	.02135	.02053	.01977	.01904	.01836	.01772
29	.02673	.02561	.02455	.02357	.02264	.02177	.02095	.02018	.01946	.01877
30	.02842	.02723	.02611	.02506	.02407	.02315	.02227	.02146	.02068	.01996
31	.03030	.02903	.02784	.02673	.02568	.02470	.02377	.02290	.02207	.02130
32	.03235	.03101	.02976	.02857	.02746	.02641	.02543	.02450	.02362	.02279
33	.03463	.03321	.03188	.03062	.02944	.02833	.02728	.02629	.02535	.02447
34	.03711	.03561	.03419	.03286	.03161	.03043	.02931	.02826	.02726	.02632
35	.03981	.03822	.03672	.03531	.03398	.03273	.03154	.03042	.02936	.02836
36	.04271	.04103	.03945	.03796	.03655	.03522	.03396	.03277	.03164	.03057
37	.04584	.04407	.04239	.04081	.03932	.03791	.03657	.03531	.03411	.03297
38	.04920	.04733	.04556	.04389	.04231	.04082	.03940	.03806	.03679	.03558
39	.05280	.05083	.04897	.04721	.04554	.04396	.04246	.04103	.03968	.03840
40	.05667	.05459	.05263	.05077	.04901	.04733	.04575	.04424	.04280	.04144
41	.06080	.05861	.05655	.05459	.05272	.05096	.04928	.04768	.04617	.04472
42	.06518	.06289	.06071	.05864	.05668	.05482	.05305	.05136	.04975	.04822
43	.06982	.06742	.06513	.06296	.06089	.05893	.05706	.05528	.05358	.05196
44	.07475	.07223	.06983	.06754	.06537	.06330	.06133	.05945	.05766	.05595
45	.07998	.07733	.07481	.07242	.07014	.06796	.06588	.06390	.06202	.06021
46	.08550	.08273	.08010	.07758	.07519	.07290	.07072	.06864	.06665	.06474
47	.09134	.08845	.08569	.08306	.08055	.07815	.07586	.07367	.07157	.06957
48	.09748	.09446	.09158	.08882	.08619	.08368	.08128	.07898	.07678	.07467
49	.10391	.10076	.09775	.09487	.09212	.08949	.08697	.08456	.08225	.08003
50	.11062	.10734	.10420	.10120	.09832	.09557	.09293	.09041	.08798	.08566
51	.11764	.11423	.11096	.10783	.10483	.10195	.09919	.09655	.09401	.09158
52	.12503	.12148	.11807	.11481	.11168	.10868	.10581	.10304	.10039	.09784
53	.13278	.12909	.12556	.12216	.11891	.11578	.11278	.10989	.10712	.10445
54	.14088	.13706	.13339	.12986	.12648	.12322	.12009	.11709	.11419	.11141

Table U(1) (continued)

Age	10.2%	10.4%	10.6%	10.8%	11.0%	11.2%	11.4%	11.6%	11.8%	12.0%
55	.14936	.14540	.14159	.13793	.13442	.13103	.12778	.12464	.12163	.11872
56	.15821	.15412	.15018	.14639	.14274	.13923	.13584	.13258	.12944	.12642
57	.16749	.16326	.15918	.15526	.15148	.14784	.14433	.14094	.13768	.13453
58	.17719	.17282	.16862	.16456	.16065	.15688	.15324	.14973	.14634	.14306
59	.18731	.18281	.17847	.17429	.17025	.16634	.16258	.15894	.15543	.15203
60	.19782	.19319	.18872	.18440	.18023	.17621	.17231	.16855	.16491	.16139
61	.20869	.20393	.19934	.19489	.19060	.18644	.18242	.17854	.17477	.17113
62	.21990	.21502	.21029	.20573	.20131	.19703	.19289	.18887	.18499	.18123
63	.23144	.22644	.22159	.21690	.21236	.20796	.20370	.19956	.19556	.19167
64	.24335	.23823	.23326	.22845	.22379	.21927	.21489	.21063	.20651	.20250
65	.25568	.25045	.24537	.24044	.23566	.23103	.22653	.22216	.21791	.21379
66	.26850	.26316	.25797	.25293	.24804	.24329	.23868	.23420	.22984	.22560
67	.28182	.27637	.27108	.26594	.26095	.25609	.25137	.24678	.24231	.23797
68	.29565	.29011	.28472	.27949	.27439	.26943	.26461	.25991	.25534	.25089
69	.30991	.30429	.29882	.29349	.28830	.28325	.27833	.27354	.26887	.26432
70	.32457	.31887	.31332	.30791	.30264	.29750	.29249	.28760	.28284	.27820
71	.33955	.33378	.32816	.32267	.31732	.31210	.30701	.30204	.29719	.29246
72	.35485	.34902	.34333	.33778	.33236	.32707	.32190	.31686	.31193	.30711
73	.37049	.36461	.35887	.35326	.34778	.34242	.33719	.33207	.32707	.32218
74	.38656	.38064	.37485	.36920	.36366	.35825	.35296	.34778	.34272	.33776
75	.40312	.39717	.39136	.38566	.38009	.37464	.36930	.36407	.35895	.35394
76	.42022	.41426	.40842	.40271	.39711	.39163	.38625	.38099	.37583	.37077
77	.43782	.43187	.42603	.42031	.41470	.40920	.40380	.39851	.39332	.38823
78	.45586	.44992	.44410	.43839	.43278	.42728	.42188	.41658	.41138	.40627
79	.47418	.46828	.46248	.45679	.45120	.44572	.44033	.43503	.42983	.42472
80	.49264	.48679	.48103	.47538	.46982	.46436	.45900	.45372	.44853	.44343
81	.51103	.50524	.49954	.49394	.48843	.48301	.47768	.47243	.46727	.46219
82	.52925	.52352	.51789	.51235	.50690	.50153	.49624	.49104	.48591	.48087
83	.54718	.54154	.53598	.53051	.52512	.51981	.51459	.50943	.50436	.49936
84	.56484	.55930	.55383	.54844	.54313	.53789	.53273	.52764	.52262	.51767
85	.58231	.57686	.57149	.56619	.56096	.55581	.55072	.54571	.54076	.53588
86	.59939	.59405	.58878	.58358	.57845	.57339	.56839	.56346	.55858	.55377
87	.61583	.61061	.60545	.60035	.59532	.59035	.58545	.58060	.57581	.57108
88	.63171	.62661	.62156	.61658	.61165	.60678	.60196	.59721	.59251	.58786
89	.64733	.64235	.63742	.63255	.62774	.62298	.61827	.61361	.60900	.60444
90	.66285	.65801	.65321	.64847	.64377	.63913	.63453	.62998	.62548	.62103
91	.67804	.67334	.66868	.66407	.65950	.65498	.65050	.64607	.64169	.63735
92	.69250	.68793	.68341	.67893	.67450	.67011	.66575	.66144	.65718	.65295
93	.70604	.70162	.69723	.69288	.68858	.68431	.68008	.67589	.67174	.66762
94	.71852	.71422	.70997	.70575	.70156	.69742	.69331	.68923	.68519	.68119
95	.72984	.72567	.72154	.71744	.71337	.70934	.70534	.70137	.69744	.69354
96	.73992	.73586	.73183	.72784	.72388	.71995	.71605	.71218	.70835	.70454
97	.74910	.74514	.74122	.73733	.73346	.72963	.72582	.72205	.71830	.71458
98	.75737	.75351	.74967	.74587	.74209	.73835	.73463	.73093	.72727	.72363
99	.76501	.76123	.75748	.75376	.75007	.74640	.74276	.73914	.73555	.73198
100	.77208	.76838	.76471	.76107	.75745	.75385	.75028	.74673	.74321	.73971
101	.77879	.77517	.77157	.76800	.76444	.76092	.75741	.75392	.75046	.74702
102	.78579	.78224	.77871	.77521	.77173	.76827	.76483	.76141	.75801	.75463
103	.79318	.78971	.78626	.78283	.77942	.77604	.77266	.76931	.76598	.76267
104	.80139	.79801	.79464	.79129	.78796	.78465	.78136	.77808	.77482	.77157
105	.81161	.80834	.80508	.80184	.79861	.79540	.79220	.78902	.78585	.78270
106	.82665	.82357	.82049	.81743	.81438	.81134	.80831	.80530	.80229	.79930
107	.84893	.84616	.84340	.84064	.83789	.83515	.83241	.82969	.82696	.82425
108	.88637	.88421	.88205	.87989	.87774	.87559	.87344	.87129	.86915	.86701
109	.94900	.94800	.94700	.94600	.94500	.94400	.94300	.94200	.94100	.94000

Table U(1) *BASED ON LIFE TABLE 80CNSMT UNITRUST SINGLE LIFE REMAINDER FACTORS ADJUSTED PAYOUT RATE*

Age	12.2%	12.4%	12.6%	12.8%	13.0%	13.2%	13.4%	13.6%	13.8%	14.0%
0	.01581	.01569	.01557	.01546	.01536	.01526	.01516	.01507	.01499	.01490
1	.00459	.00448	.00437	.00426	.00417	.00407	.00399	.00390	.00382	.00375
2	.00424	.00412	.00400	.00389	.00379	.00369	.00360	.00352	.00343	.00335
3	.00414	.00401	.00389	.00377	.00366	.00356	.00346	.00337	.00328	.00320
4	.00418	.00404	.00391	.00379	.00368	.00357	.00347	.00337	.00327	.00319
5	.00433	.00418	.00405	.00391	.00379	.00368	.00357	.00346	.00336	.00327
6	.00454	.00439	.00424	.00410	.00397	.00384	.00372	.00361	.00351	.00341
7	.00482	.00465	.00449	.00434	.00420	.00407	.00394	.00382	.00371	.00360
8	.00516	.00498	.00481	.00465	.00450	.00436	.00422	.00410	.00397	.00386
9	.00560	.00541	.00523	.00505	.00489	.00474	.00459	.00446	.00433	.00420
10	.00613	.00592	.00573	.00555	.00537	.00521	.00505	.00491	.00477	.00463
11	.00677	.00655	.00635	.00615	.00597	.00580	.00563	.00547	.00532	.00518
12	.00751	.00728	.00706	.00685	.00666	.00647	.00629	.00613	.00597	.00581
13	.00829	.00805	.00782	.00760	.00739	.00719	.00701	.00683	.00666	.00650
14	.00905	.00879	.00854	.00831	.00809	.00789	.00769	.00750	.00732	.00715
15	.00974	.00947	.00921	.00897	.00874	.00852	.00831	.00811	.00793	.00775
16	.01037	.01009	.00982	.00956	.00932	.00909	.00887	.00866	.00846	.00827
17	.01093	.01063	.01034	.01007	.00982	.00958	.00935	.00913	.00892	.00873
18	.01143	.01112	.01082	.01053	.01027	.01001	.00977	.00954	.00933	.00912
19	.01192	.01159	.01127	.01097	.01069	.01043	.01017	.00993	.00970	.00949
20	.01239	.01204	.01170	.01139	.01109	.01081	.01055	.01029	.01005	.00983
21	.01283	.01246	.01211	.01178	.01147	.01117	.01089	.01063	.01037	.01013
22	.01328	.01288	.01251	.01216	.01183	.01152	.01122	.01094	.01067	.01042
23	.01372	.01331	.01292	.01254	.01219	.01186	.01155	.01125	.01097	.01070
24	.01422	.01378	.01336	.01297	.01260	.01225	.01191	.01160	.01130	.01101
25	.01479	.01432	.01388	.01346	.01306	.01269	.01233	.01200	.01168	.01138
26	.01545	.01495	.01448	.01404	.01362	.01322	.01284	.01248	.01214	.01182
27	.01623	.01570	.01520	.01472	.01427	.01385	.01344	.01306	.01270	.01235
28	.01712	.01655	.01601	.01551	.01503	.01457	.01414	.01373	.01334	.01298
29	.01813	.01752	.01695	.01641	.01589	.01541	.01494	.01451	.01409	.01370
30	.01927	.01862	.01801	.01743	.01688	.01635	.01586	.01539	.01495	.01452
31	.02056	.01987	.01922	.01859	.01801	.01745	.01692	.01642	.01594	.01548
32	.02201	.02127	.02057	.01990	.01927	.01868	.01811	.01757	.01706	.01657
33	.02363	.02284	.02209	.02138	.02071	.02007	.01946	.01888	.01833	.01781
34	.02543	.02458	.02378	.02302	.02230	.02162	.02096	.02034	.01975	.01919
35	.02741	.02651	.02565	.02484	.02407	.02333	.02264	.02197	.02134	.02073
36	.02956	.02859	.02768	.02681	.02599	.02520	.02446	.02374	.02307	.02242
37	.03189	.03087	.02990	.02897	.02809	.02725	.02645	.02569	.02496	.02427
38	.03443	.03334	.03230	.03131	.03037	.02948	.02862	.02781	.02703	.02628
39	.03718	.03602	.03491	.03386	.03285	.03190	.03099	.03011	.02928	.02849
40	.04015	.03891	.03774	.03662	.03555	.03453	.03355	.03262	.03173	.03088
41	.04335	.04204	.04079	.03959	.03846	.03737	.03633	.03534	.03439	.03348
42	.04677	.04538	.04405	.04278	.04157	.04042	.03931	.03825	.03724	.03627
43	.05042	.04894	.04754	.04619	.04491	.04368	.04250	.04138	.04030	.03926
44	.05432	.05276	.05127	.04984	.04848	.04718	.04593	.04473	.04358	.04248
45	.05849	.05684	.05526	.05375	.05231	.05092	.04960	.04832	.04710	.04593
46	.06292	.06118	.05952	.05792	.05639	.05492	.05352	.05217	.05087	.04963
47	.06765	.06581	.06405	.06237	.06075	.05920	.05771	.05628	.05491	.05359
48	.07265	.07071	.06886	.06708	.06537	.06373	.06216	.06064	.05919	.05779
49	.07791	.07587	.07392	.07204	.07024	.06851	.06685	.06525	.06371	.06223
50	.08343	.08129	.07923	.07726	.07536	.07354	.07178	.07009	.06847	.06690
51	.08924	.08699	.08483	.08276	.08076	.07884	.07699	.07520	.07349	.07183
52	.09539	.09303	.09076	.08858	.08648	.08446	.08251	.08064	.07883	.07708
53	.10189	.09942	.09704	.09475	.09255	.09043	.08838	.08640	.08450	.08266
54	.10872	.10614	.10365	.10126	.09894	.09672	.09456	.09249	.09049	.08855

Table U(1)   (continued)

Age	12.2%	12.4%	12.6%	12.8%	13.0%	13.2%	13.4%	13.6%	13.8%	14.0%
55	.11592	.11322	.11062	.10811	.10569	.10335	.10110	.09892	.09682	.09478
56	.12350	.12068	.11796	.11534	.11281	.11036	.10800	.10571	.10350	.10137
57	.13148	.12855	.12572	.12298	.12033	.11777	.11530	.11291	.11060	.10836
58	.13990	.13685	.13389	.13104	.12828	.12561	.12303	.12053	.11811	.11576
59	.14875	.14557	.14250	.13953	.13665	.13387	.13118	.12856	.12604	.12359
60	.15799	.15469	.15150	.14841	.14542	.14253	.13972	.13700	.13436	.13180
61	.16761	.16419	.16088	.15768	.15457	.15156	.14864	.14580	.14305	.14039
62	.17758	.17404	.17062	.16729	.16407	.16094	.15791	.15496	.15210	.14932
63	.18791	.18425	.18071	.17726	.17392	.17068	.16753	.16447	.16150	.15861
64	.19862	.19484	.19118	.18762	.18417	.18081	.17754	.17437	.17129	.16829
65	.20979	.20590	.20212	.19845	.19487	.19140	.18802	.18474	.18154	.17843
66	.22149	.21748	.21359	.20980	.20612	.20253	.19904	.19564	.19233	.18911
67	.23374	.22962	.22562	.22172	.21792	.21423	.21062	.20712	.20370	.20037
68	.24656	.24234	.23822	.23422	.23031	.22651	.22280	.21919	.21566	.21222
69	.25988	.25556	.25134	.24724	.24323	.23932	.23551	.23179	.22816	.22461
70	.27367	.26925	.26493	.26073	.25662	.25261	.24870	.24488	.24115	.23750
71	.28784	.28333	.27892	.27462	.27042	.26631	.26230	.25839	.25456	.25082
72	.30241	.29781	.29332	.28893	.28464	.28044	.27634	.27233	.26841	.26457
73	.31740	.31272	.30815	.30368	.29930	.29502	.29084	.28674	.28273	.27880
74	.33291	.32817	.32352	.31897	.31452	.31016	.30589	.30171	.29762	.29361
75	.34903	.34422	.33951	.33490	.33038	.32595	.32161	.31735	.31318	.30909
76	.36581	.36095	.35619	.35152	.34694	.34245	.33805	.33373	.32949	.32533
77	.38324	.37835	.37354	.36883	.36420	.35966	.35520	.35083	.34654	.34232
78	.40126	.39634	.39150	.38676	.38210	.37752	.37302	.36861	.36427	.36001
79	.41970	.41476	.40992	.40515	.40047	.39587	.39135	.38690	.38253	.37823
80	.43842	.43348	.42864	.42387	.41918	.41456	.41002	.40556	.40117	.39685
81	.45719	.45228	.44744	.44267	.43799	.43337	.42883	.42436	.41996	.41562
82	.47590	.47101	.46619	.46145	.45677	.45217	.44764	.44317	.43877	.43443
83	.49443	.48957	.48478	.48007	.47542	.47084	.46632	.46187	.45748	.45315
84	.51279	.50798	.50324	.49856	.49394	.48939	.48490	.48048	.47611	.47180
85	.53106	.52630	.52161	.51698	.51241	.50790	.50345	.49906	.49473	.49045
86	.54902	.54434	.53971	.53514	.53062	.52616	.52176	.51741	.51312	.50888
87	.56640	.56178	.55722	.55271	.54826	.54386	.53951	.53521	.53097	.52677
88	.58326	.57872	.57423	.56979	.56541	.56107	.55678	.55254	.54834	.54420
89	.59994	.59548	.59107	.58671	.58240	.57813	.57391	.56973	.56560	.56152
90	.61662	.61226	.60794	.60367	.59944	.59526	.59112	.58702	.58296	.57894
91	.63305	.62879	.62457	.62040	.61627	.61217	.60812	.60411	.60013	.59619
92	.64876	.64461	.64050	.63643	.63239	.62839	.62443	.62051	.61662	.61277
93	.66355	.65950	.65550	.65153	.64759	.64369	.63983	.63600	.63220	.62843
94	.67722	.67328	.66938	.66551	.66167	.65786	.65409	.65035	.64664	.64296
95	.68967	.68583	.68203	.67825	.67451	.67079	.66711	.66345	.65983	.65623
96	.70076	.69701	.69330	.68961	.68595	.68231	.67871	.67513	.67158	.66806
97	.71089	.70722	.70359	.69998	.69640	.69284	.68931	.68581	.68234	.67888
98	.72001	.71642	.71286	.70933	.70582	.70233	.69887	.69544	.69203	.68864
99	.72844	.72492	.72143	.71796	.71452	.71110	.70770	.70433	.70098	.69765
100	.73623	.73278	.72935	.72594	.72256	.71920	.71586	.71254	.70924	.70597
101	.74361	.74021	.73684	.73349	.73016	.72685	.72356	.72029	.71704	.71382
102	.75128	.74794	.74463	.74133	.73806	.73480	.73157	.72835	.72515	.72198
103	.75938	.75610	.75284	.74961	.74639	.74319	.74000	.73684	.73369	.73056
104	.76835	.76514	.76194	.75877	.75561	.75246	.74934	.74623	.74313	.74005
105	.77956	.77643	.77332	.77023	.76714	.76408	.76102	.75798	.75496	.75195
106	.79632	.79334	.79038	.78743	.78449	.78157	.77865	.77575	.77285	.76997
107	.82154	.81884	.81615	.81346	.81079	.80811	.80545	.80279	.80014	.79750
108	.86487	.86274	.86061	.85848	.85635	.85423	.85210	.84998	.84787	.84575
109	.93900	.93800	.93700	.93600	.93500	.93400	.93300	.93200	.93100	.93000

Table U(1)   BASED ON LIFE TABLE 80CNSMT UNITRUST SINGLE LIFE
REMAINDER FACTORS ADJUSTED PAYOUT RATE

Age	14.2%	14.4%	14.6%	14.8%	15.0%	15.2%	15.4%	15.6%	15.8%	16.0%
0	.01482	.01474	.01467	.01460	.01453	.01446	.01440	.01433	.01427	.01421
1	.00368	.00361	.00354	.00348	.00342	.00337	.00331	.00326	.00321	.00316
2	.00328	.00321	.00314	.00308	.00302	.00296	.00290	.00285	.00279	.00274
3	.00312	.00305	.00298	.00291	.00284	.00278	.00272	.00266	.00261	.00256
4	.00310	.00302	.00295	.00287	.00281	.00274	.00268	.00262	.00256	.00250
5	.00318	.00309	.00301	.00293	.00286	.00279	.00272	.00266	.00259	.00254
6	.00331	.00322	.00313	.00305	.00297	.00289	.00282	.00275	.00268	.00262
7	.00350	.00340	.00330	.00321	.00313	.00305	.00297	.00289	.00282	.00275
8	.00375	.00364	.00354	.00344	.00335	.00326	.00318	.00310	.00302	.00294
9	.00408	.00397	.00386	.00375	.00365	.00356	.00347	.00338	.00330	.00321
10	.00450	.00438	.00426	.00415	.00405	.00394	.00384	.00375	.00366	.00357
11	.00504	.00491	.00479	.00467	.00455	.00444	.00433	.00423	.00414	.00404
12	.00567	.00553	.00539	.00527	.00514	.00503	.00491	.00481	.00470	.00460
13	.00634	.00619	.00605	.00592	.00579	.00566	.00554	.00543	.00532	.00521
14	.00699	.00683	.00668	.00654	.00640	.00627	.00614	.00602	.00590	.00579
15	.00757	.00741	.00725	.00710	.00696	.00682	.00669	.00656	.00644	.00632
16	.00810	.00792	.00776	.00760	.00745	.00731	.00717	.00703	.00690	.00678
17	.00854	.00836	.00818	.00802	.00786	.00771	.00757	.00743	.00729	.00716
18	.00892	.00873	.00855	.00838	.00821	.00806	.00790	.00776	.00762	.00748
19	.00928	.00908	.00889	.00871	.00854	.00837	.00822	.00806	.00792	.00778
20	.00961	.00940	.00920	.00901	.00883	.00866	.00849	.00833	.00818	.00804
21	.00990	.00969	.00948	.00928	.00909	.00891	.00873	.00857	.00841	.00825
22	.01018	.00995	.00973	.00952	.00932	.00913	.00895	.00877	.00861	.00845
23	.01045	.01020	.00997	.00975	.00954	.00934	.00915	.00896	.00879	.00862
24	.01074	.01049	.01024	.01001	.00978	.00957	.00937	.00917	.00899	.00881
25	.01109	.01082	.01055	.01031	.01007	.00984	.00963	.00942	.00922	.00903
26	.01151	.01122	.01094	.01068	.01043	.01018	.00995	.00973	.00952	.00932
27	.01203	.01171	.01142	.01114	.01087	.01061	.01036	.01013	.00990	.00969
28	.01262	.01229	.01197	.01167	.01138	.01111	.01084	.01059	.01035	.01012
29	.01332	.01296	.01262	.01230	.01199	.01169	.01141	.01114	.01088	.01064
30	.01412	.01374	.01337	.01302	.01269	.01237	.01207	.01178	.01150	.01124
31	.01505	.01464	.01425	.01387	.01352	.01317	.01285	.01254	.01224	.01195
32	.01610	.01566	.01524	.01484	.01445	.01408	.01373	.01340	.01307	.01277
33	.01731	.01683	.01638	.01594	.01553	.01513	.01476	.01439	.01405	.01371
34	.01866	.01814	.01766	.01719	.01674	.01632	.01591	.01552	.01514	.01479
35	.02016	.01961	.01909	.01858	.01810	.01764	.01721	.01678	.01638	.01599
36	.02180	.02121	.02065	.02011	.01959	.01910	.01862	.01817	.01774	.01732
37	.02360	.02297	.02237	.02179	.02123	.02070	.02019	.01970	.01923	.01878
38	.02557	.02489	.02424	.02362	.02303	.02245	.02191	.02138	.02088	.02039
39	.02773	.02700	.02630	.02563	.02499	.02438	.02379	.02322	.02268	.02216
40	.03007	.02929	.02854	.02782	.02714	.02648	.02585	.02524	.02465	.02409
41	.03261	.03178	.03098	.03021	.02947	.02877	.02809	.02744	.02681	.02620
42	.03534	.03445	.03360	.03277	.03199	.03123	.03050	.02980	.02913	.02848
43	.03827	.03732	.03641	.03553	.03469	.03388	.03310	.03235	.03163	.03093
44	.04142	.04041	.03943	.03850	.03760	.03673	.03590	.03509	.03432	.03358
45	.04481	.04373	.04269	.04169	.04073	.03980	.03891	.03806	.03723	.03643
46	.04843	.04728	.04618	.04511	.04409	.04310	.04215	.04124	.04035	.03950
47	.05232	.05109	.04992	.04879	.04770	.04665	.04563	.04466	.04372	.04281
48	.05644	.05515	.05390	.05270	.05154	.05042	.04934	.04830	.04730	.04633
49	.06080	.05943	.05810	.05683	.05560	.05441	.05326	.05216	.05109	.05006
50	.06539	.06394	.06253	.06118	.05988	.05862	.05740	.05622	.05509	.05399
51	.07024	.06870	.06722	.06578	.06440	.06307	.06178	.06053	.05932	.05815
52	.07540	.07377	.07220	.07069	.06923	.06781	.06644	.06512	.06384	.06260
53	.08088	.07917	.07751	.07591	.07437	.07287	.07142	.07002	.06867	.06735
54	.08668	.08487	.08313	.08144	.07981	.07823	.07670	.07521	.07378	.07239

Table U(1) *(continued)*

Age	14.2%	14.4%	14.6%	14.8%	15.0%	15.2%	15.4%	15.6%	15.8%	16.0%
55	.09281	.09091	.08907	.08729	.08557	.08390	.08229	.08072	.07921	.07774
56	.09930	.09731	.09537	.09350	.09168	.08992	.08822	.08657	.08497	.08342
57	.10619	.10409	.10206	.10009	.09818	.09633	.09454	.09280	.09111	.08947
58	.11349	.11129	.10916	.10709	.10509	.10314	.10125	.09942	.09765	.09592
59	.12121	.11891	.11667	.11451	.11240	.11036	.10838	.10646	.10459	.10277
60	.12932	.12691	.12457	.12230	.12010	.11796	.11588	.11386	.11190	.10999
61	.13780	.13528	.13284	.13047	.12817	.12593	.12375	.12163	.11958	.11757
62	.14662	.14400	.14146	.13898	.13657	.13423	.13196	.12974	.12759	.12549
63	.15580	.15307	.15042	.14784	.14533	.14289	.14051	.13819	.13594	.13374
64	.16537	.16253	.15977	.15708	.15446	.15192	.14943	.14702	.14466	.14237
65	.17540	.17245	.16958	.16679	.16406	.16141	.15883	.15631	.15385	.15145
66	.18597	.18291	.17994	.17703	.17420	.17144	.16875	.16613	.16357	.16108
67	.19712	.19395	.19087	.18786	.18492	.18206	.17926	.17654	.17388	.17128
68	.20887	.20560	.20240	.19929	.19625	.19328	.19038	.18755	.18479	.18209
69	.22116	.21778	.21448	.21126	.20812	.20505	.20205	.19912	.19625	.19345
70	.23394	.23047	.22707	.22375	.22050	.21733	.21423	.21120	.20823	.20533
71	.24716	.24358	.24009	.23667	.23332	.23005	.22685	.22372	.22066	.21766
72	.26082	.25715	.25356	.25004	.24660	.24323	.23994	.23671	.23355	.23046
73	.27496	.27119	.26751	.26390	.26037	.25691	.25352	.25020	.24694	.24375
74	.28968	.28583	.28206	.27836	.27474	.27119	.26771	.26429	.26095	.25767
75	.30508	.30116	.29730	.29352	.28982	.28618	.28262	.27912	.27569	.27232
76	.32125	.31725	.31333	.30947	.30569	.30198	.29834	.29476	.29125	.28780
77	.33818	.33412	.33013	.32621	.32236	.31858	.31487	.31122	.30763	.30411
78	.35582	.35170	.34766	.34368	.33978	.33594	.33216	.32845	.32481	.32122
79	.37400	.36985	.36576	.36174	.35779	.35390	.35008	.34632	.34261	.33897
80	.39259	.38841	.38429	.38024	.37625	.37233	.36846	.36466	.36091	.35723
81	.41136	.40716	.40302	.39894	.39493	.39098	.38709	.38325	.37947	.37575
82	.43016	.42595	.42181	.41772	.41369	.40972	.40581	.40195	.39815	.39440
83	.44889	.44468	.44053	.43644	.43241	.42843	.42451	.42064	.41682	.41306
84	.46755	.46335	.45922	.45513	.45110	.44713	.44321	.43933	.43551	.43174
85	.48622	.48205	.47793	.47387	.46985	.46589	.46198	.45811	.45430	.45053
86	.50469	.50055	.49646	.49242	.48843	.48449	.48060	.47675	.47295	.46919
87	.52262	.51852	.51447	.51047	.50651	.50259	.49873	.49490	.49112	.48738
88	.54010	.53604	.53203	.52807	.52414	.52027	.51643	.51263	.50888	.50517
89	.55747	.55347	.54951	.54559	.54172	.53788	.53408	.53033	.52661	.52293
90	.57496	.57103	.56713	.56327	.55945	.55567	.55192	.54822	.54455	.54091
91	.59229	.58843	.58461	.58082	.57706	.57335	.56966	.56601	.56240	.55882
92	.60895	.60517	.60142	.59771	.59403	.59038	.58676	.58318	.57963	.57611
93	.62470	.62100	.61733	.61369	.61009	.60652	.60297	.59946	.59597	.59252
94	.63931	.63569	.63211	.62855	.62502	.62152	.61804	.61460	.61118	.60780
95	.65266	.64912	.64561	.64212	.63867	.63524	.63184	.62846	.62511	.62179
96	.66457	.66110	.65766	.65424	.65085	.64749	.64415	.64084	.63755	.63428
97	.67546	.67206	.66868	.66533	.66201	.65870	.65542	.65217	.64894	.64573
98	.68528	.68194	.67862	.67533	.67206	.66881	.66559	.66239	.65921	.65605
99	.69435	.69106	.68780	.68457	.68135	.67816	.67498	.67183	.66870	.66559
100	.70272	.69949	.69628	.69309	.68992	.68677	.68365	.68054	.67745	.67438
101	.71061	.70743	.70426	.70112	.69799	.69488	.69180	.68873	.68568	.68265
102	.71882	.71568	.71256	.70945	.70637	.70331	.70026	.69723	.69422	.69123
103	.72745	.72436	.72128	.71822	.71518	.71216	.70915	.70616	.70319	.70023
104	.73699	.73395	.73092	.72790	.72490	.72192	.71895	.71600	.71306	.71014
105	.74895	.74596	.74299	.74004	.73710	.73417	.73125	.72835	.72546	.72258
106	.76709	.76423	.76138	.75854	.75571	.75289	.75008	.74729	.74450	.74172
107	.79486	.79223	.78961	.78699	.78438	.78178	.77919	.77660	.77402	.77144
108	.84364	.84153	.83943	.83732	.83522	.83312	.83103	.82893	.82684	.82475
109	.92900	.92800	.92700	.92600	.92500	.92400	.92300	.92200	.92100	.92000

Table U(1)   *BASED ON LIFE TABLE 80CNSMT UNITRUST SINGLE LIFE REMAINDER FACTORS ADJUSTED PAYOUT RATE*

Age	16.2%	16.4%	16.6%	16.8%	17.0%	17.2%	17.4%	17.6%	17.8%	18.0%
0	.01416	.01410	.01405	.01399	.01394	.01389	.01384	.01380	.01375	.01370
1	.00311	.00307	.00303	.00298	.00294	.00291	.00287	.00283	.00280	.00276
2	.00270	.00265	.00261	.00256	.00252	.00248	.00245	.00241	.00237	.00234
3	.00251	.00246	.00241	.00237	.00233	.00228	.00224	.00221	.00217	.00213
4	.00245	.00240	.00235	.00230	.00226	.00221	.00217	.00213	.00209	.00205
5	.00248	.00242	.00237	.00232	.00227	.00222	.00218	.00213	.00209	.00205
6	.00256	.00250	.00244	.00239	.00233	.00228	.00223	.00219	.00214	.00210
7	.00268	.00262	.00256	.00250	.00244	.00239	.00234	.00228	.00223	.00219
8	.00287	.00280	.00273	.00267	.00261	.00255	.00249	.00244	.00238	.00233
9	.00314	.00306	.00299	.00292	.00285	.00279	.00272	.00266	.00261	.00255
10	.00349	.00341	.00333	.00325	.00318	.00311	.00304	.00297	.00291	.00285
11	.00395	.00386	.00378	.00370	.00362	.00354	.00347	.00340	.00333	.00326
12	.00450	.00441	.00432	.00423	.00415	.00407	.00399	.00391	.00384	.00376
13	.00511	.00501	.00491	.00482	.00473	.00464	.00456	.00448	.00440	.00432
14	.00568	.00558	.00548	.00538	.00528	.00519	.00510	.00502	.00493	.00485
15	.00620	.00609	.00599	.00588	.00579	.00569	.00560	.00551	.00542	.00533
16	.00666	.00655	.00643	.00633	.00622	.00612	.00602	.00593	.00584	.00575
17	.00704	.00692	.00680	.00669	.00658	.00648	.00638	.00628	.00618	.00609
18	.00375	.00723	.00711	.00699	.00688	.00677	.00666	.00656	.00646	.00637
19	.00764	.00751	.00739	.00726	.00715	.00703	.00692	.00682	.00672	.00662
20	.00789	.00776	.00763	.00750	.00738	.00726	.00715	.00704	.00693	.00683
21	.00811	.00796	.00783	.00770	.00757	.00745	.00733	.00722	.00711	.00700
22	.00829	.00814	.00800	.00786	.00773	.00760	.00748	.00736	.00725	.00713
23	.00845	.00830	.00815	.00800	.00786	.00773	.00760	.00748	.00736	.00724
24	.00864	.00847	.00831	.00816	.00801	.00787	.00774	.00761	.00748	.00736
25	.00885	.00868	.00851	.00835	.00819	.00804	.00790	.00776	.00763	.00750
26	.00913	.00894	.00876	.00859	.00843	.00827	.00812	.00797	.00783	.00769
27	.00948	.00928	.00909	.00891	.00873	.00857	.00840	.00825	.00810	.00795
28	.00990	.00969	.00948	.00929	.00910	.00892	.00875	.00858	.00842	.00827
29	.01040	.01017	.00995	.00974	.00954	.00935	.00916	.00898	.00881	.00865
30	.01098	.01074	.01050	.01028	.01006	.00985	.00965	.00946	.00927	.00910
31	.01168	.01141	.01116	.01092	.01068	.01046	.01024	.01004	.00984	.00964
32	.01247	.01219	.01191	.01165	.01140	.01116	.01093	.01070	.01049	.01028
33	.01339	.01309	.01279	.01251	.01224	.01198	.01173	.01148	.01125	.01103
34	.01444	.01411	.01379	.01349	.01319	.01291	.01264	.01238	.01213	.01188
35	.01562	.01526	.01492	.01459	.01427	.01397	.01367	.01339	.01312	.01286
36	.01692	.01653	.01616	.01580	.01546	.01513	.01481	.01451	.01421	.01393
37	.01835	.01793	.01753	.01715	.01678	.01642	.01608	.01575	.01543	.01512
38	.01992	.01948	.01904	.01863	.01823	.01784	.01747	.01711	.01677	.01643
39	.02166	.02117	.02071	.02026	.01983	.01941	.01901	.01862	.01825	.01789
40	.02355	.02303	.02253	.02205	.02158	.02113	.02070	.02028	.01988	.01949
41	.02562	.02506	.02452	.02400	.02350	.02302	.02255	.02210	.02166	.02124
42	.02786	.02725	.02667	.02611	.02558	.02505	.02455	.02407	.02360	.02314
43	.03026	.02961	.02899	.02839	.02781	.02725	.02671	.02619	.02568	.02519
44	.03286	.03217	.03150	.03085	.03023	.02963	.02904	.02848	.02794	.02741
45	.03566	.03492	.03420	.03351	.03284	.03220	.03157	.03097	.03038	.02982
46	.03868	.03789	.03712	.03638	.03566	.03497	.03430	.03365	.03302	.03241
47	.04193	.04108	.04026	.03947	.03870	.03796	.03724	.03655	.03587	.03522
48	.04539	.04449	.04361	.04276	.04195	.04115	.04038	.03964	.03892	.03822
49	.04906	.04809	.04716	.04626	.04538	.04453	.04371	.04292	.04215	.04140
50	.05293	.05190	.05090	.04994	.04901	.04811	.04723	.04638	.04556	.04476
51	.05702	.05593	.05487	.05385	.05286	.05189	.05096	.05005	.04918	.04832
52	.06140	.06024	.05912	.05803	.05697	.05595	.05495	.05399	.05305	.05214
53	.06608	.06485	.06365	.06250	.06137	.06028	.05923	.05820	.05720	.05623
54	.07104	.06973	.06847	.06724	.06605	.06489	.06377	.06267	.06161	.06058

Table U(1) *(continued)*

Age	16.2%	16.4%	16.6%	16.8%	17.0%	17.2%	17.4%	17.6%	17.8%	18.0%
55	.07631	.07493	.07359	.07228	.07102	.06979	.06860	.06744	.06631	.06522
56	.08191	.08045	.97903	.07765	.07631	.07501	.07374	.07251	.07132	.07016
57	.08788	.08634	.08483	.08338	.08196	.08058	.07924	.07794	.07668	.07544
58	.09424	.09261	.09103	.08949	.08799	.08654	.08512	.08375	.08241	.08110
59	.10100	.09929	.09762	.09600	.09442	.09288	.09139	.08993	.08852	.08714
60	.10814	.10633	.10458	.10287	.10121	.09959	.09801	.09648	.09498	.09352
61	.11563	.11373	.11189	.11009	.10834	.10664	.10498	.10336	.10178	.10025
62	.12345	.12146	.11952	.11764	.11580	.11401	.11226	.11056	.10890	.10728
63	.13161	.12952	.12749	.12551	.12359	.12171	.11987	.11808	.11634	.11464
64	.14013	.13795	.13583	.13376	.13174	.12976	.12784	.12596	.12413	.12234
65	.14912	.14684	.14462	.14245	.14034	.13827	.13625	.13429	.13236	.13048
66	.15864	.15626	.15394	.15168	.14947	.14731	.14519	.14313	.14112	.13915
67	.16874	.16626	.16384	.16148	.15917	.15691	.15471	.15255	.15045	.14839
68	.17945	.17687	.17435	.17189	.16949	.16713	.16483	.16258	.16038	.15823
69	.19071	.18804	.18542	.18286	.18036	.17791	.17551	.17317	.17087	.16862
70	.20250	.19972	.19701	.19435	.19175	.18920	.18671	.18427	.18188	.17954
71	.21472	.21185	.20904	.20629	.20359	.20095	.19836	.19583	.19334	.19091
72	.22742	.22446	.22155	.21870	.21591	.21317	.21049	.20786	.20528	.20275
73	.24063	.23756	.23456	.23162	.22873	.22590	.22312	.22040	.21773	.21511
74	.25445	.25130	.24820	.24516	.24219	.23926	.23639	.23358	.23082	.22811
75	.26902	.26577	.26259	.25946	.25640	.25338	.25043	.24752	.24467	.24187
76	.28441	.28109	.27782	.27461	.27146	.26836	.26532	.26233	.25939	.25651
77	.30065	.29725	.29390	.29062	.28739	.28421	.28109	.27802	.27500	.27204
78	.31769	.31422	.31081	.30746	.30416	.30091	.29772	.29458	.29148	.28844
79	.33539	.33186	.32839	.32498	.32161	.31831	.31505	.31184	.30868	.30557
80	.35360	.35002	.34650	.34304	.33962	.33626	.33295	.32968	.32647	.32330
81	.37208	.36847	.36491	.36140	.35794	.35453	.35118	.34787	.34460	.34138
82	.39071	.38707	.38347	.37993	.37644	.37300	.36960	.36625	.36295	.35969
83	.40934	.40568	.40207	.39850	.39498	.39151	.38809	.38470	.38137	.37808
84	.42802	.42434	.42071	.41713	.41360	.41011	.40666	.40326	.39990	.39658
85	.44681	.44313	.43950	.43591	.43237	.42887	.42541	.42200	.41862	.41529
86	.46548	.46181	.45819	.45461	.45106	.44756	.44411	.44069	.43731	.43396
87	.48369	.48003	.47642	.47285	.46931	.46582	.46237	.45895	.45557	.45223
88	.50149	.49786	.49426	.49071	.48179	.48371	.48026	.47685	.47348	.47014
89	.51929	.51568	.51211	.50858	.50508	.50162	.49820	.49481	.49145	.48813
90	.53731	.53375	.53022	.52672	.52326	.51983	.51643	.51307	.50974	.50644
91	.55527	.55176	.54828	.54483	.54141	.53802	.53467	.53134	.52805	.52478
92	.57262	.56917	.56574	.56234	.55898	.55564	.55233	.54905	.54580	.54257
93	.58910	.58570	.58233	.57899	.57568	.57240	.56914	.56591	.56271	.55953
94	.60443	.60110	.59779	.59451	.59126	.58803	.58483	.58165	.57850	.57537
95	.61849	.61521	.61197	.60874	.60555	.60237	.59922	.59610	.59300	.58992
96	.63104	.62783	.62463	.62146	.61832	.61520	.61210	.60902	.60596	.60293
97	.64254	.63983	.63624	.63312	.63003	.62696	.62390	.62087	.61786	.61487
98	.65292	.64980	.64671	.64364	.64059	.63756	.63455	.63157	.62860	.62565
99	.66250	.65944	.65639	.65336	.65035	.64736	.64440	.64145	.63852	.63561
100	.67134	.66831	.66530	.66231	.65934	.65639	.65346	.65055	.64765	.64477
101	.67964	.67665	.67367	.67072	.66778	.66486	.66196	.65907	.65621	.65336
102	.68825	.68530	.68236	.67943	.67653	.67364	.67077	.66791	.66508	.66225
103	.69729	.69437	.69146	.68857	.68569	.68283	.67999	.67716	.67435	.67155
104	.70723	.70434	.70147	.69860	.69576	.69293	.69011	.68731	.68452	.68174
105	.71972	.71687	.71404	.71121	.70840	.70561	.70282	.70005	.69729	.69455
106	.73896	.73620	.73345	.73072	.72800	.72528	.72258	.71988	.71720	.71453
107	.76887	.76631	.76376	.76121	.75867	.75614	.75361	.75109	.74858	.74607
108	.82267	.82058	.81850	.81643	.81435	.81228	.81021	.80814	.80607	.80401
109	.91900	.91800	.91700	.91600	.91500	.91400	.91300	.91200	.91100	.91000

Table U(1) *BASED ON LIFE TABLE 80CNSMT UNITRUST SINGLE LIFE REMAINDER FACTORS ADJUSTED PAYOUT RATE*

Age	18.2%	18.4%	18.6%	18.8%	19.0%	19.2%	19.4%	19.6%	19.8%	20.0%
0	.01366	.01362	.01357	.01353	.01349	.01345	.01341	.01337	.01333	.01330
1	.00273	.00270	.00267	.00264	.00261	.00258	.00256	.00253	.00250	.00248
2	.00231	.00227	.00224	.00221	.00218	.00216	.00213	.00210	.00208	.00205
3	.00210	.00207	.00203	.00200	.00197	.00194	.00192	.00189	.00186	.00184
4	.00202	.00198	.00195	.00191	.00188	.00185	.00182	.00179	.00176	.00174
5	.00201	.00198	.00194	.00190	.00187	.00184	.00180	.00177	.00174	.00171
6	.00206	.00201	.00198	.00194	.00190	.00186	.00183	.00180	.00176	.00173
7	.00214	.00210	.00205	.00201	.00197	.00193	.00190	.00186	.00182	.00179
8	.00228	.00223	.00218	.00214	.00210	.00205	.00201	.00197	.00193	.00189
9	.00249	.00244	.00239	.00234	.00229	.00225	.00220	.00216	.00211	.00207
10	.00279	.00273	.00268	.00262	.00257	.00252	.00247	.00242	.00237	.00233
11	.00320	.00313	.00307	.00301	.00296	.00290	.00285	.00279	.00274	.00269
12	.00369	.00363	.00356	.00350	.00343	.00337	.00332	.00326	.00320	.00315
13	.00425	.00417	.00410	.00403	.00397	.00390	.00384	.00378	.00372	.00366
14	.00477	.00470	.00462	.00455	.00448	.00441	.00434	.00428	.00422	.00416
15	.00525	.00517	.00509	.00502	.00494	.00487	.00480	.00473	.00467	.00460
16	.00566	.00558	.00550	.00542	.00534	.00527	.00519	.00512	.00505	.00499
17	.00600	.00591	.00583	.00575	.00567	.00559	.00551	.00544	.00537	.00530
18	.00628	.00619	.00610	.00601	.00593	.00585	.00577	.00570	.00562	.00555
19	.00652	.00643	.00634	.00625	.00616	.00608	.00600	.00592	.00585	.00577
20	.00673	.00663	.00654	.00645	.00636	.00628	.00619	.00611	.00603	.00596
21	.00690	.00680	.00670	.00660	.00651	.00642	.00634	.00625	.00617	.00609
22	.00703	.00692	.00682	.00672	.00663	.00654	.00645	.00636	.00628	.00620
23	.00713	.00702	.00692	.00681	.00672	.00662	.00653	.00644	.00635	.00626
24	.00724	.00713	.00702	.00691	.00681	.00671	.00661	.00652	.00643	.00634
25	.00738	.00726	.00714	.00703	.00692	.00682	.00671	.00662	.00652	.00643
26	.00756	.00744	.00731	.00720	.00708	.00697	.00686	.00676	.00666	.00656
27	.00781	.00768	.00755	.00742	.00730	.00718	.00707	.00696	.00685	.00675
28	.00812	.00797	.00783	.00770	.00757	.00744	.00732	.00720	.00709	.00698
29	.00848	.00833	.00818	.00804	.00790	.00776	.00763	.00751	.00738	.00727
30	.00892	.00876	.00860	.00844	.00829	.00815	.00801	.00787	.00774	.00761
31	.00946	.00928	.00911	.00894	.00878	.00862	.00847	.00833	.00818	.00805
32	.01008	.00988	.00970	.00952	.00934	.00917	.00901	.00885	.00870	.00855
33	.01081	.01060	.01040	.01020	.01001	.00983	.00966	.00949	.00932	.00916
34	.01165	.01142	.01120	.01099	.01079	.01059	.01040	.01021	.01003	.00986
35	.01260	.01236	.01212	.01189	.01167	.01145	.01125	.01105	.01085	.01066
36	.01365	.01339	.01313	.01288	.01264	.01241	.01219	.01197	.01176	.01155
37	.01482	.01453	.01426	.01399	.01373	.01347	.01323	.01300	.01277	.01255
38	.01611	.01580	.01550	.01521	.01493	.01465	.01439	.01413	.01389	.01365
39	.01754	.01720	.01688	.01656	.01626	.01596	.01567	.01540	.01513	.01487
40	.01911	.01875	.01839	.01805	.01772	.01740	.01709	.01679	.01650	.01622
41	.02084	.02044	.02006	.01969	.01933	.01899	.01865	.01833	.01801	.01771
42	.02270	.02228	.02187	.02147	.02108	.02071	.02034	.01999	.01965	.01932
43	.02472	.02426	.02381	.02338	.02297	.02256	.02217	.02179	.02142	.02106
44	.02690	.02641	.02593	.02546	.02502	.02458	.02416	.02375	.02335	.02296
45	.02927	.02874	.02822	.02772	.02724	.02677	.02631	.02587	.02544	.02502
46	.03182	.03125	.03070	.03016	.02964	.02914	.02865	.02817	.02771	.02725
47	.03459	.03397	.03338	.03280	.03224	.03170	.03117	.03066	.03016	.02968
48	.03754	.03689	.03625	.03563	.03503	.03445	.03388	.03333	.03279	.03227
49	.04068	.03997	.03929	.03863	.03798	.03736	.03675	.03616	.03558	.03502
50	.04398	.04323	.04250	.04179	.04110	.04043	.03978	.03915	.03853	.03793
51	.04749	.04669	.04591	.04515	.04441	.04370	.04300	.04232	.04166	.04102
52	.05126	.05040	.04957	.04876	.04797	.04720	.04646	.04573	.04503	.04434
53	.05529	.05438	.05349	.05262	.05178	.05097	.05017	.04939	.04864	.04790
54	.05958	.05861	.05766	.05674	.05584	.05497	.05412	.05329	.05249	.05170

Table U(1)   (continued)

Age	18.2%	18.4%	18.6%	18.8%	19.0%	19.2%	19.4%	19.6%	19.8%	20.0%
55	.06415	.06312	.06211	.06113	.06017	.05924	.05834	.05746	.05660	.05576
56	.06902	.06792	.06685	.06581	.06479	.06380	.06284	.06190	.06098	.06009
57	.07424	.07308	.07194	.07083	.06975	.06870	.06767	.06667	.06570	.06475
58	.07983	.07859	.07738	.07621	.07506	.07395	.07286	.07180	.07076	.06975
59	.08579	.08448	.08320	.08196	.08074	.07956	.07840	.07728	.07618	.07510
60	.09210	.09072	.08937	.08805	.08676	.08551	.08429	.08309	.08193	.08079
61	.09875	.09728	.09586	.09447	.09311	.09178	.09049	.08923	.08799	.08679
62	.10570	.10416	.10266	.10119	.09976	.09836	.09699	.09566	.09435	.09308
63	.11297	.11135	.10977	.10822	.10671	.10523	.10379	.10238	.10100	.09966
64	.12059	.11889	.11722	.11559	.11400	.11245	.11092	.10944	.10798	.10656
65	.12865	.12686	.12511	.12339	.12172	.12008	.11848	.11692	.11538	.11388
66	.13723	.13535	.13351	.13171	.12995	.12823	.12654	.12490	.12328	.12171
67	.14637	.14440	.14247	.14059	.13874	.13693	.13517	.13343	.13174	.13008
68	.15612	.15406	.15204	.15007	.14813	.14624	.14439	.14257	.14079	.13905
69	.16643	.16427	.16216	.16010	.15808	.15609	.15415	.15225	.15039	.14856
70	.17725	.17501	.17281	.17065	.16854	.16647	.16444	.16245	.16050	.15858
71	.18852	.18619	.18390	.18165	.17945	.17729	.17517	.17309	.17105	.16905
72	.20028	.19785	.19546	.19313	.19083	.18858	.18638	.18421	.18208	.18000
73	.21254	.21002	.20754	.20511	.20273	.20039	.19809	.19584	.19362	.19145
74	.22544	.22283	.22026	.21774	.21527	.21284	.21045	.20811	.20580	.20354
75	.23912	.23641	.23376	.23115	.22859	.22607	.22359	.22116	.21876	.21641
76	.25367	.25088	.24814	.24544	.24279	.24018	.23762	.23510	.23262	.23018
77	.26912	.26625	.26342	.26065	.25791	.25522	.25258	.24998	.24741	.24489
78	.28545	.28250	.27960	.27675	.27394	.27117	.26845	.26577	.26313	.26053
79	.30251	.29950	.29653	.29361	.29073	.28789	.28510	.28234	.27963	.27696
80	.32018	.31711	.31408	.31109	.30815	.30525	.30239	.29957	.29679	.29406
81	.33821	.33509	.33200	.32896	.32597	.32301	.32009	.31722	.31438	.31158
82	.35647	.35330	.35107	.34709	.34404	.34104	.33807	.33514	.33226	.32941
83	.37483	.37162	.36845	.36533	.36224	.35919	.35619	.35322	.35029	.34739
84	.39330	.39007	.38687	.38371	.38060	.37752	.37448	.37147	.36850	.36557
85	.41200	.40874	.40552	.40235	.39920	.39610	.39303	.39000	.38700	.38404
86	.43066	.42740	.42417	.42098	.41782	.41470	.41161	.40856	.40555	.40256
87	.44892	.44565	.44242	.43922	.43605	.43292	.42983	.42676	.42373	.42073
88	.46684	.46357	.46034	.45714	.45397	.45084	.44773	.44466	.44162	.43861
89	.48483	.48158	.47835	.47516	.47199	.46886	.46576	.46269	.45965	.45663
90	.50317	.49993	.49672	.49355	.49040	.48728	.48419	.48113	.47810	.47510
91	.52155	.51834	.51516	.51201	.50889	.50580	.50273	.49969	.49668	.49369
92	.53938	.53621	.53307	.52995	.52687	.52380	.52077	.51776	.51477	.51181
93	.55638	.55325	.55015	.54708	.54403	.54101	.53801	.53503	.53208	.52915
94	.57227	.56919	.56613	.56310	.56009	.55711	.55415	.55121	.54829	.54540
95	.58686	.58383	.58082	.57783	.57487	.57193	.56900	.56610	.56323	.56037
96	.59992	.59693	.59396	.59102	.58809	.58519	.58231	.57944	.57660	.57378
97	.61191	.60896	.60603	.60313	.60024	.59738	.59453	.59170	.58889	.58611
98	.62272	.61981	.61692	.61406	.61120	.60837	.60556	.60277	.59999	.59723
99	.63272	.62984	.62699	.62415	.62134	.61854	.61576	.61299	.61025	.60752
100	.64192	.63907	.63625	.63345	.63066	.62789	.62513	.62240	.61968	.61697
101	.65053	.64771	.64492	.64214	.63937	.63662	.63389	.63118	.62848	.62580
102	.65945	.65666	.65389	.65113	.64839	.64567	.64296	.64027	.63759	.63493
103	.66877	.66601	.66326	.66052	.65780	.65510	.65241	.64973	.64707	.64443
104	.67898	.67624	.67351	.67079	.66809	.66540	.66272	.66006	.65741	.65478
105	.69181	.68909	.68638	.68369	.68101	.67833	.67568	.67303	.67040	.66777
106	.71187	.70921	.70657	.70394	.70132	.69870	.69610	.69351	.69093	.68836
107	.74357	.74108	.73860	.73612	.73365	.73118	.72872	.72627	.72382	.72138
108	.80195	.79989	.79784	.79579	.79374	.79169	.78965	.78761	.78557	.78353
109	.90900	.90800	.90700	.90600	.90500	.90400	.90300	.90200	.90100	.90000

Table U(1)   *BASED ON LIFE TABLE 80CNSMT UNITRUST SINGLE LIFE*
REMAINDER FACTORS ADJUSTED PAYOUT RATE

Age	20.2%	20.4%	20.6%	20.8%	21.0%	21.2%	21.4%	21.6%	21.8%	22.0%
0	.01326	.01323	.01319	.01315	.01312	.01309	.01305	.01302	.01299	.01296
1	.00245	.00243	.00241	.00238	.00236	.00234	.00232	.00230	.00228	.00226
2	.00203	.00200	.00198	.00196	.00194	.00192	.00190	.00188	.00186	.00184
3	.00181	.00179	.00176	.00174	.00172	.00170	.00168	.00166	.00164	.00162
4	.00171	.00168	.00166	.00164	.00161	.00159	.00157	.00155	.00153	.00151
5	.00169	.00166	.00163	.00161	.00158	.00156	.00153	.00151	.00149	.00147
6	.00170	.00167	.00164	.00162	.00159	.00156	.00154	.00151	.00149	.00147
7	.00176	.00172	.00169	.00166	.00163	.00160	.00158	.00155	.00152	.00150
8	.00186	.00182	.00179	.00175	.00172	.00169	.00166	.00163	.00160	.00157
9	.00203	.00199	.00195	.00192	.00188	.00185	.00181	.00178	.00175	.00172
10	.00228	.00224	.00220	.00216	.00212	.00208	.00204	.00200	.00197	.00193
11	.00264	.00260	.00255	.00251	.00246	.00242	.00238	.00234	.00230	.00226
12	.00310	.00304	.00299	.00295	.00290	.00285	.00281	.00276	.00272	.00268
13	.00360	.00355	.00350	.00344	.00339	.00334	.00329	.00325	.00320	.00315
14	.00409	.00404	.00398	.00392	.00387	.00382	.00376	.00371	.00366	.00361
15	.00454	.00448	.00442	.00436	.00430	.00424	.00419	.00414	.00408	.00403
16	.00492	.00486	.00479	.00473	.00467	.00461	.00456	.00450	.00445	.00439
17	.00523	.00516	.00510	.00503	.00497	.00491	.00485	.00479	.00474	.00468
18	.00548	.00541	.00534	.00528	.00521	.00515	.00509	.00503	.00497	.00491
19	.00570	.00563	.00556	.00549	.00543	.00536	.00530	.00524	.00518	.00512
20	.00588	.00581	.00574	.00567	.00560	.00553	.00547	.00541	.00534	.00528
21	.00602	.00594	.00587	.00580	.00573	.00566	.00559	.00553	.00547	.00540
22	.00612	.00604	.00596	.00589	.00582	.00575	.00568	.00561	.00555	.00549
23	.00618	.00610	.00602	.00595	.00587	.00580	.00573	.00566	.00560	.00553
24	.00625	.00617	.00609	.00601	.00593	.00586	.00578	.00571	.00564	.00558
25	.00634	.00625	.00616	.00608	.00600	.00592	.00585	.00577	.00570	.00563
26	.00646	.00637	.00628	.00620	.00611	.00603	.00595	.00587	.00580	.00572
27	.00665	.00655	.00645	.00636	.00627	.00618	.00610	.00602	.00594	.00586
28	.00687	.00677	.00667	.00657	.00647	.00638	.00629	.00620	.00612	.00604
29	.00715	.00704	.00693	.00683	.00673	.00663	.00653	.00644	.00635	.00626
30	.00749	.00737	.00726	.00714	.00704	.00693	.00683	.00673	.00663	.00654
31	.00791	.00779	.00766	.00754	.00742	.00731	.00720	.00709	.00699	.00689
32	.00841	.00827	.00814	.00801	.00788	.00776	.00764	.00752	.00741	.00730
33	.00901	.00886	.00871	.00857	.00843	.00830	.00817	.00804	.00792	.00780
34	.00969	.00953	.00937	.00922	.00907	.00893	.00878	.00865	.00852	.00839
35	.01048	.01031	.01013	.00997	.00981	.00965	.00950	.00935	.00921	.00907
36	.01136	.01116	.01098	.01080	.01062	.01045	.01029	.01012	.00997	.00982
37	.01233	.01212	.01192	.01172	.01153	.01135	.01117	.01099	.01082	.01066
38	.01341	.01319	.01297	.01275	.01255	.01235	.01215	.01196	.01178	.01160
39	.01461	.01437	.01413	.01390	.01367	.01346	.01324	.01304	.01284	.01264
40	.01594	.01568	.01542	.01517	.01492	.01469	.01446	.01423	.01401	.01380
41	.01741	.01712	.01684	.01657	.01630	.01605	.01580	.01555	.01531	.01508
42	.01900	.01868	.01838	.01809	.01780	.01752	.01725	.01698	.01673	.01648
43	.02072	.02038	.02005	.01973	.01942	.01912	.01882	.01854	.01826	.01799
44	.02258	.02222	.02186	.02152	.02118	.02085	.02054	.02023	.01992	.01963
45	.02462	.02422	.02384	.02346	.02310	.02275	.02240	.02207	.02174	.02142
46	.02682	.02639	.02598	.02557	.02518	.02480	.02443	.02407	.02371	.02337
47	.02920	.02875	.02830	.02787	.02744	.02703	.02663	.02624	.02586	.02549
48	.03176	.03127	.03079	.03032	.02987	.02943	.02899	.02857	.02816	.02776
49	.03448	.03395	.03343	.03293	.03244	.03197	.03150	.03105	.03061	.03018
50	.03735	.03678	.03623	.03569	.03516	.03465	.03415	.03366	.03319	.03272
51	.04039	.03978	.03919	.03861	.03805	.03750	.03696	.03644	.03593	.03543
52	.04367	.04302	.04238	.04176	.04115	.04057	.03999	.03943	.03888	.03835
53	.04719	.04649	.04581	.04515	.04450	.04387	.04325	.04265	.04206	.04149
54	.05094	.05019	.04946	.04875	.04806	.04738	.04673	.04608	.04545	.04484

Table U(1) *(continued)*

Age	20.2%	20.4%	20.6%	20.8%	21.0%	21.2%	21.4%	21.6%	21.8%	22.0%
55	.05494	.05414	.05337	.05261	.05187	.05115	.05044	.04975	.04908	.04842
56	.05922	.05837	.05754	.05673	.05594	.05517	.05442	.05368	.05296	.05226
57	.06382	.06291	.06203	.06117	.06032	.05950	.05870	.05791	.05714	.05639
58	.06876	.06780	.06686	.06594	.06504	.06416	.06331	.06247	.06165	.06085
59	.07406	.07303	.07203	.07105	.07010	.06917	.06825	.06736	.06649	.06564
60	.07968	.07859	.07753	.07649	.07548	.07449	.07352	.07257	.07164	.07073
61	.08561	.08446	.08333	.08223	.08116	.08010	.07908	.07807	.07708	.07612
62	.09183	.09061	.08942	.08826	.08712	.08600	.08491	.08384	.08280	.08177
63	.09834	.09705	.09579	.09456	.09335	.09217	.09102	.08989	.08878	.08769
64	.10517	.10381	.10248	.10118	.09990	.09865	.09743	.09624	.09506	.09391
65	.11242	.11098	.10958	.10820	.10685	.10554	.10424	.10298	.10174	.10052
66	.12016	.11865	.11717	.11572	.11429	.11290	.11154	.11020	.10889	.10760
67	.12845	.12686	.12530	.12377	.12227	.12081	.11937	.11796	.11657	.11521
68	.13734	.13567	.13402	.13242	.13084	.12929	.12778	.12629	.12483	.12340
69	.14677	.14501	.14329	.14160	.13994	.13832	.13672	.13516	.13362	.13212
70	.15671	.15487	.15306	.15129	.14955	.14785	.14618	.14453	.14292	.14134
71	.16709	.16517	.16328	.16142	.15960	.15782	.15606	.15434	.15265	.15098
72	.17795	.17594	.17396	.17202	.17012	.16825	.16641	.16460	.16283	.16109
73	.18931	.18721	.18515	.18312	.18113	.17918	.17726	.17537	.17351	.17169
74	.20131	.19913	.19698	.19487	.19279	.19075	.18874	.18677	.18483	.18292
75	.21410	.21183	.20959	.20739	.20523	.20310	.20101	.19895	.19693	.19493
76	.22779	.22543	.22310	.22082	.21857	.21636	.21418	.21204	.20993	.20786
77	.24241	.23997	.23756	.23520	.23287	.23057	.22831	.22609	.22390	.22174
78	.25797	.25545	.25296	.25052	.24811	.24573	.24340	.24109	.23882	.23658
79	.27433	.27173	.26917	.26665	.26417	.26172	.25931	.25693	.25458	.25227
80	.29136	.28870	.28607	.28348	.28093	.27841	.27593	.27348	.27107	.26869
81	.30883	.30610	.30342	.30077	.29815	.29557	.29303	.29052	.28804	.28559
82	.32660	.32382	.32108	.31837	.31570	.31307	.31047	.30790	.30536	.30285
83	.34453	.34171	.33892	.33617	.33345	.33076	.32811	.32549	.32290	.32034
84	.36267	.35981	.35698	.35418	.35142	.34869	.34599	.34333	.34069	.33809
85	.38111	.37822	.37536	.37253	.36973	.36696	.36423	.36153	.35885	.35621
86	.39961	.39669	.39380	.39095	.38813	.38533	.38257	.37983	.37713	.37446
87	.41776	.41482	.41192	.40904	.40620	.40338	.40060	.39784	.39511	.39241
88	.43563	.43268	.42976	.42687	.42401	.42118	.41837	.41559	.41284	.41012
89	.45365	.45070	.44777	.44487	.44200	.43916	.43634	.43355	.43079	.42805
90	.47212	.46917	.46625	.46335	.46048	.45764	.45482	.45203	.44926	.44652
91	.49073	.48780	.48489	.48201	.47915	.47632	.47351	.47072	.46796	.46522
92	.50888	.50596	.50308	.50021	.49738	.49456	.49177	.48900	.48625	.48352
93	.52624	.52336	.52050	.51766	.51485	.51206	.50929	.50654	.50381	.50110
94	.54253	.53968	.53685	.53404	.53126	.52849	.52575	.52303	.52032	.51764
95	.55753	.55472	.55192	.54915	.54639	.54366	.54094	.53825	.53557	.53291
96	.57097	.56819	.56543	.56268	.55996	.55725	.55456	.55190	.54924	.54661
97	.58334	.58058	.57785	.57514	.57244	.56976	.56710	.56446	.56184	.55923
98	.59449	.59177	.58907	.58638	.58371	.58106	.57843	.57581	.57321	.57063
99	.60481	.60212	.59944	.59678	.59414	.59151	.58890	.58631	.58373	.58117
100	.61429	.61162	.60897	.60633	.60371	.60110	.59851	.59594	.59338	.59084
101	.62313	.62048	.61785	.61523	.61263	.61004	.60747	.60491	.60236	.59984
102	.63228	.62965	.62703	.62443	.62184	.61927	.61671	.61417	.61164	.60913
103	.64180	.63918	.63658	.63399	.63141	.62885	.62631	.62377	.62126	.61875
104	.65215	.64955	.64695	.64437	.64180	.63925	.63671	.63418	.63166	.62916
105	.66516	.66257	.65998	.65741	.65484	.65229	.64976	.64723	.64471	.64221
106	.68579	.68324	.68070	.67817	.67564	.67313	.67063	.66813	.66565	.66317
107	.71895	.71653	.71411	.71170	.70929	.70689	.70450	.70211	.69974	.69736
108	.78150	.77946	.77744	.77541	.77339	.77136	.76935	.76733	.76532	.76331
109	.89900	.89800	.89700	.89600	.89500	.89400	.89300	.89200	.89100	.89000

Table U(1)   *BASED ON LIFE TABLE 80CNSMT UNITRUST SINGLE LIFE REMAINDER FACTORS ADJUSTED PAYOUT RATE*

Age	22.2%	22.4%	22.6%	22.8%	23.0%	23.2%	23.4%	23.6%	23.8%	24.0%
0	.01292	.01289	.01286	.01283	.01280	.01277	.01274	.01271	.01268	.01266
1	.00224	.00222	.00221	.00219	.00217	.00215	.00214	.00212	.00210	.00209
2	.00182	.00180	.00178	.00177	.00175	.00173	.00172	.00170	.00169	.00167
3	.00160	.00158	.00156	.00154	.00153	.00151	.00150	.00148	.00146	.00145
4	.00149	.00147	.00145	.00143	.00141	.00140	.00138	.00136	.00135	.00133
5	.00145	.00143	.00141	.00139	.00137	.00135	.00133	.00132	.00130	.00128
6	.00144	.00142	.00140	.00138	.00136	.00134	.00132	.00130	.00128	.00127
7	.00147	.00145	.00143	.00140	.00138	.00136	.00134	.00132	.00130	.00128
8	.00155	.00152	.00149	.00147	.00144	.00142	.00140	.00137	.00135	.00133
9	.00169	.00166	.00163	.00160	.00157	.00154	.00152	.00149	.00147	.00144
10	.00190	.00187	.00183	.00180	.00177	.00174	.00171	.00168	.00166	.00163
11	.00222	.00218	.00215	.00211	.00208	.00205	.00201	.00198	.00195	.00192
12	.00263	.00259	.00256	.00252	.00248	.00244	.00241	.00237	.00234	.00230
13	.00311	.00306	.00302	.00298	.00294	.00290	.00286	.00282	.00278	.00275
14	.00357	.00352	.00347	.00343	.00339	.00334	.00330	.00326	.00322	.00318
15	.00398	.00393	.00388	.00384	.00379	.00375	.00370	.00366	.00362	.00357
16	.00434	.00429	.00424	.00419	.00414	.00410	.00405	.00400	.00396	.00392
17	.00463	.00458	.00452	.00447	.00442	.00437	.00433	.00428	.00423	.00419
18	.00486	.00480	.00475	.00470	.00465	.00460	.00455	.00450	.00445	.00440
19	.00506	.00500	.00495	.00490	.00484	.00479	.00474	.00469	.00464	.00459
20	.00523	.00517	.00511	.00506	.00500	.00495	.00490	.00485	.00480	.00475
21	.00534	.00528	.00523	.00517	.00512	.00506	.00501	.00496	.00491	.00486
22	.00542	.00536	.00530	.00525	.00519	.00514	.00508	.00503	.00498	.00493
23	.00547	.00541	.00534	.00529	.00523	.00517	.00511	.00506	.00501	.00496
24	.00551	.00544	.00538	.00532	.00526	.00520	.00515	.00509	.00503	.00498
25	.00556	.00549	.00543	.00537	.00530	.00524	.00518	.00512	.00507	.00501
26	.00565	.00558	.00551	.00544	.00538	.00532	.00525	.00519	.00513	.00508
27	.00578	.00571	.00564	.00557	.00550	.00543	.00537	.00530	.00524	.00518
28	.00596	.00588	.00580	.00573	.00565	.00558	.00551	.00545	.00538	.00532
29	.00618	.00609	.00601	.00593	.00585	.00578	.00571	.00563	.00556	.00550
30	.00644	.00635	.00627	.00618	.00610	.00602	.00594	.00586	.00579	.00572
31	.00679	.00669	.00660	.00651	.00642	.00633	.00625	.00616	.00608	.00601
32	.00719	.00709	.00699	.00689	.00679	.00670	.00661	.00652	.00643	.00635
33	.00769	.00757	.00746	.00736	.00725	.00715	.00705	.00696	.00687	.00677
34	.00826	.00814	.00802	.00791	.00779	.00768	.00758	.00747	.00737	.00727
35	.00893	.00880	.00867	.00854	.00842	.00830	.00819	.00807	.00796	.00785
36	.00967	.00952	.00938	.00925	.00912	.00899	.00886	.00874	.00862	.00850
37	.01050	.01034	.01019	.01004	.00990	.00976	.00962	.00948	.00935	.00923
38	.01142	.01125	.01109	.01092	.01077	.01061	.01046	.01032	.01018	.01004
39	.01245	.01227	.01209	.01191	.01174	.01157	.01141	.01125	.01110	.01094
40	.01359	.01339	.01320	.01301	.01282	.01264	.01246	.01229	.01212	.01195
41	.01486	.01464	.01443	.01422	.01402	.01382	.01363	.01344	.01326	.01308
42	.01623	.01600	.01576	.01554	.01532	.01510	.01489	.01469	.01449	.01430
43	.01772	.01746	.01721	.01697	.01673	.01650	.01627	.01605	.01583	.01562
44	.01934	.01906	.01879	.01853	.01827	.01801	.01777	.01753	.01729	.01706
45	.02111	.02081	.02052	.02023	.01995	.01967	.01941	.01914	.01889	.01864
46	.02303	.02271	.02239	.02208	.02177	.02148	.02119	.02090	.02063	.02036
47	.02513	.02477	.02443	.02409	.02376	.02344	.02313	.02282	.02253	.02223
48	.02737	.02699	.02662	.02626	.02590	.02556	.02522	.02489	.02457	.02425
49	.02976	.02934	.02894	.02855	.02817	.02780	.02743	.02708	.02673	.02639
50	.03227	.03183	.03140	.03098	.03057	.03017	.02977	.02939	.02902	.02865
51	.03495	.03447	.03401	.03356	.03311	.03268	.03226	.03185	.03144	.03105
52	.03783	.03732	.03682	.03633	.03586	.03539	.03494	.03449	.03406	.03364
53	.04093	.04038	.03985	.03933	.03882	.03832	.03783	.03735	.03689	.03643
54	.04424	.04365	.04308	.04252	.04197	.04144	.04091	.04040	.03990	.03941

Table U(1) *(continued)*

Age	22.2%	22.4%	22.6%	22.8%	23.0%	23.2%	23.4%	23.6%	23.8%	24.0%
55	.04778	0.4715	.04654	.04594	.04535	.04478	.04422	.04367	.04313	.04260
56	.05157	.05090	.05024	.04960	.04897	.04836	.04776	.04717	.04659	.04603
57	.05566	.05494	.05424	.05355	.05288	.05222	.05158	.05095	.05033	.04973
58	.06007	.05930	.05855	.05782	.05710	.05640	.05571	.05504	.05438	.05373
59	.06480	.06399	.06319	.06241	.06164	.06089	.06016	.05944	.05873	.05804
60	.06984	.06898	.06812	.06729	.06648	.06568	.06489	.06413	.06337	.06264
61	.07518	.07425	.07335	.07246	.07159	.07074	.06991	.06909	.06829	.06751
62	.08077	.07979	.07883	.07789	.07697	.07606	.07518	.07431	.07346	.07262
63	.08663	.08559	.08457	.08357	.08259	.08163	.08069	.07977	.07886	.07798
64	.09279	.09169	.09060	.08954	.08851	.08749	.08649	.08551	.08455	.08360
65	.09933	.09816	.09702	.09589	.09479	.09371	.09265	.09161	.09059	.08959
66	.10634	.10511	.10390	.10271	.10154	.10040	.09928	.09817	.09709	.09603
67	.11388	.11258	.11130	.11004	.10881	.10760	.10641	.10524	.10410	.10297
68	.12200	.12062	.11927	.11794	.11664	.11536	.11410	.11287	.11166	.11047
69	.13064	.12919	.12776	.12636	.12499	.12364	.12232	.12101	.11973	.11848
70	.13978	.13825	.13675	.13528	.13383	.13241	.13102	.12964	.12829	.12697
71	.14935	.14775	.14617	.14462	.14310	.14160	.14013	.13869	.13727	.13587
72	.15938	.15769	.15604	.15441	.15281	.15124	.14970	.14818	.14668	.14521
73	.16989	.16813	.16640	.16469	.16301	.16136	.15974	.15814	.15657	.15503
74	.18104	.17920	.17738	.17559	.17384	.17211	.17040	.16873	.16708	.16546
75	.19297	.19104	.18914	.18728	.18544	.18362	.18184	.18009	.17836	.17665
76	.20581	.20380	.20182	.19987	.19794	.19605	.19419	.19235	.19054	.18876
77	.21961	.21752	.21545	.21342	.21142	.20945	.20750	.20558	.20370	.20183
78	.23438	.23221	.23006	.22795	.22587	.22382	.22180	.21980	.21784	.21590
79	.24999	.24774	.24553	.24334	.24118	.23906	.23696	.23489	.23285	.23083
80	.26634	.26402	.26173	.25947	.25725	.25505	.25288	.25074	.24863	.24654
81	.28318	.28079	.27844	.27612	.27382	.27156	.26933	.26712	.26494	.26279
82	.30038	.27974	.29552	.29314	.29079	.28846	.28617	.28390	.28166	.27944
83	.31781	.31532	.31285	.31041	.30800	.30562	.30327	.30094	.29865	.29637
84	.33551	.33297	.33045	.32797	.32551	.32308	.32067	.31830	.31595	.31362
85	.35359	.35101	.34845	.34592	.34342	.34095	.33850	.33608	.33369	.33132
86	.37181	.36919	.36660	.36403	.36150	.35899	.35650	.35404	.35161	.34920
87	.38973	.38708	.38446	.38187	.37930	.37676	.37424	.37175	.36929	.36684
88	.40742	.40475	.40211	.39949	.39690	.39433	.39178	.38926	.38677	.38430
89	.42534	.42265	.41999	.41735	.41474	.41215	.40958	.40704	.40452	.40203
90	.44380	.44111	.43844	.43579	.43317	.43057	.42799	.42543	.42290	.42039
91	.46251	.45982	.45715	.45450	.45188	.44927	.44669	.44414	.44160	.43908
92	.48082	.47814	.47548	.47284	.47022	.46763	.46505	.46250	.45996	.45745
93	.49842	.49576	.49311	.49049	.48788	.48530	.48274	.48019	.47767	.47516
94	.51498	.51233	.50971	.50711	.50452	.50195	.49941	.49688	.49437	.49187
95	.53028	.52766	.52505	.52247	.51991	.51736	.51483	.51232	.50983	.50735
96	.54400	.54140	.53882	.53626	.53372	.53119	.52868	.52619	.52371	.52125
97	.55664	.55407	.55151	.54897	.54645	.54394	.54145	.53898	.53652	.53408
98	.56806	.56551	.56297	.56046	.55795	.55547	.55300	.55054	.54810	.54567
99	.57862	.57609	.57358	.57108	.56859	.56613	.56367	.56123	.55881	.55640
100	.58831	.58580	.58330	.58082	.57835	.57590	.57346	.57104	.56863	.56624
101	.59732	.59483	.59234	.58987	.58742	.58498	.58255	.58013	.57774	.57535
102	.60663	.60414	.60167	.59921	.59676	.59433	.59191	.58951	.58712	.58474
103	.61626	.61378	.61131	.60886	.60642	.60400	.60159	.59919	.59680	.59443
104	.62667	.62419	.62173	.61927	.61683	.61440	.61199	.60959	.60719	.60482
105	.63972	.63724	.63477	.63231	.62986	.62743	.62501	.62259	.62019	.61780
106	.66071	.65825	.65581	.65337	.65094	.64852	.64612	.64372	.64133	.63895
107	.69500	.69264	.69029	.68794	.68560	.68327	.68094	.67862	.67631	.67400
108	.76130	.75929	.75729	.75529	.75329	.75130	.74930	.74731	.74533	.74334
109	.88900	.88800	.88700	.88600	.88500	.88400	.88300	.88200	.88100	.88000

Table U(1) *BASED ON LIFE TABLE 80CNSMT UNITRUST SINGLE LIFE REMAINDER FACTORS ADJUSTED PAYOUT RATE*

Age	24.2%	24.4%	24.6%	24.8%	25.0%	25.2%	25.4%	25.6%	25.8%	26.0%
0	.01263	.01260	.01257	.01254	.01252	.01249	.01246	.01244	.01241	.01239
1	.00207	.00206	.00204	.00203	.00202	.00200	.00199	.00197	.00196	.00195
2	.00166	.00164	.00163	.00162	.00160	.00159	.00158	.00156	.00155	.00154
3	.00143	.00142	.00141	.00139	.00138	.00137	.00135	.00134	.00133	.00132
4	.00132	.00130	.00129	.00127	.00126	.00125	.00123	.00122	.00121	.00120
5	.00127	.00125	.00124	.00122	.00121	.00119	.00118	.00117	.00115	.00114
6	.00125	.00123	.00122	.00120	.00118	.00117	.00115	.00114	.00113	.00111
7	.00126	.00124	.00122	.00121	.00119	.00117	.00115	.00114	.00112	.00111
8	.00131	.00129	.00127	.00125	.00123	.00121	.00119	.00117	.00116	.00114
9	.00142	.00140	.00137	.00135	.00133	.00131	.00129	.00127	.00125	.00123
10	.00160	.00158	.00155	.00153	.00150	.00148	.00145	.00143	.00141	.00139
11	.00189	.00186	.00183	.00180	.00178	.00175	.00172	.00170	.00167	.00165
12	.00227	.00224	.00221	.00217	.00214	.00211	.00208	.00206	.00203	.00200
13	.00271	.00268	.00264	.00261	.00257	.00254	.00251	.00248	.00245	.00242
14	.00314	.00310	.00307	.00303	.00299	.00296	.00292	.00289	.00286	.00283
15	.00353	.00349	.00345	.00341	.00338	.00334	.00330	.00327	.00323	.00320
16	.00387	.00383	.00379	.00375	.00371	.00367	.00363	.00359	.00356	.00352
17	.00414	.00410	.00406	.00402	.00397	.00393	.00389	.00385	.00382	.00378
18	.00436	.00431	.00427	.00423	.00418	.00414	.00410	.00406	.00402	.00398
19	.00455	.00450	.00446	.00441	.00437	.00433	.00428	.00424	.00420	.00416
20	.00470	.00465	.00461	.00456	.00452	.00447	.00443	.00439	.00435	.00431
21	.00481	.00476	.00471	.00467	.00462	.00458	.00453	.00449	.00445	.00441
22	.00488	.00483	.00478	.00473	.00469	.00464	.00460	.00455	.00451	.00447
23	.00490	.00485	.00481	.00476	.00471	.00466	.00462	.00457	.00453	.00449
24	.00493	.00488	.00483	.00478	.00473	.00468	.00464	.00459	.00455	.00450
25	.00496	.00490	.00485	.00480	.00475	.00470	.00466	.00461	.00456	.00452
26	.00502	.00496	.00491	.00486	.00480	.00475	.00470	.00466	.00461	.00456
27	.00512	.00506	.00501	.00495	.00490	.00484	.00479	.00474	.00469	.00464
28	.00525	.00519	.00513	.00508	.00502	.00496	.00491	.00485	.00480	.00475
29	.00543	.00536	.00530	.00524	.00518	.00512	.00506	.00500	.00495	.00489
30	.00565	.00558	.00551	.00544	.00538	.00531	.00525	.00519	.00513	.00507
31	.00593	.00585	.00578	.00571	.00564	.00557	.00551	.00544	.00538	.00532
32	.00627	.00619	.00611	.00603	.00596	.00588	.00581	.00574	.00567	.00561
33	.00668	.00660	.00651	.00643	.00635	.00627	.00619	.00612	.00604	.00597
34	.00718	.00708	.00699	.00690	.00681	.00673	.00664	.00656	.00648	.00640
35	.00775	.00765	.00755	.00745	.00735	.00726	.00717	.00708	.00699	.00691
36	.00839	.00827	.00817	.00806	.00796	.00785	.00775	.00766	.00756	.00747
37	.00910	.00898	.00886	.00875	.00863	.00852	.00842	.00831	.00821	.00811
38	.00990	.00977	.00964	.00951	.00939	.00927	.00915	.00904	.00893	.00882
39	.01080	.01065	.01051	.01037	.01024	.01011	.00998	.00986	.00973	.00961
40	.01179	.01164	.01148	.01133	.01119	.01104	.01091	.01077	.01063	.01050
41	.01290	.01273	.01256	.01240	.01224	.01209	.01193	.01178	.01164	.01150
42	.01411	.01392	.01374	.01356	.01339	.01322	.01305	.01289	.01273	.01258
43	.01541	.01521	.01501	.01482	.01463	.01445	.01427	.01409	.01392	.01375
44	.01684	.01662	.01640	.01619	.01599	.01579	.01559	.01540	.01521	.01503
45	.01840	.01816	.01793	.01770	.01748	.01726	.01705	.01684	.01663	.01643
46	.02009	.01984	.01958	.01934	.01910	.01886	.01863	.01840	.01818	.01797
47	.02195	.02167	.02140	.02113	.02087	.02061	.02036	.02012	.01988	.01964
48	.02394	.02364	.02334	.02306	.02277	.02250	.02223	.02196	.02170	.02145
49	.02606	.02573	.02541	.02510	.02480	.02450	.02420	.02392	.02364	.02336
50	.02829	.02794	.02760	.02726	.02693	.02661	.02629	.02598	.02568	.02538
51	.03066	.03028	.02991	.02955	.02920	.02885	.02851	.02817	.02785	.02753
52	.03322	.03281	.03241	.03202	.03164	.03127	.03090	.03054	.03019	.02985
53	.03598	.03554	.03512	.03470	.03429	.03388	.03349	.03310	.03272	.03235
54	.03893	.03846	.03800	.03755	.03711	.03667	.03625	.03584	.03543	.03503

Table U(1) *(continued)*

Age	24.2%	24.4%	24.6%	24.8%	25.0%	25.2%	25.4%	25.6%	25.8%	26.0%
55	.04209	.04158	.04109	.04061	.04013	.03967	.03921	.03876	.03833	.03790
56	.04548	.04494	.04440	.04389	.04338	.04288	.04239	.04191	.04144	.04098
57	.04914	.04856	.04799	.04743	.04689	.04635	.04583	.04531	.04481	.04431
58	.05310	.05247	.05187	.05127	.05069	.05011	.04955	.04900	.04846	.04793
59	.05736	.05670	.05605	.05541	.05479	.05417	.05357	.05298	.05240	.05183
60	.06192	.06121	.06051	.05983	.05916	.05851	.05787	·05723	.05662	.05601
61	.06674	.06598	.06524	.06452	.06380	.06310	.06242	.06174	.06108	.06043
62	.07180	.07100	.07021	.06944	.06868	.06793	.06720	.06648	.06578	.06509
63	.07711	.07625	.07541	.07459	.07378	.07299	.07221	.07145	.07070	.06996
64	.08268	.08177	.08088	.08000	.07915	.07830	.07747	.07666	.07586	.07508
65	.08861	.08765	.08670	.08577	.08486	.08396	.08308	.08222	.08136	.08053
66	.09499	.09397	.09296	.09197	.09100	.09005	.08912	.08820	.08729	.08640
67	.10187	.10078	.09972	.09867	.09764	.09663	.09564	.09466	.09370	.09276
68	.10930	.10815	.10702	.10592	.10483	.10375	.10270	.10167	.10065	.09965
69	.11724	.11603	.11483	.11366	.11251	.11137	.11026	.10916	.10808	.10702
70	.12566	.12438	.12312	.12188	.12066	.11947	.11829	.11713	.11599	.11486
71	.13450	.13314	.13181	.13051	.12922	.12796	.12671	.12549	.12428	.12309
72	.14376	.14234	.14094	.13956	.13821	.13687	.13556	.13427	.13300	.13174
73	.15350	.15201	.15053	.14908	.14766	.14625	.14487	.14350	.14216	.14084
74	.16386	.16229	.16074	.15921	.15771	.15623	.15477	.15334	.15192	.15053
75	.17498	.17333	.17170	.17010	.16852	.16697	.16543	.16392	.16244	.16097
76	.18700	.18527	.18357	.18189	.18023	.17860	.17699	.17541	.17385	.17230
77	.20000	.19819	.19641	.19465	.19292	.19121	.18952	.18786	.18622	.18460
78	.21398	.21210	.21024	.20840	.20659	.20481	.20305	.20131	.19960	.19790
79	.22885	.22689	.22495	.22304	.22116	.21930	.21747	.21565	.21387	.21210
80	.24448	.24245	.24045	.23847	.23651	.23458	.23268	.23079	.22894	.22710
81	.26066	.25856	.25649	.25444	.25242	.25043	.24845	.24650	.24458	.24268
82	.27726	.27510	.27296	.27085	.26877	.26670	.26467	.26266	.26067	.25870
83	.29413	.29191	.28972	.28755	.28541	.28329	.28119	.27912	.27707	.27504
84	.31133	.30906	.30681	.30459	.30239	.30022	.29807	.29594	.29384	.29175
85	.32897	.32666	.32436	.32209	.31985	.31763	.31543	.31325	.31110	.30897
86	.34682	.34446	.34213	.33982	.33753	.33526	.33302	.33080	.32861	.32643
87	.36443	.36203	.35966	.35731	.35499	.35269	.35041	.34815	.34591	.34370
88	.38185	.37942	.37702	.37464	.37228	.36995	.36763	.36534	.36307	.36082
89	.39956	.39710	.39468	.39227	.38988	.38752	.38518	.38285	.38055	.37827
90	.41790	.41543	.41299	.41056	.40816	.40577	.40341	.40106	.39874	.39643
91	.43659	.43411	.43165	.42922	.42680	.42441	.42203	.41968	.41734	.41502
92	.45495	.45248	.45002	.44759	.44517	.44277	.44039	.43803	.43568	.43336
93	.47267	.47020	.46775	.46532	.46291	.46051	.45813	.45577	.45343	.45111
94	.48940	.48694	.48450	.48208	.47968	.47729	.47492	.47256	.47023	.46791
95	.50489	.50245	.50003	.49762	.49523	.49285	.49049	.48815	.48582	.48351
96	.51881	.51638	.51397	.51158	.50920	.50684	.50449	.50216	.49984	.49754
97	.53166	.52925	.52685	.52447	.52211	.51976	.51742	.51510	.51280	.51051
98	.54326	.54087	.53849	.53613	.53377	.53144	.52912	.52681	.52452	.52224
99	.55401	.55163	.54926	.54691	.54457	.54225	.53994	.53765	.53536	.53310
100	.56386	.56149	.55914	.55680	.55447	.55216	.54986	.54757	.54530	.54304
101	.57298	.57062	.56827	.56594	.56362	.56132	.55903	.55675	.55448	.55223
102	.58238	.58003	.57769	.57536	.57305	.57075	.56846	.56619	.56392	.56167
103	.59206	.58971	.58738	.58505	.58274	.58044	.57816	.57588	.57362	.57137
104	.60245	.60009	.59775	.59542	.59310	.59079	.58849	.58621	.58393	.58167
105	.61542	.61305	.61069	.60835	.60601	.60369	.60137	.59907	.59677	.59449
106	.63658	.63421	.63186	.62952	.62718	.62486	.62254	.62023	.61794	.61565
107	.67170	.66940	.66712	.66483	.66256	.66029	.6??03	.65577	.65352	.65128
108	.74136	.73938	.73740	.73543	.73346	.73149	.72952	.72756	.72559	.72364
109	.87900	.87800	.87700	.87600	.87500	.87400	.87300	.87200	.87100	.87000

Appendix B

*ESTATE PLANNING GLOSSARY OF TERMS**

Abatement a reduction, decrease, or proportional diminution of pecuniary legacies (money) when the funds or assets out of which the legacies are payable are not sufficient to pay them in full.

Ademption the extinction or withdrawal of a legacy according to the intentions of the maker of the will. If specific property is left to a beneficiary under the terms of a will, and the property is either given to the beneficiary during the maker's lifetime, or is destroyed before the maker dies, so that there is nothing left to give to the beneficiary, this is an example of ademption.

Adjusted taxable gift the value of a gift, minus the annual exclusion amount, which is subject to payment of a gift tax; the value of all adjusted taxable gifts made after 1976 is added to the taxable estate in order to calculate the amount of federal estate tax that must be paid (the combination of all post-1976 adjusted taxable gifts and the taxable estate is referred to as the tentative tax base).

* © 1986 College for Financial Planning. This appendix is reprinted with permission of the College for Financial Planning.

Alternate valuation date   a valuation technique used to value assets in a decedent's estate; the alternate valuation date is usually 6 months after the date of the decedent's death and assets are valued as of this date rather than on the date of death.

Alternate valuation election   an election made by the executor of an estate on the federal estate tax return. By making the election, the executor chooses to have all assets included in the gross estate valued at their alternate value, which is the value the assets had on the date 6 months after the date of the decedent's death.

Annual exclusion amount   an amount which a donor can gift to a donee annually without payment of gift tax; currently, a donor can gift $10,000 to each donee per year without being subjected to gift tax liability.

Ascertainable standard   a power that is limited by some unit of measurement. A power of appointment that allows the holder to use the property for the holder's benefit, limited to use for the holder's health, education, support or maintenance is a power limited to an ascertainable standard, since it is capable of measurement. Such a power is a limited power of appointment and property or interests subject to such powers are not included in the holder's gross estate.

Available unified credit   the amount of unused unified credit that can be used either by a donor to reduce gift tax liability or by an estate to reduce estate tax liability.

Blockage discount   a valuation technique used to value publicly traded stock. The discount is calculated by determining the market factor for such stock. The discount is determined on the basis of a decrease in the realizable price of the stock below its fair market value.

Buy-sell agreement   an arrangement to dispose of a business interest in the event of the retirement, death, or disability of the business owner. If structured properly, the buy-sell agreement creates an available market and "pegs" the value of the business for estate tax purposes.

Bypass trust   a trust that is used to take advantage of the unified credit amount in a decedent's estate. Typically, an individual uses the bypass trust to provide the surviving spouse with a life income and upon the death of the surviving spouse, the property passes to children or other living heirs. This trust is usually funded in an amount equal to the exemption equivalent and remains in the gross estate of the decedent. Because it is funded in an amount equal to the exemption equivalent, the decedent's estate pays no estate tax on this trust. This trust does not qualify for the marital deduction.

Charitable deduction   a deduction that may be taken by an individual or an estate for a transfer of property to a qualified charity; if the transfer is made to the charity after the donor's death, the transfer reduces the donor's estate tax liability; if the transfer is made to the charity while the donor is alive, the transfer reduces the donor's income tax liability.

Charitable lead trust   a charitable trust that produces income or estate tax savings to the donor of the property. If structured to take effect during a donor's lifetime, the charity receives the income from the trust for a stated period of time (e.g., 20 years) and at the end of the stated time, noncharitable beneficiaries receive the remainder interest. The donor receives an income tax deduction for the charitable contribution based on a percentage of the donor's adjusted gross income. If structured to take effect upon the donor's death, the donor's estate receives a charitable deduction for the present value of the income stream passing to the charity.

Charitable remainder   the portion of a trust that passes to a qualified charity after the termination of an income stream to a noncharitable beneficiary.

Charitable remainder annuity trust (CRAT)   a form of a charitable trust in which the income (or annuity) is first paid to a noncharitable beneficiary (e.g., the spouse or children of the donor) and upon the death of the noncharitable beneficiary, or after a stated period of time (e.g., 20 years), the income stream terminates and the remainder is transferred to the charity. The amount of income passing to the noncharitable beneficiary remains constant for the period in which it is distributed to the noncharitable beneficiary. This amount must be at least 5 percent of the initial fair market value of the property. This trust can generate either income or estate tax savings for the donor.

Charitable remainder unitrust (CRUT)   a form of a charitable trust in which a stream of income is first paid to a noncharitable beneficiary and upon the death of the noncharitable beneficiary, or after a stated period of time (e.g., 20 years), the income stream terminates and the remainder is transferred to the charity. The amount of income passing to the noncharitable beneficiary increases or decreases each year, since a specific percentage (at least 5% of the corpus and income, reappraised annually) must be given to the noncharitable beneficiary. This trust can generate either income or estate tax savings for the donor.

Charitable stock bailout   a charitable contribution technique used for closely held corporations that enables the donor of the stock to take a charitable deduction. The stockholder/grantor donates stock to a qualified charity, for which contribution the donor receives a charitable contribution deduction measured by the present value of the contributed stock. Then the corporation redeems the stock from the charity and the charity receives cash as a result of the redemption.

Clifford trust   see short-term (Clifford) trust

Codicil   a document that modifies the terms of an original will without requiring the entire will to be redrafted. Codicils are often attached to the will and are executed according to the same requirements as a will.

Commercial annuity   a secured promise to pay a sum of money, issued by an insurance company or other professional organization, to an individual in exchange for receipt of property or money from the individual. The sum of money received by the annuitant, often over a period of years, depends on such variables as the health and life expectancy of the annuitant, as well as the fair market value of the property received in the exchange for the payment.

Community property   a form of property ownership used in eight states (Arizona, California, Idaho, Louisiana, Nevada, New Mexico, Texas, and Washington) to determine ownership of property held by a married couple. Generally, for property acquired by the "community" (the married couple), all income, estate, and gift taxes are prorated equally for property acquired while the couple was married. In 1986, Wisconsin adopted the legislative equivalent of community property and became the ninth state to use this form of property ownership.

Completed gift   a transfer of property in which the donor has made a total, irrevocable transfer of dominion, control, and title to the donee. A completed gift is the only type of gift that is subject to gift tax liability.

Conduit principle   the principle that allows current distributions of income from a trust to be taxed to the beneficiary. In effect, the trust reports the income and receives a deduction for income that is required to be distributed to the beneficiary. The beneficiary pays the income tax on the income, thus avoiding double taxation on the income by both the trust and the beneficiary.

Constraint   the general limitations that affect the selection of an estate planning technique which achieves a particular client objective. Constraints are universal in the sense that they have the ability to affect every estate plan; for example, the constraint "competency of beneficiaries" has the potential to affect the selection of an estate planning technique that achieves a client objective of continuing a closely held family business.

Cross-purchase agreement   an agreement which coordinates a buy-sell agreement with life insurance. In a business context, the cross-purchase agreement is used when co-owners of a business take out life insurance policies on the life of another co-owner so that each owner is insured and names the other owners as beneficiaries of the policy. When a co-owner dies, the surviving co-owners use the death benefit proceeds to purchase the deceased's interest in the business, thereby retaining their interests in the business.

"Crummey" power   a trust containing a provision that entitles the trust beneficiary to withdraw a limited amount of income, principal, or both. The power is exercisable for only a very limited time each year (e.g., 3 months per year) and is generally included in a trust in order for the withdrawn income or annual additions to the trust corpus to qualify as a gift of a present interest for purposes of the annual exclusion amount.

"Crummey" trust   a trust which has, as one of its terms, a Crummey power.

Cumulative gift tax   the nature of calculating gift tax liability on all lifetime transfers. The federal gift tax is said to be "cumulative" because gift tax liability for gifts made in the current year is imposed on the total amount of all lifetime gifts, not just on gifts made in the present year.

Current income interest trust   a trust that is required to distribute its income at least once annually to the spouse of the grantor. The spouse must be the only recipient of the income and the income is distributed to the spouse for life. Upon the death of the spouse, the trust terminates and the remainder interest passes to children or other remaindermen designated by the grantor. If the executor of the grantor's estate makes an election on the federal estate tax return, the property transferred to this trust qualifies for the marital deduction in the estate of the grantor and the value of the trust property must be included in the gross estate of the surviving spouse. This trust is also known as a Q-TIP trust.

Custodianship   a fiduciary relationship in which an adult or trust company controls and supervises property on behalf of a minor, usually in furtherance of the Uniform Gifts to Minors Act or Uniform Transfers to Minors Act. Though the custodian does not hold legal title to the property (legal title is held by the minor), the custodian has a duty to invest and reinvest the custodial property according to reasonable and prudent standards, and may use the custodial property for the support, education, and benefit of the minor without regard to the parent's obligation or resources.

Disclaimer   an exclusion technique used to reduce the size of a gross estate. It consists of an absolute, unqualified renunciation of any beneficial interest, use, enjoyment, or ownership of property. If the disclaimer is "qualified," the value of the property subject to the disclaimer is excluded from the gross estate of the individual filing the disclaimer.

Disclaimer of power   an unqualified renunciation or refusal (in writing) by a potential beneficiary to accept benefits through a testamentary or lifetime transfer. A power of appointment that is disclaimed will be treated for tax purposes as if the potential beneficiary never received the property. Thus, the value of the property subject to the power is not included in the gross estate of the disclaimant. In order to qualify as a disclaimer, the beneficiary cannot have received any benefits or income from the property subject to the power.

Disclaimer trust   an irrevocable trust established to receive assets that are disclaimed by the surviving spouse of a decedent. The trust enables the surviving spouse to disclaim the property yet receive the income produced by the trust for the life of the spouse.

Distributable net income   an amount distributed to a trust beneficiary which is subject to income taxation. The concept favors the trust beneficiary, since it gives the trust beneficiary the benefit of all trust deductions, including those allocated to the principal of the trust. For example, though a trust beneficiary might actually receive $12,000 from a trust, it is possible that only $10,000 would be distributable net income because of commissions and other expenses deductible by the trust.

Double deduction rule   the rule that prevents certain expenses of a decedent from being deducted twice, once on the federal estate tax return and again on the decedent's final income tax return. The expenses may only be deducted on either the income tax return or the estate tax return, and a written waiver of a right to claim such expenses must be filed with the return that does not claim the expenses as a deduction.

Election against the will   a statutory right of a surviving spouse to take a portion of the decedent's estate which is usually greater than the amount of property left to the surviving spouse under the terms of the will. The election to take against the will must be filed by the surviving spouse within a specified time after probate of the decedent's estate has begun.

Elective share statute   a state law that preserves the right of a surviving spouse to take a specified portion of a decedent's estate. Typically, the elective share statute allows the surviving spouse to take more property than was left to the spouse under the terms of the decedent's will.

Endowment life insurance   a life insurance policy that pays the face amount of the policy upon the maturity of the contract ("the endowment date") or upon the death of the insured, whichever occurs sooner. The cash value in such a policy builds up tax free under an endowment policy.

Estate trust   a trust that qualifies for the marital deduction, but which is structured in such a way so that the surviving spouse does not receive the corpus during his lifetime and may receive income from the trust at the discretion of the trustee. The trust terminates upon the death of the surviving spouse and the trust assets and all accumulated income are paid to the surviving spouse's estate at that time. The surviving spouse's will determines the ultimate disposition of these assets.

Executor commission   a sum of money paid to the individual who serves as executor of a decedent's estate. The commission is a deductible administrative expense for purposes of the federal estate tax and is usually determined by state law, often as a percentage of the gross estate of the decedent (e.g., 3% of decedent's gross estate if the estate is greater than $100,000 in value).

Exemption equivalent   a stated dollar amount of a gross estate on which there is no estate tax liability. If the total dollar amount of a decedent's gross estate does not exceed the exemption equivalent, the estate has no estate tax liability. In 1985, the exemption equivalent was $400,000; in 1986, the exemption equivalent equaled $500,000; in 1987 and later years, the exemption equivalent rose to $600,000.

Fair market valuation   the most commonly used valuation technique for valuing assets contained in the gross estate. It is commonly determined to be the price agreed upon between a willing seller and a willing buyer.

Family partnership   an unincorporated business association among members of the same family used primarily to split income and reduce estate taxes upon the death of one of the family partners. The association must own a capital interest and does not qualify for favorable tax treatment if its business is solely generated from the performance of personal services.

Family settlement agreement   an agreement made by family members of a decedent who consent to the division of the decedent's property in a particular fashion. The family settlement agreement is normally reached by the family members outside of court with subsequent court approval.

"5 and 5" power   a noncumulative right held by the surviving spouse in which the surviving spouse may withdraw each year from a trust the greater of: (1) 5 percent of the corpus of the trust, or (2) $5000. If exercised, only the property subject to the power is included in the gross estate of the holder. Such a power will prevent inclusion of the entire corpus of the trust as an asset in the gross estate of the surviving spouse.

Flower bonds   certain U.S. Treasury obligations owned by a decedent at death which can be used to pay federal estate taxes. The bonds can be redeemed at their par value and thus pay federal estate taxes at a discount (as opposed to redeeming the bonds at their purchase price).

Fractional interest rule   a rule for determining the portion of a jointly held asset that is included in the gross estate of a decedent joint tenant. Generally, the rule provides that if the surviving joint tenant's contributions are proved, the amount included in the decedent's gross estate is the fractional percentage of ownership in the jointly held asset, not merely the dollar value of the decedent's contribution.

Fractional share formal bequest   a bequest contained in a will which leaves the surviving spouse a fraction of a decedent's residuary estate. The formula is usually stated as a fraction in which the numerator is a particular percent of the adjusted gross estate (e.g., 50% reduced by property passing to the surviving spouse that qualifies for the marital deduction). The denominator is the value of the residuary estate.

Freeze   any technique or mechanism that prevents future appreciation of a business from accumulating in the estate of a business owner. A freeze transfers the appreciation to another individual and prevents estate tax liability from increasing in future years. The Revenue Reconciliation Act of 1990 revived many freeze techniques but subjects them to gift tax treatment when the transferor retains an interest in the transferred asset.

General power of appointment   a power that entitles the holder to transfer the property subject to the power to the holder, the holder's estate, the holder's creditors, or the creditors of the holder's estate. Generally, the holder may transfer the property to whomever the holder wishes. All property subject to this power is included as an asset in the gross estate of the holder.

Generation-skipping trust   a trust in which income from the trust is spread over more than one generation, with the corpus of the trust passing to one or more individuals who are two generations younger than the grantor's generation. A generation-skipping trust can generate estate tax savings since there is a $1 million exclusion per transferor (the $2 million exemption for direct skips of property interests to a grantor's grandchildren expired after 1989). A generation-skipping trust is one in which the grantor could provide income to be distributed to the grantor's spouse for life, with income also to be distributed to the children of the grantor and spouse for as long as the children live. Upon the deaths of all children, the trust would terminate and the principal and undistributed income would be allocated proportionally among all grandchildren of the grantor and the grantor's spouse.

Gift-leaseback   an intrafamily business transfer device which involves a gift of a property used in the donor's business to another family member. The donor frequently gifts the property to a trust, which distributes income from the trust to another family member. At the same time, the donor leases the property back from the trust and acquires an income tax deduction for the cost of leasing the property from the trust. The leaseback provides a stream of income to a family member in a lower marginal tax bracket as well as providing valuable income tax deductions to the donor. The gifted asset is also removed from the donor's gross estate.

Gift of a future interest   a gift in which the donee's possession or enjoyment begins at some time after the gift is made. Gifts of a future interest do not qualify for a gift annual exclusion amount of $10,000 per donee per year.

Gift of present interest   a gift in which the donee's possession or enjoyment begins at the time the gift is made. Gifts of a present interest qualify for the gift annual exclusion amount of $10,000 per donee per year.

Gift tax charitable deduction   a deduction allowed to a donor for gifts made to a qualified charity. The effect of the gift tax charitable deduction is to reduce gift tax liability to zero on gifts made to a qualified charity.

Gift tax marital deduction   a deduction allowed to a donor for gifts made to a spouse during the donor's lifetime. The effect of the gift tax marital deduction is to reduce gift tax liability to zero on gifts made to a spouse during the donor's lifetime.

Grantor annuity trust   an irrevocable trust into which property or money is transferred in exchange for an annuity in a fixed amount payable to the grantor for a specified period of time. The trust is used primarily to provide a stream of income to the grantor for a specific purpose.

Grantor retained annuity trust   a grantor retained income trust in which payments received by the grantor are structured as an annuity.

Grantor retained unitrust   a grantor retained income trust that is structured as a unitrust amount.

Gross estate   the total fair market value of all property and interests owned or held by the decedent at the time of death before subtractions for deductions, debts and administrative expenses, and credits.

Gross-up rule   a rule for estate taxation purposes which requires that the gift taxes paid on all lifetime gifts made within 3 years of the donor's death must be included as an asset in the decedent's gross estate.

Guardianship   a legal relationship in which an individual or co-persons are appointed by a court to take care of the needs of a minor or an incapacitated or incompetent person (the ward). The guardian has the custody and management of the ward's property and makes expenditures, with court approval, on behalf of the ward. The guardian's duty to take care of the ward's needs continues until the ward reaches the age of majority, or once again becomes competent.

Incomplete gift   a transfer of property in which the donor has failed to make an irrevocable transfer of dominion, control, or title to the donee. An incomplete gift is not subject to gift tax liability, but remains a part of the donor's gross estate and could be subject to estate tax liability.

Installment payments of estate tax   a means of paying the federal estate tax due on a decedent's gross estate in a series of payments. Under Internal Revenue Code Section 6166, the executor of an estate containing a closely held business may elect to pay the estate tax attributable to the closely held business in annual installments if the interest in the business exceeds 35 percent of the decedent's gross estate minus reductions for debts and losses, funeral expenses, and administrative expenses.

Installment sale   a sale of property to a buyer in which the buyer is not required to pay the entire purchase price at the time title is transferred to the buyer. The seller receives payments over a period of time, and the installment sale is used by a seller who wishes to spread out the income tax reportable on the receipt of the purchase price. The seller reports gain and taxable income only as it is received.

Interest-free loan   a loan of money made by a lender to a borrower without charging interest on the transaction. Though frequently used between members of one family prior to 1984, the U.S. Supreme Court and the IRS have recently declared that the use of the interest-free loan can generate gift tax liability to the lender as well as income tax liability on the income "imputed" from the interest that would have been charged on such a loan.

"Interest only" option   a settlement option upon the death of the insured in which the beneficiary of the policy receives only the interest, with the principal amount to be distributed at a later date.

Interpolated terminal reserve   a sum maintained by a life insurance company to replace the cost of a whole life insurance policy owned by a decedent on the life of another person; the interpolated terminal reserve, when added to the unexpired portion of premium payments for the current period, equals the replacement cost of a whole life insurance policy owned by a decedent on the life of another.

Intestacy   the scheme for distributing the property of an individual who dies without a will.

Intestate estate   the assets comprising the gross estate of an individual who dies without a will.

Irrevocable living trust   a trust established during the lifetime of a grantor over which the grantor has no power to alter or revoke the terms of the trust, including distributions of income to beneficiaries, terms of income distribution, conditions under which income will not be distributed, or terms under which the trust would terminate.

Joint and last survivor annuity   an annuity payment, either through a commercial annuity or through a private annuity, that pays a fixed sum of money to an annuitant until the annuitant's death, and upon the annuitant's death, continues to pay a fixed sum of money (usually lesser in amount) to a designated beneficiary.

Joint tenancy bank account   a form of will substitute created when two or more individuals open an account with a bank. Both individuals may make deposits or withdrawals. Upon the death of one depositor, the proceeds pass to the survivor and avoid probate.

Joint tenancy with right of survivorship   a form of property ownership in which two or more individuals hold an undivided interest in a property as well as in a part of the property simultaneously. Joint tenancy is characterized by full title passing to the surviving joint tenants upon the death of one of them.

Joint will   a single legal document that serves as the last will and testament for two or more individuals.

"Key individual" life insurance   a life insurance arrangement in which a corporation or partnership insures the life of a valuable employee so that, in the event of death, the corporation or partnership can more easily sustain a financial loss because of the financial protection afforded by the death benefit of the policy. In such arrangements, the business corporation or partnership is named as beneficiary on the policy and uses the death benefits to offset the loss caused by the death of a key employee.

Key personnel discount   a valuation technique used to value closely held stock; the valuation discount is frequently applied to the stock on the grounds that the value of the stock decreases when the company founder dies.

Lack of marketability discount   a valuation technique used to value closely held stock; the discount is applied to the stock on the grounds that, if the stock were to be taken public, its value would decrease because of the costs associated with taking the stock public (e.g., SEC registration fees, underwriter's commissions, and prospectus preparation fees).

Lapse   the failure to exercise or release a power of appointment within a specified time period. For example, a trust may provide that a spouse may withdraw from the corpus of a trust the greater of 5 percent of the corpus or $5000 annually. If the spouse fails to exercise the power within the calendar year, the power is said to have "lapsed."

Life insurance trust   a trust designed to accept life insurance death benefit proceeds upon the death of the insured. The trustee of such a trust, usually named as beneficiary on the life insurance policy, uses the proceeds for the specific purposes and objectives of the insured.

Low-interest loan   a loan of money made by the lender to a borrower with a stated amount of interest that is below the conventional rate of interest charged by lending institutions. The low-interest loan was frequently used between members of the same family prior to 1984. As a result of the U.S. Supreme Court's decision and the Tax Reform Act of 1984, low-interest loans may cause the lender to become subject to income tax liability and gift tax liability.

Marital deduction   a deduction that may be taken by an individual or an estate for a transfer of property to a spouse; if the transfer is made under the terms of a will or after a donor's death, the transfer reduces the donor's estate tax liability; if the transfer is made while the donor is alive, the transfer reduces the donor's gift tax liability to zero.

Marital trust   also known as a power of appointment trust, this trust provides the surviving spouse with the ability to determine the ultimate beneficiaries upon his or her death. The trust may provide the surviving spouse with income for life, or may give the spouse the unrestricted right to use, consume, or transfer the property while alive. However, all marital trusts must provide the surviving spouse's estate with the power to determine the ultimate beneficiaries of the property subject to the power. The property subject to the power qualifies for the marital deduction in the estate of the grantor, and must be included as an asset in the gross estate of the surviving spouse.

Minority interest discount   a valuation technique used to value closely held stock; the discount is applied to the stock in a minority shareholder's estate on the grounds that, as a minority shareholder, the shareholder was unable to influence corporate policy, compel dividend distributions, or force corporation liquidation, merger, consolidation, or sale. The minority interest receives a discount that reflects this lack of marketability to all but majority shareholders.

Mortmain statute   a state law that prohibits an individual from leaving more than a specified percentage of the individual's gross estate to a charity when the individual is survived by a spouse and/or children.

Mutual will   a legal document made pursuant to an agreement in which two or more individuals agree to dispose of their property in a particular way. For example, a mutual will between a husband and wife would exist where each agrees, upon death, to distribute their property to a particular charity.

Net gift   a gift for which the donee agrees to pay the gift tax liability on the amount of the gift rather than having the donor pay the gift tax liability, as is usually required.

Net gift technique   see net gift.

Noncharitable beneficiaries   individuals other than a qualified charitable organization who receive the remainder interest in a charitable lead trust, or who receive a stream of income from a charitable remainder annuity trust or charitable remainder unitrust.

Nonmarital trust   a synonym for the bypass trust. See bypass trust for further definition.

Objective   in the area of estate planning, it is a specific measurable target that a client plans to achieve through a specific course of action.

Partial interest gift   a gift that is split between a noncharitable beneficiary and a charitable beneficiary. An example of a partial interest gift is a charitable remainder annuity trust where the noncharitable beneficiary receives a gift of the stream of income for a specified time period, followed by the remainder passing as a gift to the qualified charity.

Partnership capital freeze a technique used to restructure the organization of a partnership so that the owner of a business may retain control of it in the form of a "preferred" partnership interest while transferring future appreciation of the partnership to other minority partners in the form of a "common" partnership interest. The partnership freeze guarantees the general partner of receiving a stream of income for a stated period of time while also retaining control of the business. Minority interests are provided the opportunity to work within the business and receive a percentage of income after the preferred interest has first been satisfied. As a result of the Revenue Reconciliation Act of 1990, partnership capital freezes are subject to gift tax treatment when the senior family member retains an interest in the partnership interest transferred to a junior family member.

Payable on death (POD) account a form of will substitute opened with a financial institution in which an individual deposits funds for the benefit of another, payable to the noncontributing survivor on the death of the depositor.

Pecuniary formula bequest a bequest contained in a will which leaves to the surviving spouse a fractional portion of the decedent's estate after debts, losses, funeral expenses, and administrative expenses have first been paid. For example, if the gross estate is worth $800,000, and all debts, losses, and funeral and administrative expenses total $100,000, the surviving spouse would receive $350,000 if the pecuniary formula bequest provided the surviving spouse with half of the adjusted gross estate (half of $700,000 is $350,000).

Personal holding company a corporation organized for the purpose of receiving highly appreciable assets that the grantor desires to have excluded from his or her gross estate. The newly formed corporation receives highly appreciated assets transferred to it by the donor. In exchange, the donor receives all of the new corporation's stock which is equal in value to the fair market value of the property transferred to the holding company. The stock received by the donor is divided between preferred voting and common nonvoting shares so that the donor may make gifts of the common shares to others and remove future appreciation of the stock from the donor's gross estate. The Tax Revenue Act of 1987 severely curtailed the usefulness of a personal holding company in intrafamily situations.

Pooled income fund a trust created and maintained by a public charity rather than a private donor. Each donor contributes property to the trust corpus and the contributions are pooled into a single corpus. Each donor receives a pro rata share of the income earned by the pooled funds and the income is received by the donor for life. The charity receives the remainder interest upon the death of the donor.

Pourover trust a trust into which assets are "poured over" from another source. The assets may be poured over from a will, from a qualified employee benefit plan, a Keogh plan, an IRA, or insurance proceeds.

Power of appointment a right to designate who shall use or enjoy property or an interest in the property; powers of appointment may be classified as general or special.

Precatory language language often found in a last will, codicil, or other document. The language does not give express commands to the executor of the estate; rather, the language reflects what the maker of the will would like to see accomplished or what the maker "hopes" will happen at death. The language poses special problems for the executor because it fails to make positive directions and positive dispositions of property.

Private annuity a transfer of property from one individual (the transferor) to another individual (the donee) in exchange for a payment of cash to the transferor (the annuitant). The payment is made for a specified period of time based on the following factors: the health and life expectancy of the annuitant, and the fair market value of the property exchanged in return for the annuity payment. In order to be considered a "private" annuity, neither party can be in the business of funding or financing annuities, nor can the promise to pay the annuity be secured.

Private nonoperating foundation a private organization that is neither operating nor distributing funds and does not maintain a common fund. Donations to foundations of this type made after July 18, 1984 are limited, for purposes of a charitable contribution deduction, to 30 percent of the donor's adjusted gross income or 20 percent of the adjusted gross income where donations consist of long-term capital gain property, qualified appreciated stock, or tangible personal property.

Probate the process used to make an orderly distribution and transfer of property from a decedent to a group of beneficiaries. The probate process is characterized by court supervision of property transfers, filing of claims against the estate by creditors, and publication of a last will and testament for decedents dying with wills.

Public charity a type of organization, such as a church, synagogue, nonprofit college or university, hospital or medical research organization, or governmental unit. Donations to organizations of this type are limited, for purposes of a charitable contribution deduction, to a maximum of 50 percent of the donor's adjusted gross income in any given tax year.

Q-TIP   a qualified terminable interest property trust that may qualify for the marital deduction if elected by the executor of the decedent's estate. The trust is also known as the current income interest trust and has the same characteristics as the current income interest trust. See current income interest trust for further characteristics.

"Q-TIP" election   an election made by the executor of the estate to treat certain property as qualifying for the marital deduction in the estate of the decedent. If the executor files the election box on the federal estate tax return, the property subject to the Q-TIP provision qualifies for the marital deduction in the decedent's gross estate and must be included as an asset in the gross estate of the surviving spouse.

Qualified disclaimer   a refusal by a potential beneficiary to receive property or accept the benefits of property that is recognized by the IRS. In order for the disclaimer to be "qualified," it must be an absolute irrevocable refusal to accept the property. The refusal must be in writing and, for estate tax purposes, must be filed no later than 9 months after the date of the decedent's death, or, for minors, no later than 9 months after the date on which the minor reaches the age of majority. If the disclaimer is deemed "qualified," there are no gift tax consequences to the individual who would have received the property (the disclaimant).

Qualified heir   an individual who, by definition, is the recipient of a decedent's interest in property for special use valuation purposes. The IRS has defined a qualified heir as including ancestors, lineal descendants, cousins, spouses, and sons and daughters-in-law. In order for a decedent's estate to qualify for special use valuation, the property or interest must pass to an individual who meets this definition.

Qualified organization   an organization which, for tax purposes, qualifies for a charitable contribution deduction for property donated to such an organization. The IRS maintains lists of all organizations that meet the definition of a qualified organization. Included in this list are such groups as the Boy Scouts of America, the United Way, the American Red Cross, Campfire Girls, and the American Heart Association.

Qualifying property   property that qualifies for the marital deduction. In order for property to qualify for the marital deduction, the decedent must transfer the property to the surviving spouse upon the decedent's death, or the decedent must leave the surviving spouse with a life income interest that cannot be shared with any other individual. The value of the property must be included in the gross estate of the surviving spouse.

Recapitalization   the rearrangement of a corporation's capital structure involving an exchange of voting common stock for an equal amount of voting preferred and nonvoting common stock. The recapitalization removes future appreciation of the stock from the business owner's estate while allowing the business owner to retain control of the corporation. As a result of the Revenue Reconciliation Act of 1990, recapitalizations are subject to gift tax treatment when a senior family member transfers a corporate interest to a younger family member while retaining an interest in the transferred corporate interest.

Reciprocal will   a legal document in which each maker of a separate will names the maker of another will as his or her beneficiary. Reciprocal wills are often used by spouses, with each naming as his or her beneficiary the other spouse.

Related use asset   an asset that is donated to a qualified organization that can be used by the donee organization in connection with the organization's purpose. An example of a related use asset would be a charitable donation of an art collection to an art gallery.

Residuary clause   a clause in a will that provides for the distribution of the portion of the estate remaining after specific legacies and general legacies have been determined. A residuary clause naming one or more beneficiaries is a significant way of preventing a portion of the decedent's estate from being transferred according to the rules of intestacy.

Retained interest   an interest in property that is kept by the donor for property that was transferred in the donor's lifetime. An example of a retained interest is a transfer of property to a trust in which the donor retains the right to receive income from the trust for life; another example is a transfer of a residence to another family member with the retention of a life estate by the donor in the residence.

Retained life interest   a transfer of property in which the grantor enjoys a specific benefit or interest; a transfer of property to an irrevocable living trust in which the grantor enjoys a distribution of income for the rest of the grantor's life would be a retained life interest. The retained life interest would cause the income to be taxed to the grantor, and the value of the assets would be included in the gross estate of the grantor.

Reversionary interest   a transfer of property to a donee in which the grantor has the possibility of reacquiring the property after a specific event or after a period of time. For example, a transfer of property to a donee who is the sister of the donor, and is unmarried, will revert back to the grantor if the sister dies unmarried without other living relatives or heirs. A reversionary interest is included as an asset in the gross estate of the donor if the ownership of the transferred property occurs only by surviving the donee, and only if the donor's reversionary interest in the property has a value exceeding 5 percent of the value of the transferred property.

Revocable living trust   a trust over which the grantor has the power to revoke its terms, alter one or more of its terms, or amend its terms. Retention of the power to revoke the trust provides the trust with greater flexibility to achieve the grantor's objectives. At the same time, the power to revoke the trust causes the entire corpus of the trust to be included in the gross estate of the grantor in the event of the grantor's death.

Revocable trust   see revocable living trust.

Revocation power   the authority to alter, revoke, amend or terminate a trust or any provision of a trust. Possession of the power of revocation causes the property subject to the power to be included in the gross estate of the holder of such power.

Rule against perpetuities   a rule that applies to the existence and validity of trusts. The rule provides that a trust created for a named beneficiary or class of beneficiaries can vest only within a given length of time. The trust cannot exceed the lives of any of the beneficiaries who were alive at the time the trust was created plus 21 years and 9 months. (The 9 months is for any "lives in being"—any beneficiaries who were not yet born at the time the trust was created, but who were *in vitro* at the time the trust was created.)

Sale-leaseback   an intrafamily business transfer that is similar to the gift-leaseback except the donor sells the property to a trust or other party rather than making a gift of it to the trust of other family member. It is used to accomplish the same income and estate tax savings as a gift-leaseback.

Second disposition rule   an income tax consequence that affects the original seller in an intrafamily installment sale situation. Basically, the rule provides that where the original buyer of property (usually real estate) sells the property to another intrafamily buyer within 2 years after the original sale, the initial seller from the first transaction must report the gain on the second disposition. When the sale involves marketable securities, the second disposition rule applies regardless of when the second sale occurs.

Section 303 redemption   a means of redeeming the stock of a decedent to avoid the stock being taxed as a dividend. The redemption provides cash to the executor of the estate that can be used to pay death taxes and other expenses. Though the redeemed stock is included as an asset in the gross estate of the decedent, that portion of the stock equal in value to the total of federal estate taxes, state death taxes, the interest thereon, and funeral and administrative expenses of the estate receives favorable income tax treatment (avoidance of dividend treatment).

Security   the ability of a seller of certain property to take the property back in the event the buyer defaults on payments. Technically, the property is pledged as collateral by the buyer in the event the buyer defaults so that the seller may reclaim the property with a minimum amount of inconvenience and legal action.

Short-term (Clifford) trust   an irrevocable trust that lasts for a minimum period of 10 years plus a day. The trust enables the grantor to transfer income to a trust beneficiary and allows the income to be taxed at the beneficiary's marginal tax bracket. At the termination of the trust period (10 years and a day), the principal reverts to the grantor and is included in the grantor's gross estate. This type of trust is used primarily as an income-splitting device which generates income tax savings to the grantor. Grantors can only avoid paying income tax on the income generated by such a trust if either: (1) the trust was funded prior to March 1, 1986, or (2) if the trust was funded pursuant to a binding property agreement entered into prior to March 1, 1986.

Single life annuity   a commercial annuity or private annuity that makes annuity payments to the annuitant for the life of the annuitant only. There are no survivorship features to a single life annuity and the value of the payments is excluded from the gross estate of the annuitant.

Sole ownership   a form of property ownership in which one individual holds legal title to the property and has full use, enjoyment, possession and control of the property.

Special power of appointment   a power that limits the class of individuals who may receive the property. The holder of a special power of appointment can transfer the property only to specifically designated individuals (e.g., the children of the holder or to someone other than the holder, the holder's estate, the holder's creditors, or the creditors of the holder's estate) or only under specific circumstances (e.g., only with the consent of another holder who possesses an interest adverse to that of the holder). Property subject to a special power of appointment is not included in the gross estate of the holder.

Special reduction election   an election that can be made by the donor on long term capital gain property for charitable deduction purposes. Essentially, the election allows the donor of such property to take a maximum charitable contribution deduction of 50 percent of the donor's adjusted gross income in any given tax year if the donor elects to reduce the deduction to the donor's basis in the property.

Special use valuation   a method of valuation eligible for real estate used in connection with a closely held business or a farming operation. If elected by the executor of the estate, special use valuation can result in a maximum reduction of $750,000 from the decedent's gross estate for decedents dying in 1983 and later years. To qualify for special use valuation, five qualifying tests must be met.

Special use valuation election   an election by the executor of the estate to value real estate used in a closely held business, farming operation, or other trade or business at its actual use value rather than its highest and best use. The election, made by the executor on the federal estate tax return, allows the decedent's estate to reduce the value of the property by a maximum of $750,000 if all qualifying requirements are met.

"Split-dollar" life insurance   a life insurance arrangement in which a company and an employee split the premium cost on the life of the insured employee and in which the company and the employee's beneficiaries split the proceeds on an agreed basis.

Split gift   a mechanism that allows a married donor, with the consent of the nondonor spouse, to treat a gift to a third party as though each spouse made half of the gift. The effect of gift splitting is to permit a double annual exclusion amount ($20,000) per donee, thereby reducing possible gift tax liability on the transaction.

Spousal remainder trust   a trust that provided income, estate and gift tax savings to the grantor. The trust was structured so that it distributed income to a designated beneficiary (someone other than the grantor) for a period less than 10 years and a day. At the end of this time period, the trust terminated and the remainder interest in the corpus passed to the spouse of the grantor. The grantor could not have any imputed interest in the corpus and the spouse had total dominion and control over the corpus. The property was not included in the gross estate of the grantor and the property qualified for an unlimited gift tax marital deduction so that the grantor paid no gift tax on the transfer of the property to the spouse. The trust effectively provided income, estate, and gift tax savings only if it was structured and funded at some time prior to March 1, 1986.

Stock redemption agreement   a type of buy-sell agreement that often utilizes life insurance. Basically, the stock redemption agreement provides that upon the death of a business owner or co-owner, the business itself will receive the death benefit proceeds as beneficiary of the life insurance policy on the life of the business owner. The business uses the proceeds to purchase the stock owned by the deceased business owner.

Survivorship presumption   a clause which can be inserted in a will that creates a presumption of survivorship between certain individuals in the event it cannot be determined who actually survived. The survivorship presumption is often used to avoid disputes among the families of spouses who die in a common disaster when no statutory presumption of survivorship exists.

Taxable estate   that portion of the gross estate which is subject to the payment of federal estate tax. Normally, the taxable estate is determined by subtracting debts, funeral and administrative expenses, certain unpaid taxes, certain losses, and the marital and charitable deductions from the amount of the gross estate.

Taxable gift   the amount of a gift that is subject to gift tax liability. Usually, it is the amount of the total gift minus the annual exclusion amount(s).

Tenancy by the entirety   a form of joint property ownership in which title can only be held by husband and wife. Transfer of property held in this form of ownership or severance of a tenancy by the entirety can only occur with the mutual consent of both parties.

Tenancy in common   a form of property ownership in which two or more individuals hold an undivided interest in property. Upon the death of one tenant in common, the fractional percentage of ownership of the property passes to the decedent's heirs or devisees, rather than to the surviving tenants in common.

Tentative tax   the amount of tax which is payable on the sum of the taxable estate and adjusted taxable gifts, also known as the tentative tax base. The tentative tax is further reduced by both the gift taxes which would have been payable on post-1976 gifts and by any available credits, including the unified credit, in order to determine the amount of federal estate tax payable.

Tentative tax base   the combined total of all post-1976 adjusted taxable gifts and the taxable estate. The tentative tax is calculated on this base amount.

Terminable interest   an interest in property that ends at a specific time or upon the occurrence of a specific event. The interest is less than a complete, full interest in the property. Examples of terminable interests are: (1) a life estate in property that terminates upon the death of the holder and, (2) the right to receive income from property for life. Terminable interests do not ordinarily qualify for the marital deduction.

Term insurance   a type of life insurance policy which affords protection for the insured for a given period of time. Unlike whole life insurance, term insurance does not have a cash value and does not earn dividends. At the expiration of a stated period of coverage, the insurance coverage may be renewed for an additional period of time.

Testamentary trust   a trust established under the terms of a will which takes effect upon the death of the will maker.

Testate estate   the assets comprising the gross estate of an individual who dies with a will.

Throwback rule   a rule which applies only to trusts that accumulate income and distribute it at a later time. The throwback rule causes the income beneficiary to be taxed on the income for the time period during which the trust paid the income tax on the undistributed income. The purpose of the throwback rule is to put the beneficiary in the same position as if the beneficiary had paid the income tax over the term of the trust (when income was accumulated rather than distributed).

Total gift   the amount of a gift before exclusions and deductions are applied. The total gift is the fair market value of the gift on the date of transfer.

Totten trust   a form of will substitute that is created when an individual deposits money in a bank account for another person's benefit and names himself as the "trustee" of this account. The depositor retains the right to withdraw all funds from the account at any time prior to death. At death, the funds are paid to the named beneficiary, who has no right to the funds until that time.

Transfer for value rule   a rule for calculating taxable income on a life insurance policy. Generally, where a life insurance policy has been sold or transferred for valuable consideration prior to death, the death proceeds are exempt from being taxed only to the extent of the consideration paid by the transferee and the net premiums paid by the transferee after the transfer. The balance of the proceeds are taxed at ordinary income rates to the transferee.

2503 (b) trust   a trust frequently used for minors that requires a mandatory distribution of income to the trust beneficiary on an annual basis. Gifts to a section 2503(b) trust may qualify as gifts of a present interest and are eligible for the $10,000 annual gift tax exclusion. This type of trust does not require distribution of principal and unexpended income to the beneficiary when the beneficiary reaches the age of majority.

2503 (c) trust   a trust for minors that enables a grantor to make a gift to a minor that qualifies for the $10,000 annual gift tax exclusion. The income and principal may be expended on behalf of the beneficiary prior to the time the beneficiary reaches the age of 21. When the beneficiary reaches age 21, unexpended income and principal must be available for distribution to the beneficiary. The beneficiary has the option to decline distribution, in which case the trust continues until some specified time in the trust instrument.

Unified credit   a federal estate tax credit that offsets tax liability, dollar for dollar, for both lifetime gifts and testamentary transfers. The unified credit amount decreases the amount of gift tax liability on lifetime gifts and the amount of estate tax liability on testamentary transfers. The unified credit amount for 1985 was $121,800; the amount was $155,800 in 1986, and increased again to $192,800 in 1987 and later years.

Unified credit amount   see unified credit.

Unified tax system   a single tax rate that was adopted in 1977 for both lifetime gifts and testamentary transfers. The unified tax system imposes identical tax rates on lifetime gifts and testamentary transfers that are equal in value.

Uniform Gifts to Minors Act   a model act for making gifts to minors which has been adopted, in one form or another, by all 50 states. The Uniform Act provides that an adult, while alive, may make a gift of certain types of property to a minor by having the gift registered in the name of or delivered to the donor or another adult person as custodian for the minor. These gifts qualify for the annual exclusion amount. Some states have adopted a modified version of this act, known as the Uniform Transfers to Minors Act, which allows transfers of property, including testamentary transfers, transfers of real estate, and transfers of partnership interests, and oil and gas interests, to be placed into the minor's custodial account.

Universal life insurance   a type of life insurance policy in which the cash values are invested in government securities that pay a higher rate of return than the typical life insurance policy. In addition, a universal policy allows additional premiums to be paid at the convenience of the policy holder, as well as allowing the death protection to be increased or decreased without purchasing a new policy. A universal policy can also be partly surrendered.

Unlimited marital deduction   a variation of the marital deduction that allows a decedent to qualify his or her estate for the marital deduction so long as the decedent bequeaths all property to the surviving spouse. The unlimited marital deduction allows the entire estate of the decedent to pay no federal estate tax. The unlimited marital deduction became available for surviving spouses as a result of ERTA '81. If the unlimited marital deduction is used by the estate of a decedent spouse, the decedent's estate does not use the amount of unified credit available to it to offset estate tax liability. The unlimited marital deduction only became available for the estate of a decedent dying on or after January 1, 1982.

Unrelated use asset   an asset that is donated to a qualified organization that cannot be used by the donee organization in connection with the organization's purpose. An example of an unrelated use asset would be a charitable donation of a stamp collection to a church.

Unstated interest rule   a tax rule which imputes a particular rate of interest on an installment sale between members of the same family if the contract is silent on the issue of what the interest rate should be. Basically, the rule provides that the IRS can impute an interest rate of 10 percent on the installment sale of nonreal property if the contract does not specify at least 9 percent. When sales of land are involved, the IRS can impute an interest rate of 7 percent on sales between family members that do not exceed $500,000 in one year. When the sales exceed $500,000 for one year, the IRS can impute an interest rate of 10 percent if the contract does not specify at least 9 percent.

Whole life insurance   a type of life insurance policy that provides a death protection benefit for the beneficiaries of the insured while also establishing a cash value which can be borrowed by the policyholder during lifetime. Usually, premiums are paid by the policy holder until a specified age (e.g., age 65).

Will contest   a means of disputing the validity of a will on one or more grounds, for example, the testator lacked the mental capacity to make a will, the testator inadvertently omitted one or more devisees who are heirs of the decedent, or some other grounds for disputing the validity of the document. If a will is successfully contested, it can cause a redistribution of the decedent's estate and can alter the amount of property received by an individual under the terms of the will.

"Willing buyer-willing seller" rule   the most frequently used

test applied to property to determine its fair market value. The fair market value of property is determined by what a willing buyer and willing seller would agree upon as a fair price for the property. This rule eliminates values for property that are determined as a result of a liquidation sale, forced sale, intrafamily sale, or any other sale not in the regular course of business.

Will substitute   a means of transferring title to property by the use of some mechanism other than a last will and testament. Commonly used types of will substitutes include joint tenancy with right of survivorship, Totten trusts, joint bank accounts, payable on death (POD) accounts, deeds, life insurance contracts, IRA accounts, and revocable trusts. Most will substitute forms avoid probate.

PUBLICATIONS

Author, "A Charitable Remainder Trust and a Wealth Replacement Trust Can Accomplish Income and Estate Tax Benefits," *Practical Accountant,* November, 1990.

Author, "How to Minimize State Death Tax Liabilities," *Journal of Financial Planning,* July, 1990.

Author, "Estate Planning Opportunities for the Disabled," *Iowa State Bar Association Annual Meeting,* June, 1990.

Author of 9 of 15 Assignments in *Case Studies in Estate Planning,* College for Financial Planning, June, 1990.

Author, "Estate Planning for S Corporation Shareholders," *National Public Accountant,* June, 1990.

Author, "How Lifetime Gifts Can Cut Estate Taxes," *Barron's,* March 19, 1990.

Author of 12 of 15 Assignments in *The Use of Trusts in Estate Planning,* College for Financial Planning, April, 1989.

Author, "The Unauthorized Practice of Law," *The Expert's Guide to Managing and Marketing A Successful Financial Planning Practice,* by Andrew M. Rich and Jill Arowesty, Prentice-Hall, Inc., 1988.

Author of 11 of 15 Assignments in *Estate and Insurance Planning for Business Owners,* College for Financial Planning, February, 1988.

Author, "Integration of Estate and Financial Planning with Planned Giving," a case study published for Purdue University's Insurance Planning Institute, May, 1987.

Author of 11 of 15 Assignments in *Advanced Estate Planning,* College for Financial Planning, April, 1987.

Author of three chapters in *Selected Readings in Advanced Estate Planning,* Dow-Jones-Irwin, Inc., 1987.

Co-author, "Five Reasons Why You Need to Have a Will," *Practical Accountant,* February, 1987.

Author, *The Financial Planner's Guide to Estate Planning,* Prentice-Hall, Inc., September, 1986.

Author, "Domicile, Sweet Domicile," *Financial Strategies and Concepts,* Spring 1986.

Author, "Replacing the Interest-Free Loan," *Financial Strategies and Concepts,* Summer 1985.

Author, "The Role of the Financial Planner in Estate Planning," *Financial Strategies and Concepts,* Summer 1985.

Co-author, "Community Property in the Estate Planning Process," a monograph on community property and estate planning concepts. Published by the College for Financial Planning, August, 1985.

Co-author, "Estate Planning: The Role of the Financial Planner—The Red Flag Theory of Estate Planning," *Institute of Certified Financial Planners Journal,* Spring 1985.

Author of chapters "Intrafamily Transfers" and "Estate Planning," in the publication, *Wealthbuilding through Tax Management,* a tax management guide prepared for employees of IDS/American Express by the College for Financial Planning, January 1985.

Author, "Estate Planning for the Family of the Developmentally Disabled Person," *Institute of Certified Financial Planners Journal,* Winter 1984.

Author, "Planning for the Disabled," *Financial Planning Magazine,* November 1984.

Author, "Exclusion and Valuation Techniques that Reduce the Size of the Gross Estate," *Institute of Certified Financial Planners Journal,* Summer 1984.

Author, Note, "Defendant in Criminal Trial Has Burden of Proof in Establishing an Affirmative Defense—Patterson v. New York, 432 U.S. 197 (1977)." Vol. 11 Creighton Law Review, No. 4, 1978. Cited in *The Criminal Law Bulletin,* Fall 1979.

Co-author, Annual Review of Changes in Nebraska Law (family law section), Vol. 12 Creighton Law Review, No. 1, 1978.

INDEX

U

W